Credit Rating Agencies

Mohammed Hemraj

Credit Rating Agencies

Self-regulation, Statutory Regulation and Case Law Regulation in the United States and European Union

Springer

Mohammed Hemraj
Birmingham
United Kingdom

ISBN 978-3-319-17926-1 ISBN 978-3-319-17927-8 (eBook)
DOI 10.1007/978-3-319-17927-8

Library of Congress Control Number: 2015937938

Springer Cham Heidelberg New York Dordrecht London

Printed on acid-free paper

Springer International Publishing AG Switzerland is part of Springer Science+Business Media (www.springer.com)

To my late parents, my wife Zakia and my children Amirali, Sukaina and Faiza.

Foreword

The recent world financial crisis and the consequential changes in banking and financial services regulation have inevitably drawn a great deal of attention to the causes and processes of the crisis and its aftermath. One key element in the whole saga was the role played by credit rating agencies, particularly in rating companies set up to handle long-term residential mortgage debt. Structures such as SPVs and SIVs were utilised to issue the bonds and thus restructure long-term bank lending into shorter-term bond issues. As a result, a large quantity of long-term debt was repackaged in the form of highly credit-rated grade corporate bonds. While this certainly involved excessive leveraging of the mortgage lending market and extensive exposure by certain banks to the international bond markets, the precise extent and role that securitisation played in the banking crisis is widely debated as is the fact that the ratings were virtually all issued by three firms.

This text engages in a much-needed analysis of both this process, focusing on the role of the rating agencies, and the process that it is suggested should be undergone to reduce the risks of a similar crisis happening again in the future. It considers the position in both the United States and the European Union and engages in a vital consideration of the steps that could and should be taken.

Such an analysis is a crucial part of the process of continuing to develop our understanding of the recent crisis, and avoiding a repetition and its publication are welcome.

West Midlands, UK

Professor Andrew Haynes
University of Wolverhampton

Preface

Writing a book may seem akin to locking the gate after the horse has bolted—that is, analysing the causes for the failure of the regulatory laws and their appropriateness after its occurrence and in proposing changes in the law to prevent it from recurring in future. Nevertheless, to advance the social science of law, it is necessary for a researcher to go into the underlying principles or reasons behind the law. The enquiries conducted consist of the reason(s) for adopting particular rules (or regulations) and their effects. The question of whether these regulations are suited to the present conditions is also asked, and if not, what possible improvements are required? Do the current regulations require replacing by a new set of rules?[1] Legal research requires systematically finding or ascertaining law. This can be on the identified topic (for example, in this book it is credit rating agencies) or the types of regulations introduced (for example—self-regulation, statutory regulation and case law regulation), as well as an inquiry into specific jurisdictions (the laws of the US and the EU) with a view to making advancement in the science of law. This in turn requires a legal researcher to probe systematically into the underlying principles of, and reasons for, law (or regulation).[2] However, this is difficult in practice because

> Finding law on a particular subject ... is not an easy task. There may be a number of statutes [as well as statutory provisions scattered in different statutes] with frequent amendments on the subject under inquiry. In addition, these statutes and statutory provisions may be supplemented from time to time by a bulk of rules, regulations, orders, directives and government resolutions. Similarly [particularly in the common law jurisdictions] one requires to look for pouring judicial pronouncements of the higher judicial institutions interpreting these provisions for finding 'true' meaning and ambit of the legal provisions.[3]

---

[1] Jain (1972), p. 487 at 490.

[2] Vibhute and Aynalem (2009), pp. 22–23.

[3] Ibid.

This researcher had to face and overcome the above-mentioned dilemma when conducting this research.

The regulation and law stated are those that were in force up to 31 December 2014.

References

Jain, S. N. (1972). Legal research and methodology. *Journal of the Indian Law Institute, 14*, 487.

Vibhute, K., & Aynalem, F. (2009). Legal research: Teaching material (pp. 22–23). http://chilot.files.wordpress.com/2011/06/legal-research-methods.pdf.

Acknowledgements

In writing this book, I have been indebted to several people: Dr Andromarchi Georgosouli, for her kind suggestion that I conduct research into regulation, and Professors Andrew Haynes, Peter Walton, George Alexander Walker and Charles Chatterjee, for kindly reading and commenting on my draft manuscript.

For the support that I have received in writing this book, I would like to thank Professors Barry A. K. Rider, Ian Silitoe, Glynis Cousin, Christine Hockings, Martin Dangerfield, Mike Haynes, Silke Machold, Rebecca Parry and Abbas Mithni.

Mohammed Khomail keeps asking me if I have completed my book; I can now assure him that I have.

Last but not the least, my heartfelt thanks to Anke Seyfried and to the publisher Springer for agreeing to publish my book.

Table of Cases

United States

Abu Dhabi Commercial Bank et al v. Morgan Stanley & Co et al, U.S. District Court, Southern District of New York, No. 08-07508.
Allen v. United Financial Mortgage Corporation Case No. 09-2507 SC—Dist. Court, Northern District of California (2009).
Billy v Arthur Young & Co 834 P 2d 745 (1992).
Cal. Public Employees Ret. System, No. CGC-09-490241, slip op. at 10 (Cal. Super. Ct. S.F. Cty. (2010).
Coffey v. Foamex L.P., 2 F.3d 157, 161–162 (6th Cir. 1993).
Compuware Corp. v. Moody's Investors Servs., Inc, 499 F. 3d 520—Court of Appeals (6th Circuit 2007).
County of Orange v. McGraw Hill Companies, Inc. 245 BR 151—Dist. Court, CD California, 1999.
Credit Alliance v Arthur Anderson and Co 483 Need 110 (1985).
Don King Prods., Inc. v. Douglas, 131 F.R.D. 421, 424 (S.D.N.Y.1990).
Ernst and Ernst v. Hochfelder, 425 U.S. 185, 96 S. Ct. 1375, 47 L. Ed. 2d 668 (1976).
Genesee County Employees' Retirement System et al v. Thornburg Mortgage Securities Trust 2006-3 et al, U.S. District Court, District of New Mexico, No. 09-00300 (12 Nov. 2011).
Gonzales v. Nat'l Broad. Co., Inc., 194 F.3d 29, 32 (2d Cir.1999).
Harbor Drive Condominium Ass'n v. Harbor Point, Inc., 209 Ill.App.3d 631, 154 Ill. Dec. 365, 568 N.E.2d 365, 375 (1991).
In King County, Wash. v. IKB Deutsche Industriebank AG 708 F. Supp. 2d 334—Dist. Court, SD New York (2010).
In Re Daisy Sys. Corp., 97 F.3d 1171, 1175 (9th Cir.1996).
In Re Fitch, Inc., 330 F. 3d 104—Court of Appeals, 2nd Circuit 2003, 330 F.3d 104 (2003).

In re Kingston Cotton Mills, Court of Appeal, ChD (1895) 282.
In Re Lehman Bros. Mortgage-Backed Securities 650 F. 3d 167 at 188—Court of Appeals (2nd Circuit 2011).
In Re Lehman Brothers Mortgage–Backed Securities Litigation v Moody's Investors Service, Inc. et al, US Court of Appeal (2nd Cir.) Docket Nos. 10–0712–cv, 10–0898–cv, 10–1288–cv. (11 May 2011).
In Re Merrill Lynch & Co., Inc. Research Reports 272 F. Supp. 2d 243—Dist. Court, SD New York 2003; 272 F.Supp.2d 243 (2003).
In re Moody's Corp. Securities Litigation, 599 F. Supp. 2d 493—Dist. Court, SD New York (2009).
In Re National Century Financial Enterprises, Inc., 541 F. Supp. 2d 986—Dist. 2007.
In Re Nat'l Century Fin. Enters. Inc. Inv. Litig., 580 F.Supp.2d 630, 639–640 (S.D. Ohio 2008).
In Re Pan Am Corporation 161 B.R. 577, 580–582 (S.D.N.Y. 1993).
In Re Petroleum Prods. Antitrust Litig., 680 F.2d 5, 7 (2d Cir.1982).
In Re Scott Paper Co. Sec. Litig., 145 F.R.D. 366, 370 (E.D. Pa. 1992).
Jackson v. Johnson, 5 Cal.App.4th 1350, 1355, 7 Cal.Rptr.2d 482 (1992).
Jefferson City School District No. R-1 v. Moody's Investor's Services 175 F. 3d 848—Court of Appeals 10th Circuit 1999.
Kestrel Holdings; Dartberg Pty Ltd v Wealthcare Financial Planning Pty Ltd (2007) 164 FCR 450.
King County, Washington et al v. IKB Deutsche Industrie Bank AG et al, U.S. District Court, Southern District of New York, No. 09-08387.
LaSalle Nat. Bank v. Duff & Phelps Credit Rating Co., 951 F. Supp. 1071—Dist. Court, SD New York (1996).
*LaSalle National Bank, et al., v. Duff & Phelps Credit Rating Co. and Shawmut Bank Connecticut, N.A.,*951 F. Supp. 1071 (1996).
Luce v. Edelstein, 802 F.2d 49, 56 (2d Cir.1986).
Maurice L. Quinn, Plaintiff-Appellant V. The McGraw-Hill Companies, Inc., Defendant-Appellate, No. 97-3269, United States Court of Appeals, Seventh Circuit, 168 F.3d 331 (1999).
McCormick v. Kopmann, 23 Ill. app. 2d 189, 161 N.E.2d 720 (1959).
Michaelis v. Benavides, 61 Cal.App.4th 681, 687, 71 Cal.Rptr.2d 776 (1998).
Milkovich v. Lorain Journal Co., 497 U.S. 1, 11–14, 110 S. Ct. 2695, 111 L.Ed.2d 1 (1990).
New York Times v. Sullivan, 376 U.S., 254, 269, 84 S. Ct. 710, 11 L.Ed.2d 686 (1964).
Ohio Police & Fire Pension Fund et al. v. Standard & Poor's Financial Services LLC et al Case number 2:09-cv-1054, (2009).
Ohio Police & Fire, et al. v. Standard & Poor's Fin., et al Case: 11-4203, File 12a0398p.06, Court of Appeal, (17 September 2011).
Ossining Union Free School Dist. v Anderson La Rocca Anderson, 73 NY2d 417 [1989].
Philadelphia Newspapers, Inc. v. Hepps, 475 U.S. 767, 777, 106 S.Ct. 1558, 89 L. Ed.2d 783 (1986).

Ronzani v. Sanofi S.A., 899 F.2d 195, 198 (2d Cir.1990).
S.E.C. v. Blackwell, 291 F.Supp.2d 673, 696 (S.D. Ohio 2003).
State of Connecticut v. Moody's Corporation et al. No. X04HHDCV106008836S, 54 Conn. L. Rptr. 116, (2012 WL 2149408 (Conn. Super.), May 10, 2012.
State v. Southers, 1988 Ohio App. LEXIS 4648 (Ohio Ct. App., Pickaway County, (23 November 1988).
Tellabs, Inc. v. Makor Issues & Rights, Ltd., 127 S.Ct. 2499, 168 L.Ed.2d 179 (2007).
The McGraw–Hill Companies, Inc., Fitch Inc., Defendants–Appellees, United States Court of Appeals, Second Circuit 2011 WL 1778726 (C.A.2 (N.Y.)).
Ultramares Corp. v. Touche, 255 N.Y. 170, 174 N.E. 441, 444 (1931)).
United States of America v McGraw Hill Company, Inc., and S&P, Case No. CV13-00779-Doc. (4 Feb. 2013).
United States Securities & Exchange Commission v. Citigroup Global Markets Inc. 5 Docket Nos. 11-5227-cv (Lead) 11-5375-cv (Con) 11-5242-cv (XAP), (15 March 2012).
USA v Standard and Poor's, in US District Court, California, Case No. CV13-00779 (4 Feb 2013) http://www.justice.gov/iso/opa/resources/849201325104924250796.PDF.
US Securities and Exchange Commission (SEC) v, City Group Global Markets Inc. 11 US District Court and Southern District of New York, Civ. 7387 (JSR) 2011; No. 11 Civ.7 7387, 2011 WL 5903733, (S.D.N.Y. Nov. 28, 2011).
Walburn v. Lockheed Martin Corp., 431 F.3d 966, 972 (6th Cir.2005).
Walpert, Smullian & Blumenthal, P.A. v. Katz, 361 Md. 645, at 671, 762 A.2d 582 (2000).
XL Disposal Corp. v. John Sexton Contractors Co., 168 Ill.2d 355, 213 Ill.Dec. 665, 659 N.E.2d 1312, 1316 (Ill.1995).

European Union

Enderby v. Frenchay Area Health Authority, Case 127/92 [1993] ECR 5535).
Handels-og Kontorfunktionaerernes Forbund i Danmark v. Dansk Arbejdsgiverforening (acting for Danfoss), Case 109/88, [1989] ECR 3199).

United Kingdom

Aiken v Stewart Wrightson Members Agency Limited [1995] 1 WLR 1281.
Al Saudi Banque v Clark Pixley [1990] Ch 313.
Caparo Industries Plc v Dickman [1990] 2 AC 605, [1990] 1 All ER 568, HL.
Cassa di Risparmio della Repubblica di San Marino v Barclays Bank [2011] EWHC 484 (Comm): www.bailii.org/ew/cases/EWHC/Comm/2011/484.html.

Donoghue (or McAlister) v Stevenson, [1932] All ER Rep 1; [1932] AC 562; House of Lords.
Hedley Byrne & Co Limited v Heller & Partners Limited [1964] AC 465.
Henderson v Merrett Syndicates Ltd [1994] UKHL 5.
Junior Books Co Ltd v Veitchi Co Ltd [1982] UKHL 4, [1983] 1 AC 520.
Rich (Marc) & Co AG v Bishop Rock Marine Co Ltd, The Nicholas H [1996] AC 211, [1995] 3 All ER 307 HL.
Rowling v Takaro Properties Ltd [1988] AC 473.

Australia

ABN AMRO Bank NV v Bathurst Regional Council [2014] FCAFC 65.
Bathurst Regional Council v Local Government Services Pty Ltd (No. 5) [2012] FCA 1200.
BT Australia Limited v Raine & Horne Pty Limited [1983] 3 NSWLR 221.
Caltex Oil (Australia) Pty Ltd v The Dredge "Willemstad" (1976) 136 CLR 529.
Derring Lane Pty Limited v Fitzgibbon (2007) 16 VR 563.
Esanda Finance Corp Ltd v Peat Marwick Hungerfords (reg) (1997) 142 ALR 750.
Kestrel Holdings Pty Limited v APF Properties Pty Limited (2009) 260 ALR 418.
Woolcock Street Investments Pty Limited v CDG Pty Limited (2004) 216 CLR 515.

New Zealand

Attorney-General v Carter [2003] 2 N.Z.L.R. 160.

Table of Statutes

Directive 2006/48/EC.
Investment Company Act 1940 Section 6 (a) (5).
Private Securities Litigation Reform Act of 1995.
Racketeer Influenced and Corrupt Organizations Act (RICO) (1970) Chapter 96, Title 18, United States Code, §1961–1968.
The Federal Rules of Civil Procedure 2010, Rule 8, Rule 9(b), Rule 15.
The Private Securities Litigation Reform Act of 1995.
The Sarbanes-Oxley Act of 2002.
The Securities Act 1933.
The Securities Exchange Act of 1934.
Title IX of *the Organized Crime Control Act of 1970*, Pub. L. No. 91-452, 84 Stat. 941 (Oct. 15, 1970).
U.S. Code—Title 18- Crime and Criminal Punishment, Chapter 63—*Mail Fraud and other Fraud Offences*, § 1341, § 1443, § 1444.

England

Misrepresentation Act 1967. http://www.legislation.gov.uk/ukpga/1967/7.

EU

The Credit Rating Agencies (Civil Liability) Regulations 2013.

India

Securities and Exchange Board of India (Credit Rating Agencies) Regulations, 1999.

Securities and Exchange Board of India (Procedure for holding Enquiry by Enquiry officer and Imposing penalty) Regulations, 2002.

List of Abbreviations

ASB	American Savings Bank
CDO	Collateralized Debt Obligation
CDS	Credit Default Swap
CESR	Committee of European Securities Regulators
CPR	Civil Procedure Rules
CRA	Credit Rating Agency
CRAs	Credit Rating Agencies
CRD	Capital Requirements Directive
EC	European Commission
ESMA	European Securities and Markets Authority
EU	European Union
FDIC	Federal Deposit Insurance Corporation
FHFA	Federal Housing Finance Administration
FIRREA	Financial Institutions Reform, Recovery, and Enforcement Act
FRCP	Federal Rule of Civil Procedure
FSB	Financial Stability Board
IOSCO	International Organization of Securities Commissions
MBS	Mortgage-backed Security
NCUA	National Credit Union Administration
NRSRO	Nationally Recognized Statistical Rating Organization
NRSROs	Nationally Recognized Statistical Rating Organizations
OTS	Office of Thrift Supervision
PII	Professional Indemnity Insurance
SEC	Securities and Exchange Commission
SFP	Structured Financial Products
SIV	Structured Investment Vehicle
SPV	Special Purpose Vehicle
UK	United Kingdom
US	Unites States

Contents

Chapter 1
Introduction

1.1 Aim

This book is a descriptive treaty proving a critical overview of the law of credit rating agencies (CRAs) on both sides of the Atlantic. It examines the regulations introduced, how effective the mechanisms for the enforcement of these regulations are, whether they act as a deterrent to CRAs and whether or not investors receive compensation for their losses. The book embarks on a systematic journey covering CRAs through rule and case law across countries and regulatory regime. The breadth and depth of the coverage of the topic offers a fresh perspective covering US case law, European regulation, code of conduct, etc., by objectively reviewing the law.

1.2 Need for Credit Rating

CRAs perform a useful function. They have "become a public good that serves the interest of the entire financial system".[1] They evaluate bonds and other securities issued by firms and governments to determine the likelihood that the issuers will repay the debt or can recover the losses in the event of default. CRAs also evaluate firms and governments in terms of their creditworthiness. CRAs then provide a single rating that communicates the risk associated with that security purchase. The securities rated by the CRAs are issued regularly by major global corporations and by national governments around the world.[2] Investors do not have the resources or ability to assess public and non-public information conveyed by a rating. Buyers

[1] Kelly (2012), p. 477 at 478.

[2] Kelly (2012), p. 478. See also Sinclair (2008) and Mattarocci (2013).

M. Hemraj, *Credit Rating Agencies*, DOI 10.1007/978-3-319-17927-8_1

and sellers are able drastically to reduce their transaction costs within these financial markets.[3]

1.3 Literature Review

The literature gap relates to the failure of learned scholars to conduct a holistic approach while examining and analysing regulations in place, both in the United States of America (US) and the European Union (EU). The academic trend thus far has been limited to examining either selective regulations or selective jurisdictions as illustrated by the following examples. Radzi[4] evaluates the operations of domestic credit rating agencies and is limited to Malaysia. Shin[5] examines the legal liability of CRAs in the US. Kruithof and Wymeersch[6] limit their study to examining the regulation and liability of CRAs under the law of Belgium. The study by Kaur and Kaur[7] on CRAs is limited to India, and that of Duffhues and Weterings[8] examines the quality of credit rating and liability from a Dutch perspective. The Darbellay's[9] study focuses on the interaction between regulatory intervention and competitive incentives among the "Big Three" CRAs. Mattarocci's[10] study relates to the institutional and regulatory dynamics in the business models, which give CRAs enough independence to make viable judgments without risking their own profitability.

The problem with these limited studies based on selected regulation and selected jurisdictions is that it is difficult to identify the precise defects in the regulation to enable appropriate and valid policy suggestions, as it is not possible to draw an appropriate conclusion based on a narrow and a confined study. To remedy this situation, the book will critically examine and analyse various regulations (soft laws, hard laws and case laws) introduced in the US and EU in order to fill in the gap in the literature.

---

[3] Kelly (2012), p. 478. See also Sinclair (2008) and Mattarocci (2013).

[4] See Radzi (2012).

[5] Shin (2009).

[6] Kruithof and Wymeersch (2006).

[7] Kaur and Kaur (2013).

[8] Duffhues and Weterings (2011).

[9] Darbellay (2013).

[10] Mattarocci (2013).

1.4 Need for Research

Briefly stated, the book examines the impact of the absence of a gatekeeper duty owed by CRAs in an anti-competitive environment, conflicts of interest and lack of accountability. Regulation was necessary to address and tackle these problems, and once achieved, the problem of inaccuracy in issuing ratings on the part of the CRAs would disappear. The book will examine the truth of this statement by examining regulatory options that were open to the regulators and whether or not the choices made by the regulators were effective in compelling the CRAs to act responsibly. When ratings are downgraded by the CRAs, it has an impact on the issuers in the form of borrowing becoming expensive for them and it results in losses to the investors. Therefore, both the issuers and investors demand reliable ratings and prefer CRAs to act responsibly. This will prevent likely attempts by governments to continue reducing reliance on ratings and to withdraw the rating requirements for the assessment of credit risk.[11] CRAs do perform a useful function, but will adhering to regulations introduced force CRAs to issue reliable ratings?

1.5 Research Questions

The book's intention is to fill the present potential gap in the knowledge by attempting to answer the following research questions with the expectation of contributing to the sum of present knowledge[12]: how robust are the regulations in resolving problems ranging from conflicts of interest and competition to accountability? As part of this research question, the book will consider whether regulations introduced were a success or a failure[13] and, if a failure, what the remedy is. Several questions also emerge and are worth exploring: what has been the effect of statutory regulations enacted to supplement self-regulation, especially in the US and EU? Are they complex, cumbersome and inadequate? What additional layers of statutory regulation were required to supplement them? Has the level of intrusion increased where the regulators have the power to investigate CRAs periodically to ensure that CRAs have properly conducted their business affairs? In addition, the book will explore the extent of CRAs' liability when they breach self-regulation and statutory regulations.

[11] Section 939A of the *Dodd-Frank Act 2010*.

[12] Trafford and Leshem (2008), p. 15.

[13] See Chap. 7.

1.6 Gatekeepers' Role and Accountability

The role of the gatekeeper can be perceived as that of a journalist or news editor. The gathering process can include news items winding through communication channels in a group.[14] The central aspect of a gatekeeper's role is the decision-making process, deciding what shall pass through each of the several gate sections. A CRA, as a gatekeeper and decision maker, is responsible for keeping investors informed of relevant matters relating to the securities they rate. The role of a CRA as a gatekeeper is to screen a large amount of information about an entity (e.g., an issuer) and to convey to the recipients (e.g., an investor) information that a gatekeeper believes is important. It is a gatekeeper who decides which information will go forward and which will not.[15] Gatekeeping is therefore a "process of culling and crafting countless bits of information into the limited number of messages that reach people every day... This process determines not only which information is selected, but also what the content and nature of the messages, such as news [or ratings], will be".[16] A CRA does this by issuing ratings to the debt instruments. The CRAs, acting as gatekeepers, are in an excellent position to identify the creditworthiness of individual corporations (i.e., issuers) issuing debt securities and to inform the investors interested in buying these securities about a corporation's ability to meet their commitments to pay interest and the capital sum advanced at maturity. The word gatekeeper may also mean one who monitors or oversees the actions of others. In this respect, it includes regulators who are required to act as a watchdog for the authorisation and supervision of CRAs stipulated under the Regulation.

When investors make investment decisions to purchase corporate securities, especially when based on favourable ratings issued by CRAs, they believe that the ratings issued are reliable and therefore do not expect to suffer losses. By introducing regulation that aims to make CRAs gatekeepers, regulators expect to protect investors. CRAs as intermediaries, or gatekeepers, provide important services that benefit investors by vetting issuers' creditworthiness. The questions that arise are whether CRAs are gatekeepers and the reasons for the absence of gatekeeper accountability, which is needed to protect investors. In the previous investors-pay model, investors used to pay CRAs by subscribing to their magazines, which published ratings of various debt instrument issued by various corporations. In such a scenario, there was a real possibility of liability if CRAs failed to act responsibly; as agents, they owed contractual duties to the investors. This is no longer the position based on the present issuers-pay model. In the strictest sense, the CRAs are agents of the issuers and not investors, and arguably this has played a big role in absolving the CRAs from liability to investors.

[14] Shoemaker et al. (1991).

[15] Lewin (1947), p. 145.

[16] Shoemaker et al. (2009).

CRAs were essential cogs in the wheel of financial devastation. The Financial Crisis Inquiry Commission[17] concluded that both the CRAs and investors were to blame. At the heart of the crisis, the marketing and selling of the mortgage-related securities depended on CRAs' seal of approval. Investors (some of whom were obligated to use them for regulatory capital standards) relied on them blindly.

The word "gatekeeper" appeared too late in the US regulation (first mentioned in the *Dodd-Frank Act 2010*) for it to have had a major impact in the regulation, and it does not appear in the EU regulation. Perhaps, in hindsight, the regulators ought to have introduced gatekeeper accountability on the part of CRAs much earlier for it to achieve an important milestone. There was a need to strengthen it with appropriate enforcement mechanisms if CRAs breached the regulations to ensure that they did act as responsible gatekeeper.

1.7 Research Method

1.7.1 Doctrinal Analysis and Black Letter Law

The doctrinal analysis in this book is based on traditional legal methodology.[18] Doctrinal research is research that provides a systematic exposition of the rules governing a particular set of legal propositions and/or duties. It analyses the relationship between rules, explains areas of difficulty and, perhaps, predicts future developments.[19] The black letter method "focuses almost entirely on the law's own language of statutes and case law to make sense of the legal world" [20] and does so by systemising and rationalising the law. On black letter law, Brownsword states:

> So-called 'black-letter' lawyers stick pretty close to the primary source materials, to the Constitution [where legal systems have one], to legislation [statutes, statutory instruments, and so on) and to the leading case decisions (the precedents]. Distinctively, there is a reluctance to move far beyond these mainstream materials [for example, to consider 'soft law' regulations such as that found in codes of practice].[21]

Chynoweth does not see doctrinal research and "black letter law" as distinct methodologies, but rather he finds them complementing each other.[22] On law reform, Morris and Murphy suggest that it "should take place within the premises of doctrinal analysis" and how "the law can be made ordered and stable".[23]

---

[17] Final Report of the National Commission on the Causes of Financial and Economic Crisis in the United States (2011), p. xxv.

[18] Morris and Murphy (2011), pp. 30–31.

[19] Clark (1997).

[20] Morris and Murphy (2011), p. 31.

[21] Brownsword (2006), p. 4.

[22] Chynoweth (2008).

[23] Morris and Murphy (2011), p. 31.

The chosen research question is topical; it examines the regulation introduced in the US and EU critically in order to dwell on law reform; that is, what improvements are required. In this respect, the book will examine if better regulation is achieved through legal accountability. Policy research on regulation would seek to provide some level of explanation as to what led to the enactment of particular regulations in the US and EU. The book will examine gatekeeper theory as the main theory, to throw some light on the regulations introduced. Using the doctrinal method, the aims and objectives that the regulators were trying to pursue when introducing the existing regulations in relation to CRAs are examined; where aims and objectives have not been realised, the book will highlight flaws in the policy pursued. In addition to adopting a black letter law approach,[24] the book will analyse the US Constitution (in the form of the US First Amendment), legislation and case decisions. It will also examine "soft law" regulation found in codes of practice.

1.8 The Research Agenda

The book investigates the effectiveness of the regulations introduced in the US and EU on three fronts. First, prohibiting the issuance of triple-A ratings as a matter of course and ensuring prompt downgrading when circumstances change; second, prohibiting CRAs from participating in the rating of new securities or financial products for which they lack relevant expertise; third, considering the part played by the CRAs in the sub-prime crisis and the attempts made by the current regulations to prevent its future recurrence. On the success of regulations introduced, the answer may lie in two important considerations. First, regulation should be sufficiently robust in making CRAs the investors' gatekeeper, and second, there ought to be appropriate sanction in place when breaches of these regulations occur. "Financial crisis and regulation are closely linked. Good regulation . . . should prevent the outbreak of financial crisis".[25]

1.9 Regulation

The criticism levelled against CRAs is their serious deficiency "in providing an assessment of the true state of affairs in the markets generally and, more particularly, in relation to issuers and their issuances of securities".[26] It was due to

> their policies and lack of transparency, the criteria that they employed in rating issuers and transactions, the failure to take account of the wider perspective, such as in relation to

[24] Brownsword (2006), p. 4.
[25] Cassis (2011), p. 88.
[26] McKnight (2009), p. 5.

> possible deleterious market influences which might affect overall asset values when rating a transaction, and possible conflicts of interest, particularly with respect to the way they earned their remuneration through competitive tendering for fees charged to and paid by issuers.[27]

The demand for regulation is felt immediately after a severe financial crisis; this is when the opportunity for real change presents itself. Financial innovation, like bundling of subprime mortgages, led to the crisis, but no one could foresee the exact form it would take and the timing of its onset and its ferocity, which in turn led to regulating CRAs. The question remains: what is a good regulation? It is difficult to find the right answer based on the 2007–2009 subprime debacle. Past financial crises have brought strong demands for change in the regulatory environment, and yet crises recur.[28] The reason is that measures taken to contain one crisis are inadequate to contain the next. "Striking the right balance between insufficient or excessive control, self- or state regulation, national or international compliance has historically proved a huge challenge".[29]

1.10 The Research Boundaries

The study is limited to an examination of the role of CRAs in the subprime mortgage crisis in relation to corporate credit ratings (debt instruments issued by the issuers and rated by CRAs). Discussion of personal ratings will not feature, and the ratings of sovereign debts will feature briefly. The study concentrates on the "Big Three" to allow analysis of the issues of subprime mortgages, corporate rating and the regulation of CRAs in the US and EU in detail.

The book will examine internal restriction and the operational aspects of the "Big Three" CRAs (Moody's, Standard & Poor's and Fitch) on how they comply with the regulation and will largely ignore the medium and smaller sized CRAs. The reason for this is that the Big Three carry out the majority of ratings: 95 % between them. All have headquarters in New York (but Fitch is dual headquartered in New York and London) with over 50 offices worldwide. Fitch Ratings is a global rating agency dedicated to providing value beyond the rating through independent and prospective credit opinions, research and data. Fitch Solutions provides a range of fixed-income products and professional development services to the global financial community.[30] The Big Three all operate worldwide and rate tens of trillions of dollars in securities. Moody's and Standard & Poor's (S&P) adjusted the way they graded securities after Goldman Sachs Group Inc., UBS AG and at least six more banks pressured them. They made exceptions to rules when bankers

---

[27] Ibid.

[28] Ibid.

[29] Ibid.

[30] Fitch Ratings, http://www.fitchratings.com/web/en/dynamic/contact-us.jsp.

asked for better safety ratings on complex mortgage-backed securities.[31] About 90 % of triple-A securities backed by subprime mortgages from 2006 and 2007 were later downgraded to junk status. Such revisions forced banks, pension funds and insurance companies to sell holdings, contributing to US $2 trillion in losses and asset write-downs worldwide.[32]

Moody's, from 2000 to 2007, "rated nearly 45,000 mortgage-related securities as triple-A. This compares with six private-sector companies in the US that carried this coveted rating in early 2010. In 2006 alone, Moody's put its triple-A stamp of approval on 30 mortgage-related securities every working day".[33] The end result was disastrous, as "83 % of the mortgage securities rated as triple-A in 2006 ultimately were downgraded".[34] From the first quarter of 2005 to the third quarter of 2007, of S&P's collateralized debt obligation (CDO) ratings of asset-backed securities, 66 % were downgraded and 44 % were downgraded from investment grade to speculative grade, including default.[35] In July 2007, S&P downgraded US $7.3 billion of securities sold in 2005 and 2006. Moody's gross revenue from rating the complex products quadrupled to US $260 million in 2006 from US $61 million in 2002, and for S&P, the number also quadrupled to US $265 million in 2006 from US $64 million in 2002.[36]

1.11 Book's Contribution to Knowledge

If another financial crisis were to occur, the question would be whether the CRAs were a part of the problem or a part of the solution. The book's contribution will be in critically examining the sum total of current regulations, comprising soft laws contained in the codes of conduct and hard laws contained in the statutory regulations. The book will also analyse common law defences[37] available to CRAs to exculpate them from liability. It will examine to what extent deterrence is necessary to prevent a gatekeeper failure of CRAs. The research findings of this book will be useful to the regulators, policymakers, investors, issuers, CRAs and legal researchers.

---

[31] Ibid.

[32] Faux (2011).

[33] Final Report of the National Commission on the Causes of Financial and Economic Crisis in the United States (2011), p. xxv.

[34] Ibid.

[35] Crouhy et al. (2007), p. 8.

[36] Faux (2011).

[37] See Chap. 6.

1.12 Outline

The book consists of seven chapters in all. This chapter has provided a framework for this research study; the rest of this academic work proceeds as follows: Chap. 2 examines the role of CRAs in general and then specifically examines their role in ratings relating to subprime mortgages and corporations, Chap. 3 examines self-regulations based on the Code of Conduct devised by the International Organization of Securities Commission (IOSCO), Chap. 4 examines statutory regulations introduced in the US and analyses the statutory provisions of the *Credit Reform Act of 2006* and the *Dodd-Frank Wall Street Reform* and *Consumer Protection Act 2010*, Chap. 5 analyses statutory regulation introduced in the EU, Chap. 6 critically examines the civil liabilities (and especially the legal defences) of CRAs in the US and the pros and cons of liability, and the book concludes in Chap. 7 by revealing the research findings of whether regulation has been a success or a failure and makes recommendations.

References

Brownsword, R. (2006). An introduction to legal research (Chapter 1). http://www.scribd.com/doc/14260230/An-Introduction-to-Legal-Research.

Cassis, Y. (2011). *Crises & opportunities: The shaping of modern finance* (pp. 88–110). Oxford: OUP.

Chynoweth, P. (2008). Legal research (Chapter 3). In A. Knight & L. Ruddock (Eds.), *Advanced research method in the build environment*. Chichester: Blackwell Publishing Ltd. http://www.lawlectures.co.uk/legal-research.pdf.

Clark, E. (1997). Report: Australian legal education a decade after the Pearce report. *Legal Education Review, 8*, 213.

Crouhy, M. G., Jarrow, R. A., & Turnbull, S. M. (2007, July 4). The subprime credit crisis of 07. http://www.fdic.gov/bank/analytical/cfr/bank_research_conference/annual_8th/Turnbull_Jarrow.pdf.

Darbellay, A. (2013). *Regulating credit rating agencies*. Cheltenham: Edward Elgar.

Duffhues, P. J. W., & Weterings, W. C. T. (2011). The quality of credit ratings and liability: The Dutch view. *IJDG, 8*(4), 1–21. http://arno.uvt.nl/show.cgi?fid=121277; (October 2010). http://dx.doi.org/10.2139/ssrn.1689868.

Faux, Z. (2011, April 14). Moody's, S&P caved in to ratings pressure from Goldman. UBS over mortgages. http://www.bloomberg.com/news/2011-04-13/moody-s-s-p-caved-to-mortgage-pressure-by-goldman-ubs-levin-report-says.html.

Final Report of the National Commission on the Causes of Financial and Economic Crisis in the United States (2011). http://c0182732.cdn1.cloudfiles.rackspacecloud.com/fcic_final_report_full.pdf; http://www.gpo.gov/fdsys/pkg/GPO-FCIC/pdf/GPO-FCIC.pdf.

Kaur, K., & Kaur, R. (2013). *Credit rating agencies in India: An appraisal*. LAP LAMBERT. Germany: Academic Publishing.

Kelly, T. F. (2012). The ethics of credit rating agencies: What happened and the way forward. *Journal of Business Ethics, 111*(4), 477–490.

Kruithof, K., & Wymeersch, E. O. (2006, March 31). *Regulation and liability of credit rating agencies under Belgian Law* (Ghent University Financial Law Institute Working Paper No. 2006-05, p. 1). http://dx.doi.org/10.2139/ssrn.894820.

Lewin, K. (1947). Frontiers in group dynamics. *Human Relations, 1*(2), 143–153.

Mattarocci, G. (2013). *The independence of credit rating agencies: How business models and regulators interact*. Waltham, Massachusetts, US: Academic Press Inc.
McKnight, A. (2009). A review of 2008: Part 1. *L.F.M.R., 3*(1), 3–30.
Morris, C., & Murphy, C. (2011). *Getting a PhD in law*. Oxford, Oxford and Portland: Hart.
Radzi, R. M. (2012). *Rating the ratings: An evaluation of the operations of credit rating agencies in Malaysia* (Unpublished Ph.D. thesis). University of South Australia.
Shin, H. T. (2009, December 17). *Legal liabilities of credit rating agencies in structured finance (CDO): Based upon the business ethics for investor protection* (Unpublished Doctoral Dissertation). U.C. Berkeley School of Law. http://dx.doi.org/10.2139/ssrn.1549225.
Shoemaker, P., Riccio J., & Johnson, P. (1991). Communication gatekeeping. http://www.oxfordbibliographies.com/view/document/obo-9780199756841/obo-9780199756841-0011.xml.
Shoemaker, P. J., Pamela, J., & Vos, T. P. (2009). *Gatekeeping theory*. New York: Routledge.
Sinclair, T. J. (2008). *The new masters of capital: American bond rating agencies and the politics of creditworthiness*. Ithaca, New York: Cornell University Press
Trafford, V., & Leshem, S. (2008). *Stepping stones to achieving your doctorate: Focusing on your viva from the start*. Berkshire: Open University Press.

Chapter 2
Theories, Rating Failure and the Subprime Mortgage Crisis

2.1 Introduction

Investors, before making a decision on whether to invest in a debt security from a company (or foreign country), must determine whether the issuing entity will be able to meet its obligations. Credit rating agencies (CRAs)[1] help in this process by providing an independent objective assessment of the creditworthiness of companies (and countries) and help investors decide on how risky it is to invest money in a security.[2] CRAs "perform an important intermediary function in the global financial markets. They rate debt obligations based on the ability of issuers to make timely payments".[3] Borrowers, investors, pension funds, banks and governments from around the world use ratings in order to make informed investment and financing decisions. Money market funds are restricted to investing only in triple-A assets; pension funds and municipalities are restricted to investing in investment grade assets and base their investment decision on the rating attributed by the rating agencies.[4] "Critics have argued that CRAs failed to perform their function as institutional 'gatekeepers' during the recent crisis by giving favourable ratings on the creditworthiness of historically unproven and structurally unstable financial instruments".[5]

In the three sections of this chapter, Sect. 2.2 examines various models and theories relating to CRAs as they supplement a gatekeeper theory, which this book adopts. Section 2.3 examines the part played by CRAs in the 2007–2008 subprime

[1] See Partnoy (2006a), p. 61; Hunt (2009a), pp. 114–115. See also, Egan (2008), p. 1. Reisberg (2011), pp. 169–212. Nye (2014); Eborall (2012), pp. 549–580.

[2] "What is a Corporate Credit Rating?" (26 September 2009). http://www.investopedia.com/articles/03/102203.asp.

[3] Bunjevac (2009), p. 40.

[4] Crouhy et al. (2007), p. 11.

[5] Ibid. Bunjevac (2009), p. 40.

M. Hemraj, *Credit Rating Agencies*, DOI 10.1007/978-3-319-17927-8_2

mortgage crisis that in turn led to the financial crises not only in the US but also globally and that necessitated the regulation of CRAs. Section 2.4 will examine the involvement of CRAs in the sagas of Enron and Lehman Brothers in the US and Northern Rock in the UK. The premise of this book is that the crisis was due to the gatekeeper failure of the CRAs; the regulations will be examined to find out if the regulators have succeeded in preventing future gatekeeper failure. The detail of these regulations in the US and EU will then be analysed in subsequent chapters. The discussion first examines the rationale for regulation.

2.2 Regulatory Models and Theories

2.2.1 The Rationale for Regulation

The quotation

> CRAs analyse masses of data and supply credit information to investors, underwriters, and traders and as a result they "have become more than an advisory opinion; they have become a standard of value and a tool of financial regulation"[6]

suggests that the responsibilities of CRAs have slowly progressed from expressing a mere opinion, through providing an advisory opinion, to provision of a standard of value. In reality, a dilemma of the regulators in regulating CRAs is their insistence that they are expressing a mere opinion. Generally, a rationale for regulation is to preserve law and order (that is, the rule of law, the desire to control and show respect for the rule of law). Another rationale is that regulation maintains an ethic of good behaviour for both the law and the civilisation it serves.[7] An ethical approach to regulation ensures that CRAs abide by ethical behaviour, which encompasses transparency, avoiding conflicts of interest and ensuring reliable high-quality ratings.

What regulation does is creates, limits or constrains a right; creates or limits a duty; or allocates a responsibility. Regulation is a fact (of life) in any civilisation and is often necessary to make systems work better; there are four types: arbitrary regulations, good faith regulations, goal conflict regulations and process regulations.[8] Regulation takes many forms; examples are legal restrictions promulgated by a government authority, contractual obligations that bind parties, self-regulation by an industry, social regulation (e.g., norms), co-regulation, third-party regulation or market regulation. In its legal sense, Levi-Faur[9] distinguishes regulation from primary legislation (by Parliament or other elected legislative bodies) on the one

[6] Forbes et al. (1974), p. 1.

[7] Hudson (2009), p. 832.

[8] "Four Types of Regulation", http://bounds.net.au/node/65.

[9] Levi-Faur (2010), p. 2.

hand and judge-made law on the other. Regulation is necessary to protect public interest. Levi-Faur suggests

> [T]he study of regulatory governance should proceed beyond states, markets and societies into the identification of hybrid forms of regulation and towards the creation of autonomous regulatory spaces that blur the distinctions between the global and the national.[10]

> Regulation mandated by a state attempts to produce outcomes that might not otherwise occur, produce or prevent outcomes in places different from those that might otherwise occur, or produce or prevent outcomes in different timescales than would otherwise occur. In this way, regulation implements artefacts of policy statements.[11]

Litan[12] notes that regulation consists of requirements a government imposes on private firms and individuals to achieve the government's purposes. These include controls on market entries, prices, wages, better and cheaper services and goods, cleaner water and air, and safer workplaces and consumer products. Failure to meet regulations can result in fines, orders to cease doing certain things or, in some cases, even criminal penalties.[13]

Ground rules of good regulation range from proportionality, accountability, consistency, transparency and targeting.[14] Regulation is not straightforward in nature as it is diverse and at times contradictory, and therefore different models and theories, discussed below, have emerged. Regulation based on hit and misses or resulting from knee-jerk reactions (which means doing something quickly and spontaneously and without too much thought or deliberation) will require the introduction of new regulation occasionally, but even then it may not produce the desired result. Regulation may hinder competition; it may serve either a public interest or a private interest.[15]

The role played by the CRAs in the 2007–2009 global market turmoil has prompted a number of international reviews, including those of the International Organization of Securities Commissions (IOSCO), the Financial Stability Forum (FSF), the Committee of European Securities Regulators (CESR), the European Commission (EC) and the US Securities and Exchange Commission (SEC).[16] The regulatory objective in relation to CRAs is not as pronounced as found under the provision of legal services.[17] Equally important, as mentioned below, is the thorny

---

[10] Ibid.

[11] "Regulation" http://en.wikipedia.org/wiki/Regulation.

[12] R. Litan, "Regulation", http://www.econlib.org/library/Enc/Regulation.html.

[13] Ibid.

[14] Chapter 5: Principles of Regulation, http://www.scotland.gov.uk/Publications/2008/12/29155017/6.

[15] Levi-Faur (2010), p. 3.

[16] A joint report by the Treasury and the Australian Securities and Investments Commission (2008), p. 4.

[17] "Regulatory Objectives" is a defined term in the first section of the *English Legal Services Act 2007* C. 29 and encompasses many issues. See http://www.legislation.gov.uk/ukpga/2007/29/section/1.

issue of whether or not CRAs are gatekeepers. Academic writers do agree on the issue of CRAs being involved in scandals. It will be a mistake on the part of regulators and CRAs alike not to accede to the fact that CRAs do play a gatekeeper role in the market and that there is an urgent need to address the problem of gatekeeper failure. Fuchita and Litan[18] note that corporate financial reporting scandals in the US and elsewhere in recent years have called into question the sufficiency of the legal framework governing these gatekeepers. This has led to a multiple rounds of regulatory reform since the Enron-era scandals.

Policymakers have since responded by imposing a series of new obligations, restrictions and punishments—all with the purpose of strengthening investor confidence in financial gatekeepers (auditors, financial analysts and CRAs).[19]

2.2.1.1 Ethical Regulatory Model (ERM)

The ERM features in professions (accountants and lawyers) that are expected to demonstrate the highest standards of professional conduct and take into consideration the public interest. Ethical behaviour plays a vital role in ensuring public trust in business practices and upholding their reputation. An ethical code is distinct from a moral code. Like professional codes of conduct, the ERM is self-regulatory, promulgated by CRAs to regulate their own conduct. The IOSCO rules have further supplemented them by requiring the incorporation of additional clauses. It is suggested that for ethical rules to be effective, the regulators should be able to take appropriate actions against those CRAs that breach these ethical rules. As will be seen in Chap. 3, a disclaimer of liability clause inserted by CRAs protects them from such breaches. The dominant aim of regulation ought to be to prevent gatekeeper failure by the CRAs. The contentious issue is how to make CRAs perform an effective role as the investors' gatekeeper rather than try to please issuers who pay their fees based on the issuers-pay model. In the case of accountants/auditors, the aims of the accounting standard and the common law were to prevent auditors from acting as mere lapdogs. When developing common law, the judges were cautious and equated auditors to a watchdog (a moderate standard) and avoided making them a bloodhound (a very high standard) or a lapdog (a low standard).[20]

If liability is found to be non-existent, it may be because regulators prefer to impose fines rather than de-registering CRAs from nationally recognized statistical

---

[18] Fuchita and Litan (2006).

[19] Ibid.

[20] Lopes L. J. *In re Kingston Cotton Mills*, Court of Appeal, ChD (1895), had stated that an auditor is a watchdog and not a bloodhound, at 288. The tripartite test of foreseeability, proximity and policy issues were enunciated by the House of Lords in *Caparo Industries Plc v Dickman* [1990] 2 AC 605. See also Windal (1980).

rating organization (NRSRO) status, then the book will propose that ERM be supplemented with the legal regulatory model (LMR) considered below.

2.2.1.2 Legal Regulatory Model (LMR)

Prima facie, the basis for the LRM is akin to legal liabilities for professions (e.g., auditors, lawyers, securities analysts, etc.) for their failure to act as responsible gatekeepers. Judges, based on awarding damages, have penalised professionals for their failure to act as their clients' gatekeeper. What the judges have done is to lay down a body of laws as precedents for future use by litigants and their lawyers.[21] They then scrutinise the acts of gatekeepers (auditors, solicitors, etc.), give rulings based on acceptable acts as distinguished from unacceptable ones and examine the defences that are available to the gatekeepers. Judges have been very cautious, and rightly so, in not imposing liability on the gatekeepers "in an indeterminate amount for an indeterminate time to an indeterminate class".[22] However, total absolution from liability would make gatekeepers complacent in discharging their duties.

2.2.1.3 Reputation Capital Model and Reputation Theory

Reputation Capital

"Reputation mechanisms operate in the credit rating industry to solve problems of information asymmetry".[23] Partnoy[24] is in favour of the imposition of both regulation and liability that relates to CRAs as reputational intermediaries. As a key limitation on gatekeeper behaviour, scholarship on gatekeepers has focused attention on reputation in the belief that reputation-related incentives alone would suffice to lead gatekeepers to screen against fraudulent transactions and improper disclosure in an optimal way. On this basis, there is no need for the imposition of regulation or civil liability on the CRAs. The evidence based on the worldwide credit crisis suggests otherwise. It has thrust CRAs into the spotlight, with attention focused on their ratings of novel structured finance products. "The mortgage-related assets, particularly securities, spread to U.S. and global investors, and the permeation of these assets made a global financial crisis inevitable when the assets became 'toxic'".[25] The New York Attorney General's office in 2010 started investigating not only whether Wall Street banks manipulated the process of achieving a

---

[21] See Cross and Harris (1991).

[22] The classic words of Cardozo C. J. made in *Ultramares Corporation v. Touche* (1931) 174 N.E. 441 at 444.

[23] Bonewitz (2010), p. 391, http://scholarship.law.wm.edu/wmblr/vol1/iss2/4.

[24] See Partnoy (2003a).

[25] Cox et al. (2010).

triple-A rating on securities built from packages of subprime mortgages but also whether the CRAs allowed themselves to be co-opted in that process.[26] The basis of a dominant academic theory of CRAs is the reputational capital model that implies that under the right circumstances, a well-functioning reputation mechanism will act as deterrence and prevent low-quality ratings from being issued. As policy initiators, regulators have to make efforts in fixing discrete problems within the ratings market so that the reputation mechanism can work properly. This requires policymakers to take a number of initiatives intended to address various perceived problems, including the need for enhancing competition, promoting transparency, reducing conflicts of interest and reducing ratings-dependent regulation, in order to achieve the aim of preventing gatekeeper failure.

Coffee notes:

> Characteristically, the professional gatekeeper essentially assesses or vouches for the corporate client's own statements about itself or a specific transaction. This duplication is necessary because the market recognizes that the gatekeeper has a lesser incentive to lie than does its client and thus regards the gatekeeper's assurance or evaluation as more credible. To be sure, the gatekeeper as watchdog is typically paid by the party that it is to watch, but its relative credibility stems from the fact that it is in effect pledging a reputational capital that it has built up over many years of performing similar services for numerous clients. In theory, such reputational capital would not be sacrificed for a single client and a modest fee.[27]

Hunt argues that reform efforts consistent with the reputational capital model of CRAs are incomplete. His reasoning is that a well-functioning reputation mechanism will still not guarantee high-quality ratings of new products. When rating novel products, CRAs have no reputation at stake for rating them. While low-quality ratings on new products could harm the reputation of the agency for rating other products, CRAs will not hesitate in rating a novel product if it is lucrative based on the high volume of that product.[28]

In theory, should CRAs intentionally issue or maintain inaccurate ratings they will damage their reputation and, as a result, their business would suffer. In practice, "when thousands of structured debt securities proved to hold inflated ratings during the run-up to the credit crisis",[29] CRAs continued to maintain their position in the global financial system. CRAs had the ability to rate more accurately, and the criticism levelled against them is that they intentionally failed to do so.[30] In reality, CRAs' reputation with investors has never been a cause of concern, partly because the majority of credit ratings given were accurate. However, inaccurate ratings that are too high act to the advantage of the issuers in their ability to raise money cheaply by offering low interest rates on their debt instruments but act

[26] Farrell (2010).

[27] Coffee Jr (2002), pp. 5–6.

[28] Hunt (2009a), p. 109 at 181.

[29] Bonewitz (2010), p. 391.

[30] See "Credit Rating Agencies and the Financial Crisis on Oversight and Gov't Reform", 111th Cong. 41 (2008).

to the disadvantage of investors who accept riskier debt paper than they wish to hold. Even if, for the sake of argument, CRAs do earn comparatively small fees for each opinion they provide, there is no justification for the CRAs' immunity from liability should they get their ratings wrong. The statutory and regulatory regime governing CRAs ought to tackle barriers to accuracy that are due to "regulatory and market factors [which] may increase the short-term profitability of falsifying ratings or diminish the long-term profitability of reputation-building".[31]

The role of CRAs in ratings for asset-backed securities and those collateralised by and associated with subprime residential mortgages has cast a doubt over their ability, as gatekeepers, to provide reliable ratings to enable other parties such as investors, financial institutions and regulators to make informed decisions. It seems CRAs are competent gatekeepers when performing their role as they do not need to stake their reputational capital behind the judgments they make, and therefore the notion of reputation capital influencing CRAs can be rejected.[32] Some take the view that the judgments CRAs make relate either to withholding their seal of approval or to acknowledging publically their endorsement.[33] The reason attributed to the demise of reputation capital is the CRAs' shift from a relationship with investors to one with issuers, which may be a contributing factor to the crisis. The evidence does suggest that a shift from the investors-pay model to the issuer-pay model has led CRAs in issuing higher ratings.[34] CRAs claim that they thrive by their reputation, and if that were the case, CRAs would have been cautious in issuing ratings and the problems seen in the subprime mortgages and financial markets prevented.

Reputation Theory

Having scrutinised the reputation capital model above, it is time to examine reputational theory. In reality, investors were persuaded to make investment decisions and buy subprime mortgage products based on favourable ratings issued by CRAs, and when these ratings turned out to be faulty they suffered losses. The CRAs, as intermediaries or gatekeepers, do provide important services by vetting issuers' creditworthiness for the benefit of investors. Previously, under the investors-pay model, investors used to pay CRAs by subscribing to their magazines, which published ratings of various debt instrument issues by various corporations. Under this model, CRAs were agents of the investors. An agent is a person who acts on behalf of another. This is no longer the case based on the present issuers-pay model, and in the strictest sense CRAs are the agents of the issuers, and arguably this scenario plays a big role in absolving CRAs from liability to investors. The adoption of the issuers-pay model created the possibility that a CRA will

[31] Bonewitz (2010), p. 391.

[32] Partnoy (1999), pp. 627 ff. Hunt (2009a) footnote 68 (and sources cited therein).

[33] Coffee (2006).

[34] Jiang (Xuefeng) et al. (2012).

compromise the integrity of its ratings to appease the issuer—its paying customer—by either issuing an undeservedly high rating or by failing to downgrade a security when changes in circumstances warrant it.[35] However, the issuer-pays conflict did not create a problem when rating non-securitised products; as will be seen later, it only became intensified when CRAs started rating securitised products[36]; initially they gave high ratings, but then they had to downgrade them at the beginning of 2007.[37]

The reason for such a problem arising is, firstly, CRAs had underestimated the risk that the issuers of certain, more complicated, financial instruments may not be able to repay the debts; secondly, they gave the highest possible ratings to complex instruments even in cases where it could not be justified by economic fundamentals[38]; and, thirdly, when the market conditions worsened, they failed to reflect this promptly in their ratings. Various inexperienced investors in the US and abroad felt encouraged to purchase financial instruments relying on given ratings without first having properly assessed the risks and thereby suffered irrecoverable losses. The present applicable laws tend to protect CRAs against suits filed by the investors.[39]

Dennis views the situation differently in that the question is whether CRAs' "underestimation of the risks of mortgage backed securities" was due to a mistake on their part or was deliberate. It was deliberate if the underestimation was due to an "economically rational response to legal, regulatory, and market incentives".[40] In reality, "revenues from rating mortgage backed securities and other structured finance products grew exponentially between 2001 and 2006, so much so that by 2006, these ratings accounted for a significant part of rating agencies' total revenues".[41] However, "the costs of inaccurate certification were declining as a result of judicial and regulatory actions favouring limited rating agency liability".[42] Based on the cost/benefit analysis, if "the benefits of overrating mortgage backed securities were greater than the costs"[43] of issuing reliable ratings, then the CRAs would opt for issuing higher ratings, even if they turned out to be unreliable. This proposition suggests that CRAs' "behaviour in the months and years preceding the credit crisis, calls for regulatory overhaul and additional liability [to] be imposed on rating agencies".[44]

A mistaken assumption is that making the credit rating industry more transparent, more competitive and less conflicted will *per se* restore the quality of credit

---

[35] Darcy (2009), p. 623.

[36] Ibid.

[37] Ibid.

[38] Europa Press Releases (2009).

[39] More discussion is in Chap. 6.

[40] See Dennis (2008–2009), p. 1111.

[41] Ibid.

[42] Ibid.

[43] Ibid.

[44] Ibid.

ratings.[45] Merely by providing investors with more information and more choices, as required by regulation, may not be "adequate for guarding against compromised rating".[46] It may not be a good option if investors are unable to assess accurately CRAs' reputations, and CRAs have no legal accountability for issuing or maintaining inaccurate ratings. The suggestion that a successful reform effort must restore the role of reputation in the credit rating industry and if this is unachievable, then the regulatory need for ratings ought to be dispensed with[47] is taking an extreme position. The solution may lie elsewhere in the form of making CRAs legally accountable for their actions in those situations where they issue unreliable ratings, especially when the issuer is raising a large amount of money from the marketplace. When an issuer is trying to raise a large amount of money, it requires CRAs, when rating a debt instrument, to exercise extra caution. In the absence of liability for issuing unreliable ratings, the chances are that CRAs will not exercise any caution.

2.2.2 Various Other Theories

Besides reputation theory, there are various other theories. The dominant theory is gatekeeper theory, which is examined below to see what light it throws on the regulation and CRAs as actors.

2.2.2.1 Gatekeeper Theory

This book will examine CRAs' gatekeeper role by analysing regulation introduced in the US and EU. The basis of the book's assumption is that the regulators were trying to prevent the gatekeeper failure of CRAs. Partnoy, in his seminal article "How and why CRAs are not like other gatekeepers",[48] briefly touches on the negative traits of CRAs; in Partnoy's opinion, they are more serious when one compares them with other professional gatekeepers. The reasons put forward by Partnoy relate to the fact that in spite of CRAs performing at least as poorly as other gatekeepers, it had a positive rather than a negative impact on their market value, which has skyrocketed.

The answer as to why CRAs are very different from other gatekeepers is that "unlike auditors, analysts, investment bankers, corporate attorneys, stock

[45] SEC's regulations under the Reform Act of 2006. The U.S. Congress passed the Credit Rating Agency Reform Act of 2006, Pub. L. 109–291, 120 Stat. 1327; it was enacted on 29 September 2006.

[46] Darcy (2009), p. 645.

[47] Bonewitz (2010), p. 392.

[48] Partnoy (2006b), pp. 60–61.

exchanges, and others – [the CRAs] literally regulate admission to bond markets, and possess the power to articulate public policy . . . with no straightforward form of accountability to constrain them".[49] CRAs exist in a position of profitable limbo somewhere between market journalist and state authority. In addition, CRAs continue to face conflicts of interest and have benefited from an oligopoly market structure reinforced by regulation registering few CRAs as NRSRO and thus providing them with "regulatory licences". CRAs had previously merely assigned ratings to debt and companies in which they had no active role. However, the increased complexity and introduction of mortgage-backed securities (MBSs) and collateralized debt obligations (CDOs) created a unique conflict of interest.[50] This puts CRAs in a position of incredible power with little accountability as they have been largely immune from civil and criminal liabilities for malfeasance, an issue the book will examine later.

The claim of Hunt,[51] based on the positive traits, is that CRAs are the investors' gatekeeper. His reasons are that, first, investors look to them for high-quality assessment of credit risk; second, the financial regulatory system has incorporated ratings issued by agencies that enjoy the government-recognised status of NRSRO; and third, many fixed-income instruments and structural products require ratings to be conducted by CRAs and have to meet the rating criteria. The basis for regarding CRAs as the investors' gatekeeper is the likelihood of an adverse effect on the investors' interest when the ratings issued are defective, unreliable or sham. Either as a gatekeeper who performs the job of a watchdog or a referee, CRAs mediate between the clashing of the interests of both the issuers and investors as players. Drawing from the analogy of the audit profession, CRAs discharge an important function, which has enabled issuers to raise money by issuing various debt instruments. Investors likewise rely on ratings issued by CRAs in making investment decisions.[52] Using a football match analogy, "[w]hen the referee is being paid by the players; no one should be surprised when the game spins out of control. That is what happened on Wall Street when credit rating agencies . . . sold their independence to the highest bidder".[53] Levitt suggests that CRAs "are playing both coach and referee in the debt game. They rate companies and issuers that pay them for that service".[54]

The reason why CRAs may not wish to act as the investors' gatekeeper is perhaps their fear of courts imposing liability, which at present does not exist. The policymakers, based on the theory that CRAs are gatekeepers, are able to legitimise their position in being able to regulate the CRAs. The legitimacy comes

[49] Bruner (2008).

[50] Krebs (2009–2010), p. 141.

[51] Hunt (2009b), pp. 1–2.

[52] See Shore (2000), p. 387.

[53] Statement of Rep. Christopher H. Shays, H. Comm. on Oversight and Government Reform, p. 12. http://beta.congress.gov/110/crpt/hrpt930/CRPT-110hrpt930.pdf.

[54] Levitt (2007).

from the regulators' ability to introduce regulation. Initially, the book will show in Chap. 3 that policymakers adopted soft laws; this was easy as CRAs already had in place codes of conduct to regulate their behaviour. Later chapters will examine the deficiencies found in the soft laws that necessitated regulators in the US and EU supplementing them by enacting statutory regulations.

2.2.2.2 Yield Hunt Theory

To try to understand and explain the reason why the commercial banks in the US and global investors had turned towards mortgage-related instruments as their investment vehicle in the first place, the Yield Hunt Theory can be examined.[55] The premise underlying the Yield Hunt Theory relates to a double-edged shield (which later on turned out to be a double-edged sword): investors wanted to invest in assets that were meant to be very safe yet at the same time produced high yields.

Banks had an incentive to seek low-risk assets. They needed to meet the capital adequacy requirements set by the Basel Committee on Banking Regulation.[56] To meet these requirements, they had to keep a certain amount of capital on their books to guard against the risk attached to the assets they held. The less risky the asset, the less capital the banks were required to keep to satisfy regulatory requirement.[57] Commercial banks in the US and worldwide and in the EU were incentivised to purchase assets that were considered to be of little risk. At the same time, it eliminated the requirement of the need to keep large amounts of capital on hand required under Basel II and III, and their risk was measured by the credit ratings given to a particular borrower of debt issue. The purpose of Basel II is to create an international standard that banking regulators can use when creating regulations about how much capital banks need to put aside to guard against the types of financial and operational risks banks face.[58] Basel III is a comprehensive set of reform measures, developed by the Basel Committee on Banking Supervision, to strengthen the regulation, supervision and risk management of the banking sector.[59] The attention by the Federal Reserve Bank in the US and Central Banks in the EU to Basel's need for higher capital ratios and liquidity requirements for financial institutions is probably because of the bad state of these institutions in spite of being under their watch.

In reality, it was not sufficient for banks to hold only low-risk assets as they also wanted assets that produced high yields or returns on their investment, in order to

---

[55] The "yield hunt theory" has been devised by Cox et al. (2010), p. 1.

[56] See "Basel II" in the Glossary.

[57] Cox et al. (2010), pp. 1–2, note 27.

[58] "Basel 2", https://www.enisa.europa.eu/activities/risk-management/current-risk/business-process-integration/governance/frameworks/basel-2.

[59] "International regulatory framework for banks (Basel III)", https://www.bis.org/bcbs/basel3.htm.

increase profit. The securitisation process produced financial instruments that seemingly allowed banks to satisfy both of these needs:

> Through securitization and re-securitization, U.S. investment banks and other financial institutions pooled many different types of assets, including risky subprime mortgages, to make assets that were "safer" and would thus appeal to commercial banks . . . These assets produced higher yields than other types of assets, such as U.S. Treasury bonds, with comparable credit ratings.[60]

To obtain a greater yield for the same amount of risk, the US banks invested heavily in subprime mortgage-backed securities. When yield hunting becomes a global phenomenon, it leads to financial crises. European banks also became involved when they invested in triple-A-rated asset-backed securities (that is, subprime mortgage-backed securities) produced in the US.

2.2.2.3 Agency Theory

The CRAs' claim is that they are not investors' fiduciaries, but rather they are issuers' agents whose securities they rate. The reason why CRAs are not investors' agents is that they simply rely on credit ratings to make investment decisions.[61] Such a claim of the absence of an agency relationship would protect CRAs from legal accountability to investors. What is, however, not appreciated is that when the investors do buy securities offered by issuers, the price paid by investors, *inter alia*, includes the cost of rating that the issuers have to pay to the CRAs. Investors are therefore indirectly paying for the services of CRAs, thus creating, at least in theory, a privity of contract between the CRAs and investors and thus giving rise to an agency relationship. The US judges have readily upheld the First Amendment defence in favour of CRAs, thus depriving the investors (or their lawyers) from presenting an argument of indirect privity, and the judges, on their part, have had no chance of deciding on the validity of such an argument.

2.2.2.4 Deterrence Theory

The book will examine to what extent the various regulations introduced have acted as a deterrent to CRAs and have protected the interest of investors; this demands an examination of a deterrence theory. From a behavioural psychology perspective, deterrence is a theory about preventing or controlling actions or behaviour through fear of punishment or retribution. From a criminal perspective, deterrence is the use of punishment as a threat to deter people from offending.[62] Deterrence is often

---

[60] Cox et al. (2010), p. 2, note 27.

[61] Standard & Poor's Ratings Services, "Role and Function of Credit Rating Agencies in the U.S. Securities Markets", U.S. Securities and Exchange Commission Public Hearing—15 November 2002. http://www.sec.gov/news/extra/credrate/standardpoors.htm.

[62] Wright (2010).

contrasted with retribution, which holds that punishment is a necessary consequence of a crime (or a misdeed in the form of an error) and should be calculated based on the gravity of the wrong done.

The concept of deterrence has two key assumptions: the first is that specific punishments imposed on offenders will deter or prevent them from committing further crimes; the second is that fear of punishment will prevent others from committing similar crimes.[63] The basis of deterrence theory as a concept is that if the consequence of committing a crime outweighs the benefit of the crime itself, then it will deter an individual from committing that crime. The basis of the foundation of this idea is that all individuals are aware of the difference between right and wrong and the consequences associated with wrong or criminal behaviour.[64] Based on economic cost/benefit analysis,[65] a CRA will factor the cost (time, staff and expenses) involved in ensuring the issuance of reliable ratings and the possible damages they would have to pay if found liable for issuing unreliable ratings. If the expected payment of damages by CRAs in terms of fines imposed by a regulator were smaller than the sum it would cost them to issue reliable ratings, then the CRAs may be tempted to issue unreliable ratings. The basis is in utilising the easiest or the least expensive method, and if held liable they would take a risk of being required to pay damages.

The aims of civil action and criminal action differ. In a civil action for damages against the perpetrator of the wrongdoing, the aim is compensation, as opposed to the criminal prosecution where punishment is the aim.[66] The objective of tort law is to compensate the claimant at the expense of the tortfeasor. It is unclear as to whether the payment of compensation is for educational purposes or atonement for wrongdoing.[67] The law of tort is also an expression of a moral principle[68] in that one who by his fault has caused damage to another ought, as a matter of justice, to compensate.[69]

Utilitarian philosophy[70] advocates that the damages awarded to investors must not be punitive by being far greater than the losses sustained by them. Windfall gains are not the norm and are few.[71] From the investors' perspective, they want to be "made whole" (that is, to remain in a position they would have been in had they not invested in the unreliable and negligent ratings). Investors are seeking

---

[63] See Glossary for the definition of "deterrence".

[64] For the assumptions, implications and alternative, see Kennedy (1983). For a historical perspective, see Summerfield (2006).

[65] For the definition of "cost and benefit analysis", see Glossary.

[66] Williams (1951), p. 137.

[67] Ibid.

[68] Pound (1914), p. 195.

[69] Williams (1951), p. 140.

[70] Ibid., p. 146.

[71] Von Hirsch (1992), pp. 55–98. See also http://law.jrank.org/pages/9576/Punishment-THEORIES-PUNISHMENT.html.

compensation for losses arising from their reliance on ratings negligently issued by CRAs, and their intention is not to make CRAs mere scapegoats. They are not asking for punitive damages for this will amount to a "windfall" gain, which even the judges generally despise. If CRAs are required to act responsibly, then compensating investors will act as a deterrent and would compel them to organise their affairs responsibly. Compensation will prevent other CRAs from cutting corners (i.e., taking shortcuts to save staff time and money or use less time in conducting ratings) resulting in issuing unreliable ratings. Investors, like other professions (auditors, doctors and solicitors), expect CRAs always to uphold the highest standards and to be held to account for their actions when they issue unreliable ratings. The solution may lie in making regulation have a deterrent effect on the part of CRAs by continuing to enact more regulation rather than removing the need for ratings or replacing rating with something else.

2.3 An Introduction to Credit Ratings

2.3.1 Introduction

2.3.1.1 Functions and the Role of CRAs

CRAs publish ratings and research about the creditworthiness of issuers and the credit quality of specific debt instruments. They can generally perform credit analyses more efficiently and economically because they are specialised in that activity and devote substantial resources to it.[72] CRAs disseminate rating assessments about the relative creditworthiness of, *inter alia*, issuers and debt issuances. The usefulness of credit ratings depends on them enhancing market efficiency and providing a globally comparable, authoritative measure of creditworthiness.[73] However, what CRAs do is to issue opinions on the creditworthiness of a particular issuer or financial instrument. They assess the likelihood that an issuer will default either on its financial obligations generally (issuer rating) or on a particular debt or fixed income security (instrument rating).[74] Credit ratings from CRAs provide predictive opinions on an isolated characteristic of a company, which is the likelihood that an issuer will be able to repay its rated debt in a timely manner.[75]

Although credit rating is the main factor for banks and other investors to consider in making investment decisions, credit rating has its own limitations. It

[72] Standards & Poor's, "Credit Rating Agencies Evaluate Credit Risk", http://www.standardandpoors.com/aboutcreditratings/.

[73] MIS EU Transparency Report, at 2, http://www.moodys.com/PublishingImages/MCO/EU%20Trans%2011.pdf.

[74] Official Journal of the European Union, "Communications form the Commission on Credit Rating Agencies", 2006/C 59/2, C59/2.

[75] Macey (2006), p. 21.

is neither an indication of market liquidity of a debt security nor its price in the secondary market. CRAs guarantee neither credit quality nor the future credit risk.[76] Rather, credit ratings offer predictions as to the likelihood of repayment of a particular debt instrument, in part or as a whole. Credit ratings that relate to general corporate debts require CRAs to analyse the overall financial health of that company. CRAs also conduct ratings on the credit risk of assets within a pooled security, such as a mortgage-backed security.[77]

2.3.1.2 What Is a Credit Rating?

A CRA is a private independent company that attributes and publishes credit ratings.[78] For those investors who do not have the knowledge or time to investigate, monitor and evaluate the quality of available financial instruments, credit ratings provide simple, easy-to-use information that can help them make rational investment decisions.[79] A CRA examines a specific security to determine the likelihood that the security's issuer will meet its obligation by repaying the purchasers, as investors, their principal and interest.[80] The CRA's determination about the security's respective stability or risk when converted into a rating ranges from triple-A to D. Triple-A rating indicates that there is little chance of default, whereas ratings of BB and lower mean they are of a speculative grade and are often referred to as junk bonds.[81] The advantage of "[h]igher ratings [is] not just [that it] allow [s] for lower borrowing costs but can be a magnet for additional business and better terms from suppliers".[82] CRAs, by analysing and rating a security's creditworthiness, indicate the issuing entity's ability to meet its financial obligations. CRAs provide investors with valuable information that is utilised in determining proper pricing of a security. CRAs are an essential cog in the wheel of the transferability of securities,[83] which also trade on a secondary market.

Having established that CRAs are in the business of analysing and rating securities and debt offerings, when one of its clients—for example, a corporation or a bank—is planning to issue a security, it contracts a CRA to rate that security. This rating may take into consideration various factors, including the likelihood of default or the expected rate of return. The Big Three CRAs, as private organisations operating globally, make their credit ratings available to investors globally on a comparative basis by charging issuers fees that have resulted in conflicts of interest.

[76] Ibid; see also Partnoy (2006b), http://ssrn.com/abstract=900257; Blaurock.

[77] Akins and Calabria (2012), p. 3.

[78] Kruithof and Wymeersch (2006), p. 1.

[79] Santomero (2008), pp. ix–xi. Langohr and Langohr (2008), pp. 89–125.

[80] Schwarcz (2001).

[81] Kisgen (2007), pp. 56–64.

[82] Hackel (2010).

[83] Brooke (2009–2010), p. 738.

However, CRAs do rate sovereign debts publicly and free of charge, thus avoiding any such conflict.[84]

2.3.1.3 The Business of Credit Rating Agencies[85]

CRAs "provide investors, large and small, a signpost in assessing the likelihood of default by a bond issuer, be it a foreign or local government, or a Wall Street bank offering a sophisticated engineered product".[86] CRAs are for-profit entities, and they exist due to governments' blessings. They play a public interest role.[87] Although they may have misaligned incentives, legal requirements are such that any company or country that wants to raise money by issuing debt instruments (e.g., bonds) has to be evaluated by CRAs. CRAs are responsible for providing investors with information about an organisation's creditworthiness. CRAs differ from a credit-reporting agency in that whereas a credit-reporting agency is responsible for compiling financial data that is necessary for loan decisions, CRAs conduct all the statistical assessments that are involved in placing a rating on a company or organisation's credit history. [88] CRAs have received a lot of criticism over the years for the quality of their research, and the basis for these criticisms relate to their errors in judgment when rating structured products in the past.

The desire for yield runs deep. Globally, in the week ending 24 July 2013, investors pumped money into junk bond funds and US $5.4 billion flew into speculative-grade bonds. Investors "prefer high-yield vs. investment-grade due to the extra coupon cushion it provides".[89] There is, therefore, a demand for junk investments, but issuers have to pay high interest rates based on the associated risk. Some managers of unit trusts or pension funds may decide to hold a combination of low-risk and high-risk investments on behalf of their investors. CRAs arrive at the ratings by applying a combination of some science and some art. Science relates to the mathematical modelling of the entity's financial performance (in case of a government, its economy) and art based on analysts' assessments of the prospects of the entity's business and its place in the economy generally.[90] In the conduct of securities market, like bond markets, CRAs assign ratings by way of letter grades.[91]

Most importantly, when assigning ratings, a CRA will examine an issuer's company position. It includes financial statements, audit report, past financial

[84] Detrixhe (2011).

[85] For a detailed discussion, see Langohr and Langohr (2008); White (2010), pp. 211–226.

[86] Doyle et al. (2013), para 6.

[87] For Raison d'Etre of Credit Ratings and their Market, see Langohr and Langohr (2008), pp. 89–160.

[88] "Credit Rating Agencies – How They Work", http://creditratingagency.net/.

[89] Farzad (2013), paras 1 and 3.

[90] Hudson (2009), p. 915.

[91] McVea (2010), p. 701 at 704.

dealings, timely repayment capabilities; amount of debt to equity, cash flow and other disclosed/undisclosed contingencies that could affect the company; and application of standards and procedures to ensure the credibility of the ratings issued. Investors use these credit ratings as a valuable yardstick in identifying good investment opportunities and in assessing the risks associated with their investment decisions. A credit rating (sometimes also called a debt rating) is an opinion based on whether an issuer of a credit commitment, a debt or debt-like security, is likely to make timely repayment of its financial obligations generally or a particular financial obligation.[92]

2.3.1.4 Opinion not a Guarantee

A credit rating is neither an indication of the market liquidity of a debt security or its price in the secondary market nor a guarantee of credit quality or of future credit risk.[93] In the modern capital markets, investors and others are bound to look for someone who can do several things—shift vast amounts of information, analyse the credit risk and express opinions—to enable investors to gauge the potential credit risk of issuers of securities and their financial obligations. This is required when lending to a particular borrower or when purchasing an issuer's debt and debt-like securities.[94] Lenders and investors in fixed income securities similarly use credit ratings in assessing the likely risks they face when lending money to, or investing in, the securities of a particular issuer.[95] Ratings may apply to a variety of entities, including sovereigns, financial institutions and corporations, and to the securities or other obligations they issue, as well as to structured finance securities backed by receivables and other financial assets.[96] In the US, the State laws require State funds and employment pension funds to meet credit rating requirements and the banking regulations to determine regulatory capital requirements based on the credit ratings of the securities that banks own.[97] In that respect, judicial decisions should protect fiduciaries that rely on credit ratings.[98]

---

[92] A joint report by the Treasury and the Australian Securities and Investments Commission (2008), p. 4.

[93] Ibid; see also Partnoy (2006a, b); Blaurock; Akins and Calabria (2012), p. 3.

[94] The Technical Committee of International Organization of Securities Commissions, "IOSCO Code of Conduct Fundamentals for Credit Rating Agencies" (Revised May 2008) at 1. http://www.cmvm.pt/CMVM/Cooperacao%20Internacional/Docs%20Iosco/Documents/CodCondutaIOSCOCRA.pdf.

[95] A joint report by the Treasury and the Australian Securities and Investments Commission (2008), pp. 6–7.

[96] Fitch Code of Conduct (January 2014) at 4. https://www.fitchratings.com/web_content/ratings/fitch_ratings_definitions_and_scales.pdf.

[97] Hunt (2008), p. 1. http://paers.ssrn.com/so13/papers.cfin?abstractid–1267625.

[98] Ibid.

2.3.1.5 Conduct of Ratings

Both Standard & Poor's (S&P) and Moody's have provided some details as to how they conduct their ratings.[99] The CRAs mainly rely on information they receive from the company that subscribes to it in issuing and maintaining the credit rates.[100] In addition, CRAs conduct an appropriate investigation ranging from verifying the authenticity of the information through financial statements, their rating methodologies, audit reports, legal issues and information obtained from independent sources. CRAs issue and maintain credit by gathering information from the companies with which the business has had financial relationships.[101] A rating is analysed by using financial statements, audit reports and lawsuits. The credit report also contains a brief history of the company, the number of its employees, and its size and structure.[102] The profile of the company, which is contained in the rating, also helps creditors to gauge the size and potential of the companies they are dealing with or hope to deal with in future. The CRAs do not search for fraud, nor do they perform audits of rated companies. The analysis of their credit ratings largely depend on the quality of information they receive from corporations, which they do not verify. This would cast doubt on the reliability of such ratings. The CRAs generally make these ratings available to both the subscribers as well as to non-subscribers; the only difference is that subscribers have access to detailed reports.

2.3.1.6 Reliance on Ratings and the Need for Higher Ratings

The main reason why investors rely on CRAs' ratings is their perceived reputation and credibility. There are diverse users of credit ratings, and they are issuers, borrowers, investors and regulators. Issuers and corporate borrowers on their part rely on and, in many cases, pay for opinions issued by CRAs to help them raise necessary capital. Investors and lenders naturally want to be compensated for uncertainty, and, when taking on debt, issuers pay for this uncertainty through higher interest rates. Institutional and private investors use credit ratings to help them allocate investments in a diversified risk portfolio. Government regulators use credit ratings for a variety of purposes, including setting capital charges for financial institutions according to the credit risks paused by the institutions' various investments portfolio.[103]

---

[99] For S&P see http://www.standardandpoors.com/aboutcreditratings/RatingsManual_PrintGuide.html, and for Moody's see http://www.moodys.com/Pages/amr002001.aspx.

[100] IOSCO (2003), p. 1.

[101] Ibid.

[102] Standard and Poor's, "About Credit Ratings", http://www.standardandpoors.com/aboutcreditratings/RatingsManual_PrintGuide.html.

[103] A joint report by the Treasury and the Australian Securities and Investments Commission (2008), pp. 6–7.

The corporate issuers rely on a continuing and growing need for credit and are more sensitive to the analyses of the Big Three with NRSRO status. For those firms that scarcely deal in the credit market, their cost for standby lines of credit, bankers' acceptances or other facilities will be higher than that for lower rated credits. Moreover, pledges tied to debt will be more restrictive for lower rated credits, forcing up their cost of capital based on secure bank lending. Low-rated firms may have no option but to consider raising capital from non-traditional lenders, including private equity and hedge funds. In numerous ways, credit ratings have an effect on the cost of companies' capital and on stock valuation. Higher ratings would not only allow for lower borrowing costs but also attract additional business and better terms from suppliers. In that respect, the credit rating has a significant effect on the cost of doing business.

Many companies dealing with overseas companies rely on the credit rating when making their purchase decisions. Companies will have their cost of debt significantly raised or lowered due to a change in their rating. Ratings also affect the entity's supplier and customer decisions, with regard to their willingness to supply goods or place purchase orders.

Downgrading impinges on the creditworthiness of a company and results in an adverse outcome on its valuation. An adverse downgrade affects the financial aspect of the business as creditors, and counterparties would then demand additional collateral. Many pension funds cannot own debts below a certain grade, while other funds may own only a small allocation of lower grades. Banks prefer to hold higher graded debt instruments in calculating their capital adequacy requirements because of the requirements of Basel II and III. A higher rating will create a greater potential demand for an issuer's fixed income instruments and correspondingly will lower the cost of debt.

2.3.1.7 Limitation of Credit Rating

CRAs publish credit ratings and research reports on securities, and in that respect they occupy a narrow but important niche in the investment information industry. They prefer to keep it that way and do not wish to undertake an extra burden and responsibility by providing other services like authenticating information supplied by companies and carrying out due diligence, which would increase the cost of rating but would be very beneficial to investors. Their role is to disseminate information about the relative creditworthiness of, among other things, financial obligations of corporations, banks, governmental entities and pools of assets collected in securitised or "structured finance" transactions.[104] The credit ratings so issued are forward-looking opinions that address solely the probability that a debt

[104] Memorandum from Moody's (2008) http://www.parliament.the-stationery-office.co.uk/pa/cm200708/cmselect/cmtreasy/56/56we32.htm.

instrument will default and the amount of loss the debt holder will incur in the event of default.[105]

The turmoil in the credit markets has adversely affected investor confidence on the ratings issued.[106] However, there is consensus among the Big Three CRAs about the limit on what they can offer. In their view, the credit ratings do not address many other factors in the investment decision process, including the price, term, likelihood of prepayment, liquidity risk or relative valuation of particular securities. When rating a corporation, a credit rating analyses the intrinsic financial strength of that corporation on a stand-alone basis and then factors in the likelihood and extent of external support in the event of financial difficulty.[107] According to Moody's, a rating system is not a "pass-fail" system because the future is uncertain and, therefore, it is difficult to ascertain which corporation will be able to pay its debts and which will not. Rather, ratings are an assessment of the relative risk of credit loss as measured by the increasing probability of such loss with each lower rating level.[108]

2.3.2 *Moody's and Fitch: Ratings Volume and Revenue Generated*

Fitch Ratings currently maintains wide ratings coverage, ranging from approximately 6,000 financial institutions (including over 3,500 banks and 1,400 insurance companies). Other coverage, including finance and leasing companies, broker-dealers, asset managers, managed funds and bonds, makes up the remainder of its financial institution coverage. In addition, it rates more than 2,000 corporate issuers, 100 sovereigns, 200 sub-sovereigns, 300 global infrastructure ratings and 46,000 US municipal transactions. Moreover, it also "maintains surveillance on over 6,500 US, 1,300 European and 800 Asian structured finance transactions".[109]

Moody's is the oldest bond-rating agency, having introduced ratings in 1909.[110] Today, it is one of the world's most widely utilised sources for credit ratings, research and credit risk analysis. Its ratings and analysis track debt covering more than 100 sovereign nations, 12,000 corporate issuers and 96,000 structured finance obligations. They maintain offices in most of the world's major financial centres and employ approximately 3,000 people worldwide, including more than 1,000 analysts.[111] Moody's, from 2000 to 2008, rated nearly 45,000 mortgage-related

[105] Ibid. Paras 1, 2.

[106] Ibid. Para 7.

[107] Ibid. Paras 3, 4.

[108] Ibid. Para 13.

[109] http://www.fimalac.com/Fitch-ratings-GB.html.

[110] Parnoy (2009), p. 3.

[111] Additional information about Moody's is available at www.moodys.com.

securities as triple-A. This compares with six private-sector companies in the US that carried this coveted rating in early 2010. In 2006 alone, Moody's had put its triple-A stamp of approval on 30 mortgage-related securities every working day. The results were disastrous: 83 % of the mortgage securities rated triple-A that year ultimately were downgraded.[112] The reasons are "the flawed computer models, the pressure from financial firms that paid for the ratings, the relentless drive for market share; the lack of resources to do the job despite record profits, and the absence of meaningful public oversight"[113]; and the skill with which investment banks learned to present financial statements to get triple-A ratings for clients. What this means is that "without the active participation of the CRAs, the market for mortgage-related securities could not have been what it became".[114] With regard to revenue generated:

> From 2000 until 2007, the growth of structured finance drove an exponential increase in revenue for the major rating agencies. Moody's—the only agency that is also a reporting company—had its net income rise "from $159 million in 2000 to $425 million in 2004, while its stock price increased by 300% between 2001 and 2006." Over roughly the same period, the share of Moody's revenue generated by structured finance rose to 44 percent.[115]

Moody's makes its credit ratings widely and publicly available at no cost to investors and the public. It publicly disseminates its ratings through press releases and makes them available on their website. Moody's makes ratings issued simultaneously available to all market participants regardless of whether or not they purchase their products or services. The public availability of ratings helps in creating a "level playing field" between, for example, large and small investors; enhances the transparency and efficiency of financial markets; and allows the market and all users of ratings to assess independently the aggregate performance of our rating system.[116]

In the first half of 2013, Fitch reported revenue of €378.4 million (US $497.2 million), a 19.3 % increase from €317.1 million (US $411.4 million) from the previous period. In the ratings segment, Fitch Ratings turned in a good performance with a first-half revenue of €308.1 million (US $404.9 million). Fitch Solutions, Fitch's second business segment, which is a subscription-based research service, in the first half of 2013 reported revenue of €55.3 million (US $72.6 million), which represented around 15 % of consolidated revenue, and it is maintaining its steady growth.[117]

When compared to 2007, Moody's and S&P had a combined market share of 80 % and Fitch had 15 %,[118] which meant that the credit rating industry was

---

[112] Benmelech and Dlugosz, p. 161.

[113] The Financial Crisis Inquiry Report (2011) at 25.

[114] Ibid.

[115] Bonewitz (2010), p. 405.

[116] Moody's Memorandum (2008), para 14.

[117] http://finance.yahoo.com/news/fimalac-first-half-2013-revenue-163303606.html.

[118] "Rating agencies: Measuring the measurers – Credit rating could do with more competition, and a bit more rigour" The Economist (31 May 2007) http://www.economist.com/node/9267952.

dominated by just two agencies, Moody's and S&P, and this led to legislative and regulatory calls for increased competition. Fitch believes in the power of competition:

> [O]ur emergence as a global, full service rating agency capable of competing against Moody's and S&P across all products and market segments has created meaningful competition in the ratings market for the first time in years. Fitch's challenge to the Moody's/S&P monopoly has enhanced innovation, forced transparency in the rating process, improved service to investors and created much needed price competition.[119]

However, the entry of Fitch in the market seems to have produced the opposite effect:

> The material entry of a third rating agency (Fitch) to the competitive landscape ... coincides with lower quality ratings from the incumbents: rating levels went up, the correlation between ratings and market-implied yields fell, and the ability of ratings to predict default deteriorated.[120]

Although Fitch has become a competitor to Moody's and S&P in providing rating services and has increased competition, the reliability of ratings issued has yet to improve because of conflict of interest as they are paid by issuers.[121]

2.3.3 Conclusion

Downgrading a rating by CRAs is not easy as it can create severe problems for the corporation (e.g., lenders may demand repayment or higher interest rates, it may be harder and more expensive to borrow money from other lenders, share prices may fall, etc.), which can then lead to further downgrades. Such a chain reaction has played an important part in the current financial crisis.[122] Investors and issuers perceive the importance of ratings differently. For investors, the high ratings given by CRAs act as an assurance that a borrower will be creditworthy and will not default on the debt.[123] This allows the issuers to give low interest and thus raise money cheaply. Any future downgrading affects both the investors (who would lose money spent in purchasing securities) and borrowers (forced to accept a higher interest rate on future securities).

Credit ratings have a significant impact on the operation of the markets and on the trust and confidence of investors and consumers. CRAs play an important role in global securities and banking markets, as investors, borrowers, issuers and

[119] 'Fitch Ratings', letter addressed to US SEC (12 November 2002) https://www.sec.gov/news/extra/credrate/fitchratings1.htm.

[120] Becker and Milbourn (2011), p. 493.

[121] Levin and Coburn (2011), p. 7. http://www.hsgac.senate.gov//imo/media/doc/Financial_Crisis/FinancialCrisisReport.pdf?attempt=2.

[122] Ibid.

[123] Cambridge.

governments as part of making informed investment and financing decisions use credit ratings.[124] The US subprime mortgage crisis highlighted the systemic relevance of the rating agencies and the deficiencies in their activities. The criticism of CRAs relates to their role in the financial crisis by understating credit risk. Rousseau postulates that lawmakers, regulators and commentators have questioned the role of CRAs in the market turmoil.[125] An international consensus then emerged that regulatory intervention was required, and this paved the way to regulating the rating business.[126]

CRAs are required to conduct their activities in accordance with the principles of integrity, transparency, responsibility and good governance.[127] This in turn will ensure that resultant credit ratings used in the US and EU will be independent, objective and of adequate quality. Thus, "a number of reform initiatives are under way in Canada, Europe and the United States to address the concerns raised by credit rating agencies' activities in the context of structured finance products".[128] The CRAs should realise that investors and issuers appear to be demanding, based on a common sense approach, both realistic and stable rating that will stand the test of time.

2.4 The Subprime Mortgage Crisis

2.4.1 What Is Structured Finance?

Structured finance involves the use of highly complex financial instruments and techniques by pooling of assets and the subsequent sale to investors of claims on the cash flows backed by these pools. Structured finance includes mortgage-backed securities (MBS), asset-backed commercial paper (ABCP), collateralized debt obligations (CDOs) and credit default swaps (CDS). Typically, several classes (or tranches) of securities are issued, each with distinct risk-return profiles.[129] Structured finance, in a narrow sense, is used interchangeably with securitisation[130] and needs further explanation:

[124] Regulation (EC) No 1060/2009 of the European Parliament and of the Council on Credit Rating Agencies of 16 September 2009, Reported in Official Journal of European Union (17.11.2009) at 1. http://eur-lex.europa.eu/LexUriServ/LexUriServ.do?uri=OJ:L:2009:302:FULL:EN:PDF.

[125] Rousseau (2009).

[126] Alcubilla and Pozo (2012).

[127] Seminar on "Benchmarks and Credit Rating Agencies" held on 4–5 June 2013 at St. Petersburg. http://www.g20.org/news/20130605/781392881.html.

[128] Rousseau (2009).

[129] Criado and Rixtel (2008), p. 11.

[130] Ibid. Criado and Rixtel (2008), p. 11.

> The term securitization refers to the transfer of financial assets from the original lender to others, often via a special purpose company. It does not refer to collateral or security for payment. Financial institutions find securitization attractive because it lowers the risk of funding by isolating risk. Furthermore, businesses find it attractive because it enables them to borrow more cheaply and obtain a better return than more conventional means of obtaining finance. In addition, this practice is sometimes used by financial institutions that are short of working capital or that must satisfy the capital adequacy ratios of the Bank of England or by those seeking to make a strategic move.[131]

> When securitisation started 25 or 30 years ago, it was to solve a crisis. Then, in 2008, it became the scapegoat for a crisis. The problem was not the tool but how it was used in some cases. Securitisation was initially about channelling capital market funding to lending, not about complex arbitrage products and collateralised debt obligations [CDO] squared. That principle remains and is being recognised now.[132]

The securitisation industry owes its very existence to the willingness of CRAs to rate asset-backed securities (ABS) based on "extravagantly hedged" true-sale opinions. The parties to a securitisation transaction are knowingly assuming a serious legal risk.[133] "'Securitisation' involves transferring pools of assets such as mortgage loans into a special purpose vehicle, which then issues 'asset backed securities' or marketable debt instruments".[134] Securitisation is based on statistical analysis and involves benchmarking by means of a rating to satisfy capital market investors. Securitisation takes pools of illiquid assets and turns them into liquid securities, and one of the big rating agencies (Moody's, Fitch or S&P) rates them. Once securities receive ratings, it is possible to fund them in the capital markets by issuing rated bonds (long term) or commercial paper (short term). One of the key advantages of ABS is that it is possible to borrow directly from the capital markets. The market for such securities was large and growing. ABS bonds issued in 2005 (prior to the 2007–2008 crisis) were worth US $797 billion (£419 bn) in the US and €408 billion (£282 bn) in Europe. The amount of commercial paper issued exceeded US $1 trillion. The most popular asset class securitised was mortgages, which accounted for 58 % of the market.[135] This was because, at that time, they related to many small individual assets with a clear payment history, which made obtaining ratings easier.

Some firms have other motives for securitisation, including "off balance sheet" treatment and risk management. On the sale of assets, a firm cannot lose more than the retained risk, which is 1.5 % of the pool for mortgages. Historically, banks had reasons to securitise, as the Basel I regulation required that corporate risk be backed by 8 % capital, mortgages by 4 % and banks by 1.6 %. The bank capital treatment of

---

[131] Chandler and Davies (1993), p. 48.

[132] Fabrice Susini, head of securitisation at BNP Paribas., quoted by Hart (2013b); see also Hart (2013a).

[133] K. Kettering, quoted in "USA finance: Securitisation – false security?" EIU ViewsWire (18 June 2003).

[134] Atkins (2012).

[135] R. Senior, Financial Management (October 2006), pp. 28–29.

ABS bonds (8 % capital) led to many banks setting up repackaging vehicles to buy ABS bonds and fund them via commercial paper. This required virtually no bank capital, compared with 8 %. Many ABS bonds ended up in these vehicles.[136] Securitisation had expanded rapidly before the global economic crisis of 2007. The securitised products in the EU soon after the crisis shrank to €1.68 trillion due to a combination of factors ranging from slow economic growth and the bursting of housing market bubbles to declining investor demand and banking reforms, which adversely affected Europe's securitisation business.[137]

The advantage of securitisations is that they allow the sponsor, typically a bank or other financial company, to speed up cash realisation from financial assets, including mortgages. The bank lends to homeowners whose homes are taken as collateral with the expectation that their wages/salaries will be sufficient to service the mortgage debts. The bank then takes a pool of mortgages and transfers them to an entity, created specifically for this purpose, called a special purpose vehicle (SPV) in exchange for cash. The SPV raises cash by issuing securities to investors. The sole purpose of an SPV is to issue securities funded by the bank's transferred loan portfolio. A typical strategy adopted is to have at least one of the SPV securities of a very high credit quality (rated as triple-A) with stable cash flows from the mortgage pool. Creating such low-risk, premium tranche securities necessarily concentrates the risk of the mortgage pool in other claims on the pool.[138] The advantages of securitisation include allowing the bank to spread some of its risks to other financial institutions or to investors and increasing the supply of credit in the economy.

Since mid-2007, arguably the waves of structured finance downgrading conducted by CRAs marked the start of the crisis with securitised products at the receiving end; part of this was due to regulatory pressure. Since January 2011, issuers have been unable to outsource all risk, as they are required to retain some risk. Banks placing securitisation deals with European investors have to retain at least 5 % of the nominal value of the underlying exposures under EU rules.[139] In total, European structured finance in every year from 2012 to 2014 was about €200 billion compared to €310 billion in 2011 and more than €600 billion in the years before the financial crisis.[140] More generally, the likely downgrade of a number of securitisation of issuers raises questions about the ability of securitisation deals to obtain the highest triple-A ratings in future.[141]

---

[136] R. Senior (2006), pp. 28–29.

[137] Atkins (2012).

[138] O'Brien (2011), pp. 39–50.

[139] Pengelly (2012), pp. 44–47.

[140] Hart (2013a, b).

[141] Pengelly (2012), pp. 44–47.

2.4.2 What Led to the Crisis?

What started as a financial crisis in 2007–2009[142] quickly transformed into a deep economic and social crisis that spread across the world and affected most countries. The crisis led to the debt crisis that engulfed some Eurozone members and gave rise to dramatic and controversial measures to keep the euro together.[143] The increase in the delinquency and foreclosure rates for subprime mortgage loans in the US at the beginning of 2007 created turmoil in the markets.[144] Taking S&P as an example, it had originally assigned the US $1.6 billion CDOs its top rating of triple-A in August 2007 as the housing market was showing signs of collapse and downgraded the deal to junk status 6 months later. In July 2007, S&P downgraded US $7.3 billion of securities sold in 2005 and 2006.[145] On the revenue side, the deal was lucrative. On the basis of the 2002–2007 period, by providing ratings on CDOs and other structured finance deals, S&P's revenue more than tripled on an annual basis and totalled more than US $2.3 billion.

An intriguing analysis relates to why the bursting of the housing bubble brought the financial system—rather than just the housing sector of the economy—to its knees. Banks used two methods to evade regulatory capital requirements.[146] First, they had temporarily placed assets, such as securitised mortgages, in off-balance-sheet entities so that they did not have to hold significant capital buffers against them. Second, the capital regulations also allowed banks to reduce the amount of capital they held against assets that remained on their balance sheets if those assets took the form of triple-A-rated tranches of securitised mortgages. Thus, by repackaging mortgages into MBSs, whether held on or off their balance sheets, banks were able to reduce the amount of capital required against their loans, significantly increasing their ability to make more loans. The principal effect of this regulatory arbitrage, however, was to concentrate the risk of mortgage defaults in the banks and render them insolvent when the housing bubble burst.

2.4.3 The Housing Market

Low interest rates led to the availability of cheap money, which fuelled a demand in the housing market. Lower taxes were due to the US government's deliberate policy of rewarding entrepreneurs and business persons. Subprime borrowers with bad

---

[142] For causes and remedies of financial crises, see Richardson (2009), pp. 57–60, and Remedies' at pp. 1–56.

[143] Klinz (Chairman).

[144] Klinz (2008).

[145] Crouhy et al. (2007), p. 11. http://www.fdic.gov/bank/analytical/cfr/bank_research_conference/annual_8th/Turnbull_Jarrow.pdf.

[146] Acharya et al. (2009).

credit risks received large loans. Based on borrowers' fixed incomes and rapidly growing house prices, it was difficult to imagine how they could repay their loans. The loans given were worth more than the cost of the houses taken as security. Lenders were least concerned with the borrowers' wages not keeping pace with the cost of houses; they were content with their security as the house prices were expected to rise further, and with the sale of these houses, the borrowers were expected to redeem their mortgages[147] and also make a good profit. When the US housing market began to decline and with the economic slowdown, borrowers failed to keep up with their repayments. When lenders resorted to selling the repossessed houses, they were unable to recover the amount of money lent. This required lenders to carry out a reappraisal of their mortgage property portfolios. They had no choice but to write down a large amount of their profits and in some cases suffer straightforward losses.[148]

2.4.4 *Financial Engineering*

Hill opines that "financial engineers are always thinking creatively, devising ways to securitise new assets".[149] These innovations are only important if they help in utilising money raised for the economic development of the countries where they operate. As mortgage-backed securities (backed by prime mortgages) were long standing, there was an attempt to find a new means through subprime mortgage securities. The financial engineers had little past performance to refer to in terms of data, and yet they went ahead and constructed/designed elaborate algorithms to assist them in structuring the transactions.[150] With hindsight, subprime mortgages were an example of financial engineering that was bound to lead to disaster.

The lenders had been less than eager to make loans to subprime borrowers because the performance of such loans was not well known and eventually it was to prove a disaster.[151] Lenders became enthusiastic when they discovered they could sell these loans to someone else. It resulted in the transaction volume reaching an epic proportion leading to subprime issuances in hundreds of billions of dollars.[152] The financial engineers did not rest on their laurels, and they went much further, crafting exotic structures, not just using mortgages and other "real" assets but also betted on the performance of certain assets—so-called synthetic instruments. That instrument is CDOs. Did CDOs cause the financial crisis, or was it blindness, greed and the need for riskier assets? CDOs provided investors with

[147] Hudson (2009), p. 833.
[148] Ibid., p. 834.
[149] Hill (2010).
[150] Ibid.
[151] Ibid.
[152] Ibid.

desired investments (cash flow streams) at reduced transaction costs. "European banks and investors bought sub-prime housing loan portfolios from original US lenders to diversify their investment portfolio before the sub-prime crisis. At that time, it seemed a lucrative investment avenue . . . Most of these loans [mortgage-backed securities] were bought as part of CDOs".[153]

2.4.5 *The Role of Investment Bankers*

While the CRAs had rated many of the CDO products as triple-A quality, they were in fact exaggerated as they were based on mortgages many of which were later defaulted on.[154] Borrowers with poor credit histories received mortgages for the sole purpose of creating more mortgages, for securitisation purposes, simply because in the past securitisation had proved a profitable source of funds. Large investment bankers, like Lehman Brothers Holdings Inc., started selling security bonds, which acted as insurance to the investors and was very profitable to Lehman. However, when securitisation started to fail, Lehman was landed with an obligation worth US $400 billion. This led to its insolvency as the CDOs and CDO markets had augmented the effect of the subprime mortgage crisis.[155] The situation became aggravated when banks stopped lending to each other due to loss of trust, and it was doubtful if customers would be able to continue to pay instalments on their loans, which inevitably led to a liquidity crisis. Banks, on their part, began demanding higher interest rates in order to lend, thus exacerbating the crisis. It led to the freezing of the credit markets. Three reasons emerged as to why interbank lending had stopped, which led to the commencement of the global financial crisis. Firstly, the fact that banks had to write down the value of the assets on their balance sheets meant that they had less capital on their books and lending became more difficult; secondly, there was a widespread sense of uncertainty regarding how widely and to what extent toxic assets had spread through the banking system; and, lastly, banks were concerned about other banks' creditworthiness, which led to credit freeze and resulted in a drastic reduction in lending to companies and individuals who depended on loans to pursue important economic activity. [156]

---

[153] "What is collateral debt obligation", http://articles.timesofindia.indiatimes.com/2009-02-01/open-space/28008882_1_cdos-mutual-funds-toxic-assets.

[154] Hudson (2009), pp. 834–835.

[155] For Lehman's saga, see Field (2010).

[156] For more details, see Cox et al. (2010).

2.4.6 Globalisation

The quotations

> The world economy faces a severe downturn as a result of the financial crisis happening in the United States that has now spilled into most of the other advanced and developing economies.[157]

> Today, most countries' economies are linked tightly because of free international trading; opportunities in overseas market; and investment diversification for governments, corporations, and even individuals, which makes those markets very sensitive to each other.[158]

suggest that what happened in the US had worldwide repercussions. "The financial market crisis has since then infected the rest of the world economy resulting in a crisis of confidence, credit rationing and widespread de-leveraging that has had major impacts on wealth, output, trade, employment and standards of living across the globe".[159] In addition, "[t]he global financial system remains under severe stress as the crisis broadens to include households, corporations, and the banking sectors in both advanced and emerging market countries".[160] Globalisation has its own advantages and disadvantages:

> For years many people benefitted from the advantages of the international market, however, the time when things got extremely profitable was followed by the crisis of the US sub-prime mortgage fiasco. This type of crisis most often happens in one place and spreads to other places, even across continents, as a 'domino effect'.[161]

Both the developed and developing nations and their economies have felt the impact of the subprime mortgage crisis.

In order to get a better understanding of what caused the crisis, one needs to understand the hype of the subprime mortgage crisis in the US, which this section will analyse in detail. Financial institutions and CRAs embraced mathematical models as reliable predictors of risks. In many instances, it led to the suspension of judgment and the "risk management" became "risk justification".[162] Lenders made loans that they knew borrowers could not afford and that such borrowings could cause massive losses to investors in mortgage securities. Lenders also knew that a significant percentage of loans did not meet their own underwriting standards or those of the originators, but nonetheless they sold those securities to investors.[163]

---

[157] "The Impact of the Sub-prime Mortgage Crisis and a Global Economic Slowdown on Malaysia" (19 February 2009), http://cloudchronicler.net/2009/02/19/the-impact-of-the-sub-prime-mortgage-crisis-and-an-global-economic-slowdown-on-malaysia/.

[158] Abdullah (2012).

[159] Legg and Harris (2009), p. 350.

[160] IMF (2009), pp. xi–xii. See also "The global financial system is facing a once-in-a-century event, where credit risks have risen to extremely high levels": at 3.

[161] Abdullah (2012), note 177.

[162] The Financial Crisis Inquiry Commission (US) (2011), p. xix.

[163] Ibid. at xxii.

Before the actual housing bubble, lenders noted that certain high-risk loans they were making could result not only in foreclosures but also in financial and reputational catastrophes for the firm, but they did not stop lending.[164] The mortgages the commercial banks had purchased from other firms in 2006 and then sold to investors were defective; nearly half were sold to investors regardless.[165]

The major financial institutions went on purchasing high-risk loans in order to package and sell them to investors.[166] Major firms and investors had blindly relied on CRAs as their arbiters of risk.[167] The consequence was that investors had to hold bonds and other securities that had dramatically declined in value. When the housing bubble did finally burst, the US found itself in the deepest recession since the Great Depression. Despite the collapse of Lehman Brothers and the massive government bailout of AIG, Bank of America and others in the US in 2008, it seems not much has really changed.[168]

2.4.7 *The Lenders' Role*

In early 2000, the global excess of capital led to investment managers' concern about where to invest their money in order to get a decent return. The possibility of a global financial crisis was unthinkable. A great amount of money found its way straight into the US mortgage market via securitisation. Mortgage-backed securities (MBSs)[169] seemed like a perfect solution to the great demand for assets. MBSs work when an individual gets a mortgage from a broker, who then sells the mortgage back to the bank, which in turn sells the mortgage to an investment firm on Wall Street. These firms collected thousands of mortgages in huge quantities. This represented thousands of mortgage cheques coming in each month, a monthly income that was supposed to continue for the life of the mortgage.[170] The firm in turn sold shares of that income to investors who were willing to buy. Initially, MBSs were considered safe investments as they comprised mortgages with down payments, proven steady income and money in the bank. Investors, not

---

[164] Ibid.

[165] Nasiripour (2012).

[166] The Financial Crisis Inquiry Commission (US) (2011), p. xxii.

[167] Ibid., p. xix.

[168] Hon. Edolphus Towns (2009) at 2.

[169] For the definition of "MBS", see Glossary.

[170] "Stock Market Investors, Stock Investment Risks, The Subprime Mortgage Crisis Explained", at 1. http://stock-market-investors.com/stock-investment-risk/the-subprime-mortgage-crisis-explained.html. See also "Stock Market Investors, Stock Investment Risks, What Caused the Current Financial Crisis?" http://stock-market-investors.com/stock-investment-risk/what-caused-the-current-financial-crisis.html; "Stock Market Investors, Stock Investment Risks, The Credit Crisis (Credit Crunch)" http://stock-market-investors.com/stock-investment-risk/the-credit-crisis-credit-crunch.html.

only in the US but also all over the world, had shares in such securities. The high demand for mortgages considered safe but were in the form of MBSs meant that in the US in 2003 anyone who qualified for a mortgage got one, and still global funding wanted more. This led to the change in the mortgage qualification guidelines, and borrowers did not have to prove their income; instead, they had to state their income and show that they had money in the bank. In order to keep pace with the demand, borrowers were able to borrow money without having to prove or state anything. A good credit score was sufficient to enable a borrower to obtain a mortgage.[171]

Between 2002 and 2007, The Big Three CRAs gave top ratings on debt pools that "included $3.2 trillion of loans to homebuyers with bad credit and undocumented incomes", many of which defaulted.[172] With regard to Moody's

> The rating of structured finance products such as mortgage-backed securities made up close to half of Moody's rating revenues in 2005, 2006, and 2007. By the fall of 2005, Moody's market capitalisation had grown to US $15 million ... Moody's had 2,500 employees and US$1.6 billion of revenue. From 2000 to 2007, revenues from rating such financial instruments increased more than fourfold.[173]

As a public company, in "February 2007, its [Moody's] stock had risen 340 per cent. Structured finance was approaching 50 % of Moody's revenue – up from 28 % in 1999".[174] Moody's and S&P rated the same collateralized debt obligations, which they both initially gave triple-A ratings.[175] However, based on the evidence, the CRAs cannot claim that the majority of the triple-A ratings issued by them were reliable.[176]

2.4.8 Market Turmoil

Financial crises have an adverse impact on the economy. Financial crises can destroy wealth, and the instability produced by a financial crisis can be significant.[177] The blame for contributing to the 2007–2009 market turmoil in the US is attributed to CRAs.[178] They underestimated the credit risk of structured credit products, which resulted in a worldwide impact as the banks and other investors had a stake in such products.[179] The CRAs gave the highest ratings to the great

[171] Stock Market Investors, Ibid, at 2.

[172] Smith (2008).

[173] The Financial Crisis Inquiry Commission (US) (2011), p. 118.

[174] McLean and Nocera (2010), p. 123.

[175] See Senate Subcommittee Report, http://online.wsj.com/article/SB10001424052970203721704577156963813900028.html.

[176] Chan (2012).

[177] Biglaiser et al. (2011), p. 68.

[178] Jaffee et al. (2009), pp. 61–82.

[179] See Arora (2010), pp. 670–669.

majority of subprime mortgage products, which implies that they had clearly underestimated the major risks inherent in these instruments. The causes and consequences of the US subprime mortgage crisis led to a generalised credit crunch in other financial sectors that ultimately affected the real economy.[180] Furthermore, when market conditions worsened, the CRAs failed to adapt the ratings promptly[181] by downgrading them. The role of CRAs in inflating the bubble can be discerned in that "without the active participation of the rating agencies [by awarding triple-A ratings to complex, unsafe asset-backed securities and other derivatives, thereby magnifying the financial shock when the housing bubble finally burst] the market for mortgage-related securities could not have been what it became".[182]

2.4.8.1 Downgrading

CRAs have failed (a) to reflect the risks that were inherent in certain credit instruments (especially structured obligations) and (b) to adjust their credit ratings in time following the deepening market crisis. Evidence suggests two reasons for the market turmoil. First, CRAs underestimated the credit risk of structured credit products, and the great majority of subprime products were given the highest ratings. When market conditions worsened, the CRAs failed to downgrade the ratings promptly.[183] Second, the changes in the financial environment meant that the issuers were persuaded to approach those CRAs that were, in the past, generous with their ratings. For example, many observers blame the CRAs for being too generous in their ratings of the mortgage-backed securities at the core of the housing bubble[184] and had a positive impact on their business. In addition, there were shortcomings in the CRAs' communication with the users of credit ratings.[185] The problems with regard to disclosure relate, first, to their failure to adequately disclose information about their procedures; second, material information was selectively disclosed to their subscribers; and, third, they inadvertently disclosed confidential information about the entities they rated.[186] As a result, after the onset of the global crisis, the market participants' confidence in the performance of CRAs

[180] Claessens et al. (2014), pp. 1–277; Mah-Hui (2008), pp. 3–13.

[181] Lowenstein (2008).

[182] The Financial Crisis Inquiry Commission (US) (2011), p. xxv.

[183] Proposal for a Regulation of the European Parliament and of the Council on Credit Rating Agencies, Brussels (12 November 2008) at 2, http://ec.europa.eu/internal_market/securities/docs/agencies/proposal_en.pdf, The proposed Regulation was adopted in Regulation (EC) No 1060/2009 of the European Parliament and of the Council on Credit Rating Agencies of 16 September 2009, http://eur-lex.europa.eu/LexUriServ/LexUriServ.do?uri=OJ:L:2009:302:0001:0031:EN:PDF.

[184] Sinclair (2013).

[185] European Commission (2010).

[186] Frost (2007), pp. 475–476. European Commission (2010).

and in the reliability of ratings has suffered.[187] It was felt that unless the regulators are able to rectify this situation, it will create uneasiness in the minds of investors.

The credit crunch and the collapse of the financial markets were due to many of the asset-backed securities being given solid investment grade ratings in the form of triple-A ratings[188] by the CRAs that could not survive in the meltdown. Downgrading did have an impact on the issuers and investors alike but not a major impact on CRAs' business. The figures for downgrading are astounding. As of February 2008, Moody's had downgraded at least one tranche of 94.2 % of the subprime residential mortgage-backed security (RMBS) issues it rated in 2006, including 100 % of the 2006 RMBSs backed by second lien loans and 76.9 % of the issues rated in 2007. Overall, Moody's has downgraded 53.7 and 39.2 % of all of its 2006 and 2007 subprime tranches, respectively.[189] As of March 2008, S&P had downgraded 44.3 % of the subprime tranches it rated between the first quarter of 2005 and the third quarter of 2007.[190] This included 87.2 % of securities backed by second lien mortgages.[191] As of December 2007, Fitch had downgraded approximately 34 % of the subprime tranches it rated in 2006 and in the first quarter of 2007. In February 2008, Fitch placed all of the RMBSs it rated in 2006 and the first quarter of 2007 backed by subprime first lien mortgages on Ratings Watch Negative.[192] Between late 2007 and mid-2008 (after the housing bubble burst), the CRAs collectively downgraded US $1.9 trillion in mortgage-backed securities.

As a result of the decline in the housing market, CRAs downgraded their ratings for an unprecedented number of RMBSs and collateralized debt obligations (CDOs) from initially high ratings; this resulted in investors suffering substantial losses, thus necessitating the increase of the Securities and Exchange Commission's (SEC) oversight of CRAs. These downgrades led to forced selling by the institutions, magnifying the panic and preventing other investors from buying the distressed debt.[193] The blame for the financial crisis is found in the regulations that were in place. These regulations interacted with each other to foster the issuance and securitisation of subprime mortgages, and it was impossible to predict the disastrous outcome of these interacting regulations.[194] It resulted in the system pushing many big investors to buy high and sell low, and this led to losses. Investors and issuers of the debt instruments had mixed feelings. Investors felt that the CRAs

[187] Proposal for Regulation, (2008) at 2.

[188] Pagano and Volpin (2009).

[189] See 'U.S. Subprime RMBS 2005–2007 Vintage Rating Actions,' Update (January 2008), Moody's Investors Service (1 February 2008).

[190] "U.S. RMBS Update", Fitch Ratings (20 February 2008).

[191] See "Transition Study: Structured Finance Rating Transition and Default Update as of March 21, 2008", Standard & Poor's Ratings Services (28 March 2008).

[192] See Fitch Ratings "Update on U.S. Subprime and Alt-A: Performance and Rating Reviews" (20 March 2008).

[193] Surowiecki (2009).

[194] Friedman (2009), pp. 127–185, http://www.criticalreview.com/crf/pdfs/Friedman_intro21_23.pdf.

were too slow to respond to changes in the financial environment for them to be able to take any prompt action and cover their position. The issuers felt that CRAs were too quick, which meant paying higher interest rates for their future borrowings.

The implication for the decrease in 2006 of subprime mortgages' market value resulting in the write-down of billions of dollars in the value of mortgage securities is that CRAs had either not rated the structured products accurately or subsequently failed to reassess their credit ratings.[195] The multiple blames attributed to CRAs consist of being weak as financial forecasters, being too slow to spot negative trends, tracking things too late to revise their ratings and not downgrading companies quickly enough. As was discussed earlier, the lowering of a credit score by a CRA can create a vicious cycle, an increase in expenses and a decrease in creditworthiness.[196] In spite of criticisms levelled against the CRAs due to various shortcomings on their part, CRAs play an important role and the regulations in the US and EU were required to rectify these shortcomings.[197]

2.4.9 General Criticisms

Out of a hundred CRAs currently operating[198] worldwide, the Big Three have over 90 % of the market share of conducting ratings. Commentators have levelled the following criticisms against them: they do not downgrade issuers' high ratings promptly when circumstances change[199]; they have had too familiar a relationship with company management, possibly opening them up to undue influence or to the vulnerability of being misled by taking at face value a company's explanations on issues without verifying them[200]; the regulators have implicitly allowed CRAs to fill a quasi-regulatory role[201]; conflicts of interest arise due to the current issuers-pay model; the companies issuing the securities pay the CRAs, and this arrangement leads to a disincentive for the CRAs to act vigilantly on behalf of investors.[202]

Owing to high barriers to market entry and the fact that the CRAs' business is reputation based, large corporations prefer to appoint the Big Three CRAs. In reality, CRAs hold an oligopolistic position. Errors of judgment in rating structured

[195] U.S. Securities and Exchange Commission at iii.

[196] "Credit Rating Agencies" (2013) http://taxfreegold.co.uk/creditratingagencies.html.

[197] For what these reforms should be, see Black Rock, View Point "Credit Rating Agencies: Reform, Don't Eliminate" (July 2013) pp. 1–6. https://www.blackrock.com/corporate/en-gb/literature/whitepaper/viewpoint-credit-rating-agencies-reform-dont-eliminate.pdf.

[198] "World Credit Rating Agencies", http://www.whichwaytopay.com/world-credit-rating-agencies.asp.

[199] See Borrus (2002); E Wyatt (8 February 2002).

[200] Partnoy (2006a), p. 13. http://papers.ssrn.com/sol3/papers.cfm?abstract_id=900257.

[201] Kruck (2013), pp. 141–176.

[202] Alessi et al. (2013).

finance products[203] and in CDOs[204] meant CRAs either had subsequently to downgrade them or in a large number of cases led to default.[205] With regard to the use of securitisation and special purchase vehicles (SPVs),[206] it seems everyone was passing the risk to the next buyer in the chain. All tended to economise on due diligence and ignore signs that assets were not creditworthy.[207]

The SEC may have contributed to this decline by softening its disclosure and due diligence standards for asset-backed securitisation.[208] The reasons for its poor performance[209] are attributed to the dominant position of the Big Three CRAs, which restricted competition and not facing the threat of liability. CRAs have a political incentive to show they do not need stricter regulation by being overly critical in their assessment of governments they regulate.[210] The book will not examine the issue of sovereign debt, but arguably the government's reluctance to regulate CRAs on legal liability might be their fear that if this was done, then the CRAs might be reluctant to give high ratings to the debt instruments issued by the government, leading to the cost of government borrowing going up.

Giving high ratings to risky subprime mortgages may be because the CRAs had little incentive to take the necessary or extra precautions as an absence of any liability meant there was neither a deterrent effect nor fear of tarnishing their reputation. CRAs' main concern was to appease issuers (90 % of their income came from the corporate issues), which would then ensure a steady flow of future income. The lack of competition, the issuer-pay model that led to conflicts of interest and the rise of structural finance were the reasons for CRAs being instrumental in producing ratings inflation.[211] The collapse of structured bond ratings during the 2007–2008 financial crises had brought attention to the possibility of rating inflation due to lowered rating standards and rating shopping. In the wake of the financial crisis, the companies that rate bonds have been criticised strongly for being asleep at the switch and for assigning optimistic ratings to questionable mortgage bonds in order to win business. Arguably, issuers still conduct a "ratings shop" among firms for the most favourable opinions on their deals.[212]

---

[203] According to Coffee (2009), p. 53.

[204] See Glossary for the meaning of "CDO".

[205] Wadden IV, William "Biv" (2002). See also Norris (2007), Buiter (2007) and Kerr (2007).

[206] For the meaning of "SPV", see Glossary.

[207] Coffee Jr.; Coffee (2009), p. 12. http://ssrn.com/abstract=1372194.

[208] Mendales (2009), p. 1359 at 1362.

[209] Coffee (2009), pp. 10–11.

[210] "Will Financial Reform Negatively Bias U.S. Sovereign Credit Ratings?" *Thoughtsworththinking.net* (21 May 2010). http://www.thoughtsworththinking.net/2010/05/will-financial-reform-negatively-bias-us-sovereign-credit-ratings/.

[211] See Coffee (2006) and Partnoy (2006b).

[212] Lucchetti and Ng (2010).

2.4.10 The Blunder

The crisis was partly at least due to errors committed by CRAs in their rating risk analysis. Moody's, S&P and Fitch have admitted this but have refused to apologise for their shortcomings.[213] In oral evidence regarding the financial crisis, the testimonies given by Moody's was of not being satisfied with their rating performance, which were associated with the US mortgage housing market. S&P regretted the assumptions it had used and built into their subprime models, which, when compared with what actually had happened in the market, proved not to be true. Fitch admitted its failings with regard to rating structured finance products.[214] The blame attributed to the Big Three CRAs in general is that they were the key enablers of the financial meltdown.[215]

It was the failures of CRAs, as essential cogs in the machine, that resulted in the financial crisis. The inquiry failed to pick up the fact that the Big Three's motive was to have a healthy relationship with the issuers and their need to earn a continuous stream of money. It required appeasing issuers at the expense of investors who have had to bear the losses. This section will scrutinise below the occurrence of these failings. The emerging question, however, is how to ensure these failings do not occur in future. These CRAs had, perhaps, answers on how to tackle the problem. The regulators and the government inquiries could have relied on these answers to form the basis of the regulatory footings regulating the CRAs, instead of simply resorting to blaming the CRAs.

2.4.11 The Credit Crunch

Modern credit crunches are due to an unexpected exogenous shock that destroys market confidence. Moody's does not accord the cause of the modern credit crunch to bank credit or interest rates but rather ascribes it to sudden changes in market risk premium as expressed in credit spreads and credit availability.[216] The 2007 shock, relating to US subprime mortgages and the consequent problems of global credit market liquidity, has, as with previous shocks, invited comment about the role, function and performance of CRAs. The unprecedented combination of forces that drove mortgage delinquencies in the US were the decline and eventual reversal in

---

[213] According to the Chairman of the inquiry Mr. A. Tyrie, House of Commons oral evidence taken before the Treasury Committee Inquiry into Credit Rating Agencies (7 March 2012). http://www.publications.parliament.uk/pa/cm201012/cmselect/cmtreasy/uc1866-ii/uc186601.htm.

[214] See Jobst (2005). http://www.ruralfinance.org/fileadmin/templates/rflc/documents/1217520036684_what_is_structured_finance.pdf. For the definition of "structured products", see Glossary.

[215] The Financial Crisis Inquiry Report (2011) at 25.

[216] Memorandum from Moody's (2008), para 35, see http://www.parliament.the-stationery-office.co.uk/pa/cm200708/cmselect/cmtreasy/56/56we32.htm.

home price appreciation, the sharp contraction in credit available for refinancing, the deterioration in mortgage underwriting processes and the now apparent extent of misrepresentation in the mortgage application process.[217] As recognised by Moody's, markets can change rapidly and dramatically. This requires CRAs to pursue vigorously credit analysis and credit rating processes, including transparency, thus restoring confidence in, and the healthy operation of, credit markets.[218] The boom in the financial markets continued from the mid-1990s through to 2007, with occasional reverses. During this period, new financial products such as financial derivatives, credit default swap (CDS) and securitisation (CDOs) began to emerge and created speculative opportunities and optimism that led to the surging market for real estate and securities,[219] which resulted in the crash and the credit crunch. The reality in a capitalist system is that with every boom, there is bound to be an inevitable periodic recession. It is, however, difficult to predict when precisely the boom will end and the recession will start and vice versa.

2.4.12 *The Result of the Crisis*

White[220] blames the three major CRAs for having played a central role in the subprime mortgage debacle of 2007–2008. Rather than being accidental, eight decades of financial regulation propelled these CRAs into the centre of the bond information market by elevating their judgments about the creditworthiness of bonds so that those judgments attained the force of law. In addition, the SEC exacerbated this problem by erecting a barrier to entry into the credit rating business in 1975, by granting four CRAs (the Big Three and Dominion Bond Rating Service Ltd) NRSRO status.[221]

The subprime mortgage crisis became a global crisis when soon after mid-2007 Europe became the first area affected and where there was a call for the introduction of regulation. Thereafter, its toxicity spread to the rest of the world. Shirai[222] finds that the nature of the global financial crisis is unprecedented in terms of, first, the scale of the problems in the financial sector (particularly in the US and Europe); second, the depth and speed of contagion of the crisis spread worldwide (through financial sector and trade linkages); and, third, it caused the severity of the recession (particularly in emerging market economics, small countries and East Asia).

[217] Ibid., para 36.

[218] Ibid., para 37.

[219] Hudson (2009), p. 833.

[220] White (2009).

[221] SEC.

[222] Shirai (2009).

2.4.13 The Culprits Blamed for the Crisis

Various factors can be identified that contributed to the subprime mortgage credit crisis. They range from the search for yield enhancement, agency problems, lax underwriting standards, failure of the CRAs to identify a changing environment, poor risk management by financial institutions, lack of transparency to the limitation of existing valuation models and the failure of regulators to understand the implications of the changing environment for the financial system.[223] The effect of the subprime crisis started to spread across other asset markets. The austerity measures taken by the US government and the EU did not succeed in halting an impending recession and caused a global credit crunch and an economic downturn in major parts of the world.[224]

It is difficult to identify precisely those who should bear investors' loss—the CRAs, governments or those who resorted to innovative products. The major banks and other investors lost hundreds of billions of dollars simply because of their misplaced belief in the value of residential MBSs, including subprime securities.[225] Some have put the blame for the financial crisis, which began in the summer of 2007, on CRAs for badly underestimating the risk of newly structured investment vehicles, their casualness in certifying novel financial instruments as being investment grade, their insufficient understanding of the risks involved and quickness in giving these vehicles their highest investment grade ratings.[226] Perhaps rather than being casual, ratings were done extremely carefully but on a flawed basis.[227]

2.4.14 Causes and Complexity of the Financial Crisis[228]

"There is no single cause and thus no simple remedy, the sheer number of causal factors tends to suggest that the current financial situation is not yet fully understood in its full complexity".[229] "The proper functioning of ... capital markets depends on good corporate governance – and good corporate governance depends on gatekeepers who serve ... investors with honesty and integrity".[230] CRAs as intermediaries (often called gatekeepers through their role in evaluating a company's creditworthiness) provide important services for the benefit of investors. They play crucial roles in the capital markets because they are more able to gather

[223] Turnbull et al. (2008).
[224] Cf. Klinz (2008), p. 7.
[225] Ellsworth and Porapaiboon (2009), p. 1.
[226] Hurst (2009), p. 63.
[227] A. Haynes, Discussion (2012).
[228] For details, see Foster and Magdoff (2009).
[229] Jickling (2009).
[230] Walter and Daigler (2010).

information about companies than most investors have the time or inclination for. Investors trust and rely on gatekeepers as long as their independence and integrity remain intact; otherwise, market confidence suffers.[231] Cardinute notes:

> Anytime something goes wrong, it is only a matter of time before the blame-game starts. With the events of the recent sub-prime mortgage crisis, there is no single person or entity that can solely be blamed for this misstep in society. Alternatively, it was a combined effort from the potential and current homeowners, lenders, underwriters, and investors.[232]

The above statement needs further elaboration. Underwriters can be blamed for packaging risky subprime loans that did not fulfil the intended objective of reducing risks through diversification. Investors are to be blamed for inadequately understanding the true risks involved and having blind faith when investing in these products.[233] Lenders, as gatekeepers, failed when they started granting loans to potential homeowners without proof of assets or verifying evidence of a stable income. The gatekeeper function collapsed when lenders let borrowers through the gate, irrespective of their ability to repay mortgage loans.[234] The Big Three CRAs' role in the 2007–2008 market crises was that of giving triple-A ratings to risky subprime mortgages products, and this may have facilitated excessive risk taking by the investors. Investment banks' balance sheets had "toxic assets" comprising subprime mortgages, which is one reason why they were incapable of lending to businesses and individuals.[235]

Financial institutions are blamed for claiming to have found a way of eliminating risk when in reality it was not true, as the risk was not eliminated.[236] Central bankers and other regulators are blamed for tolerating this imprudence.[237] The years of low inflation and stable growth had stimulated complacency and risk taking, and a "savings glut" in Asia had reduced global interest rates.[238] Low interest rates created an incentive for banks, hedge funds and other investors to begin hunting for riskier assets that offered higher returns.[239] The low volatility increased the temptation to "leverage", and some investors borrowed in the money markets to buy longer dated, higher yielding securities.[240]

---

[231] Walter and Daigler (2010).

[232] Cardinute (2011).

[233] Walter and Daigler (2010).

[234] Block-Lieb and Janger (2009), p. 474.

[235] 'So What's A Toxic Asset?', CBSNews (23 March 2009) http://www.cbsnews.com/news/so-whats-a-toxic-asset/.

[236] Sabato (2009).

[237] Goldfarb and Dennis (2011).

[238] Xafa (2007).

[239] "Economists still disagree over whether these low rates were the result of central bankers' mistakes or broader shifts in the world economy". See 'Financial crises and Singapore,' (16 September 2013) http://leongszehian.com/?p=5986.

[240] 'The origins of the financial crisis,' The Economist (7 September 2013) http://www.economist.com/news/schoolsbrief/21584534-effects-financial-crisis-are-still-being-felt-five-years-article.

European banks borrowed in the US money markets before the 2007 crisis and used the extra cash to increase their investments by wrongly assuming that the returns would exceed the cost of borrowing funds to buy securities.[241] It raised a surge of debt that was perceived to be a less risky investment but which later proved to have less value than the original investment.[242]

The years before the crisis saw a flood of irresponsible mortgage lending in the US by financiers. These risky mortgages were passed on to financial engineers at the big banks, which turned them into supposedly low-risk securities by putting large numbers of them together in pools. The pooled mortgages were used to back securities called collateralized debt obligations (CDOs),[243] which were divided into tranches by degree of exposure to default. It transpired that loans were given to "sub-prime" borrowers who had poor credit histories and had struggled to repay them[244] and considering that, starting in 2006, the US suffered a nationwide house-price slump.[245]

Investors had believed that they were buying safer tranches of investment products as these were based on CRAs' high ratings with the additional benefit that they provided higher returns in an era of low interest rates. Investors trusted the triple-A credit ratings assigned by CRAs (Moody's, S&P and Fitch), but, as they were paid by the banks that created the CDOs, arguably they were inclined to be generous in their assessments.[246]

The uncertainty of the US housing market led to a chain reaction causing instabilities in the financial system[247]; neither pooling nor financial engineering assisted in providing investors with the promised protection.[248] Mortgage-backed securities fell in value, and despite the CRAs' seal of approval, allegedly safe CDOs lost a lot of their original value.[249] It became difficult to sell doubtful assets even at low price or to use them as collateral for the short-term funding that so many banks had relied on in the past. It affected banks' capital based on "mark-to-market" accounting rules, which required them to revalue their assets at current prices and thus acknowledge losses on paper.[250] Trust within the banking system started to suffer in 2007—a year before Lehman's bankruptcy—as they started questioning the viability of their counterparties.[251] The wholesale funding withdrew short-term

[241] Debts, Deficits and Dilemmas (2014), p. 12.
[242] Pettinger (2013).
[243] Murphy (2008).
[244] Mah-Hui (2008).
[245] Henwood (2006).
[246] Utzig (2010), pp. 1–3.
[247] Utt (2008).
[248] 'The origins of the financial crisis,' The Economist (7 September 2013) http://web.econ.unito.it/bagliano/macro3/economist_financialcrisis_sept13.pdf.
[249] Murphy (2008).
[250] Ibid.
[251] Shell.

credit, causing those most reliant on it to suffer, and, as has already been discussed, Northern Rock was an early victim in 2007.[252]

Although the long period of economic and price stability encouraged risk taking, central bankers and regulators bear responsibility for mishandling the crisis. They failed to keep economic imbalances in check and in exercising proper oversight of financial institutions. Regulators let Lehman Brothers go bankrupt, which resulted in more intervention by the government. It created a panic in markets, and the regulators had to rescue some of the companies[253] to prevent them from becoming insolvent and going bankrupt. The regulators' mistakes, pre-Lehman bankruptcy, were to tolerate global current account imbalances and the housing bubbles that they helped to inflate. Banks, under pressure from shareholders to increase returns, operated with inadequate equity, thus leaving them vulnerable when things went wrong.[254] The mistake of the banks, from the mid-1990s, was to use their own internal models to assess risk—in effect, they set their own capital requirements and judged their assets to be safe, thus allowing balance sheets to inflate without a proportionate rise in capital.[255] The cause of crises in large part was because of incompatible incentives regarding securitisations. Banks made money from fees rather than the performance of loans. They did not take adequate care in originating loans because they wanted to pass them on quickly. CRAs underestimated the risk of the products, often keen to earn fees in rating products. Banking regulation gave financial institutions incentives to hold securitised loans in "off balance sheet" vehicles, and these products were excessively complex.[256]

There were multiple causes for the global financial crisis,[257] and it is important to note that risk may be perception based.[258] The blame attributed to CRAs relates to their assessment of the risk on subprime mortgages and to investors for recklessly relying, rather than carrying out due diligence, on the favourable triple-A ratings given by CRAs. Risk perception is the subjective judgment that people make about the characteristics and severity of a risk, and therefore people respond to a risk or

---

[252] House of Commons Treasury Committee, "Banking Crisis: dealing with the failure of the UK banks", Seventh Report of Session 2008–2009, London, The Stationery Office Limited (1 May 2009) at 45.

[253] The claim is that the "Collapse of Lehman Brothers, a sprawling global bank, in September 2008 almost brought down the world's financial system. It took huge taxpayer financed bail-outs to shore up the industry". See "Debts, Deficits and Dilemmas – A crash course on the financial crisis and its aftermath", Economist (2014) at 11. http://www.waterstones.com/wat/images/special/pdf/9781781253786.pdf.

[254] A study shows that (1) before the crisis, differences in capital did not have much impact on stock returns and (2) during the crisis, a stronger capital position was associated with better stock market performance, most markedly for larger banks. See Demirguc-Kunt et al. (2010).

[255] Ibid.

[256] Giles (2009).

[257] See Helleiner et al. (2010).

[258] See the Basel Report 2011 on this matter—Operational Risk—Supervisory Guidelines for the Advanced Measurement Approaches (AMA) and Supervisory Guidelines for AMA.

hazard in ways consistent with their perception of that risk. It is their perception that influences behaviour or action.[259] "Risk management, and the identification of risk levels, hinge on the assessment of probability and consequence. Yet people, including experts, differ in their perceptions especially with regard to the probability and consequence of events. Risks are often rated inconsistently as a result".[260] The departures from codes of conduct by brokers and other related people also contributed to the crisis. The crisis was therefore not simplistic[261] but complex and multifaceted in nature, and no consensus emerges (as opinion, interpretation and analysis differ) as to the reasons that led to the crisis in the first place.

2.5 The Saga of Enron, Lehman Brothers and Northern Rock

This section, rather than being an exhaustive study of all corporate ratings undertaken by CRAs, presents a sample of corporate ratings carried out by CRAs as brief case studies drawn from Enron and Lehman Brothers in the US and Northern Rock in England as they had become a matter of interest to the regulators. There might be different reasons for the downfall of each, but they are typical of the crisis. CRAs need to exercise care when awarding over-optimistic ratings and ought to promptly downgrade ratings when the circumstances changes. Enron Epic predates financial crisis of 2007–2009 and led to the enactment of the Sarbanes-Oxley law.[262] Enron's saga highlights the mistakes made and shows how the same mistakes, instead of being avoided, were repeated in Lehman Brothers and in Northern Rock. SEC's "Report addresses certain issues regarding rating agencies, such as allegations of anticompetitive or unfair practices, the level of diligence of credit rating agencies, and the extent and manner of Commission oversight, that go beyond those specifically identified in the Sarbanes-Oxley Act".[263]

[259] Mileti and Sorensen (1987).

[260] 'From Risk Perception to Safe Behaviour,' https://www.sia.org.au/downloads/SIGs/Resources/From_Risk_Perception_to_Safe_Behaviour.pdf.

[261] Miller et al. (2009).

[262] The Sarbanes-Oxley Act of 2002 (for short SOX) is a legislation passed by the US Congress to protect shareholders and the public from accounting errors and fraudulent practices in the enterprise, as well as improve the accuracy of corporate disclosures, corporate governance and accountability. The SOX was enacted in response to a series of high-profile financial scandals that occurred in the early 2000s at companies including Enron, WorldCom and Tyco that distraught investor confidence. M. Rouse, "Sarbanes-Oxley Act (SOX)", http://searchcio.techtarget.com/definition/Sarbanes-Oxley-Act.

[263] Report on the Role and Function of Credit Rating Agencies in the Operation of The Securities Markets As Required by Section 702(b) of the Sarbanes-Oxley Act of 2002, at 1. http://www.sec.gov/news/studies/credratingreport0103.pdf.

2.5.1 Enron's Saga

"Regulatory interest in the [rating agency] industry has been ongoing since 2003 in the wake of the Enron scandal with a renewed interest since the subprime crisis".[264] The gatekeepers (that is, Enron's board of directors, its regulators, its banks and investors, CRAs and investment analysts) have essential roles to play. The gatekeepers having fallen short in the performance of their duties, enabled Enron to use transactions and institutional structures to manipulate the firm's financial reports and to avoid regulation.[265] Credit ratings influenced Enron's business as investors use ratings as an indicator of the company's strength. Enron used its stock to support a number of structural financial transactions. What Enron, as a parent company, did was to rely on special-purpose entities (SPEs) to expand access to capital and to manage debts for its subsidiaries based on its higher credit rating.[266] However, Partnoy[267] sees Enron's trouble as not being due to its fraudulent involvement in SPEs but being due to derivatives.[268]

Any drop in the credit rating of issuers, like Enron, would have a catastrophic effect by depressing the stock/share price. This required the borrower to maintain its rating by legitimate means rather than unduly influencing CRAs to maintain the *status quo*. When a rating fell below a certain level, as in the case of Enron, it triggered repayment; Enron, as a parent company, was obliged to meet accelerated financial obligations for its subsidiary borrowings. When Moody's downgraded Enron from BBB+ to BBB in November 2001, it was obliged to repay US $690 million within 15 days for the money it had borrowed for its subsidiary.[269] Had Enron survived, the implication for downgrading its credit rating was that the future cost of borrowing would have increased, as it would have had to pay higher interest on future loans. Enron, after repaying its present loans on maturity, would have had to pay higher interest rates on its future debts in order to attract future investors. What transpired was that Enron's rating remained investment grade 4 days before the company went bankrupt, despite the fact that CRAs had been aware of the company's problems for months.[270] CRAs feared that lowering a credit score could create a vicious cycle, as not only interest rates for that company would go up, but also other contracts with financial institutions would have had an adverse effect by causing an increase in expenses due to an ensuing decrease in creditworthiness. These rating triggers were instrumental in the collapse of Enron.

---

[264] Langer and Langer, p. 373.

[265] Dembinski et al. (2006), pp. 1 and 19.

[266] Schwarcz (2002), p. 1309.

[267] Partnoy (2003b), p. 1245.

[268] For definition of "derivatives", see Glossary.

[269] Slater (2008), p. 220.

[270] "Credit Agencies Waited Months to Voice Doubt About Enron" http://bodurtha.georgetown.edu/enron/Credit%20Agencies%20Waited%20Months%20to%20Voice%20Doubt%20About%20Enron.htm.

The role played by CRAs in the Enron scandal was that the investment grade given provided Enron with the stability to operate and expand its trading business, as well as the opportunity to access the capital markets to meet its liquidity needs. Enron repeatedly sought improved ratings, and the CRAs obliged despite the fact that it embarked on a business that involved substantial amounts of risk.[271] Moody's, for its part, blames Enron for withdrawing information. Its claim is that even though it had asked for significant amounts of information, it received only some.[272] Enron had carried out an extremely clever financial fraud assisted by its auditor, Arthur Anderson, that was difficult to spot by CRAs.[273] Perhaps Moody's did not scrutinise Enron's finances sufficiently because of the lucrative fees received, which may have led to Enron lobbying for better ratings. In this context, it does not mean that Moody's deliberately issued false ratings to keep its business but that it should have exercised caution. Moody's had earned an annual fee of between US $1.5 million and US $2.00 million per year for rating Enron's publicly and privately issued debts.[274] It seems Moody's was tempted to hang on to a lucrative deal even if it meant issuing unjustified favourable ratings (bearing in mind that there are no adverse legal implications to Moody's for issuing unreliable ratings).

The reason why CRAs do not verify information is that they assign hundreds of thousands of ratings globally. Placing a verification obligation on them would be both overly burdensome and redundant. Others in the market, like auditors, who are responsible for certifying the accuracy of the data, are better able to do so.[275] It is understandable if CRAs' protocols are not designed to verify information asked for by them and given by an issuer, but in Enron's case, it had withheld a lot of information.[276] Yet Moody's, instead of declining, went ahead and rated Enron. The CRAs were in the best position to raise red flags to the market but failed to do so.[277]

The real trouble started when Enron's share price started a free fall, and this meant Enron was looking for a white knight and begged the Big Three not to downgrade it. Dynegy, as a bidder, appeared to be the only serious contender initially wanting to purchase Enron for US $8.9 billion, but then it withdrew when it could not trust the restated financial statement of Enron.[278] When the prospect of a bailout had finally disappeared, the CRAs had no choice but to downgrade Enron to junk status, and this led to its ultimate demise:

---

[271] Coskun (2008), p. 264 at 266. http://www.kvdl.nl/wp-content/uploads/2013/01/Deniz-Coskun-credit-rating-agencies-in-a-post-Enron-world.pdf.

[272] Slater (2008), p. 225, note 228.

[273] Coffee (2002).

[274] Slater (2008), p. 224.

[275] A. M. Best, DBRS Ltd, Finch, Moody's and S&P, p. 2.

[276] Slater (2008), p. 225.

[277] Coskun (2008), p. 266.

[278] See Fusaro and Miller (2002), pp. 121–123.

> [The] collapse of companies such as Enron and WorldCom in the aftermath of the internet bubble demonstrated the central role of accounting in good corporate governance. Both companies manipulated their figures and then persuaded their auditors (Arthur Andersen in both cases) to sign off on accounts that were at best misleading, at worst downright criminal.[279]

Presumably, the CRAs do rely on audited accounts and will take comfort from the auditors having signed Enron's accounts (profit and loss account and balance sheet) as true and fair.

Growth for Enron was rapid. In 2000, the company's annual revenue reached US $100 billion, and it ranked as the seventh-largest company on the Fortune 500 and the sixth-largest energy company in the world. The company's share price had peaked at US $90. However, cracks began to appear when in October 2001 Enron reported a loss of US $618 million—its first quarterly loss in 4 years. By late November, the company's share price was down to less than US $1.00. Investors had lost billions of dollars. On 2 December 2001, Enron filed for bankruptcy protection but did not survive the then biggest case of bankruptcy in the US (later overtaken by the collapse of WorldCom). Around 5,600 Enron employees subsequently lost their jobs.[280] Others see the collapse of Enron as an unfortunate incident. The tremendous financial losses that the company had incurred were due to "arrogance, greed, and foolishness from the top management, all the way down ... [M]any of the company's losses started the collapse that could have been avoided, if someone had had the nerve and the foresight to put a stop to it".[281] While Enron's CEO Jeffrey Skilling had a role to play in hiding financial losses of the trading business and other operations of the company,[282] CRAs cannot escape their share of the blame. CRAs' functional duty is not to give optimistic high ratings, and if they do so, then CRAs should downgrade them promptly when circumstances changes. On both counts, CRAs had failed in the case of Enron with devastating consequences to the corporation that led to its demise, to the shareholders (including pension funds) who had lost their investment money and to its employees who had lost their jobs and their shareholdings, which many had held.

2.5.2 Lehman Brothers

"The collapse of Lehman Brothers, a sprawling global bank, in September 2008 almost brought down the world's financial system. It took huge taxpayer-financed

---

[279] *Economist*, "True and Fair", 22 September 2008, http://www.economist.com/node/12284475.

[280] 'The rise and fall of Enron: a brief history,' (Updated 25 May 2006). http://www.cbc.ca/news/business/story/2006/05/25/enron-bkgd.html.

[281] 'Enron: The Fall of a Wall Street Darling' (5 December 2011), http://www.investopedia.com/articles/stocks/09/enron-collapse.asp.

[282] Ibid.

bail-outs to shore up the industry".[283] Lehman Brothers (founded in 1850 by three immigrants from Germany) was ranked as the fourth largest investment bank in the US.[284] It remained a prominent investment bank for decades and one of Wall Street's biggest dealers in fixed-interest trading. Its core business was buying and selling shares and fixed income assets, trading and research, investment banking, investment management and private equity. It dealt, as a wholesale operator, "with governments, companies and other financial institutions, employing 25,000 people worldwide, including 5,000 in the UK".[285]

Lehman had heavily invested in securities linked to the US subprime mortgage market[286] and had US $54 billion of exposure to hard-to-value mortgage-backed securities. Lehman finance deteriorated when property prices crashed and repossessions and arrears increased rapidly. In its third-quarter results of 2008, Lehman had to write down US $2.5 billion due to its exposure to commercial real estate. Lehman's total losses in 2008 were US $6.5 billion, but more "toxic waste" remained to be uncovered.[287]

Lehman being the largest underwriter of property loans in 2007 was heavily exposed to the US real estate market. In 2008, Lehman had over $60 billion invested in commercial real estate, exposure in subprime mortgages (loans to risky homebuyers) in collateralized debt obligations (CDO) and credit default swaps (CDS).[288] Lehman became vulnerable to worsening market conditions as it had a high leverage (the ratio of total assets to shareholders' equity) and due to being the second-largest underwriter of mortgage-backed securities. "On March 17, 2008, following the near-collapse of Bear Stearns – the second-largest underwriter of mortgage-backed securities – Lehman shares fell as much as 48 % on concern it would be the next Wall Street firm to fail".[289]

On 9 June 2008, Lehman announced a second-quarter loss of US $2.8 billion, and it had raised US $6 billion from investors. Lehman, to rectify the problem, took several measures, including selling some of its assets and reducing exposure to residential and commercial mortgages by 20 %, but it proved to be too little too late. Lehman's stock fell 77 % in the first week of September 2008 as equity markets worldwide fell[290]:

> Lehman "reported a loss of [US] $3.9 billion, including a write-down of [US] $5.6 billion, and also announced a sweeping strategic restructuring of its businesses... Moody's Investor Service announced that it was reviewing Lehman's credit ratings, and also said that

---

283 'The origins of the financial crisis,' *The Economist* (7 September 2013) http://www.economist.com/news/schoolsbrief/21584534-effects-financial-crisis-are-still-being-felt-five-years-article.

284 For what led to the demise of Lehman, see Tibman (2009); Mawutor (2014).

285 Q&A: Lehman Brothers bank collapse, BBC News (16 September 2008) http://news.bbc.co.uk/1/hi/business/7615974.stm.

286 Ibid.

287 D'Arcy (2009).

288 D'Arcy (2009).

289 Investopedia Staff.

290 Ibid.

Lehman would have to sell a majority stake to a strategic partner in order to avoid a rating downgrade. These developments led to a 42% plunge in the stock on September 11 [2008]."[291]

As the crisis in financial markets gathered pace, Lehman saw its share price collapse from US \$82 to less than US \$4.[292] Lehman had only \$1 billion left in cash by the end of that week. Last-minute efforts aimed at the takeover of Lehman by Barclays PLC and Bank of America did not materialise;[293] on 15 September 2008, its shares had plunged 93 % from its previous close, and it declared bankrupt[294]:

> The bankruptcy of Lehman rocked the financial system to its core, not least because it was the biggest corporate bankruptcy in US history. With over \$600 billion in assets to administer, Lehman's bankruptcy was many times more complex than Enron's failure in 2001. Also, as a leading investment bank, Lehman was deeply plumbed into the global financial system, thanks to a spider web of companies, contacts and contracts around the world.[295]

Lehman's was the largest victim of the US subprime mortgage-induced financial crisis that swept through global financial markets. On 15 September 2008, Lehman Brothers failed to be rescued by a buyer or a government bailout and filed for Chapter 11 bankruptcy[296] with \$639 billion in assets and \$619 billion in debt. Lehman's assets far exceeded those of previous bankrupt giants such as WorldCom and Enron.[297] Lehman's collapse had wider implication as it greatly deepened the 2008 crisis and contributed to the loss of "close to \$10 trillion in market capitalisation from global equity markets in October 2008, the biggest monthly decline on record at the time".[298]

Frydman and Goldberg blame regulators, bankers and CRAs for the crisis, and they question: how could reputable ratings agencies—and investment banks—misjudge things so badly?[299] The investment banks had paid rating agencies to rate CDOs, and they rated them as high-grade investments when in fact many of

---

[291] Ibid.

[292] Q&A (2008).

[293] 'Financial Crisis 2007/2008 Overview', http://www.wallstreetoasis.com/financial-crisis-overview.

[294] For resolution of Lehman Brothers Holdings Inc. in the US Bankruptcy Court, see Fleming and Sarkar (2014), p. 20.

[295] D'Arcy (2009).

[296] Named after the US bankruptcy code 11, Chapter 11 is a form of bankruptcy that involves a reorganisation of a debtor's business affairs and assets. It is generally filed by corporations that require time to restructure their debts. Chapter 11 gives the debtor a fresh start, subject to the debtor's fulfilment of its obligations under its plan of reorganisation. http://www.investopedia.com/terms/c/chapter11.asp.

[297] Enron's total assets of US \$ 65.5 billion in 2000 were reduced to US \$47.3 in 2001. See Li (2010), p. 41; WorldCom's assets were US \$107 billion in 2002. See Beltran (2002).

[298] Investopedia Staff.

[299] Frydman and Goldberg (2013).

them had included high-risk mortgage loans (called subprime).[300] With regard to the role of CRAs, S&P, until 6 days before Lehman's collapse, had maintained the firm's investment-grade rating of "A". The situation for Moody's was worse as it waited even longer, downgrading Lehman one business day before it collapsed. Frydman and Goldberg view that the near meltdown in 2008 was not due to the failure of capitalism but due to "a failure of contemporary economic models' understanding of the role and functioning of financial markets".[301]

The reasons for the failure of Lehman are many, and in addition to those already mentioned, they range from "dubious accounting practices, unethical management practices, over investment in risky unsecured investments, laxity on the part of regulators"[302] to the failure of external auditors in detecting financial statement malpractices perpetrated by the Lehman managers.[303] The financial crisis of 2007–2008 led to the crisis of confidence of the financial markets, and once undermined it is difficult to restore quickly. The crisis had worldwide implications. After every crisis in the past, markets have come out strong to forge new beginnings,[304] but this time around, one can expect to take it a long time to recover.

2.5.3 *The Northern Rock Fiasco*

Since the failure of Northern Rock, "the world has experienced what is arguably its most serious financial crisis ever..."[305] Northern Rock had a strong presence in the UK's mortgage market. With regard to the new financial instruments, the CRAs had little history on which to base their analysis.[306] In the first years for which such instruments existed, default rates were very low since rising house prices meant that the vast majority of mortgages would be paid. When assessing risk, CRAs do not seem to have allowed for the possibility that house prices could decline in future.[307] As a result, the CRAs often gave high investment ratings of triple A to CDOs that were largely filled with assets that were in turn backed by high-risk mortgages. For example, the Financial Services Authority's stress test of Northern Rock 6 months before it failed showed it should survive a house price fall of 25 %.[308] CDOs are

[300] Who is to Blame for the Financial Crisis', Wall Street Economist, http://www.economicpredictions.org/who-is-to-blame-for-the-financial-crisis.htm.

[301] Frydman and Goldberg (2013).

[302] Mawutor (2014).

[303] Ibid.

[304] Singh.

[305] Bruni and Llewellyn (2009), p. 7.

[306] Baker (2000).

[307] Ibid.

[308] For detailed discussion, see Bruni and Llewellyn (2009).

seen as the cause of the subprime crisis and recession as CDOs became toxic assets for these banks and investors.[309]

Moody's had been rating Northern Rock since 1996 and maintained a published rating opinion on the bank. Prior to the 2008 summer's market turmoil, Moody's had rated Northern Rock as Aa3, lower than triple A, for deposits and senior bonds. The bank's specific factors that supported this opinion were the nationwide mortgage franchise of the bank, its good asset quality, a history of stable earnings and satisfactory profitability. Moody's rating also factored in the possibility of support from the UK government[310] should Northern Rock face the problem of finance. It is questionable if the above bases under which Moody's had issued a higher rating is justifiable. Following the announcement by Northern Rock on 14 September 2008 of the problem associated with interbanking lending, Moody's placed Northern Rock's rating on review based on uncertain direction. This rating action reflected Moody's opinion that the arrangements put in place by the Bank of England would mitigate the liquidity problems. Northern Rock's model was dependent on the continuation of interbank lending and the Bank of England meeting its obligation as lender of last resort[311] if it faced any difficulty. As a precedent, in October 2008 the European Central Bank (ECB) was forced to increase massively liquidity to save the banking system. The ECB did not hesitate to serve as lender of last resort to the banking system, despite fears of moral hazard, inflation and the fiscal implications of its lending.[312]

Moody's did not consider the probability of interbank lending drying up and the fact that the depositors would lose confidence when the news of the Bank of England stepping in to assist Northern Rock became public. This led to Moody's giving an investment grade rating to Northern Rock.[313] Doubts about depositors ever getting their deposited money led to the unprecedented withdrawal of money and led to Northern Rock's eventual collapse.[314]

The credit crunch exposed the shortcomings of the Basel II rules governing bank capital.[315] Strict focus on capital meant Northern Rock and others banks were considered to have adequate capital[316] and the problem of liquidity (cash or near cash on the balance sheet) was overlooked. The banks took advantage of Basel II and the less transparent flexibility to set up off-balance-sheet financing, which,

---

309 For definition of collateral debt obligation, see Glossary of Terms. http://articles.timesofindia.indiatimes.com/2009-02-01/open-space/28008882_1_cdos-mutual-funds-toxic-assets.

310 Memorandum from Moody's (2008), Para 5. http://www.parliament.the-stationery-office.co.uk/pa/cm200708/cmselect/cmtreasy/56/56we32.htm.

311 Hubbard et al. (2009).

312 De Grauwe (2011).

313 "Northern Rock: Lessons from the Fall", *The Economics*, http://www.economist.com/node/9988865.

314 Mayes and Wood; Bruni and Llewellyn (2009), pp. 13–30.

315 For details on Basel II, see Chernobai et al. (2007), pp. 35–64.

316 Brummer (2009), p. 223.

although heavily leveraged and risky, received favourable treatment in calculating banks' capital ratios.[317]

Northern Rock's business model approved by the UK regulators was particularly over-dependent on "borrowing substantial amount[s] of money in the inter-bank market".[318] "There was a mismatch between the borrowings – which could, and did vanish overnight – and the lack of understanding in the market place"[319] by the board[320] and the regulators. Northern Rock relied "on customer deposits for a quarter of its money".[321] The press leak that Northern Rock had applied to the Bank of England, as a lender of last resort, led to the run on the bank by depositors withdrawing their deposits, which exacerbated the situation.[322] Several villains emerged. The FSA had failed in supervising Northern Rock. Search for economic growth meant the UK government opted for lax regulation and low interest rates (sacrificing financial stability), which led banks to look around for better returns, and bank borrowing got out of control and caused a housing bubble.[323] Northern Rock developed rapidly with few checks and balances in place and became the most leveraged bank in Europe.[324] The survival of Northern Rock ultimately depended on taking it into public ownership; it was nationalised. The refinancing "had cost the [UK] taxpayer some £22 billion of advances to Northern Rock", which was necessary to preserve confidence in the institution;[325] a new management team was recruited, and the UK government recapitalised it.[326]

2.5.4 Reliance by Investors

Many financial institutions and investors, rather than undertake their own analysis, simply outsourced their risk management by relying on the CRAs to do the essential work of risk analysis for them.[327] The question is where the blame lies. Is it the investors in general and institutional investors in particular for having relied too heavily on credit ratings in their investment guidelines and choices? The CRAs, for their part, have conceded that ratings are useful for limiting the credit risk that investors take as they monitor and communicate their findings. Credit ratings do not

[317] Ibid., p. 234.

[318] Redwood (2009), p. 27.

[319] Brummer (2009), pp. 213–214, note 251.

[320] Redwood (2009), p. 27, feels the mistake made by the Northern Rock is not to borrow long term.

[321] Ibid.

[322] Ibid., p. 24.

[323] Turner (2008), p. 191.

[324] Ibid., p. 192.

[325] Redwood (2009), p. 1, note 248.

[326] Brummer (2009), p. 230, note 251.

[327] Blankfein (2009), p. 7.

directly address any risk other than credit risk.[328] Such a limitation of credit ratings means investors are required to carry out their own independent risk assessment and due diligence and ought not to rely exclusively on ratings for valuation.[329] Arguably, investors may have been encouraged to rely overly on ratings based on international and official recognition of credit ratings in various regulatory and supervisory frameworks, and in the process investors may have failed to pay close attention to what the ratings actually mean.[330] The market practice has also come to rely on the ratings given by CRAs, and investors naturally do expect CRAs to do a proper job based on their expertise.

By issuing unjustified higher ratings, CRAs had misled the investors into thinking their investments were safe when they were not. This led to a view that there was a need to regulate CRAs. Views differ on the need for additional regulation and on extensive supervision. For example, neither the European Securities and Markets Authority (ESMA) nor any other public authority is allowed to interfere with the content of credit ratings or methodologies.[331] Schwarcz's[332] view is that CRAs should remain unregulated, as additional regulations, which will mean unnecessary regulatory costs, would not enhance the role of CRAs in the international market regulations. Jackson[333] sees the regulatory incorporation of private credit rating and whether CRAs ought to be subjected to extensive supervision as presenting a new and difficult question of public policy.[334] No clear answer emerges as to the benefit and extent of regulation and supervision.

2.5.5 Conclusion

CRAs issue opinions on creditworthiness of companies, governments and sophisticated financial structures, and investors' protection requires that they act as gatekeepers. CRAs provide independent opinions on the probability of default or expected losses of companies, governments and a wide range of financial instruments. Investors, borrowers, issuers and governments use the Big Three CRAs, and therefore they play an important role in financial markets. Undoubtedly, the subprime mortgage led to the financial crisis, and the CRAs have escaped any blame, despite their culpability. The CRAs have made errors of judgment in rating

[328] Fitch Rating, "Understanding Credit Rating – Limitations and Usage" https://www.fitchratings.com/jsp/general/RatingsDefinitions.faces?context_ln=5&detail_ln=500&context=5&detail=509.

[329] A joint report by the Treasury and the Australian Securities and Investments Commission and Review of credit rating agencies and research houses (October 2008), p. 20.

[330] Ibid.

[331] See Chap. 5.

[332] Schwarcz (2001), p. 310.

[333] Jackson (2001), p. 311.

[334] For discussion on the supervision of CRAs, see Chaps. 4 and 5.

structured products, particularly in assigning triple-A ratings to structured debt, which in a large number of cases were subsequently downgraded or defaulted.[335] Many of the structured financial products that the CRAs were responsible for rating consisted of lower quality triple-B rated loans, but when pooled together into CDOs, a triple-A rating emerged.[336] In reality, there would not have been a demand for these products had CRAs resisted giving higher ratings. However, the blame does not lie squarely on the shoulders of CRAs because although high ratings had encouraged investors to invest, the government and the investors should bear a proportionate part of the blame. The US government's affordable housing policy led to the erosion of mortgage lending standards; that rests squarely on the shoulders of the policymakers who had advocated these ill-conceived policies in the first place. Borrowers, irrespective of their socio-economic status, quite naturally responded to the incentives given, and risky lending had spread to the wider mortgage market.[337] The fear is that the "rest of the world will not be immune to the slowdown in the United States, especially if it becomes serious". The "financial crisis started in a relatively small part of the U.S. financial system – the subprime mortgage market – but has now become a global problem".[338]

Sinclair[339] sees the situation differently in that the subprime crisis is not a direct consequence of subprime mortgage delinquencies as the subprime securities market was worth only US $0.7 trillion in mid-2007, out of a total global capital market of US $175 trillion. The impact of subprime assets is out of all proportion to their actual weight in the financial system. He submits that it is not possible to explain or deduce a systemic crisis in rational terms. Although the problem is essentially subprime in origin, however, the complex inter-linkages between financial markets and economic activity have put the global economy at risk. Regulation introduced should, therefore, aim to prevent the same crisis from occurring in future. The reason for unreliable ratings issued, which led to the subprime mortgage crisis, appears to be due to the gatekeeper failure of CRAs. CRAs are required to take on an obligation of acting as a responsible gatekeeper to avoid future crises. In subsequent chapters, various regulations will be critically analysed to see the extent to which regulators are able to address the tripartite problems of conflicts of interest, lack of competition and absence of regulation that the regulators in the US and EU had identified.

335 See Wadden IV, William "Biv" (2002). See also Norris (2007), Buiter (2007) and Kerr (2007).

336 Li (2000), pp. 43–54.

337 Affordable Housing Policy, at 12.

338 Ibid.

339 Sinclair (2010), p. 6.

References

A joint report by the Treasury and the Australian Securities and Investments Commission, Review of credit rating agencies and research houses (October 2008). http://www.asic.gov.au/asic/pdflib.nsf/LookupByFileName/rep143.pdf/$file/rep143.pdf.

Abdullah. (2012, April 17). Dominos effect of U.S. sub-prime mortgage crisis. http://pu33les.com/2012/04/17/dominos-effect-of-u-s-sub-prime-mortgage-crisis/.

Acharya, V. V., Viral, V., Richardson, M. P., & Matthew, P. (2009). Causes of the financial crisis. *Critical Review, 21* (2, 3), 195–210. http://ssrn.com/abstract=1514984.

Akins, E. M., & Calabria, M. A. (2012). Regulation, market structure, and role of the credit rating agencies. *Policy Analysis, 704*, 1–35.

Alcubilla, R. G., & Pozo, J. R. (2012). *Credit rating agencies on the watch list*. OUP: Oxford.

Alessi, C., Wolverson, R., & Sergie, M. A. (2013, October 22). The credit rating controversy. http://www.cfr.org/financial-crises/credit-rating-controversy/p22328.

Arora, A. (2010). The global financial crisis: A new global regulatory order? *Journal of Business Law, 8*, 670–690.

Atkins, R. (2012, November 19). Eurozone securitisation hits crisis low. *FT.com.*

Baker, D. (2000). The housing bubble and the financial crisis. *Real-World Economics Review, 46*, 73–81. http://paecon.net/PAEReview/issue46/Baker46.pdf.

Becker, B., & Milbourn, T. (2011, November 3). How did increased competition affect credit ratings? *Journal of Financial Economics, 101*, 49 (Harvard Business School Working Paper). http://hbswk.hbs.edu/item/6517.html.

Beltran, L. (2002, July 22). WorldCom files largest bankruptcy ever: Nation's no. 2 long-distance company in Chapter 11 – Largest with $107 billion in assets. *CNN/Money*. http://money.cnn.com/2002/07/19/news/worldcom_bankruptcy/.

Benmelech, E., & Dlugosz, J. (2010). The credit rating crisis (Chapter 3), 161. http://www.nber.org/chapters/c11794.pdf.

A. M. Best, DBRS Ltd, Finch, Moody's and S&P. Joint Response to the Technical Committee of the International Organization of Securities Commissions' Consultation Report on the Role of Credit Rating Agencies in Structured Finance Markets', p. 1. http://www.fitchratings.com/creditdesk/reports/report_frame.cfm?rpt_id=384044.

Biglaiser, G., DeRouen Jr, K., & Archer, C. C. (2011). Politics, early warning systems, and credit rating agencies. *Foreign Policy Analysis, 7*(1), 67–87.

Blankfein, L. (CEO of Goldman Sachs). (2009, February 8). Do not destroy the essential catalyst of risk. *Financial Times*, 7.

Blaurock, U. (2007). Control and responsibility of credit rating agencies. http://ejcl.org/113/article113-16.pdf.

Block-Lieb, S., & Janger, E. (2009). Demand-side gatekeepers in the market for home loans. *Temple Law Review, 82*, 474.

Bonewitz, P. L. (2010). Implications of reputation economics on regulatory reform of the credit rating industry. *William & Mary Business Law Review*, *1*, 391. http://scholarship.law.wm.edu/wmblr/vol1/iss2/4

Borrus, A. (2002, February 8). The credit-raters: How they work and how they might work better. *Business Week.* http://www.ba.metu.edu.tr/~adil/BA-web/bus%20press/credit%20raters.pdf.

Brooke, M. A. (2009–2010). Credit rating immunity – How the hands-off approach toward credit rating agencies led to the subprime credit crisis and the need for greater accountability. *Oklahoma Law Review*, 62, 735

Brummer, A. (2009). *The crunch: How greed and incompetence sparked the credit crisis*. London: Random House.

Bruner, C. M. (2008). States, markets, and gatekeepers: Public-private regulatory regimes in an era of economic globalization. *Michigan Journal of International Law, 30*, 125, 168.

Bruni, F., & Llewellyn, D. T. (Eds.). (2009). The failure of northern rock: A multi-dimensional case study. The European Money and Finance Forum Vienna (pp. 13–30). http://www.suerf.org/download/studies/study20091.pdf.

Buiter, W. (2007, September 21). Basel II: back to the drawing board? *The Financial Times*. http://blogs.ft.com/maverecon/2007/09/basel-ii-back-t.html.

Bunjevac, T. A. (2009). Credit rating agencies: A regulatory challenge for Australia. *Melbourne University Law Review, 33*, 40.

Cambridge. 'AAA rating,' Professional English Online. http://peo.cambridge.org/index.php?option=com_content&view=article&id=164:aaa-rating&catid=10:jargon-buster&Itemid=4.

Cardinute, M. (2011, November 4). Who's to blame for sub-prime mortgage crisis? http://mg312.wordpress.com/2011/11/04/who%E2%80%99s-to-blame-for-sub-prime-mortgage-crisis/.

Chan, E. (2012, January 20). Credit Rating Agencies: How much should we trust them? http://www.arbitragemagazine.com/general/236credit-rating-agencies-trust-them/.

Chandler, R. A., & Davies, I. R. (1993). Securitisation – The buzzword that means business. *Banking World, 11*(7), 48.

Chernobai, A. S., Rachev, S. T., & Fabozzi, F. J. (2007). Basel II capital accord (Chapter 3). In *Operational risk: A guide to Basel II capital requirements, models, and analysis*. Hoboken, NJ: Wiley.

Claessens, S., Kose, M. A., Laeven, L., & Valencia, F. (2014). *Financial crises: Causes, consequences, and policy responses*, 1–277, Kindle Edition.

Coffee, J. C. Jr. (2009, March 10). *Enhancing investor protection and the regulation of securities markets* (Working Paper No. 348). The Centre for Law and Economic Studies Columbia University School of Law.

Coffee, J. C. (2002, July 30). *Understanding Enron: It's about the gatekeepers, stupid* (Columbia Law School Working Paper No. 207). http://mba.tuck.dartmouth.edu/mdm/AlumniLearningLinks/CoffeeOnEnron.pdf.

Coffee, J. C. (2006). *Gatekeepers: The professions and corporate governance*. Oxford: Business & Economics, OPU.

Coffee, J. C. Jr. (2009, March 10). Congressional testimony. http://ssrn.com/abstract=1372194.

Coskun, D. (2008). Credit rating agencies in a post-Enron world: Congress re-visits NRSRO concept. *Journal of Banking Regulation, 9*(4), 264. http://www.kvdl.nl/wp-content/uploads/2013/01/Deniz-Coskun-credit-rating-agencies-in-a-post-Enron-world.pdf.

Cox, J., Faucette, J., & Lickstein, C. V. (2010, March). Part 5-II: Why did the credit crisis spread to global markets? http://blogs.law.uiowa.edu/ebook/uicifd-ebook/part-5-ii-why-did-credit-crisis-spread-global-markets.

Credit Rating Agencies – How they work. http://creditratingagency.net/.

Criado, S., & Rixtel, A. V. (2008, August 29). *Structured finance and the financial turmoil of 2007–2008: An introductory overview* (Banco de Espana Occasional Paper No. 0808). http://dx.doi.org/10.2139/ssrn.1260748.

Cross, R., & Harris, J. W. (1991). *Precedents in English law*. In Clarendon law series (4th ed.). Oxford: Oxford University Press.

Crouhy, M. G., Jarrow, R. A., & Turnbull, S. M. (2007, July 4). The subprime credit crisis of 07. http://www.fdic.gov/bank/analytical/cfr/bank_research_conference/annual_8th/Turnbull_Jarrow.pdf.

D'Arcy, C. (2009, September 14). Why Lehman Brothers collapsed. https://www.lovemoney.com/news/3909/why-lehman-brothers-collapsed.

Darcy, D. (2009). Credit rating agencies and the credit crisis: How the issuer pays conflict contributed and what regulators might do about it. *Columbia Business Law Review, 2009*(2), 605.

De Grauwe, P. (2011, August 18). The European Central Bank as a lender of last resort. http://www.voxeu.org/article/european-central-bank-lender-last-resort.

Debts, Deficits and Dilemmas – A crash course on the financial crisis and its aftermath. *Economist*, 11 (2014). http://www.waterstones.com/wat/images/special/pdf/9781781253786.pdf.

Dembinski, P. H., Lager, C., Cornford, A., & Bonvin, J.-M. (Eds.). (2006). *Enron and world finance: A case study in ethics*. Basingstoke: Palgrave Macmillan. http://www.strongwindpress.com/pdfs/TuiJian/Enron%20and%20World%20Finance%20-%20A%20Case%20Study%20in%20Ethics.pdf.

Demirguc-Kent, A., Detragiache, E., & Merrouche, O. (2010, November 30). Bank capital: Lessons from the financial crisis. In *Unpublished Working Paper WP/10/286*. International Monetary Fund, Washington, DC.

Dennis, K. (2008–2009). Rating game: Explaining rating agency failures in the build-up to the financial crisis. *University of Miami Law Review, 63*, 1111.

Detrixhe, J. (2011, October 18). Credit rating companies favoring borrowers paying most Bloomberg. http://www.bloomberg.com/news/2011-10-28/credit-rating-companies-favor-firms-paying-most.html.

Doyle, M., Gordon, G., & Hall, K. G. (2013, February 5). U.S. suit against standard & poor's raises stakes for wall street. *McClatchy Newspapers*. http://www.mcclatchydc.com/2013/02/05/182055/us-sues-standard-poors-claims.html.

Eborall, C. (2012). Credit rating agencies (Chapter 19). In M. Blair, G. Walker, & S. Willey (Eds.), *Financial markets and exchanges law* (pp. 549–580). Oxford: OUP.

Egan, S. J. (2008, October 22). *Statement of Sean J. Egan, Hearing before the Committee on Oversight and Government Reform, House of Representatives, One Hundred Tenth Congress, Second Session*, Serial No. 110–155, pp. 45–60. http://www.gpo.gov/fdsys/pkg/CHRG-110hhrg51103/html/CHRG-110hhrg51103.htm.

Ellsworth, L. P., & Porapaiboon, K. V. (2009). Credit rating agencies in the spotlight: A new casualty of the mortgage meltdown. *Business Law Today, 18*(4), 1.

Enron: The Fall of a Wall Street Darling, 5 December 2011. http://www.investopedia.com/articles/stocks/09/enron-collapse.asp.

Europa Press Release. (2009, April 23). Approval of new regulation will raise standards for the issuance of credit rating used in the community, Brussels. http://europa.eu/rapid/pressReleasesAction.do?reference=IP/09/629.

European Commission. (2010, November 5). Public consultation of credit rating agencies. http://ec.europa.eu/internal_market/consultations/docs/2010/cra/cpaper_en.pdf.

Farrell. (2010, May 14). Credit rating agencies in the spotlight. *Financial Times*. http://www.ft.com/cms/s/0/b3f59f8e-5ee8-11df-af86-00144feab49a.html#axzz2cb5JaS6K.

Farzad, R. (2013, July 30). Investors are hungry for junk. *Bloomberg Business Week*.

Field, A. (2010, March 14). Lehman report: The business decisions that brought Lehman down. Updated 15 March 2010. http://www.dailyfinance.com/2010/03/14/lehman-report-the-business-decisions-that-brought-lehman-down/.

Financial Crisis 2007/2008 Overview. http://www.wallstreetoasis.com/financial-crisis-overview.

Financial Crises and Singapore. (2013, September 16). http://leongszehian.com/?p=5986.

Fitch Ratings. Update on U.S. Subprime and Alt-A: Performance and Rating Reviews (20 March 2008).

Fitch Ratings, letter addressed to US SEC. (2002, November 12). https://www.sec.gov/news/extra/credrate/fitchratings1.htm.

Fleming, M., & Sarkar, A. (2014). The failure resolution of Lehman Brothers. *Federal Reserve Bank of New York Economic Policy Review, 20*(2), 175–206.

Forbes, R., Frankle, A., & Hierl, A. (1974). Municipal bond credit ratings: A suggested methodology. *Journal of Financial Quantitative Analysis* (November 1974 Proceedings).

Foster, J. B., & Magdoff, F. (2009). *The great financial crisis: Causes and consequences*. New York: Monthly Review Press.

Friedman, J. (2009). A crisis of politics, not economics: Complexity, ignorance, and policy failure. *Critical Review, 21*(2–3), 127–185. http://www.criticalreview.com/crf/pdfs/Friedman_intro21_23.pdf.

From risk perception to safe behaviour. https://www.sia.org.au/downloads/SIGs/Resources/From_Risk_Perception_to_Safe_Behaviour.pdf.

Frost, C. A. (2007). Credit rating agencies in the capital markets: A review of research evidence on selected criticism of the agencies. *Journal of Accounting, Auditing & Finance, 22*(3), 469.

Frydman, R., & Goldberg, M. D. (2013, September 13). Lehman Brothers collapse: Was capitalism to blame? *Theguardian.com.* http://www.theguardian.com/business/2013/sep/13/lehman-brothers-was-capitalism-to-blame.

Fuchita, Y., & Litan, R. E. (Eds.). (2006). *Financial gatekeepers: Can they protect investors?* Baltimore: The Brooking Institute, Brooking Institute Press.

Fusaro, P. C., & Miller, R. M. (2002). *What went wrong at Enron; Everyone's guide to the largest bankruptcy in US history.* Hoboken: John Wiley & Sons Inc.

Giles, C. (2009, September 21). IMF defends securitisation markets. *Financial Times.*

Goldfarb, Z. A., & Dennis, B. (2011, January 27). Government report blames regulators and financial institutions for economic crisis. *Washington Post.* http://www.washingtonpost.com/wp-dyn/content/article/2011/01/27/AR2011012702940.html.

Hackel, K. (2010, October 5). Why credit rating are still important in determining stock valuation. http://seekingalpha.com/article/228415-why-credit-ratings-are-still-important-in-determining-stock-valuation.

Hart, J. (2013, March). Report: Debt capital markets – Securitisation – The redemption of securitisation? *The Banker.*

Hart, J. (2013, March 1). Securitisation seeks redemption in Europe. *The Banker.* http://www.thebanker.com/World/Securitisation-seeks-redemption-in-Europe?ct=true.

Helleiner, E., Pagliari, S., & Zimmermann, H. (Eds.). (2010). *Global financial crisis: The politics of international regulatory change.* London and New York: Routledge.

Henwood, D., et al. (2009, August 21). Leaking bubble. *The Nation.*

Hill, C. A. (2010). Why did rating agencies do such a bad job rating sub-prime security? *University of Pittsburgh Law Review, 71* (20) (University of Minnesota Law School, Legal Research Paper Series, Research Paper No. 10–18, 2010, p. 6). http://ssrn.com/abstract=1582539.

Hubbard, G., Scott, H., & Thornton, J. (2009). The Fed's independence is at risk. *Financial Times,* 1–2.

Hudson, A. (2009). *The law of finance.* London: Sweet & Maxwell.

Hunt, J. P. (2008, September 3). Credit rating agencies and the 'Worldwide Credit Crisis': The limits of reputation, the inefficiency of reform, and a proposal for improvement (p. 1). http://paers.ssrn.com/so13/papers.cfin?abstractid–1267625.

Hunt, J. P. (2009a). Credit rating agencies and the worldwide "Credit Crisis": The limits of reputation, the insufficiency of reform, and a proposal for improvement. *Columbia Business Law Review, 1*(1), 109–209. http://www2.wiwi.hu-berlin.de/finanz/skript_semfin/t12.pdf; http://works.bepress.com/john_hunt/1.

Hunt, J. P. (2009b, September 3). Summary credit rating agencies and the 'Worldwide Credit Crisis': The limits of reputation, the inefficiency of reform, and a proposal for improvement. *Columbia Business Law Review, 1,* 1–2. http://ssrn.com/abstract=1267625.

Hurst, T. (2009). The role of credit rating agencies in the current worldwide financial crisis. *The Company Lawyer, 30*(2), 61–64.

IMF. (2009, April). Global financial stability report: Responding to the financial crisis and measuring systemic risks, xi–xii.

Investopedia Staff. Case study: The collapse of Lehman Brothers. http://www.investopedia.com/articles/economics/09/lehman-brothers-collapse.asp

IOSCO. (2003, September). Report on the activities of credit rating agencies (p. 1). https://www.iosco.org/library/pubdocs/pdf/IOSCOPD153.pdf.

Jackson, H. E. (2001). The role of credit rating agencies in the establishment of capital standards for financial institutional in a global economy (Chapter 19). In E. Ferran & C. A. E. Goodhart (Eds.), *Regulating financial services and the markets in the 21st century.* Oxford/Portland, OR: Hart.

Jaffee, D., Lynch, A. W., Richardson, M., & Van Nieuwerburgn, S. (2009). Mortgage originations and securitization in the financial crisis (Chapter 1). In V. Acharya & M. Richardson (Eds.),

Restoring financial stability: How to repair a failed system (pp. 61–82). Hoboken: John Wiley & Sons Inc.

Jiang, J. (X)., Stanford, M. H., & Xie, Y. (2012). Does it matter who pays for bond ratings? Historical evidence. *Journal of Financial Economics*, *105*(3), 607–621. http://dx.doi.org/10.1016/j.jfineco.2012.04.001.

Jickling, M. (2009). *Causes of the financial crisis*. Washington, DC: Congressional Research Service. http://digitalcommons.ilr.cornell.edu/key_workplace/600.

Jobst, A. A. (2005, September). *What is Structured Finance?* (Working Paper). http://www.securitization.net/pdf/publications/structuredfinance_20oct05.pdf.

Kennedy, K. C. (1983, January 1). A critical appraisal of criminal deterrence theory. Michigan State University College of Law. http://digitalcommons.law.msu.edu/cgi/viewcontent.cgi?article=1036&context=facpubs.

Kerr, D. (2007, October 18). Banks learn to reprice risk in post-crisis credit market. http://www.financialnews-us.com/?page=ushome&contentid=2448964990.

Kisgen, D. (2007). The influence of credit ratings on corporate capital structure decisions. *Journal of Applied Corporate Finance, 19*, 65.

Klinz, W. (Chairman) (2011). European Parliament Special Committee on the Financial, Economic and Social Crisis. Documentation relating to the Committee's work from October 2009 to July 2011. http://www.europarl.europa.eu/document/activities/cont/201109/20110901ATT25750/20110901ATT25750EN.pdf.

Klinz, W. (2008, February 27). The International Financial Crisis: Its cause and what to do about it. In *Liberal and Democratic Workshops*, p. 7. https://www.coursehero.com/file/1649782/Finance-bookEN/.

Krebs, J. D. (2009-2010). Rating agencies: Where we have been and where do we go from here. *Journal of Business, Entrepreneurship & the Law, 3*, 133.

Kruck, A. (2013). The regulatory use of credit ratings in Germany and the US: A resource dependence view on the transfer of (quasi-) regulatory authority. *German Policy Studies, 9*(1), 141–176.

Kruithof, K., & Wymeersch, E. O. (2006, March 31). *Regulation and liability of credit rating agencies under Belgian law* (Ghent University Financial Law Institute Working Paper No. 2006-05, p. 1). http://dx.doi.org/10.2139/ssrn.894820.

Langohr, H., & Langohr, P. (2008). The raison d'Etr of credit ratings and their markets (Chapter 3). In H. Langohr & P. Langohr (Eds.), *The rating agencies and their credit ratings: What they are, how they work and why they are relevant* (pp. 89–125). Chichester: Wiley.

Legg, M., & Harris, J. (2009). How the American dream became a global nightmare: An analysis of the causes of the global financial crisis. *University of New South Wales Law Journal, 32*, 350.

Levi-Faur, D. (2010, February). Regulation and regulatory governance. Jerusalem Papers in Regulation and Governance, No. 1. http://regulation.huji.ac.il/papers/jp1.pdf.

Levin, C., & Coburn, T. (2011, April 13). Wall Street and the financial crisis: Anatomy of a financial collapse. http://www.hsgac.senate.gov//imo/media/doc/Financial_Crisis/FinancialCrisisReport.pdf?attempt=2.

Levitt, A. (2007, September 7). Conflicts and the credit crunch. *WSJ*. http://online.wsj.com/article/SB118912606193520154.html.

Li, Y. (2010). The case analysis of the scandal of Enron. *International Journal of Business and Management, 5*(10), 41. http://www.ccsenet.org/journal/index.php/ijbm/article/viewFile/7627/5855.Free.

Li, D. X. (2000). On default correction: A Copula function approach. *Journal of Fixed Income, 9*, 43–54.

Lowenstein, R. (2008, April 17). Triple a failure. *The New York Times*. http://www.buildingthepride.com/faculty/blgordon/630%20Documents/Article%20-%20Triple_A_Failure.pdf.

Lucchetti, A., & Ng, S. (2010, May 24). "Rating Shopping" lives on as congress debates on fix. *The Wall Street Journal*. http://online.wsj.com/news/articles/SB10001424052748703315404575250270972715804.

Macey, J. R. (2006). Polarisation of American corporate governance. *Virginia Law and Business Review, 1*(1), 21.

Mah-Hui, M. L. (2008). Old wine in new bottles: Subprime mortgage crisis – Causes and consequences. *Journal of Applied Research in Accounting and Finance, 3* (1), 3–13. http://ssrn.com/abstract=1263280.

Mawutor, J. K. M. (2014). The failure of Lehman Brothers: Causes, preventive measures and recommendations. *Research Journal of Finance and Accounting, 5*(4), 85–91.

Mayes, D. G., & Wood, G. Lessons from the northern rock episode. http://economix.fr/pdf/profs/Mayes-LESSONS-FROM-THE-NORTHERN-ROCK-EPISOD.pdf.

McLean, B., & Nocera, J. (2010). *All the devils are here: The hidden history of the financial crisis*. New York, London: Penguin.

McVea, H. (2010). Credit rating agencies, the subprime mortgage debacle and global governance: The EU strikes back. *International and Comparative Law Quarterly, 59*(3), 701.

Memorandum from Moody's. (2008). http://www.parliament.the-stationery-office.co.uk/pa/cm200708/cmselect/cmtreasy/56/56we32.htm.

Mendales, R. (2009). Collateralized explosive devices: Why securities regulation failed to prevent the CDO meltdown and how to fix it. *University of Illinois Law Review, 5*, 1359. http://illinoislawreview.org/wp-content/ilr-content/articles/2009/5/Mendales.pdf.

Mileti, D., & Sorensen, H. (1987). Natural hazards and precautionary behavior. In N. D. Weinstein (Ed.), *Taking care: Why people take precautions*. New York: Cambridge University Press.

Miller, F. P., Vandome, A. F., & McBrewster, J. (Eds.) (2009). *Causes of the financial crisis of 2007–2009*. Mauritius (Printed in USA, UK, Germany): Alphascript Publishing (A trademark of International Book Market Service Ltd.).

Murphy, A. (2008, November 4). An analysis of the financial crisis of 2008: Causes and solutions. Available at SSRN: http://ssrn.com/abstract=1295344 or http://dx.doi.org/10.2139/ssrn.1295344.

Nasiripour, S. (2012, June 27). Financial crisis commission finds cause for prosecution of Wall Street. *Huss Post Business*. http://www.huffingtonpost.com/2011/01/24/financial-crisis-commissi_2_n_813415.html.

Norris, F. (2007, November 2). Being kept in the dark on Wall Street. *The New York Times*. http://www.nytimes.com/2007/11/02/business/02norris.html?ref=business.

Nye, R. P. (2014). *Understanding and managing the credit rating agencies: A guide to fixed income issues*. London: Euromoney Institutional Investor Plc.

O'Brien, P. C. (2011). Securitisation, transparency and failure risk. *The Irish, Accounting Review, 18*(1), 39–50.

Official Journal of the European Union. Communications form the Commission on Credit Rating Agencies, 2006/C 59/2, C59/2.

Pagano, M., & Volpin, P. (2009, September). Credit ratings failures and policy options. http://www.eief.it/files/2009/12/credit-ratings-failures-and-policy-options.pdf.

Parnoy, F. (2009). *Overdependence on credit ratings was a primary cause of the crisis* (Legal Studies Research Paper Series, University of San Diego, Research Paper No. 09-015).

Partnoy, F. (1999). The Siskel and Ebert of financial markets: Two thumbs down for the credit rating agencies. *Washington University Law Quarterly, 77*, 619–712. http://dx.doi.org/10.2139/ssrn.167412.

Partnoy, F. (2003a). Strict liability for gatekeepers: A reply to professor coffee (Spring 2003). University of San Diego Law and Economics Research Paper No. 3. http://dx.doi.org/10.2139/ssrn.417262.

Partnoy, F. (2003b). A revisionist view of Enron and the sudden death of may. *Villanova Law Review, 48*, 1245.

Partnoy, F. (2006a). How and why credit rating agencies are not like other gatekeepers. In Y. Fuchita & R. E. Litan (Eds.), *Financial gatekeepers: Can they protect investors?* (p. 59). Washington, DC: Brookings Institute.

Partnoy, F. (2006b). How and why credit rating agencies are not like other gatekeepers (University of San Diego Legal Studies Research Paper Series, No. 07-46, pp. 59–102). http://ssrn.com/abstract=900257.

Pengelly, M. (2012). Reviving securitisation. *Risk, 25*(6), 44–47.

Pettinger, T. (2013, May 16). The great recession 2008–13. *Economicshelp*. http://www.economicshelp.org/blog/7501/economics/the-great-recession/

Pound, R. (1914). The end of law as developed in legal rules and doctrines. *Harvard Law Review, 27*, 195.

Proposal for a Regulation of the European Parliament and of the Council on Credit Rating Agencies. Brussels (12 November 2008). http://ec.europa.eu/internal_market/securities/docs/agencies/proposal_en.pdf.

Q&A: Lehman Brothers bank collapse. *BBC News*, 16 September 2008. http://news.bbc.co.uk/1/hi/business/7615974.stm.

Redwood, J. (2009). *After the credit crunch: No more boom or bust*. London: Middlesex University.

Reisberg, A. (2011). The future role of credit rating agencies in contemporary financial markets – A theoretical perspective (Chapter 7). In D. Prentice & A. Reisberg (Eds.), *Corporate finance law in the UK and EU* (pp. 169–212). Oxford: Oxford University Press.

Richardson, M. (2009). Causes of the financial crisis of 2007–2009. In V. Acharya & M. Richardson (Eds.), *Restoring financial stability: How to repair a failed system* (pp. 57–60). New York: Wiley.

Rousseau, S. (2009, July 23). *Regulating credit rating agencies after the financial crisis: The long and winding road toward accountability* (Capital Markets Institute Research Paper 15). http://dx.doi.org/10.2139/ssrn.1456708.

Sabato, G. (2009, August 24). Financial crisis: where did risk management fail? Available at SSRN: http://ssrn.com/abstract=1460762 or http://dx.doi.org/10.2139/ssrn.1460762.

Santomero, A. M. (2008). Foreword. In H. Langohr & P. Langohr (Eds.), *The rating agencies and their credit ratings* (pp. ix–xi). Chichester: Wiley.

Schwarcz, S. L. (2002). Enron and the use and abuse of special purpose entities in corporate structure. *University of Cincinnati Law Review, 70*, Corporate Law Symposium.

Schwarcz, S. L. (2001). The role of rating agencies in global market regulations (Chapter 18). In E. Ferran & C. A. E. Goodhart (Eds.), *Regulating financial services and the markets in the 21st century*. Oxford, Portland/Oregon: Hart.

SEC. Concept release: rating agencies and the use of credit ratings under the federal securities laws. https://www.sec.gov/rules/concept/33-8236.htm.

Shell, A. (n.d.). Lehman Bros. collapse triggered economic turmoil. New York, *USA TODAY*. http://abcnews.go.com/Business/lehman-bros-collapse-triggered-economic-turmoil/story?id=8543352.

Shirai, S. (2009, April). *The impact of the US subprime mortgage crisis on the world and East Asia: Through analyses of cross-border capital movements* (ERIA Discussion Paper Series). http://www.eria.org/ERIA-DP-2009-10.pdf.

Shore, K. E. (2000). Watching the watchdog: An argument for auditor liability to third parties. *SMU Law Review, 53*, 387.

Sinclair, T. J. (2010). Credit rating agencies and the global financial crisis. *Economic Sociology the European Electronic Newsletter, 12*(1), 4–9. http://econsoc.mpifg.de/archive/econ_soc_12-1.pdf.

Sinclair, T. J. (2013, February 18). Should we care about Moody's. http://speri.dept.shef.ac.uk/2013/02/28/care-moodys/.

Singh, M. (n.d.). The 2007–08 Financial crisis in review. http://www.investopedia.com/articles/economics/09/financial-crisis-review.asp.

Slater, M. S. (2008). *Innovation corrupted: The origins and legacy of Enron's collapsed*. Cambridge: Harvard University Press.

Smith, E. B. (2008, September 24). Bringing down wall street as ratings let loose subprime scourge. *Bloomberg*. http://www.bloomberg.com/apps/news?pid=newsarchive&sid=ah839IWTLP9s.

So what's a toxic asset? *CBSNews*, 23 March 2009. http://www.cbsnews.com/news/so-whats-a-toxic-asset/.

Summerfield, M. (2006, May 18). Evolution of deterrence crime theory: A journey with an end. http://voices.yahoo.com/evolution-deterrence-crime-theory-37965.html?cat=37.

Surowiecki, J. (2009, September 28). Ratings downgrade (The talk of the town). *The New Yorker*, 297–310.

The Financial Crisis Inquiry Commission. (2011, January). Final report of the National Commission on the causes of the financial and economic crisis in the United States. http://www.gpo.gov/fdsys/pkg/GPO-FCIC/pdf/GPO-FCIC.pdf.

The impact of the sub-prime mortgage crisis and a global economic slowdown on Malaysia. (19 February 2009). http://cloudchronicler.net/2009/02/19/the-impact-of-the-sub-prime-mortgage-crisis-and-an-global-economic-slowdown-on-malaysia/.

The origins of the financial crisis. *The Economist*, 7 September 2013. http://www.economist.com/news/schoolsbrief/21584534-effects-financial-crisis-are-still-being-felt-five-years-article.

The rise and fall of Enron: a brief history. Updated 25 May 2006. http://www.cbc.ca/news/business/story/2006/05/25/enron-bkgd.html.

Tibman, J. (2009). *The murder of Lehman Brothers: An insider's look at the global meltdown*. New York: Brick Tower Press.

Turnbull, S. M., Stuart, M., Crouhy, M., & Jarrow, R. A. (2008, July 9). The subprime credit crisis of 07. http://ssrn.com/abstract=1112467.

Turner, G. (2008). *The credit crunch: Housing bubbles, globalisation and the worldwide economic crisis*. London: Pluto Press.

U.S. Securities and Exchange Commission. (2009, August 27). The SEC's Role Regarding and Oversight of National Recognised Statistical Rating Organisation (NRSROs), Report No. 458. http://www.sec-oig.gov/Reports/AuditsInspections/2009/Report458.pdf.

Utt, R. D. (2008, April 22). The subprime mortgage market collapse: A primer on the causes and possible solutions. *The Heritage Foundation*. http://www.heritage.org/research/reports/2008/04/the-subprime-mortgage-market-collapse-a-primer-on-the-causes-and-possible-solutions.

Utzig, S. (2010, January). *The financial crisis and the regulation of credit rating agencies: A European banking perspective* (ADBI Working Paper Series No. 188, pp. 1–3).

Von Hirsch, A. (1992). Proportionality in the philosophy of punishment. *Crime and Justice, 16*, 55–98.

Wadden IV, William "Biv" (2002). Interpreting Moody's Historical Default Rate Data. http://www.cs.williams.edu/~jpw1/Docs/Ev_Hist_Moodys_Defaults.pdf.

Walter, E. B., & Daigler, M. A. (2010, June 22). Gatekeepers are the key to good governance. *Fobes.com*. http://www.forbes.com/2010/06/21/shareholders-risk-gatekeepers-elisse-walter-leadership-governance-ethisphere_print.html.

White, L. J. (2009, April 8). The credit rating agencies: Understanding their central role in the subprime debacle of 2007–2008. http://dx.doi.org/10.2139/ssrn.1434483.

White, L. J. (2010). Markets – The credit rating agencies. *The Journal of Economic Perspectives, 24*(2), 211–226.

Who is to blame for the financial crisis. *Wall Street Economist*. http://www.economicpredictions.org/who-is-to-blame-for-the-financial-crisis.htm.

Williams, G. (1951). The aims of the law of tort (Chapter 7). *Current Legal Problems, 4*, 137.

Windal, F. W. (1980). *The accounting professional: Ethics, responsibility and liability*. London: Englewood Cliffs, Prentice-Hall.

Wright, V. (2010, November). Deterrence in criminal justice: Evaluating certainty vs. severity of punishment. The Sentencing Project.

Xafa, M. (2007, March 1). *Global imbalances and financial stability – Issues 2007–2111* (Working Paper). International Monetary Fund.

Chapter 3
US and EU Soft Law: Self-Regulation

3.1 Introduction

The Big Three credit rating agencies (CRAs), Fitch, S&P and Moody's, had in place their own ethical code of best practices, but it seems the regulators felt that in some respect they did not address the problem of gatekeeper failure, which had arisen as a result of conflicts of interest, lack of competition and lack of accountability. The basis for the foundations of the code of conduct introduced by the regulators after the crisis (whether through the International Organization of Securities Commissions (IOSCO) in the US and the EU) was the assumption that these regulations would go a long way to make CRAs responsible gatekeepers. "IOSCO's Code of Conduct aims to improve investor protection, improve the fairness, efficiency and transparency of securities markets and to reduce systemic risk".[1] The IOSCO Code uses "comply or explain" principles[2] that are based on a code of moral conduct. Those CRAs with nationally recognized statistical rating organization (NRSRO)[3] status were compelled to adopt "soft law"—a code of conduct promulgated by IOSCO, as a global benchmark, based on the self-regulatory approach for industry oversight. Those CRAs without NRSRO status had to register with the regulators but were not required to adopt the IOSCO Code.[4]

This chapter will examine the success of self-regulation in enabling CRAs to issue reliable ratings, the steps taken by regulators in trying to use a voluntary code of conduct in regulating CRAs and CRAs' willingness to abide by these regulations. The chapter is in three sections. The first, Sect. 3.2, examines important provisions and the purposes of the IOSCO Code of Conduct. The second, Sect. 3.3, examines the adoption of the IOSCO Code of Conduct by the Big Three CRAs and the

[1] Prada (2008).

[2] Langer and Langer (2008), pp. 440, 443–444, 446.

[3] See Chap. 4.

[4] See Elkhoury (2008), p. 2.

M. Hemraj, *Credit Rating Agencies*, DOI 10.1007/978-3-319-17927-8_3

difference it has made to the way CRAs operate. The third, Sect. 3.4, deals with deficiencies, sanctions and a conclusion.

3.1.1 What Is Soft Law?

Historically, CRAs operated in a self-regulated environment in the US and EU. "Despite the significance of credit ratings, prior to the global credit crisis, the general consensus in the market was that self-regulation was sufficient for the credit rating industry".[5] As it is difficult to cover every facet of regulation through legislation in the form of hard statutory law, soft law does play an important role. Soft law refers to rules that have legal significance but are in the form of guidelines, policy declarations or codes of conduct, which set standards of conduct.[6] However, a party bound by a soft law may exclude third parties from getting benefit when breaches occur. Soft law refers to quasi-legal instruments and commitment made by negotiating parties, in contrast to hard law (e.g., a statutory law) being imposed upon the parties. Soft law often contains aspirational goals aimed at producing the best possible scenarios and may contain elements such as statements, principles, codes of conduct or codes of practice often found as part of framework treaties. In the European Union (EU), the term soft law is used to describe various kinds of quasi-legal instruments, for example, codes of conduct, guidelines and communications. The EU soft law instruments are used to indicate how the European Commission intends to use its powers and perform its tasks within its area of competence.

The concept of soft law has existed for many years, and the three main reasons for its use are that, first, "states may use soft law to solve straightforward coordination games in which the existence of a focal point is enough to generate compliance".[7] Second, "[s]tates will choose soft law when the marginal costs in terms of the expected loss from violations exceed the marginal benefits in terms of deterred violations. Third, under the delegation theory, states choose soft law when they are uncertain about whether the rules they adopt today will be desirable in the near future and when it is advantageous to allow a particular state or group of states to adjust expectations in the event of changed circumstances".[8] Legal consequences may flow from a range of non-binding international instruments, just as from non-binding documents in a domestic setting.[9]

---

[5] Shields and Gillen (2008).

[6] US Legal Definition, http://definitions.uslegal.com/s/soft-law/.

[7] Guzman and Meyer (2010), pp. 171–225.

[8] Guzman and Meyer (2010), pp. 171–225.

[9] Ibid.

3.2 IOSCO Code of Conduct

3.2.1 Background

In September 2003, the IOSCO published Principles Regarding the Activities of CRAs, along with a report briefly describing what CRAs do and regulatory issues that arise regarding their activities. The revised 2004 IOSCO CRA Code Fundamentals were as a result of

> an extensive consultation process involving rating agencies, issuers, investors, academics and financial institutions. It represent[ed] a global, converged view of specific mechanisms CRAs can use to protect their analytical independence, eliminate or manage conflicts of interest, and help ensure the confidentiality of certain types of information shared with them by issuers.[10]

"The Code Fundamentals offer a set of robust, practical measures that serve as a guide to and a framework for implementing the Principles' objectives". It "address[es] measures that CRAs should adopt to help ensure that the CRA Principles are properly implemented".[11] These broad Principles were designed to be a useful tool in regulating CRAs. The 2004 IOSCO Code was inclined towards detailed macro-regulations but then changed to micro-regulation, as found in the revised Code of 19 May 2008, to provide elaborate guidance to the CRAs as to their responsibilities. They laid out high-level objectives that CRAs, regulators, issuers and other market participants had to strive to achieve in order to improve investor protection and the fairness, efficiency and transparency of securities markets and to reduce systematic risk.[12] Although the IOSCO Principles were to apply to all types of CRAs operating in various jurisdictions, its implementation was left open, based on the different market, legal and regulatory circumstances in which CRAs operate and the varying size and business models of CRAs. The IOSCO Principles contemplated the use of a variety of mechanisms, including both market mechanisms and regulation.[13] IOSCO's Technical Committee published a report on the activities of CRAs outlining their activities, the types of regulatory issues that arise relating to these activities and how the Principles address these issues. The IOSCO Report highlighted the growing and the sometimes controversial importance placed on CRA assessment and opinions, and, in some cases, CRAs' activities are a mystery to both investors and issuers alike.[14] In addition to the lack of understanding, there was little formal regulation or oversight in most jurisdictions. The concern related to "the manner in which CRAs protect the integrity of the rating process, ensure that

[10] Media Release, "IOSCO releases Code of Conduct Fundamentals for Credit Rating Agencies" (23 December 2004) http://www.fsa.go.jp/inter/ios/f-20041224-3/02.pdf.

[11] Ibid., p. 2.

[12] IOSCO Code (revised May 2008), p. 1. http://www.iosco.org/library/pubdocs/pdf/IOSCOPD271.pdf.

[13] IOSCO Code (2008), p. 1.

[14] IOSCO Code (2008), p. 1.

investors and issuers are treated fairly, and safeguarding confidential information provided to CRAs by issuers".[15] The promulgation of the IOSCO Code was to address these concerns.

The IOSCO Code, based on the IOSCO Principles, was adopted by the international securities regulatory authorities with discussion among IOSCO members, representatives of the Basel Committee on Banking Supervision, the International Association of Insurance Supervisors and the public at large (that is, CRAs, issuers, investors and market participants).[16] While the IOSCO Code deals with CRAs' duties to issuers, its purpose is to promote investor protection by safeguarding the integrity of the rating process.[17] Although there are numerous other users of credit ratings, the IOSCO members recognise that they exist primarily to help investors assess the credit risks they face when making certain kinds of investments[18] and, therefore, CRAs should maintain independence vis-à-vis the issuers they rate to achieve this goal. The emphasis on CRAs' obligations to issuers is to improve the quality of credit ratings and their usefulness to investors.[19] Care was, therefore, required in interpreting the IOSCO Code as being pro-CRA independence and CRAs' ability to issue timely ratings.[20] Although the intention of the IOSCO Code was to be useful to all types of CRAs relying on a variety of business models, there is no indication of preference for one business model over another.[21]

The IOSCO Code can be broken down into three main sections, namely, quality and integrity of the rating process, CRA independence and avoidance of conflicts of interest, and CRA responsibilities to the investing public and issuers (all considered below).

3.2.1.1 Quality and Integrity of the Rating Process

The CRAs are required to devote sufficient resources to carry out high-quality credit assessments of all obligations and issuers they rate.[22] These resources are to maintain internal records to support its credit opinions; to establish a review function where one or more senior managers with appropriate experience are to review the feasibility of providing a credit rating, which did not fall under the normal category of rating; and to periodically review the methodologies and models and significant changes. Where issuance of credit ratings relates to a complex "new type of structured product" or where there is the "lack of robust data about the assets

[15] IOSCO Code (2008), p. 1.
[16] IOSCO Code (2008), p. 2.
[17] IOSCO Code (2008), p. 3.
[18] IOSCO Code (2008), p. 3.
[19] IOSCO Code (2008), p. 3.
[20] IOSCO Code (2008), p. 3.
[21] IOSCO Code (2008), p. 3.
[22] IOSCO Code (2008) Section 1.A. 1.7, p. 4.

underlying the structured product",[23] it should refrain from issuing a credit rating. This is particularly important given the increasing complexity of securities markets and financial instruments.[24] There is no provision as to what steps the regulators can take against CRAs if they rate complex products or where there is a lack of data.

A CRA is required to structure its rating teams to promote continuity and to avoid bias in the rating process[25] and to ensure that adequate personal, human and financial resources are allocated to monitoring and updating its ratings.[26] Presumably, this will allow a CRA to keep track by regularly reviewing issuers' creditworthiness. Under the sub-heading of integrity of the rating process, CRAs and their employees are required to "comply with all applicable laws and regulations"[27] relevant to the jurisdictions in which they operate. In addition, in order to deal fairly and honestly with issuers, investors, other market participants and the public,[28] analysts are required to have a high standard of integrity.[29] In a way, CRAs' hands are tied in that they cannot give any assurance or guarantee of a particular rating prior to a rating assessment.[30] In this respect, a CRA has to prohibit its analysts from making proposals or recommendations regarding the design of structured finance products that a CRA rates.[31] In addition, a CRA should specify clearly the person responsible for rating with an independent employee ensuring compliance with the Code of Conduct and with applicable laws and regulations,[32] and a CRA employee is duty bound to report any illegal or unethical acts by another employee that are contrary to the provisions of the Code to a compliance officer.[33]

3.2.1.2 Independence

Independence can be compromised by the amount of revenue a CRA derives from issuers that the analyst rates. To avoid this, a CRA is required to conduct formal and periodic reviews of compensation policies and procedures.[34] The CRA employees are prohibited from soliciting money, gifts or favours and accepting gifts or cash offers over a minimal monetary value from anyone with whom the CRA does business.[35]

[23] IOSCO Code (2008) Section 1.A. 1.7-3, p. 5.

[24] Annex on IOSCO Code of Conduct Fundamentals for Credit Rating Agencies, p. 1.

[25] IOSCO Code (2008) Section 1.A. 1.8, p. 5.

[26] IOSCO Code (2008) Section B 1.9, p. 5.

[27] IOSCO Code (2008) Section C 1.11, p. 6.

[28] IOSCO Code (2008) Section C 1.12, p. 6.

[29] IOSCO Code (2008) Section C 1.13, p. 6.

[30] IOSCO Code (2008) Section C 1.14, p. 6.

[31] IOSCO Code (2008) Section C 1.14-1, p. 6.

[32] IOSCO Code (2008) Section C 1.15, p. 6.

[33] IOSCO Code (2008) Section C 1.16, p. 6.

[34] IOSCO Code (2008) Section C 2.11, p. 8.

[35] IOSCO Code (2008) Section C 2.15, p. 9.

3.2.1.3 Market Participants

Market participants, including investors, issuers, investment bankers, broker-dealers and governments, all naturally expect rating analyses to be of high quality, produced through a process involving high integrity as nothing less would be acceptable. This obliges a CRA to ensure that the ratings given to a debt instrument are reasonable and do not exaggerate the worth of securities issued, and ratings are continually being updated in line with the issuer's current financial condition and prospect to prevent market participants from being misled. CRAs have moral responsibilities not only towards issuers (like protecting confidential information) but also to the investing public.[36]

The IOSCO Principles led to the IOSCO Code, which was meant to ensure that the opinions issued by CRAs help in reducing the asymmetry of information that exists between borrowers or securities issuers on the one hand and lenders or investors on the other. Tang submits that "[i]nformation asymmetry lies at the heart of explanations for why economic outcomes such as investment decisions could be inefficient. Financial intermediaries such as banks, credit rating agencies, and advisory financial service providers exist on the pretext of partially resolving the adverse effect of information asymmetry".[37] Reducing information asymmetry requires the issuance of reliable credit ratings, but this requires CRAs to act as a responsible gatekeeper towards investors. The next section examines the way the CRAs have adopted the IOSCO Code.

3.3 Adoption of the IOSCO Code

3.3.1 Introduction

Soft laws, as opposed to hard laws that are enshrined in the statutory provisions and case laws discussed in subsequent chapters, are self-regulations and are normally enshrined in the business/professional codes of conduct. All the Big Three CRAs (Moody's, Standard & Poor's and Fitch) already had their own established code of conduct in place before the crisis, and it seems the regulators felt that they were neither detailed nor comprehensive enough. Regarding the activities of CRAs, the IOSCO Principles[38] produced the broad standards developed by the international regulatory community. These broad principles were designed to be a useful tool to regulate CRAs by laying out high-level objectives that the CRAs, regulators, issuers and other market participants ought to strive to achieve in order to improve investor

---

[36] IOSCO Code (2008), pp. 3–4.

[37] Tang (2009), p. 325.

[38] IOSCO Principles (2008).

protection and the fairness, efficiency and transparency of securities markets and to reduce systematic risk.[39] The Big Three CRAs adopted the IOSCO Principles in their own codes of conduct in December 2004 and simultaneously retained and added to their own previous provisions; since then, they have been continuously updating them. "The Code Fundamentals offer a set of robust, practical measures that serve as a guide to and a framework for implementing the Principles' objectives and are to be included in individual CRA codes of conduct".[40] This section will selectively analyse the adoption of the IOSCO Code of Conduct by the three main CRAs and, in addition, examine some of the remaining unresolved contentious issues.

3.3.2 Adoption of the IOSCO Principles

The S&P Rating Services readily embraced the IOSCO Code in their October 2005 Code of Conduct before the crisis.[41] The 2005 Code statement stated that "S&P strives for analytic excellence at all times, evaluates its rating criteria, methodologies, and procedures on a regular basis; and modifies or enhances them as necessary to respond to the needs of the global capital markets".[42] This was omitted from the Code in 2013. Now, as appears in its mission statement, it states that its purpose is to provide high-quality, objective, independent and vigorous analytical information to the marketplace. The fear was that investors who lost money and the US government might use the failure of adhering to its 2005 statement of the Code in their legal proceedings.[43]

The structure of Moody's Code intends to track the IOSCO Code as closely as possible in its Code of Professional Conduct,[44] aiming at enhancing market understanding and confidence in its credit ratings.[45] Moody's seeks to protect the integrity of the rating process, to ensure fair treatment of investors and issuers and to safeguard the confidential information provided by issuers.[46] Moody's responsibility is to be as transparent as practicable with regard to its analytical methodologies, rating policies and practices and overall record of

[39] Ibid., p. 1.

[40] IOSCO (2008), p. 2.

[41] Standard & Poor's, "Rating Service Code of Conduct" (30 June 2011), http://www.maalot.co.il/publications/PAR20120116151628.pdf.

[42] Contained in its revised 2008 Code of Conduct, p. 3.

[43] United States of America, vs. McGraw-Hill Companies, Inc.; Standard and Poor's Financial Services LLC, United States District Court Central District of California Southern Division.

Case 2:13-cv-00779-DOC-JCG Document 34 Filed 07/16/13, pp. 1–18. http://www.cooley.com/files/sandpdismiss0717.pdf.

[44] Moody's Code of Professional Conduct (2013) (footnote 3 of the Code), p. 2.

[45] Moody's Code of Professional Conduct (2013) Preamble, p. 2.

[46] Moody's Code of Professional Conduct (2013), p. 2.

accomplishment.[47] Moody's regards credit ratings as probabilistic opinions about future creditworthiness. Moody's endeavours to provide forward-looking opinions on the relative creditworthiness of issuers of debt and debt instruments[48] in order to help reduce the information asymmetry that exists between those issuers and potential purchasers of their debt.[49] Moody's mission is to develop and maintain rigorous and systematic rating.[50] The Credit Policy Group within Moody's is responsible for monitoring the appropriateness and completeness of rating methodologies and procedures and for approving any significant changes to Moody's rating methodologies and procedures.[51] In addition, a rating committee determines credit rating and not an individual analyst.[52] Moody's uses separate analytical teams for assigning initial credit ratings and for monitoring structured finance credit ratings. It ensures that each team has the requisite level of experience and resources to perform its respective functions in a timely manner.[53]

Fitch Ratings ("Fitch") claims that it is committed to providing the world's markets with objective, timely, independent and forward-looking credit opinions that are dedicated to several core principles such as objectivity, integrity and transparency.[54]

3.3.3 Conflicts of Interest

Conflicts of interest arise when issuers approach CRAs to rate debt instruments, which they want to offer to public investors. Investors have no say as issuers negotiate the payment with CRAs. Independence is compromised as a CRA has a relationship with issuers, investors and other interested entities. In the past, CRAs used to help the issuers in packaging a debt instrument while rating them at the same time. Such action(s) undoubtedly compromises CRAs' independence. Moody's standpoint is that it neither has a fiduciary relationship with the issuers whose security it is rating (or any other party), nor does it act as advisor to the issuers it rates, which means it does not participate in the actual structuring of any security under consideration for a credit rating.[55] As a matter of policy, and in keeping with its role as an independent and objective publisher of opinions,

[47] Moody's Code of Professional Conduct, p. 2.

[48] Moody's Code of Professional Conduct, Preamble, p. 2.

[49] Moody's Code of Professional Conduct, Section 1, p. 8.

[50] Moody's Code of Professional Conduct, Section 1.2, p. 8.

[51] Moody's Code of Professional Conduct, Section 1.2, p. 8.

[52] Moody's Code of Professional Conduct, Section 1.5, p. 8.

[53] Moody's Code of Professional Conduct, Section 1.11, p. 9.

[54] Fitch Ratings—Code of Conduct—20 June 2013, p. 3. https://www.fitchratings.com/web_content/credit_policy/code_of_conduct.pdf.

[55] Moody Code of Professional Conduct (2008) Section II, 4th Para, p. 7.

Moody's retains complete editorial control over the content of its credit ratings, credit opinions, commentary and all related publications. Moody's reserves the right at any time to suspend, modify, lower, raise or withdraw a credit rating or place a rating on the watch list in accordance with Moody's policies and procedures.[56]

3.3.4 *Quality of the Rating Process*

A CRA should use rating methodologies that are rigorous, systematic and, where possible, result in ratings that can be subjected to some form of objective validation based on historical experience.[57] Although Fitch publishes its rating opinions on a variety of subjects, the most common is providing credit ratings to sovereigns, financial institutions and corporations.[58] Fitch claims to use rigorous and systematic rating methodologies, and, where possible, ratings are subjected to some form of objective validation based on historical experience.[59] Such a claim, even post-financial crisis, appears to be a mere public relations exercise. A CRA and its analysts should take steps to avoid issuing any credit analyses or reports that contain misrepresentations or are otherwise misleading as to the general credit-worthiness of an issuer or obligation.[60] Had the CRAs discharged their duties completely, then arguably the problem relating to the subprime mortgage crisis would not have arisen.

"[R]atings should reflect all information known, and believed to be relevant, to the CRA, consistent with its published methodology".[61] Fitch's undertakings consists of (a) taking steps to avoid issuing any credit analysis or reports that knowingly contain misrepresentations or are otherwise misleading as to the general credit-worthiness of an issuer or obligation[62] and (b) ensuring that it devotes sufficient resources to carry out high-quality credit assessments of all obligations and issuers it rates.[63] Moreover, Fitch does assess the appropriateness of the existing methodologies and models it uses as a process of determining the ratings of structured products and does refrain from issuing a rating on a new, complex type of structured product, unless it has sufficient information and expertise to analyse such a product.[64] Furthermore, Fitch structures its rating team in such a way that will promote

[56] Moody Code of Professional Conduct, Section II, 5th Para, p. 7.

[57] IOSCO Code (2008), p. 4.

[58] Fitch Code of Conduct (2013) section 1.2, p. 3.

[59] Fitch Code of Conduct, Section 2.1.2, p. 4.

[60] 1.6 IOSCO Code (2008), p. 4.

[61] 1.4 IOSCO Code (2008), p. 4.

[62] Fitch Code of Conduct, Section 2.1.6, p. 4.

[63] Fitch Code of Conduct, Section 2.1 A. 2.1.7, p. 5.

[64] Fitch Code of Conduct (2013) Section 2.1.7-3, p. 5.

continuity in the rating process and avoid bias.[65] Fitch asserts that it does not provide advice—be it financial, legal, auditing, accounting, appraisal, valuation or actuarial services—to any party, nor does it constitute a replacement for such advice or services.[66] When assigning a rating to a security, Fitch does not consent to the use of its name in connection with any registration statement, offering document or other filings under any relevant securities laws.[67]

3.3.5 Unsolicited Ratings

A CRA is required to disclose its policies and procedures regarding unsolicited ratings.[68]

An unsolicited rating is one without the backing of an issuer or arranger. Presently, unsolicited ratings are a rare phenomenon but are more common with regard to ratings given to the sovereign countries. CRAs personally initiate unsolicited ratings based on their reliance on publicly available information, although on rare occasions it may involve the participation of the issuer's management. "[T]he issuance of unfavorable unsolicited credit ratings enables rating agencies to extract higher fees from issuers by credibly threatening to punish those that refuse to solicit a rating".[69] Unlike solicited ratings where an issuer approaches a CRA to carry out the rating of debt instruments and pays for it, for unsolicited ratings the issuers make no payment to a CRA. Also, there is an absence of any inputs from the issuer's management with regard to any concern CRAs may have that may raise some doubt on the reliability of the unsolicited rating that is being conducted. In relation to corporate debt issues, a concern is that CRAs issue unsolicited and unfavourable credit ratings to ply for the business, but there is no official record on the number of times they have succeeded. S&P has omitted its previous claim that it "issues unsolicited ratings only when it believes that it has sufficient information to be able to form a robust credit opinion"[70] as a safeguard from potential liability.

Moody's reserves the right to publish unsolicited ratings under certain conditions, for example, if there is a meaningful credit market or investor interest is served by the publication of such a rating, and it has sufficient information to support adequate analysis and, if applicable, ongoing monitoring.[71] When a credit

---

[65] Fitch Code of Conduct, Section 2.1.8, p. 5.

[66] Fitch Code of Conduct, Section 4.8, p. 18.

[67] Fitch Code of Conduct, Section 4.9, p. 18.

[68] 3.9 IOSCO Code of Conduct, Revises May 2008, p. 11. http://www.iosco.org/library/pubdocs/pdf/IOSCOPD271.pdf.

[69] Fulghieri et al. (2010).

[70] Contained in its 2008 Code of Conduct, p. 14.

[71] Moody Code of Professional Conduct (2011) Section 3.12, p. 14.

rating is unsolicited, Moody's will not seek or accept remuneration for its analytical services from the issuer for at least 1 year after the publication of such a credit rating,[72] but this is applicable to corporate and not to sovereign rating. The Big Three CRAs have traditionally been able to take advantage of economies of scale in ways that may inhibit entry for smaller competitors. They can afford to provide unsolicited ratings in an attempt to discourage new entrants building a niche position.[73] Obviously, the manner of conducting unsolicited ratings is based on limited information resulting in them being less positive than solicited ratings, which then may encourage a corporate issuer to request a solicited rating from the same provider.[74] As unsolicited ratings are distinguishable from solicited ratings in that while unsolicited ratings in particular may qualify as mere opinions, it is submitted that a court ought to hold a CRA to a higher standard of care based on payment received from an issuer. Such a move would compel a CRA to issue reliable ratings.

3.3.6 Transparency

Transparency, according to the IOSCO's Principles, requires providing public information regarding the issuers and the securities it rates. However, S&P's claim is that it cannot guarantee that all the information it receives and uses is complete or accurate.[75] It means S&P is not obliged to perform any due diligence or independent certification of any information submitted to, or obtained by it, in connection with its rating and surveillance process. S&P will differentiate credit ratings of structured finance products from other credit ratings through additional disclosures or the use of different rating symbols.[76] S&P will not issue a credit rating unless certain conditions are met; for example, it has (a) information of satisfactory quality to determine the credit rating, (b) sufficient analysts with appropriate knowledge and experience to determine the credit rating and (c) sufficient historical experience or information to appropriately rate a new type of structure or a new entity, when applicable.[77]

Furthermore, S&P will clearly define its rating symbols and apply those symbols in a consistent manner.[78] S&P will disclose required information in a consistent and timely manner, but this is limited to its regulatory requirements.[79] S&P will not

---

[72] Ibid.

[73] Deb et al. (2011), p. 7.

[74] Ibid., p. 11.

[75] S&P's Rating Service Code of Conduct (2011) Section 7.3, p. 8.

[76] S&P's Rating Service Code of Conduct (2011) Section 1.1, p. 3.

[77] S&P's Rating Service Code of Conduct (2011) Section 1.1, p. 4.

[78] S&P's, Rating Service Code of Conduct (2011) Section 1.1, p. 3.

[79] S&P's, Rating Service Code of Conduct (2011) Section 4.1, p. 6.

misrepresent the nature of the credit rating or make any statements that could reasonably mislead potential users of the credit rating.[80] What if S&P does mislead the investors, do investors have any recourse? The answer is no, as S&P stipulates in a disclaimer that it will not assume any responsibility or liability to any third party arising out of or relating to the Code. The Code does not form a part of any contract with any third party, and no third party has the right (contractual or otherwise) to enforce any of this Code's provisions, either directly or indirectly, and S&P has the sole discretion to revise the Code.[81] Moody's believes that promotion of transparency requires letting the market be the best judge of the aggregate performance of credit ratings on debt instruments by publishing, *inter alia*, sufficient information about the historical default rate of its credit rating.[82]

3.3.7 Expectation Gap

The Big Three CRAs have not explicitly indicated that they are aware of either an expectation gap—which is the difference in perception between the public (including shareholders) and CRAs based on rating services provided by them—or what the term means to them. S&P, in its Code of Conduct, went a long way to narrow and bridge the expectation gap on what CRAs actually do and what the public, as third parties, think they do. With regard to ratings, the Big Three CRAs' positions are similar in that ratings are current opinions regarding the creditworthiness of issuers and are based on the information supplied to them by issuers or agents and information obtained by them from other sources they consider reliable.[83] Moreover, CRAs rely on several sources (issuers, accountants, counsels, advisors and other sources) "for the accuracy, completeness, and timeliness of the information submitted in accordance with the rating and surveillance processes".[84] Most importantly, credit ratings do not constitute investment, financial or other advice. Credit ratings are not recommendations to purchase, hold or sell a particular security or to make any other investment decision as credit ratings do not comment on the suitability of an investment for a particular investor and, therefore, should not be relied on when making any investment decision. CRAs have categorically denied being in a fiduciary relationship with any issuer, investor or any other person.[85]

---

[80] S&P's, Rating Service Code of Conduct (2011) Section 1.10, p. 4.

[81] S&P's, Rating Service Code of Conduct (2011), p. 8. Similar provision is found in Moody's Code of Conduct (December 2013) footnote 2, p. 2.

[82] Moody Code of Professional Conduct (2011) Section 3.10, p. 14.

[83] Standard and Poor's, "What are ratings and how do they work?", p. 3. http://www.unite.it/UniTE/Engine/RAServeFile.php/f/File_Prof/MALAVOLTA_1250/SP_CreditRatingsGuide.pdf.

[84] S&P's, Rating Service Code of Conduct (2011) Section 7.1, p. 8.

[85] Ibid.

The above was a standard claim made even before the onset of the global financial crisis and is a great weapon in the armoury of CRAs. What the investors do in practice is to rely on triple-A ratings given by CRAs, arguably based on the market practice, as it implies that the corporate debt rated is of a good investment grade and as such has a lower chance of default. Based on this belief, perhaps the investors are treating ratings as akin to financial advice or recommendations. It may be that investors need to undertake their own due diligence, but it is not clear what sort of due diligence the CRAs want the investors to carry out and what would be appropriate.

As "Credit Ratings are not verifiable statements of fact",[86] it is contended that the reliability of the ratings is questioned when they are unverifiable and when CRAs do not guarantee accuracy, completeness and timeliness. Verification is an important issue, but CRAs contend that ratings are statements of opinion and not fact and it follows from this that they remain unverifiable. Then, on what do CRAs base their opinion in the first place? What are the investors supposed to do when a rating agency issues triple-A ratings? Moreover, it is absurd if investors are not meant to have faith in the market practice of ratings but at the same time are required to carry out their own due diligence, and if so, on what basis? Is it on the basis that CRAs cannot be trusted with their ratings? This is not the case as CRAs do not categorically state that investors cannot rely on their ratings, as this would be detrimental to them.

In assigning a credit rating, Moody's in its 2011 Code claims for the first time that it in no way provides a guarantee with regard to the accuracy, timeliness or completeness of factual information reflected, or contained, in the credit rating or in any related Moody's publication.[87] Moody's now categorically states in its 2011 Code that it does not provide consulting services.[88] In cases involving new types of financial products, Moody's has also decided to refrain from providing a credit rating unless it believes that it has sufficient information and the appropriate analytical skills to do so.[89]

It seems the general practice of CRAs is not to verify the facts of the information asked for and supplied by issuers, which are then relied upon by them in issuing suitable ratings. Their contention is that this will require them to audit the information, a task that they do not undertake. It also allows S&P at any time to suspend, modify, lower, raise or withdraw a credit rating or place a credit rating on CreditWatch in accordance with its policies.[90] In addition, CRAs do not address the risks associated with, *inter alia*, liquidity risk, market value risk or price volatility. The intention is perhaps to curb any public expectation of the types of risk they address. Other matters that the Big Three CRAs do not represent are

[86] Ibid.

[87] Moody Code of Professional Conduct (2011) Section II, p. 7.

[88] Ibid. Section 2.8a, p. 11.

[89] Ibid. Section 1.7, p. 8.

[90] S&P's, Rating Service Code of Conduct (2011) Section 7.4, p. 8.

statements of current or historical fact constituting investment or financial advice and recommendations to purchase, sell or hold particular securities.[91] Most importantly, credit ratings do not comment on the suitability of an investment for any particular investor.[92] The above-mentioned factors help in clearing the expectation gap by CRAs, making it explicitly clear to potential investors the limits of credit rating, what tasks they undertake and which ones they do not.

The legal issue relates to whether or not investors' reliance is reasonable and justifiable under the circumstances and the reasonableness of CRAs' exclusion clauses.[93] Whether or not any exclusion clause should be upheld is adjudicated by a court.[94] Fear of legal accountability may incentivise CRAs to take steps to caution the users about the hazards of using their credit ratings (similar to those adopted by cigarette companies that, after their unhappy legal experience from various legal actions, have now inserted warnings), which is presently lacking. Exclusion clauses contained in the Code may not be sufficient. Warnings about the possible hazards identified by CRAs need to be explicitly drawn to the attention of investors. As CRAs are not examining several risks with regard to debt instruments, investors should exercise caution when relying on the credit ratings they issue. The IOSCO Principles do not mention anywhere or comment on the weaknesses arising from the investors' confusion/failure to understand the functions and purposes of credit ratings provided by CRAs.

3.3.8 Due Diligence

In practice, prior to giving a rating, CRAs have to gather information, and they rely on the issuers and their agents to provide accurate, timely and complete information. Fitch, in issuing and maintaining its ratings, relies on information it receives from issuers and underwriters and from other sources that Fitch believes to be credible.[95] Fitch conducts a reasonable investigation of the information relied upon by it in accordance with its ratings methodology and obtains reasonable verification of that information from independent sources to the extent such sources are available for a given security or in a given jurisdiction.[96] However, as a proviso, Fitch states that users should understand that neither an enhanced factual investigation nor any third-party verification could ensure that all information Fitch relies on in connection with the rating is accurate and complete.[97] Fitch puts the onus and

[91] Ibid. Section 7.2, p. 8.

[92] Ibid.

[93] Under the UK *Unfair Contract terms Act 1977*.

[94] Lehmann (2014).

[95] Fitch Code of Conduct (2013) Section 4.4, p. 16.

[96] Fitch Code of Conduct, Section 4.4, pp. 16–17.

[97] Fitch Code of Conduct, Section 4.4, p. 17.

responsibility on the issuers and its advisors to provide accurate information to them and to the market,[98] which, it seems, Fitch does not verify. In addition, lack of verification may mean ratings are associated with information containing misrepresentation or otherwise misleading information, which CRAs do take at face value and are thereby misleading the public. Fitch categorically states that when it assigns a rating to any issuer or security, such an act is not to be viewed as a guarantee of the accuracy, completeness or timeliness of the information issuers have supplied to them and its advisers and Fitch are not responsible for their accuracy.[99] Fitch further states that, because of any changes in accuracy, unavailability or inadequacy of the information for any reason, it may change, qualify or place the rating on Rating Watch.[100] Fairness requires making the CRAs account for their failure in not acting quickly enough when deciding to change ratings, and in the majority of the cases changes have involved downgrading many securities simultaneously.

Another unresolved issue is what happens if the issuers or their agents do provide misleading information in order to get a higher credit rating and, as a result, the rating turns out to be unreliable. As there is a contract between the issuers and CRAs, it is unknown if the contract provides any remedy when and if the issuers do provide unreliable or false information to the CRAs. Presently, based on the several defences available that exempt CRAs from liability and as investors do not have a legal recourse by suing them,[101] the CRAs are relatively unconcerned, except for their reputation damage. However, if a liability regime is introduced in future, it will motivate the CRA to do two things: either verify the information received from the issuer or as a precaution take a contractual indemnity. The indemnity will state that the information supplied by the issuer is correct, and if it turns out to be incorrect then an issuer, and not the CRA, will be personally liable to third parties (including investors). The previously mentioned wise course of action that the CRAs will be able to take will absolve them from potential liability. Related to the issue of liability is the fact that when publicly disclosing their code for the sake of transparency, Moody's "does not assume ... any responsibility or liability to any third party".[102] At present, issuers are absolved from liability to any investor when supplying misleading, defective, faulty or distortive information to CRAs. As to whether a court would find CRAs' contention of a need for investors to exercise caution and carry out their own diligence as reasonable, there is no clear-cut answer.

[98] Fitch Code of Conduct (2013) Section 4.4, p. 17.

[99] Fitch Code of Conduct, Section 4.4, p. 17.

[100] Fitch Code of Conduct, Section 4.7, p. 17.

[101] See Chap. 6.

[102] Moody Code of Professional Conduct (2011) contained in footnote 2, p. 2.

3.3.9 *Opinion Shopping and Credit Spotting*

Opinion shopping and credit spotting are thorny issues. Opinion shopping occurs when an issuer approaches a CRA with a view to finding out, in advance of a rating, whether it is prepared to assign the highest rating on their debt instruments. This may result in issuers approaching more than one CRA and the one who has agreed to give the highest rating task gets that job. Although the chances of opinion shopping occurring remain, the absence of fierce competition among CRAs, due to the oligopoly position of the Big Three CRAs, means that opinion shopping may not be widespread. In reality, even if the IOSCO Code had an explicit statement mirrored in the CRAs' codes of conduct requiring CRAs to refrain from participating in opinion shopping, it would be impracticable for the regulators to police them. Related to opinion shopping is the issue of credit spotting. Credit spotting occurs when the issuers move to agencies known for giving higher ratings to the debt paper they are holding. Similarly, as the credit crisis started to emerge, banks and others started credit spotting by moving to agencies with the highest ratings. According to Hill,[103] such practices do occur based on conflict of interest situations as ratings receive payment from the issuers and not investors, and issuers could and do buy high ratings from willing sellers, the CRAs.

3.3.10 *Sanctions*

A code of conduct, being voluntary, depends on the goodwill of CRAs for its proper implementation. The issue is what happens when CRAs breach any provision of their code and the possible sanctions regulators can impose on them. In publishing their code of conduct, a CRA is at liberty to amend the code at its sole discretion at any time. One expects sanctions imposed by the regulators either to be in the form of a substantial fine or, better still, a bar for the CRA from issuing ratings. However, failure to observe soft law is not in itself a breach of an enforceable obligation. It may, therefore, be desirable to transform these principles into hard law if regulators have to apply sanctions.[104] Even then, CRAs have legal defences at their disposal to exculpate them from liability. The barring of a CRA is an unheard of phenomenon as the Big Three CRAs command an oligopolistic position and operate in a wider marketplace. As such, they are too big for any regulator to implement a disciplinary measure to bar them from carrying out its activities, which renders the regulators toothless.

What CRAs have to do is to give reasons if they do not comply with the IOSCO Code, based on the "comply or explain" approach. A CRA is required to disclose to the public its code of conduct and describe how the provision of its code fully

[103] Hill (2009–2010), p. 585.

[104] Alexander et al. (2006), p. 139.

implements the provisions of the IOSCO Principles regarding the activities of CRAs. Should a CRA code of conduct deviate from the IOSCO provisions, the CRA should explain where and why these variations exist and how they are able to achieve the objectives contained in the IOSCO provisions.[105] The Big Three CRAs have made a shrewd move by including an exclusion clause in their own codes denying any responsibility or liability to third parties, who obviously include investors. For example, Moody's does not assume any responsibility or liability to any third party arising out of or relating to its Code of Professional Conduct. The Code is not part of any contract with any third party, and no third party shall have any right to enforce any of its provisions.[106] S&P and Fitch have adopted a similar stand. This means third parties can neither enforce any rights (contractual or otherwise) nor enforce the Code's provisions, assuming breaches—either directly or indirectly—do occur.

3.3.11 Provisional Conclusion

As self-regulators, the Big Three CRAs implemented the requirement of incorporating the main provisions of the IOSCO Principles in their codes of conduct. CRAs' practices before the global financial crisis were somehow ineffective, and they contributed to the giving of unreliable ratings. The main provisions of the IOSCO were *prima facie* an attempt by the regulators to impose a gatekeeper duty and to prevent the issuance of unreliable ratings. The Big Three, on their part, have had no problem in adopting the provisions of IOSCO's Code of Conduct into their own codes, although in some matters, as when S&P deviated from the Code, it had to explain the reasons. To protect themselves from incurring liability and their own interests, a concerted effort has been made by the Big Three to ensure that their codes of conduct address the matters such as the expectation gap, what their actual obligations are and the limitations of ratings issued by them. More important is the non-acceptance of legal liability for any breaches of their own codes and placing the onus on the investors to carry out their own due diligence. It is a win–win situation for the CRAs only.

[105] Provision 4.1 of the IOSCO Code (Revised May 2008).

[106] Moody's investment service, "Code of Professional Conduct", (December 2013), p. 2. https://www.moodys.com/uploadpage/Mco%20Documents/Documents_professional_conduct.pdf.

3.4 Deficiencies, Sanctions and Conclusion

3.4.1 Deficiencies of the IOSCO Code

The Big Three CRAs' practices before the global financial crisis may have been ineffective, possibly contributing to the issuance of unreliable ratings. The main provisions included in the IOSCO Code of Conduct were an attempt by the regulators to prevent the issuance of unreliable ratings. Based on "comply or explain" approach, CRAs are either required to comply with the provisions of the IOSCO Code or required to explain by giving reasons for any deviation.

The drawback of self-regulation based on voluntary compliance with the IOSCO Code is that it appears not to offer an adequate, reliable solution to the structural deficiencies of the business. Most of these have not been robust and/or stringent enough to cope with their severe problems and to restore confidence in the markets.[107] Moreover, individual approaches by some of the CRAs would not have had the market-wide effect necessary to establish a level playing field across the EU and presumably the world.[108] Although the Commission[109] considered the revised IOSCO Code as a global benchmark, the Code had some limitations that had to be tackled to make its rules operational.[110] It was felt that the application of the rules was not easy in practice as some were quite abstract and generic and needed to be concreted and consolidated. In some other cases, rules that were more efficient were called for. Most importantly, the IOSCO Code was found to be deficient in not providing any enforcement mechanism as it only invites CRAs to give reasons if they do not comply with it (based on the "comply or explain" approach). "In short, comply or explain does not impose 'one-size-fits-all' solutions".[111] The Code itself was open to be complemented by enforceable rules.[112] However, the central purpose of the Code was its use as a foundation for CRAs' codes of conduct and as a template for regulation to facilitate the convergence of approaches to CRA regulation and to address conflicts of law issues. In addition, the two main purposes of the Permanent IOSCO CRA Committee were, namely, to review and update the international consensus regarding CRA oversight and as a forum for regular interaction between regulators and CRAs.

---

[107] Proposal for a Regulation of the European Parliament and of the Council on Credit Rating Agencies, Brussels (12.11.2008), p. 3. http://ec.europa.eu/internal_market/securities/docs/agencies/proposal_en.pdf.

[108] Ibid.

[109] Commission on Credit Rating Agencies, OJ C 59 (11.3.2006), p. 2. http://eurlex.europa.eu/LexUriServ/LexUriServ.do?uri=OJ:C:2006:059:0002:0006:EN:PDF.

[110] Proposal for a Regulation (2008), p. 3.

[111] See "When is comply or explain the right approach?" http://www.icaew.com/en/technical/corporate-governance/dialogue-in-corporate-governance/when-is-comply-or-explain-the-right-approach.

[112] Ibid.

3.4.2 Sanctions for Breaches of the Code

The IOSCO Code depends on the goodwill of CRAs for its proper implementation. The question that arises relates to the sanctions regulators can impose on CRAs when they breach any provision of the Code. One expects sanctions to be in the form of a fine or a rating agent being barred from acting as a CRA. In India, a CRA that contravenes the provisions of Securities and Exchange Board of India (Credit Rating Agencies) Regulations, 1999, shall be dealt with in the manner provided under the Securities and Exchange Board of India (Procedure for holding Enquiry by Enquiry officer and Imposing penalty) Regulations, 2002. In Singapore, the breach of the Code (which is non-statutory in nature) or non-compliance is not a criminal offence. However, the relevant authority would consider such a failure by a member of a CRA as an indication of the person not being fit or proper to hold a licence. The Singapore Monetary Authority (SMA) would then determine whether to revoke their licence or suspend it. Similarly, the regulation goes further by allowing the SMA to take into account a failure by a representative of a CRA to comply with the Code and to determine if the representative is a fit and proper person to remain so appointed or whether imposing any conditions or restrictions on the representative is the right solution.[113]

In the US and EU, CRAs are free not to abide by the IOSCO Code, based on the comply-or-explain approach, provided reasons are given. A CRA is required to disclose its code of conduct to the public and describe how the provisions of its code fully implement the provisions of the IOSCO Principles. Regulators in the US and EU ought to consider appropriate sanctions such as imposing a fine or suspension, similar to the Indian Code, when regulations are breached. The Singapore Code has chosen the right of suspension or revocation of a licence as a means of disciplining CRAs that breach the Code's provisions.

3.4.3 Conclusion

This chapter has examined why self-regulation based on soft law was an uncomplicated, easy option where compliance has not been difficult for CRAs. The IOSCO Code relies upon disclosure as a "compliance" mechanism so that when individual CRAs publish their code, market participants will be able to evaluate the degree to which the IOSCO provisions have been incorporated and then be in a position to decide for themselves how much weight to give to the ratings opinions offered by

[113] Code of Conduct for Credit Rating Agencies is issued by the Monetary Authority of Singapore pursuant to section 321 of the Securities and Futures Act (Cap. 289). See Monetary Authority of Singapore (2012), p. 1.

that CRA.[114] The IOSCO Code has, to some extent, tried to address the problem of conflicts of interest. However, CRAs are free to decide for themselves on the appropriateness of the methodology they wish to adopt in credit rating and at the same time maintain their oligopolistic position in the marketplace. Self-regulation could have partially prevented the gatekeeper failure of CRAs in the US and EU if they were, absent disclaimer, held liable for breaching the provisions of the Code.

To date, CRAs have escaped liability for issuing unjustified high ratings as they practically enjoy immunity from civil law liability, mostly on the grounds of freedom of speech and freedom of the press,[115] which may be the reason for the gatekeeper failure of CRAs. Arguably, CRAs *are* gatekeepers as they decide which security receives an investment grade, which gives a signal to investors to invest in that security.[116] If CRAs are fulfilling the position of gatekeepers, then *ipso facto* one would have expected ratings to reflect reality, but this was not the case with subprime mortgages. The irony is that the CRAs want investors and others to rely on mere opinion as a means of protecting themselves should they fail to act as the investors' gatekeeper. Therefore, with respect to structured finance products and asset-backed securities, ratings are valuable to both issuers and investors and CRAs have merely acted as conduits of information.[117]

There could be a valid reason as to why a CRA does not follow a specific provision of the Code and under the comply-or-explain principles "they are not bound to follow the provisions of the Code on any given item", but if a CRA "deems it preferable to set aside a specific provisions of the Code, they may do so provided they state reasons".[118]

The evidence suggests that the IOSCO Code chose to deal with CRAs' duties to issuers and not to investors. A move that concentrates on CRAs' duties to issuers would in theory ensure that CRAs produce reliable ratings, thereby promoting investors' interests by safeguarding the integrity of the rating process; thus, they would act as a responsible gatekeeper.[119] Such a move by the regulators was necessary as possibly CRAs would have resisted IOSCO's moves to promulgate rules that directly tried to protect the interests of investors. Otherwise, based on the issuers-pay model,[120] CRAs would have argued that their contract is with the issuers and not the investors and therefore IOSCO had to resort indirectly to protect investors by ensuring that CRAs do fulfil certain obligations. Investors' protection under IOSCO concerns "misleading, manipulative or fraudulent practices,

[114] IOSCO—International Cooperation in oversight of Credit Rating Agencies—Note Technical Committee of Internal Organisation of Securities Commission (March 2009), p. 2.

[115] Coskun (2009), p. 254. See also Chap. 6.

[116] Ibid.

[117] Rousseau (2009), p. 15.

[118] Wymeersch (2006), p. 148.

[119] Technical Committee of the International Organization of Securities Commissions (2009). See also Alcubilla and Pozo (2012), pp. 36–46.

[120] See Chap. 2.

including insider trading, front running or trading ahead of customers and the misuse of client assets",[121] which are already covered under various statutory laws in the US and EU. It was felt that investors are better able to assess the potential risks and rewards of their investments and, thus, to protect their own interest if CRAs made full disclosure of information material to investors' decisions.[122] The Indian Code, on the other hand, expressly states, "A credit rating agency shall make all efforts to protect the interests of investors",[123] which *prima facie* means that CRAs have to exercise caution as unreliable ratings may jeopardise the interest of investors.

The provisions regarding transparency, independence and conflicts of interest contained in the IOSCO Code seem not to have gone far enough. The glaring omission was the absence within the Code of a need for CRAs wishing to provide credit ratings to register. In addition, the IOSCO Code does not touch on the jurisdictions that have different laws or the need for other relevant regulations for different jurisdictions. In addition, there were other issues like accountability and transparency of the CRAs, which were absent and which needed further regulation. This led to the enactment and implementation of statutory provisions in the US and EU, which will be analysed in Chaps. 4 and 5.

References

Alcubilla, R. G., & Pozo, J. R. (2012). *Credit rating agencies on the watch list* (pp. 36–46). Oxford: OUP.

Alexander, K., Dhumale, R., & Eatwell, J. (2006). *Global governance of financial systems: The international regulation of systematic risk* (p. 139). Oxford: OUP.

Coskun, D. (2009). Supervision of credit rating agencies: The role of credit rating agencies in finance decisions. *Journal of International Banking Law and Regulation, 24*(5), 254.

Deb, P., Manning, M., Murphy, G., Penalver, A., & Toth, A. (2011, March). *Whither the credit ratings industry?* (Financial Stability Paper No. 9, p. 7). Bank of England. http://www.bankofengland.co.uk/research/Documents/fspapers/fs_paper09.pdf.

Elkhoury, M. (2008, January). *Credit rating agencies and their potential impact on developing countries* (United Nations Conference on Trade and Development, Discussion Paper, No. 186, p. 2). http://unctad.org/en/Docs/osgdp20081_en.pdf.

Fulghieri, P., Strobl, G., & Xia, H. (2010, December 20). The economics of solicited and unsolicited credit ratings. http://faculty.haas.berkeley.edu/mopp/conference/strobl.pdf.

Guzman, A. T., & Meyer, T. L. (2010). International soft law. *Journal of Legal Analysis, 2*(1), 171–225.

Hill, C. A. (2009–2010). Why did rating agencies do such a bad job rating subprime securities? *University of Pittsburgh Law Review, 71*, 585.

[121] IOSCO (2003), p. 5.

[122] Ibid.

[123] "Third Schedule" Securities and Exchange Board of India (Credit Rating Agencies) Regulations, 1999 [Regulation 13] Code of Conduct, Cl. 1.

IOSCO. (2003, May). Objectives and principles of securities regulation (p. 5). http://www.cssf.cl/cssf/docs/ti-IOSCOPD154.pdf.

IOSCO. (2008). Code of conduct fundamentals for credit rating agencies (p. 2) (Revised May 2008). http://www.cmvm.pt/CMVM/Cooperacao%20Internacional/Docs%20Iosco/Documents/CodCondutaIOSCOCRA.pdf.

Langer, H., & Langer, P. (2008). *The rating agencies and their credit ratings: What they are, how they work, and why they are relevant* (pp. 440, 443–444, 446). Chichester: John Wiley & Sons Ltd.

Lehmann, M. (2014, June 20). Civil liability of rating agencies: An insipid sprout from Brussels. In *LSE Legal Studies Working Paper No. 15/2014*. Available at SSRN: http://ssrn.com/abstract=2456953 or http://dx.doi.org/10.2139/ssrn.2456953.

Monetary Authority of Singapore. (2012, January 17). Code of conduct of credit rating agencies (p. 1). http://www.mas.gov.sg/~/media/resource/legislation_guidelines/securities_futures/sub_legislation/Codes/CRA%20Code_Final.pdf.

Prada, M. (2008). Chairman of IOSCO's Technical Committee, in IOSCO Media Release, 'IOSCO to implement changes to Code of Conduct for Credit Rating Agencies' (18 May 2008) http://www.fsa.go.jp/inter/ios/20080609-1/03.pdf.

Rousseau, S. (2009, July 23). *Regulating credit rating agencies after the financial crisis: The long and winding road toward accountability* (Capital Markets Institute Research Paper, p. 15). http://dx.doi.org/10.2139/ssrn.1456708.

Shields, L. K., & Gillen, O. (2008, October 31). The credit crunch breeds a rating agency watchdog. *European Union*. http://www.lexology.com/library/detail.aspx?g=c3b3d7b2-e40f-4d92-957b-4d95edf30d00.

Tang, T. T. (2009, August). Information asymmetry and firms' credit market access: Evidence from Moody's credit rating format refinement. *Journal of Financial Economics, 93*(2), 325.

Technical Committee of the International Organization of Securities Commissions. (2009, March). A review of implementation of the IOSCO code of conduct fundamentals for credit rating agencies. http://www.fsa.go.jp/inter/ios/20090318-2/03.pdf.

Wymeersch, E. (2006). How can corporate governance codes be implemented? In G. Ferrarini & E. Wymeersch (Eds.), *Investor protection in Europe: Corporate law making, the MiFid and beyond* (p. 148). Oxford: OUP.

Chapter 4
US Statutory Regulation

4.1 Introduction

Chapter 3 dealt with the self-regulation of credit rating agencies (CRAs) based on their own codes of conduct supplemented by the International Organization of Securities Commissions (IOSCO) Code. "The 'worldwide credit crisis' has thrust credit rating agencies into the spotlight, with attention focused on their ratings of novel structured finance products".[1] "Policymakers have undertaken a number of initiatives intended to address perceived problems with such ratings – enhancing competition, promoting transparency, reducing conflicts of interest, and reducing ratings-dependent regulation".[2] This chapter will examine additional statutory reforms that were necessary to adjust shortcomings to ensure CRAs do act as responsible gatekeepers. In this regard, this chapter will focus on two important statutory regulations introduced in the US. Section 4.2 will analyse the provisions of the *Credit Rating Agency Reform Act 2006* (Reform Act). Section 4.3 will analyse the provision of the *Dodd-Frank Wall Street Reform and Consumer Protection Act 2010* (Dodd-Frank), and the assessment of these regulations appears in Sect. 4.4.

4.2 Credit Rating Agency Reform Act 2006

4.2.1 Introduction

In the past four decades, regulators of credit ratings were limited to helping monitor the risk of investments held by regulated entities and to providing an appropriate

[1] Hunt (2009).

[2] Ibid.

M. Hemraj, *Credit Rating Agencies*, DOI 10.1007/978-3-319-17927-8_4

disclosure framework for securities of differing risks.[3] However, since 1975 the US Security and Exchange Commission (SEC) has relied on ratings by market-recognised NRSROs for distinguishing between grades of creditworthiness in various regulations contained within Federal Securities laws. [4]

Moody's, S&P and Fitch issued favourable credit ratings of WorldCom bonds just 3 months before it declared bankruptcy, and, more disturbingly, Moody's and S&P continued to rate Enron bonds favourably just 4 days before its bankruptcy. The unexpected collapse of these issuers cost investors billions of dollars. This raised the question: why did credit rating agencies issue favourable bond ratings that did not appear accurately to reflect the likelihood of these bankruptcies?[5] The *Sarbanes-Oxley Act of 2002* mandated the Securities and Exchange Commission (SEC) to study the role of CRAs in securities markets.[6] The Reform Act aimed to increase competition among CRAs while extending SEC oversight authority. The policymakers, regulators and market participants had begun to raise latent concerns about the reliability of ratings and the ratings process.[7] There was a need for improving "the quality of credit ratings by fostering competition, transparency, and accountability in the credit rating industry and to address concerns regarding the current 'NRSRO' designation process".[8] Increased competition, appropriate SEC oversight, greater transparency and heightened accountability were the objectives for the reform of the credit rating industry.[9] The discussion will centre on NRSROs as, most importantly, the Reform Act involves granting NRSRO status to the registered CRAs, the term introduced in 1975.[10] This section will determine the extent to which the provisions of the Reform Act do protect investors by requiring CRAs to act in the public interest.

4.2.2 *Background to Regulation*

For almost a century, CRAs have been providing opinions on the creditworthiness of issuers of securities and their financial obligations. The importance of these opinions to investors and other market participants has significantly increased the influence of these opinions on the securities markets. The attributed reason is the

[3] Nazareth (2003).

[4] SEC Concept Release No. 33-8236 (2003), p. 1.

[5] Carroll (2005).

[6] Section 702(b).

[7] Cox (2008).

[8] Stevens (2005), p. 1.

[9] Ibid.

[10] U.S. Securities and Exchange Commission, "The SEC's Role Regarding and Oversight of National Recognised Statistical Rating Organisation (NRSROs), Report No. 458 (27 August 2009)" at i. http://www.sec-oig.gov/Reports/AuditsInspections/2009/Report458.pdf.

globalisation of the financial markets that led to expanding the role of credit ratings to countries other than the US, where reliance on credit ratings was largely confined to the first half of the twentieth century. Presently, credit ratings affect securities markets in many ways, including an issuer's access to capital, the structure of transactions and the ability of fiduciaries and others to make particular investments.[11]

4.2.3 *NRSRO as a* De Facto *Oligopoly*

Originally, the use of the term "NRSRO" was for a narrow purpose meant solely to provide a method for determining capital charges on different grades of debt securities.[12] Over time, as the reliance on CRAs' rating increased, so too did the use of the NRSRO concept.[13] The SEC Commission staff recognised Moody's, S&P and Fitch as NRSROs, on 24 September 2007 through the no-action letter process[14] for the purpose of net capital rule.[15] The reason was that the Big Three were widely recognised and widely accepted in the US as issuers of credible and reliable ratings and by their operational capacity and reliability.[16] It then inadvertently created a *de facto* oligopoly.

4.2.4 *Corporate Governance*

Since the early twentieth century, CRAs have been issuing ratings on the likelihood of issuer default on debt payments. The crisis and the fact that dominant CRAs did not accurately predict Enron and WorldCom's[17] financial condition meant a need arose to reform the CRAs' industry practice in the US. The urgency of the

[11] Nazareth (2003).

[12] Under the Commission's net capital rule for broker-dealers, Rule 15c3-1 under the Exchange Act (the "Net Capital Rule").

[13] Rating Agencies and the Use of Credit Ratings under the Federal Securities Laws (2003).

[14] "'No-action' process [is] a mechanism permitting the public and practitioners to obtain the informal views of the SEC staff on proposed transactions that appear to raise compliance issues under applicable federal securities laws and the rules thereunder". See Lemke (1986–1987), p. 1019.

[15] Net capital rule is Securities and Exchange Commission rule that requires all broker/dealers to maintain no more than a 15-to-1 ratio between indebtedness and liquid assets. Akins and Calabria (2012).

[16] SEC, "Definition of NRSRO", http://www.sec.gov/rules/proposed/33-8570.pdf, pp. 8–10. See also Kotz (2010).

[17] Gannon Jr. (2011–2012), pp. 1015–1051. http://www.bu.edu/law/central/jd/organizations/journals/banking/archives/documents/volume31/HelpCreditRatingAgencies.pdf.

regulation was due to ratings by NRSROs being "widely used as benchmarks in federal and state legislation, rules issued by financial and other regulators, foreign regulatory schemes, and private financial contracts".[18] The bankruptcies of Enron, WorldCom and other corporations meant that NRSROs were not providing investors with timely and accurate ratings.[19] The scenario, prior to the Reform Act, was that "credit rating agencies were essentially unregulated by the federal government and the SEC had no authority to make rules governing their business, or to subject them to examinations as NRSROs".[20] After Enron had filed for bankruptcy in 2001, CRAs were strongly criticised for their failure to warn the public of Enron's precarious financial situation until 4 days before it declared bankruptcy.[21] The "Reform Act was one of several reforms that followed corporate scandals in the early 2000s, most notably Enron and WorldCom where both had filed for bankruptcy amidst revelations of widespread accounting fraud".[22] The ratings failure in relation to Enron, while outside the area of banking rating, does reflect ratings failure in a parallel environment. The difference with Enron was that its directors engaged in a deliberate attempt to mislead the ratings agencies.[23] Criticism of CRAs is justified where they continued to rate companies highly even when the circumstances had changed; they ought to have downgraded ratings promptly but took a while to do so. The expectation of the Reform Act was that it would improve the quality of credit rating, thereby protect investors and act in the public interest by fostering accountability, transparency and competition in the credit rating industry.[24] On 29 September 2006, President George W. Bush Junior acted promptly by signing the Reform Act to bring it into law just three weeks after the introduction of the legislation.[25]

4.2.5 *Regulating Credit Rating Agencies*

It is true that CRAs carry out an important function. As total money market mutual fund assets are US $2.710 trillion,[26] the importance of sound credit ratings and

18 SEC Concept Release No. 33-8236 (2003).

19 Egan-Jones Ratings Company points out several failures of the Big Three CRAs. http://www.sec.gov/news/extra/credrate/eganjones2.htm.

20 Cox (2008).

21 U.S. Securities and Exchange Commission (2009), p. ii.

22 Baker (Committee Chairman) (2005).

23 A. Haynes, University of Wolverhampton, discussion (21 February 2012).

24 U.S. SEC (2009) at ii.

25 Soucy (2010).

26 "Total money market mutual funds rise by $7.45 billion in latest week: ICI", *Reuters* (12 December 2013). http://www.reuters.com/article/2013/12/12/us-total-money-market-idUSBRE9BB18E20131212.

rating agencies to investors cannot be overstated. "CRAs are employed in a variety of ways – to help make investment decisions, to define investment strategies, to communicate with their shareholders about credit risk, and to inform the process for valuing securities".[27] Prior to the introduction of the Reform Act in the US, there were several steps that regulators could have taken "[t]o promote the integrity and quality of the credit ratings process and, in turn, [this would have] served the interests of investors who utilise credit ratings".[28] These steps, which were not taken, were, first, to reform the NRSRO designation process in order to facilitate the recognition of more CRAs, thus introducing much-needed competition in the credit rating industry; second, the SEC ought to carry out regulatory oversight of CRAs in order to ensure that the credibility and reliability of credit ratings remain intact; third, to give investors regular and timely access to information about NRSROs and an opportunity to evaluate the ratings CRAs produced; and, most importantly, fourth, to introduce NRSRO accountability for their ratings, which would have acted as a deterrent.

There was also a need for NRSRO regulations to deal with important issues such as introducing competition and regulatory oversight, thus ensuring the credibility and reliability of credit ratings. It would have an added advantage of allowing investors to evaluate the ratings produced by CRAs as NRSROs. In addition, introduction of some sort of accountability would have incentivised CRAs "to analyse information critically and to challenge an issuer's representation".[29] Having already examined the measures for ideal regulation above, the actual steps taken by the regulators are analysed next.

4.2.6 Abusive Practices

The Big Three were and still are the major players, dominating the global credit rating industry. The emerging consensus about conflicts of interest is due to a change from the investors-pay model to the issuers-pay model[30] which also resulted in various abusive practices. An illustration of this would be when a CRA sends a company a free, unsolicited low rating, along with a bill to enable the issuer to purchase additional non-rating services that would result in an upward rating for the

[27] P.S. Stevens, President Investment Company Institute, Statement on H.R. 2990, the *Credit Rating Agency Duopoly Relief Act of 2005* Before the Committee on Financial Services United States House of Representatives (29 November 2005). http://www.idc.org/policy/ici_testimony/ci.05_house_nrsro_tmny.idc.

[28] Ibid.

[29] Ibid.

[30] Bai submits, "conflicts of interest are perceived as a major problem plaguing the credit rating industry", Bai (2010), p. 253 at 312. http://dev.nyujlpp.org/wp-content/uploads/2012/11/Lynn-Bai-On-Regulating-Conflicts-of-Interest-in-the-Credit-Rating-Industry.pdf; on how conflicts of interest can be addressed, see Aguilar; Deb and Murphy (2009).

benefit of the issuer. A second example relates to the practice of discounting (or "notching"). When rating structured products, CRAs use bait by promising the issuers higher ratings for asset-backed securities packages if they give them the task of rating the underlying assets.[31] A third example is where a CRA does not have a contract with a company but nevertheless goes ahead and rates that company anyway and sends a bill with an implicit threat to downgrade the company's rating if the bill is not paid. A fourth example relates to when a CRA suggests that a company would get a higher rating if it purchased other services from the same agency, such as consulting services.[32] The *Duopoly Act*[33] was more concerned about lack of competition that might have led to abuses and the need for preventing them[34], but it never became law as the Reform Act replaced it.

4.2.6.1 Rating Shopping

The other issue relates to opinion shopping, rating catering or rating shopping. Rating catering is a phenomenon where rating agencies inflate ratings in order to match competitor ratings.[35] Rating shopping occurs when a security issuer touts its deal to various CRAs to see who will assign the highest rating. A CRA that will assign the best rating then gets the job and receives the rating fee.[36] As an illustration, a real estate investment firm, Redwood Trust Inc., had approached two different CRAs in 2010 to rate a new mortgage bond offering. S&P expressed reservations about parts of the deal and could not give a triple-A rating. Redwood then chose Moody's, received a triple-A rating and, in April 2010, sold more than US $200 million of bonds. Redwood's explanation was that S&P could not meet their deadlines, and Moody's has claimed to have "conducted a thorough review of the deal" in awarding a triple-A rating.[37] This throws into doubt rating consistency, and a possibility exists that different CRAs use different rating criteria.

4.2.7 The Need for the Reform Act

Instead of the SEC Commission adopting specific standards for determining which CRAs were nationally recognised, it addressed the question on a case-by-case

[31] Cox (2008).

[32] See Soucy (2010).

[33] *Credit rating Agencies Duopoly Relief Act of 2006* H.R. 2990 (109th). This bill was introduced in Congress and was passed by the House on 12 July 2006 but was never passed by the Senate.

[34] Section 4 (ii) Ibid.

[35] Griffin et al. (2012).

[36] Long (2013).

[37] Lucchetti and Ng (2010).

basis.[38] The use of the term NRSRO began in 1975 when the SEC Commission promulgated rules regarding bank and broker-dealer net capital requirements.[39] The CRAs the SEC Commission registered were subject to its oversight authority. It had no statutory authority to regulate them. The Reform Act[40] tries to remedy the problems in relation to the credit ratings involvement in the billions of dollars' worth of residential mortgage-backed securities (RMBSs) and collateralized debt obligations (CDOs) that created the crisis, requiring an ongoing examination.

The ratings process used by CRAs to rate the RMBS and CDO products became less quantitatively developed when these products became more complicated and involved different types of loans than was generally believed.[41] Congress, in passing the Reform Act, was responding to the concern about the reliability of ratings and the ratings process that policymakers, regulators and market participants had already started to raise. The enactment of this law marked a major increase in the responsibilities and authority of the SEC. The drawback of the Reform Act is that the SEC Commission's authority to regulate did not extend to the *substance* of credit ratings or the procedures and methodologies by which an NRSRO determines credit ratings. A critic sees no "reason to suppose that they [Commission] would have done any better than the rating agencies [implying that] the staffs [of the Commission] are worse paid and it is reasonable to assume [they] have less depth of knowledge than those at the ratings agencies".[42] The results of the ongoing Commission examination of the past failures of CRAs is to provide significant and useful new information that will help not only the SEC but also issuers and users of credit ratings to address the problems Americans had experienced regarding the ratings of subprime-related products.

4.2.7.1 Enabling Rules

In order to make its authority effective, the Reform Act stipulated that the Commission could write enabling rules. This was subject to the public notice and comment process of the *Administrative Procedure Act of 1946*. The Commission promulgated final rules with the establishment of a formal regulatory programme for NRSROs in June 2007, and CRAs were required to register with the SEC if they wished to become NRSROs.[43] The Commission actively participated in the drafting

[38] U.S. Securities and Exchange Commission (2003). http://www.sec.gov/news/studies/credratingreport0103.pdf.

[39] Adoption of Amendments to Rule 15c3-1 and Adoption of Alternative Net Capital Requirement for Certain Brokers and Dealers", Exchange Act Release 34-11497 of June 26, 1975; 40 F.R. 29795 of 16 July 1975.

[40] Findings under Section 2(6) of the Reform Act.

[41] Elkhoury (2008), p. 4.

[42] A. Haynes, University of Wolverhampton, Discussion (21 February 2012).

[43] Cox (2008).

of the Working Group's "Policy Statement on Financial Market Developments" in March 2008.[44] The policy, *inter alia*, examines the impact of CRAs on lending practices, how their ratings are used and how securitisation changed the mortgage industry and related business practices. Since the purpose of the Reform Act is to improve ratings quality by fostering accountability, transparency and competition in the credit rating industry, the Commission proposed rules to advance these objectives, as examined below.

4.2.7.2 Accountability

To strengthen accountability, the new rules require enhanced disclosures about ratings performance to enable market participants to be in a better position to compare one NRSRO with another. Prohibition related to prescribing performance measures, which would either bias the ratings process or indirectly prescribe ratings methodologies, or rules that may conflict with the Reform Act's goal of increasing competition in an effort to develop accurate credit ratings.[45] To ensure NRSROs' accountability in managing their conflicts of interest, the Commission's new rules include specific prohibitions on certain practices, as well as the establishment of requirements designed to address potential conflicts that could impair the process for rating structured products. It was realised that the provision of consulting services by CRAs to the issuers of securities they rate, and rating structured securities that the NRSRO itself helped design, gives rise to a conflict of interest. To enhance the responsibility of the NRSROs' designated compliance officers, a rule requires CRAs to furnish the Commission with annual reports describing their internal reviews on how well they were able to adhere to their procedures for determining ratings, managing conflicts of interest and complying with the securities laws.[46]

4.2.7.3 Transparency

To enhance transparency, the Commission's new rules require the disclosure of information about the assets underlying the RMBSs, CDOs and other types of structured finance products they rate. This would allow market participants to better analyse the assets underlying structured securities and reach their own conclusions about their creditworthiness. Such availability of data could particularly benefit subscriber-pays NRSROs, who could use it to perform independent assessments of the validity of the ratings by their competitors who use the issuer-pays model. The

[44] This was done as a member of the President's Working Group on Financial Markets; see http://www.law.du.edu/images/uploads/presidents-working-group.pdf.

[45] Cox (2008).

[46] Ibid.

reason for enhanced disclosures about how NRSROs determine their ratings for structured products is to improve transparency. Rules requiring the disclosure of ratings information in a manner that would make it possible for investors to distinguish easily between ratings for different types of securities, such as structured products, corporate securities and municipal securities, are a step in the right direction.[47]

4.2.7.4 Information Flow and Due Diligence

There was a need to explore ways to improve the quality of information available to the users of credit ratings. The status of "concept release" is to investigate diverse issues (like conflicts of interest between the agencies and the corporations whose debt they rate to the red tape that hinders the entry of new players). Based on comments received on concept release, SEC would then issue rules that would address the issues, for example that affect the controversial credit rating business.

Concept Release 5[48] has introduced several conditions.[49] The first condition for NRSRO recognition required a CRA to implement procedures to assure appropriate disclosure of key information about its ratings and rating processes. It included (a) widespread public dissemination of its ratings, (b) identifying an unsolicited rating as such, (c) annual disclosure of specified ratings performance information and (d) public disclosure of the key bases of, and assumptions underlying, the ratings decision (pursuant to generally accepted industry standards developed by a broad-based committee of market participants). The second condition was to assure appropriate public notification when it ceases rating an issuer.

Additional rules include provisions designed to ensure that enhanced disclosure about a firm's rating performance affords other CRAs, including newly recognised NRSROs, an opportunity to identify flaws, or opportunities for improvement on their competitor's approach, or to demonstrate to investors that their credit ratings performance is better. NRSRO-designated CRAs were free to devise their own additional rules of good corporate governance, and the Commission can rely on them. It meant investors should only use NRSRO ratings that they (investors) deemed to be credible, along with other information available or disclosed by the CRAs, in conducting their due diligence. The expectation was that it would likely encourage greater competition among the CRAs and that this in turn would produce high-quality and the most reliable ratings.[50]

---

[47] Ibid.

[48] P. L. Green "Features: Rating Agencies On Watch" (1 March 2003) http://www.gfmag.com/archives/86-86-march-2003/605-features.html#axzz2chrA4myR.

[49] Securities and Exchange Commission, "Concept Release: Rating Agencies and the Use of Credit Ratings under the Federal Securities Laws", https://www.sec.gov/rules/concept/33-8236.htm.

[50] Cox (2008).

4.2.7.5 Power to Designate NRSRO Status

SEC's "no-action letter" approach, which allowed the granting of NRSROs status to the Big Three, was opaque, and it provided SEC with too little regulatory oversight of these NRSROs. The Reform Act requires the SEC to establish clear guidelines for determining which CRAs qualify as NRSROs. It also gave the SEC the power to regulate NRSROs' internal processes in relation to record keeping and CRAs' guarding against conflicts of interest. NRSRO determination became subject to a Commission vote (rather than through SEC staff determination). The Reform Act specifically prohibits the SEC from regulating an NRSRO's rating methodology. In June 2007, the SEC promulgated new regulations that implemented the provisions of the Reform Act.[51] In February 2009, the SEC promulgated amended regulations designed to address concerns about the integrity of the process by which NRSROs rate structured finance products, particularly mortgage-related securities.[52]

Changes in rules have to be appropriate and simple, and this meant that any CRA that meets certain stipulated standards should be able to register itself with the SEC. Although the SEC retained its power to inspect CRAs' work, such power was limited. The SEC did not have the authority to regulate the way CRAs used and applied methodologies to arrive at their ratings. Currently, the Reform Act lacks provisions that would enable the SEC to outlaw certain practices by CRAs that are tantamount to an abuse of power, as seen earlier.

4.2.7.6 Barrier to Entry

The dominant position of the Big Three and NRSRO rules acts as a barrier to entry. Over a century ago, Mr John Moody (1868–1958) founded the modern ratings business when he first published ratings on railroad bonds in 1909.[53] Moody's along with S&P and Finch remain the dominant companies. There are several reasons why CRAs have since then assumed increased importance. They range from regulatory decisions, the development of complex financial products such as asset-backed securities and credit derivatives, and the globalisation of financial markets. In recent years, the increase in securitisation has been responsible for explosive revenue growth of the Big Three rating agencies.[54]

[51] "Oversight of Credit Rating Agencies Registered as Nationally Recognized Statistical Rating Organizations", Exchange Act Release 34-55857 of June 5, 2007; 72 F.R. 33564 of 18 June 2007.

[52] "Amendments to Rules for Nationally Recognized Statistical Rating Organization", Exchange Act Release 34-59342 of 2 February 2009; 74 F.R. 6456 of 9 February 2009.

[53] For a history of Moody's, see Langohr and Langohr (2008), pp. 394–398.

[54] Senate Report Number 109-326 (2006) at 3.

NRSROs and the First Amendment

Although NRSRO designation acts as a barrier to entry into the credit rating business, the Commission's legal authority to regulate or impose requirements on NRSROs is challengeable. On 19 April 2005, the SEC released for comment a proposed rule for NRSROs because it felt it might not have legal authority to regulate or impose requirements on NRSROs. The proposed rule focuses on a comprehensive definition of the term NRSRO. The SEC believes the definition is to "strike a balance within the confines of the [SEC's] existing legal authority".[55] The NRSRO rating activities are journalistic in nature, and consequently CRAs get a high level of protection against liability under the First Amendment free-speech guarantee to the credit rating opinions they give.[56] The Commission's power to inspect or otherwise impose regulatory burdens on NRSROs may presumably fall foul of the NRSROs' First Amendment protection rights as it may restrict CRAs' activities. New legislation providing the Commission with additional authority over NRSROs may also face the same First Amendment challenges as the Commission did not have an explicit regulatory authority over NRSROs and it would be inappropriate for the Commission, absent legislation, to impose a more comprehensive regulatory framework for rating agencies.[57]

Nevertheless, the Reform Act establishes fundamental reform and improvement of the NRSRO designation process. Most notably, the Act replaces the artificial barriers to entry created by the current approval system by SEC staff with a transparent and voluntary registration system. It does not favour any particular business model, thus encouraging purely statistical models to compete with the qualitative models of the dominant CRAs and for investor-subscription-based models to compete with a fee-based model. The CRAs that choose to register as NRSROs are compelled to disclose important information such as ratings performance, conflicts of interest and the procedures used in determining ratings to the regulators.[58] The CRAs have also to update annually their rating performance statistics. Such a move is meant to facilitate informed decision-making by giving investors the opportunity to compare the ratings quality of different firms.[59]

4.2.7.7 Conflicts of Interest

Sinclair attributes the subprime crisis to fundamental dilemmas involving the gatekeeper's role of CRAs in a market system, rather than breaking implicit

[55] See 17 CFR Part 240, "General Rules and Regulations, Securities Exchange Act of 1934" at 55.

[56] Jones (2009).

[57] SEC Concept Release No. 33-8236 (2003), p. 1.

[58] Section 4(1) (B) of the Reform Act.

[59] Fitch Ratings, http://www.fitchratings.com/jsp/marketfocus/MarketFocus.faces?marketFocusArea=CreditMarketResearch&selectedTab=Research&selectedLeftNav=all.

regulative rules about conflicts of interest.[60] The evidence seems to suggest otherwise. The problem of conflicts of interest emerged in 1970 when the model for payments for CRAs services changed from investors to issuers. Nazareth notes, "[T]he dependence of rating agencies on revenues from the companies they rate could induce them to rate issuers more liberally, and temper their diligence in probing for negative information".[61]

Conflicts of interest arise in many ways. Some examples are (a) the way the obligor compensates CRAs, (b) when CRAs provide consultancy advisory services to the obligor and (c) the business and financial relationship between CRAs and the obligor. CRAs on their part deny that conflicts exist by asserting that their processes, procedures and market competition are sufficiently robust to address these concerns.[62] Conflict also arises as CRAs have developed ancillary fee-based businesses to complement their core ratings business. In the case of the ratings assessment service, where, for an additional fee, issuers present hypothetical scenarios to the CRAs to determine how their ratings would be affected by a proposed corporate action (for example, a merger, asset sale or stock repurchase) as an ancillary business, it has created a potential conflict of interest for CRAs. While it is difficult to eliminate conflict of interest, effectively managing it requires, according to the Credit Rating Information Services of India Limited,[63] adequate disclosures and a strong governance architecture comprising codes of conduct and robust firewall mechanisms. A.M. Best Company, Inc., is headquartered in Oldwick, New Jersey, and, as a CRA, is committed to being fair and honest when dealing in all facets of its business through their firewall policy.[64]

A step taken to manage conflicts of interest is requiring the CRAs, in the form of registration, to disclose conflicts of interest relating to their issuance of credit ratings.[65] In addition, CRAs are required to establish, maintain and enforce written policies and procedures to manage conflicts of interest.[66] The Commission has the mandate to adopt rules prohibiting conflicts of interest or to require the management and disclosure of such conflicts in the public interest or for the protection of investors.[67] Deb and Murphy[68] suggest that the most efficient way of aligning the incentives of rating agencies is to return to an investor-pay system.

---

[60] Sinclair (2010).

[61] Nazareth (2003).

[62] S&P, "Rating Policies and Code of Conduct", http://www.standardandpoors.com/ratings/code-of-conduct/en/us.

[63] "How CRISIL Manages Conflict of Interest", http://crisil.com/pdf/ratings/how-CRISIL-manages-conflict-of-interest.pdf.

[64] See A. M. Best Company Inc. (2011).

[65] Section 4(3) (h) of the Reform Act.

[66] Under sub-section (1) of Section 4(3) (h) of the Reform Act.

[67] Under sub-section (2) of Section 4(3) (h) of the Reform Act.

[68] Deb and Murphy (2009), p. 5.

4.2.7.8 The Issue of Competition

Pure competition, also called perfect competition, is an economic situation where a market has many sellers, none of whom have a significant amount of market power. In perfect competition, goods are homogeneous and there are no barriers to entry or exit, meaning new firms can enter the market easily. The net effect of these factors is that under perfect competition, individual firms have no power to influence prices; the market determines prices. However, perfect competition does not exist in reality because a market does not have perfect information to be perfectly competitive. In perfect information, consumers are aware of any differences in quality and prices between producers. In addition to an absence of perfect information about prices, most markets have at least some barriers to entry and some differentiation between products.[69]

In an ideal world, competition puts businesses under constant pressure to offer the best possible range of goods and services at the best possible prices, and if they do not do so, consumers have the choice to buy elsewhere. In a free market, business should be a competitive game with consumers as the beneficiaries. Sometimes companies try to limit competition in several ways: (a) by agreements between companies that restrict competition, e.g., by cartels or other unfair arrangements in which companies agree to avoid competing with each other and try to set their own prices[70] (cartels are illegal in the US and the EU[71]); (b) by abuse of a dominant position, whereby major players try to squeeze smaller/medium-sized competitors out of the market; and (c) by mergers and acquisitions that are legitimate provided they expand markets and benefit consumers.[72] The Office of Fair Trading (OFT) has continued to prevent anti-competitive activity in the UK by imposing heavy fines on offending businesses.[73] *The Enterprise Act 2002*[74] introduced tougher sanctions as a powerful incentive for individuals themselves not to engage in anti-competitive behaviour. The prospect of a fine is to deter individuals within the business from breaching competition laws.

To preserve a well-functioning product market, authorities like the Commission are in a position to prevent or correct anti-competitive behaviour as mentioned above, but there are no known instances of any action being taken against CRAs in this regard. The reason is that "[t]he largest NRSROs, S&P and Moody's, wield enormous power in the global Capital market system. Their ratings affect the cost of capital and the structure of transactions for debt issuers, and determine which securities may be purchased by money market mutual funds, banks, credit unions,

---

[69] Hamel.

[70] For a definition of cartel, see Glossary.

[71] "Cartel", http://www.investorwords.com/745/cartel.html#ixzz2ZKB5rYoS.

[72] For a definition of mergers and acquisition, see Glossary.

[73] For actions taken by OFT, see "Anti-competitive behaviour under the Enterprise Act", http://www.out-law.com/page-403.

[74] The Act came into force in June 2003.

insurers, state pension funds, local governments, and local school boards".[75] The problem facing small/medium-sized CRAs is either (1) because of their inability to acquire NRSRO status or (2) that if they are able to do so the big market players will "swallow" them up to get rid of any competition in the marketplace.[76]

In comparison, in the UK (which is a part of the EU) the government, on 15 March 2012, announced its plans to reform the UK's competition regime. The reforms included creating a new single Competition and Markets Authority taking on the functions of the Competition Commission and the Office of Fair Trading's competition functions and consumer enforcement powers.[77] Encouraging competition and preventing takeovers of smaller CRAs by the Big Three players through monitoring such deals by the Mergers and Acquisition Commissioner and the approval of the deal should preferably depend on satisfying the criterion of serving the public interest. US federal securities laws, in particular the *Securities Act of 1933* (the Securities Act) and the *Securities Exchange Act of 1934* (the Exchange Act), and the rules and regulations of the US Securities and Exchange Commission (the SEC) contain requirements that affect the structure and process of many acquisition transactions. The Takeover Directive 2004/25/EC is an EU directive dealing with European company law's treatment of mergers and acquisitions.

Anti-competitive and unfair practices arise when the largest CRAs, in order to win business, abuse their dominant position by engaging in certain aggressive competitive practices. In the case of the News Corporation, it seems that monopolistic practices did cause damage to the Corporation and have an effect on the value of its stock.[78] To win the business, a CRA lowers its ratings of issuers or refuses to rate securities issued by certain asset pools (e.g., CDOs), unless it is allowed also to rate the assets within those pools. With respect to unsolicited ratings, there are some allegations that CRAs may have used strong-arm tactics, for example, by compelling payment for a rating that an issuer did not request (e.g., sending a bill for an unsolicited rating or sending a fee schedule and "encouraging" payment).[79]

In theory, a competitive disadvantage occurs due to lack of access to the information on the assets underlying the structured credit product. Occasionally, organisations make mistakes through "blunder, lapse and misjudg[ment]. They [at times] fail to capture opportunities, fail to imitate imitable resources, fail to solve solvable problems, and fail to execute fundamental strategies".[80] Therefore, to enhance competition requires designing rules to ensure that all NRSROs have

---

[75] Senate Report Number 109-326 (2006), p. 3.

[76] Several CRAs were absorbed by the Big Three: see "Credit Rating Agencies Globally", http://www.defaultrisk.com/rating_agencies.htm.

[77] Competition Commission, "Policy: Institutional Reform" http://www.competition-commission.org.uk/policy#sthash.g1Tc6mGk.dpuf.

[78] Grimes and Smith (2013).

[79] Section 4 of the *Duopoly Act* prohibited such acts and practices.

[80] Powell and Arregle, p. 2.

access to the information underlying credit ratings, regardless of whether the NRSRO follows the issuer-pays model or the subscriber-pays model.

There is a need for both the models in a marketplace to act as a healthy competitive check on the other. In addition, given the dominance of the issuer-pays model currently in place, such rules could create an equal opportunity for NRSROs not paid by issuers to rate securities, to issue their own unsolicited ratings and, thereby, to develop a record of accomplishment for rating these products. In 2006, about 130 companies were in the business of assigning credit ratings, whereas the Big Three (S&P, Moody's and Fitch Ratings) controlled 95 % of the market.[81] Although smaller/medium-sized CRAs would not have achieved a better result (than the Big Three whose claim is that Enron deceived them), they are unable to break the barrier because the SEC has the sole power to decide which companies qualify as NRSROs. The NRSRO designation is important as it brings credibility and is crucial in the CRA's ability to grow its market share. Small/medium-sized companies are being disadvantaged in that although they are required to register as CRAs, they do not have the SEC's stamp of authority in the form of NRSRO status, which carries a great deal of weight and acts as a status symbol.

4.2.8 *Nationally Recognized Statistical Rating Organization (NRSRO)*

4.2.8.1 Definition of the NRSRO

The SEC, in the past, had attempted to devise a regulatory scheme for CRAs, but it had failed to define the term NRSRO. The definition appears, for the first time, in the Reform Act 2006. Section 3(61) defines an NRSRO as an entity that satisfies the following three criteria: first, it issues publicly available credit ratings that are current assessments of the creditworthiness of obligors with respect to specific securities or money market instruments; second, the predominant users of securities ratings generally accept it in the financial markets as an issuer of credible and reliable ratings, including ratings for a particular industry or geographic segment; third, it uses systematic procedures designed to ensure credible and reliable ratings, manage potential conflicts of interest, prevent the misuse of public information and has sufficient financial resources to ensure compliance with these procedures.[82] There are merits to CRAs being able to satisfy the important criteria needed for NRSRO status; however, it was easy for the Big Three to satisfy them compared to the small/medium-sized CRAs. In relation to subprime mortgages, it is worth noting that the Big Three had failed to meet the criterion of providing credible

---

[81] Wrobel (2013).

[82] See Senate Report Number 109-326 (2006) at 6.

and reliable ratings as they gave overoptimistic triple-A ratings to such debt instruments.

4.2.8.2 Insight into the NRSRO

Prior to 1975, the SEC had adopted the term NRSRO solely for determining capital charges on different grades of debt securities under the SEC's net capital rule for broker dealers.[83] There was a need to address the problem in that Commission NRSRO designation had become a sensitive and controversial issue of global significance, particularly in the absence of published standards for such designation.[84] In reality, "globalization and securitization of the international financial markets have expanded the role of credit ratings in countries other than the United States".[85] As already mentioned, the US NRSROs are today widely used as benchmarks in federal and state legislation, rules issued by financial and other regulators, foreign regulatory schemes and private financial contracts.[86] A number of additional SEC rules and regulations relate to the NRSRO concept, including rules issued under the *Securities Act of 1933*, the *Securities Exchange Act of 1934* and the *Investment Company Act of 1940*. Congress, too, has used the NRSRO concept in legislation, as have other regulatory bodies, including banking regulators both at home and abroad.[87]

SEC responded to a Congressional directive under the *Sarbanes-Oxley Act of 2002* and issued a report on the role of CRAs in the securities markets. The report identified a number of substantive issues. They were as follows: (1) a need for improved information flow in the credit rating process, (2) potential conflicts of interest, (3) alleged anti-competitive or unfair practices, (4) potential regulatory barriers to entry into the credit rating business and (5) ongoing regulatory oversight of credit rating agencies. The SEC also reviews the operational capability and reliability of the CRAs. It includes CRAs' organisational structure, their financial resources, their size and experience and training of rating agency staff, their independence from the companies they rate, their procedures and internal procedures to prevent the misuse of non-public information to minimise possible conflicts of interest and whether those procedures are followed.[88] It follows that the procedure adopted by SEC in recognising CRAs as NRSRO is to review their

[83] Exchange Act Rule 15c3.1, see Adoption of Amendments to Rule 15c3-1 and Adoption of an Alternative Net Capital Requirement for Certain Brokers and Dealers, Exchange Act Release No. 11497 (26 June 1975).

[84] Roberts (1992).

[85] Ibid., p. 5.

[86] Nazareth (2005a).

[87] Ibid.

[88] See Sec. B—Recognition Criteria in EC Concept Release: Rating Agencies and the Use of Credit Ratings under the Federal Securities Laws. http://www.sec.gov/rules/concept/33-8236.htm.

operational capability and the reliability of their credit rating. The intention of these criteria is to reflect the view of the marketplace on the credibility of the CRAs. It is a catch-22 situation in that "You cannot be widely accepted by the predominant users unless you are an NRSRO, but you cannot become an NRSRO unless you are already widely accepted!"[89]

The basis for objection to NRSRO status was that the recognition process was not sufficiently transparent; it led to barriers to entry, and there were concerns regarding the training and qualifications of CRAs' analysts.[90] The retention of NRSROs was preferred as eliminating them would be disruptive to the capital markets and it would be costly and complicated to replace them. As to the objection that NRSROs create a barrier to entry, this could be addressed by improving the transparency of the NRSRO recognition process and the Commission by making rules that oblige CRAs to ensure their analysts are properly trained and qualified. Moreover, CRAs could improve their performance with an appropriate introduction of accountability on their part. Obviously, there was a need to improve the clarity of the process to identify NRSROs to the extent that credit ratings are obliged to rely upon Commission's rules and regulations.

The Reform Act prohibits reliance on SEC no-action letters identifying NRSROs with effect from 26 June 2007. The CRAs "supported the Commission's suggestions to specify in more detail what credit rating agencies need to provide to obtain an NRSRO no-action letter".[91] The current NRSROs and others have also raised concerns about the extent of the SEC authority to impose requirements on NRSROs.[92] The CRAs contend that the SEC do "not have explicit regulatory authority over NRSROs and that NRSRO rating activities are journalistic [in nature] and are afforded a high level of protection under the First Amendment".[93]

4.2.8.3 Qualifying as an NRSRO

Naturally, prospective CRAs want a better understanding of whether they qualify as an NRSRO based on the Commission's definition of an NRSRO under Section 3 (61), mentioned above. An NRSRO is an entity that issues publicly available credit ratings that are current assessments of the creditworthiness of obligors with respect to specific securities or money market instruments. This "would also require a credit rating agency to issue credit ratings that are 'current assessments' of the creditworthiness of specific securities or money market instruments".[94] The reason

[89] A. Pollock (American Enterprise Institute) quoted by Carnahan (2005).

[90] SEC Concept Release (2003).

[91] SEC "No Action Letters" http://www.sec.gov/answers/noaction.htm.

[92] Amy B.R. Lancellotta (Senior Counsel) Letter addressed to J.G. Kutz, "Definition of NRSRO", Investment Company Institute (9 June 2005) at 1.

[93] Nazareth (2005b).

[94] Ibid.

is that "anyone relying on a rating for regulatory purposes in Commission rules and regulations would have confidence, at any given time, that the rating reflects the credit rating agency's current view".[95] The SEC's interpretation of "current assessments" should go beyond a CRA's published credit ratings, expressing an opinion. Until the "rating is changed or withdrawn, it continues to represent the rating agency's view as to the creditworthiness of such security or money market instrument".[96] The aim is to ensure that the CRAs are obliged to ensure the ratings given to a debt instrument are currently valid and to change them, say by downgrading, when the circumstances change, based perhaps on the lessons learnt from the subprime mortgage and Enron sagas.[97]

What this does is to link the evaluation of a CRA's ratings to the views of the predominant users of securities ratings, and this is a sensible approach. Major users generally include financial market participants who hold large inventories of proprietary debt securities, preferred stock and commercial paper, such as broker-dealers, mutual funds, pension funds and insurance companies. Credit ratings are important to the business of these market participants and to the stability of the financial markets as a whole as they provide a certain level of credibility and reliability to NRSRO ratings. The acceptance of CRAs in the financial markets provides some level of assurance to those relying on ratings about the dependability and consistency of the ratings for a variety of regulatory purposes.[98]

The designation of an NRSRO is to ensure that a CRA uses systematic procedures to ensure credible and reliable ratings, manages conflicts of interest and prevents the misuse of non-public information. To meet the requirements of such a definition requires CRAs to have sufficient financial resources, for example in engaging competent staff to ensure compliance with such procedures. This will assist the NRSRO-designated CRAs to produce credible and reliable ratings, thus furthering the purposes underlying the regulatory users of NRSRO ratings,[99] but does not prevent them from adopting unethical behaviours.

4.2.9 Oversight

Given the importance of credit ratings to investors and the influence ratings have on the securities markets, there is a need for the SEC to play a more active role in reviewing the operation of CRAs on an ongoing basis, including jurisdiction, feasibility, resources and other considerations. This oversight could include, *inter*

[95] Ibid.

[96] Ibid.

[97] See Chap. 2.

[98] Nazareth (2005b).

[99] Ibid.

alia, record-keeping requirements designed for the credit rating business and a programme of regular SEC inspections and examinations.[100]

CRA analysts seem to have been less than thorough in their review of Enron's public filings. The reasons relate to the rating analysts having paid insufficient attention to the detail in Enron's financial statements, failure to probe opaque disclosures, failure to review Enron's proxy statements, failure to take into account the overall aggressiveness of Enron's accounting practices and failure to use the necessary rigour in ensuring the sound analysis of Enron, which was a complex company. In the aftermath of Enron, concerns were raised regarding the training and qualifications of CRA analysts.[101] An important aspect of oversight is whether CRAs should be required to incorporate general standards of diligence in performing their ratings analysis and develop standards for the training and qualifications of credit rating analysts. The issues regarding what oversight authority the SEC has in mind and what the potential impact is on the credit ratings market of any action the SEC may take would need to be resolved.[102]

4.2.10 Barriers to Entry

The aim of the *Duopoly Act*[103] (which remained a bill and was replaced by the Reform Act) was to improve ratings quality by fostering competition, transparency and accountability in the credit rating agency industry. In the Act, the Congress had acknowledged that through its staff designation of CRAs as NRSROs, it had created an artificial barrier to entry for new participants.[104] Market participants have expressed concerns about the concentration of CRAs in the US securities markets resulting in undue barriers to entry.[105] Significant natural barriers already exist, particularly given the longstanding dominance of the credit rating business by a few firms—essentially the NRSROs—as well as the fact that the marketplace may not demand ratings from more than two or three CRAs. Arguably, the regulatory use of the NRSRO concept and the process of Commission recognition of NRSROs have increased the natural barriers to entry. The users of securities ratings have a regulatory incentive to obtain ratings issued by NRSROs, and without NRSRO status new entrants encounter great difficulties in achieving the "national recognition" necessary to acquire the NRSRO designation.[106] Users of credit ratings and

[100] Nazareth (2003).

[101] U.S. Securities and Exchange Commission (2003), p. 32.

[102] Nazareth (2003).

[103] H.R. 2990 (109th) *Credit Rating Agency Duopoly Relief Act of 2006* (the Duopoly Act), https://www.govtrack.us/congress/bills/109/hr2990/text.

[104] Section 2(2) (A) of the *Duopoly Act 2006*.

[105] Nazareth (2003), Section 4.

[106] Ibid.

others want substantive threshold standards for achieving NRSRO status for that term to have any meaning.[107] Haynes notes:

> Once you [have] good dominant players, the big clients [tend] to use them (as with [the big] accountancy [firms]). For a new entrant to succeed it needs the backing of another entity. McGraw Hill [S&P] could have developed further for this reason if finance were the only issue. However ... there [is no] evidence they would have done any better. *There always seems to be a herd instinct in human behaviour*[108] [emphasis added].

As an extreme case, Nazareth submits that "an obvious way to avoid potential regulatory barriers to entry is to eliminate the regulatory use of the NRSRO concept".[109] White[110] also suggests that the SEC should abolish the NRSRO category entirely but for different reasons. His reasoning for elimination is to allow the financial markets to reach their own conclusions. The basis for these conclusions depends on "which organizations are the most reliable raters of debt, which have the best track records in predicting insolvencies, which organizations are free of serious conflicts of interest, and what business models and methods are the most conducive to yielding good results".[111]

Should, hypothetically, the NRSRO be abolished, a key issue is whether one can find a better viable and suitable alternative in the current approach of relying on ratings by CRAs recognised by the SEC. The answer is in the negative. In addition, given the widespread use of the NRSRO concept in other federal and state laws and regulations, the difficulty lies in developing substitutes by authorities, other than the SEC, which would effectively eliminate any regulatory barriers to entry. Ensuring a CRA performs a rating service competently requires conducting an appropriate assessment by a regulator to review the operational capability and reliability of each rating organisation.

4.2.11 Tackling CRAs

Congress mentions in the *Credit Rating Agency Reform Act of 2006* that CRAs are of national importance.[112] The reasons, *inter alia*, are that the rating transactions occur in such volume as to affect interstate commerce, the securities markets, the national banking system and the national economy substantially. Regulation tackling an oversight of CRAs would serve the interest of investor protection. On the issue of competition, the hitherto two largest CRAs (S&P and Moody's) served the vast majority of the market, and competition was required in the public interest. On

---

[107] Ibid.

[108] A. Haynes, University of Wolverhampton, email exchanges (21 February 2012).

[109] Nazareth (2003).

[110] L. J. White, Comments at 2. http://www.sec.gov/rules/proposed/s70405/ljwhite6694.pdf.

[111] Ibid.

[112] Section 2 of the Reform Act.

whether the arrival of Fitch as a serious competitor has really opened the door to competition, Baker thinks it has.[113] However, based on the evidence credit rating is a highly concentrated industry where the three major rating agencies hold a collective market share of roughly 95 %. The two largest CRAs, Moody's and S&P, have an 80 % market share globally, while Fitch, which dominates the bond market, has 15 % of the market share.[114] The SEC needed statutory authority to oversee the credit rating industry. Section 3 of the Reform Act defines the terms credit rating, credit rating agency, NRSRO, persons associated with NRSRO and qualified institutional buyer. Section 4 contains the registration process and procedures of NRSROs. It amended the *Securities Exchange Act of 1934* to require NRSROs to register with the SEC.

The SEC is required to grant registration unless the applicant does not have adequate financial and managerial resources to produce consistent credit ratings with integrity and to comply materially with the procedures and methodologies disclosed in the application. Most importantly, it grants the SEC exclusive enforcement authority over any NRSRO that issues credit ratings in material contravention of the procedures included in its registration application. SEC is suing the CRA Egan-Jones because in its NRSRO application made in 2008, it had exaggerated its skills by overstating its experience in rating government bonds and ABS.[115]

The Reform Act has its own limitation. It prohibits the SEC or any state or local government from regulating the substance of credit ratings or the procedures and methodologies by which an NRSRO determines credit ratings. SEC rules are to be personalised narrowly. The SEC cannot regulate either the substance of credit ratings or the procedures and methodologies used by NRSROs to determine credit ratings. Each NRSRO is required to establish and enforce written policies and procedures to prevent the misuse of non-public information and manage conflicts of interest.

4.2.11.1 NRSROs' Practices

The SEC is to issue final rules to prohibit unfair, coercive or abusive acts or practices by NRSROs. It includes conditioning or threatening to condition an issuer's credit rating on the purchase of other services or products, lowering or threatening to lower a credit rating or refusing to rate securities or money market instruments issued by an asset pool unless a portion of the assets in the pool is also rated by the NRSRO; and modifying or threatening to modify a credit rating based on whether the issuer or an affiliate will purchase other services from the NRSRO.

---

[113] Baker and Milbourn (2010).

[114] SEC Staff Report (2012), p. 5.

[115] Tchirp, "What the TF? The SEC, NRSRO, Free Speech, and Lawsuits" TF Market Advisors (2013). http://www.tfmarketadvisors.com/2012/04/25/what-the-tf-the-sec-nrsro-free-speech-and-lawsuits/.

The NRSROs are required to fulfil two further obligations. These obligations are (1) to designate a compliance officer to ensure compliance with securities laws, rules and regulations and (2) to furnish the SEC with financial statements certified by an independent public accountant. Registration under the Reform Act became the sole method of NRSRO registration. Those CRAs that had obtained NRSRO status based on no-action relief had to reapply for registration. This prevents any state and local law requiring the registration, licensing or qualification of an NRSRO (or any employee or contractor) as a CRA or an NRSRO.

However, the SEC (or similar agency or office) has power to investigate and bring about enforcement action with respect to fraud or deceit against any NRSRO or associated person. It directs the SEC to report annually to specified congressional committees on several matters. These matters are (1) applicants for NRSRO registration, (2) actions taken on the applications and (3) the views of the SEC on the state of competition, transparency and conflicts of interest among NRSROs.[116]

The Comptroller General is required to study and report to certain congressional committees on the impact of the Reform Act concerning certain issues: the impact upon the quality of credit ratings issued by NRSROs, the financial markets, competition between credit rating agencies, the incidence of inappropriate conflicts of interest and sales practices by NRSROs, the process for registering NRSRO and other matters the Comptroller General deems necessary to bring to the attention of Congress.[117]

4.2.11.2 Enforcements

Undoubtedly, a robust enforcement programme is critical to fulfilling the SEC's mission to instill confidence in those who invest in our markets and to make the markets fair and honest.[118] In theory and in my submission, simply enacting rules is not sufficient; "teeth" are required to enforce these rules. Following NRSRO registration, the SEC is able to control CRAs and legitimise their position. Once registered, CRAs then immediately become subject to various Commission authorities, including the SEC's right to examine their books and records and to take enforcement action against an NRSRO. Such action would include placing limitations on an NRSRO's activity, censuring the NRSRO or revoking or suspending NRSRO registration. The law required the Commission to review and act on any such registration applications within 90 days. Initially, seven firms had applied to become NRSROs, and the Commission approved all seven registrations within the time allowed by the Reform Act. As a result, as of the end of September 2007, seven credit rating agencies—including those that were most active in rating subprime RMBSs and CDOs—became subject to the Commission's new oversight authority,

[116] Section 6 of the Reform Act.

[117] Section 7, Ibid.

[118] White (2013).

and subject as well to the newly adopted rules.[119] Many professionals supported the Reform Act based, *inter alia*, on creating competition and received favourable comments.[120] The reason for Fitch's support, which is a jointly owned subsidiary of the Hearst Corporation and Fimalac SA, may be explained by the fact it is a main competitor to Moody's and S&P.

Placing limitations on NRSROs is understandable, but the problem is how the Commission or SEC would go about censuring NRSROs. Common sense suggests this should be through imposing fines on CRAs, and other such impositions of penalties relating to their compliance failures.[121] The question that then arises relates to what constitutes a reasonable fine when either the SEC imposes a fine or when a fine is tendered by a defendant as an out-of-court settlement. In *US Securities and Exchange Commission (SEC) v, City Group Global Markets Inc.*[122] Judge J. S. Rakoft refused to approve a meagre civil penalty of US $95 million offered by City Group as payment to the SEC for securities fraud without a full court hearing. The district Judge "concluded that the proposed consent judgment was not fair, adequate, reasonable, or in the public interest because Citigroup had not admitted or denied the allegations".[123]

It is understandable that the penalty has to be harsh enough to act as a deterrent. However, on appeal, the Court of Appeal (CA) held that judges do not decide on policy matters, and this led to the reversal of the decision.[124] The CA did not consider the issue of whether the fine was reasonable or not, and the judges left it for the SEC to decide. Presently in the US, the fines imposed on CRAs go into the coffers of the regulators to defray regulatory expenses, rather than compensating investors for their losses. The same scenario exists in the EU, as under Article 8, fines imposed on CRAs go to the EU budget under general revenue[125] rather than used in compensating investors.

[119] Cox (2008).

[120] Senate Report Number 109-326 (2006), pp. 8–9.

[121] Commission Announcements –"SEC Penalizes Investment Advisers for Compliance Failures", *SEC News Digest* (28 November 2011). See http://www.sec.gov/news/digest/2011/dig112811.htm.

[122] 11 US District Court and Southern District of New York, Civ. 7387 (JSR) 2011; No. 11 Civ.7 7387, 2011 WL 5903733, (S.D.N.Y. November 28, 2011).

[123] "*SEC v. Citigroup Global Markets Inc.*" http://law.justia.com/cases/federal/appellate-courts/ca2/11-5227/11-5227-2012-03-15.html.

[124] United States Securities & Exchange Commission v. Citigroup Global Markets Inc. 5 Docket Nos. 11-5227-cv (Lead) 11-5375-cv (Con) 11-5242-cv (XAP) (Submitted: January 17, 2012 Decided: March 15, 2012), http://docs.justia.com/cases/federal/appellate-courts/ca2/11-5227/11-5227-2012-03-15.pdf.

[125] Official Journal of the European Union, "Commission Delegated Regulation (EU) No 946/2012 of 12 July 2012" (16.10.2012) L 282/23. http://eur-lex.europa.eu/LexUriServ/LexUriServ.do?uri=OJ:L:2012:282:0023:0026:en:PDF.

4.2.11.3 Methodology

From comments and objections the SEC had received, two other changes were made.[126] First, the Reform Act prevents the SEC from regulating the rating methodologies. It is unknown whether each of the Big Three uses their own unique methodologies and the extent to which they are on a par with each other. The EU regulation requirement is that the methodologies used by CRAs should be rigorous, systematic, continuous and subject to validation.[127] It is puzzling, therefore, as to how the SEC is able to determine the adequacy or otherwise of a methodology used by the diverse range of CRAs that it cannot regulate. Second, the Reform Act retains the right, privilege or defence that CRAs have under state or federal law.

4.2.12 The Issue of Competition

4.2.12.1 Competition Versus Competency Theory

There are three reasons for lack of competition. First, only a few CRAs are able to register as NRSROs, and those CRAs that find it difficult to register as NRSROs provide ancillary services to investors and issuers. As of 2011, there were 76 registered CRAs carrying on business worldwide, and the majority of them were not registered as NRSROs.[128] A second reason is due to investors and issuers trusting the incumbent CRAs and the possibility of CRAs charging lower fees to issuers for issuing second-rate ratings.[129] A third reason relates to the absorption by the Big Three of other CRAs operating within and outside of the US, some CRAs are becoming redundant and others providing non-rating services. The reasons for de-listing CRAs were as follows: (a) they were absorbed by the Big Three, (b) other CRAs decided to provide non-rating services and (c) the CRAs are becoming redundant.[130]

It appears that regulators were trying to achieve two conflicting aims: to increase competition and at the same time ensure competency on the part of CRAs. The regulators might have feared that allowing competition might backfire in that it might sacrifice competency in the provision of services by the CRAs, and this would make the situation worst. Competition *per se* is not necessarily a good thing. Becker and Milbourn tested the potential problem of raters who compete for business favouring the issuers and providing less reliable ratings. Their finding was that an increase in competition among raters would lead to "friendlier", poorer

---

[126] Senate Report Number 109-326 (2006) at 9.

[127] ESMA (2010).

[128] See "Credit Rating Agencies Globally". http://www.defaultrisk.com/rating_agencies.htm.

[129] See Jeon and Lovo (2011).

[130] See "Credit Rating Agencies Globally", http://www.defaultrisk.com/rating_agencies.htm.

quality ratings.[131] This may lead CRAs to undercut each other to get the available rating jobs from the limited pool of issuers, and this would mean cutting corners and sacrificing the type of services that CRAs provide under the regulation.

Flight believes in enhancing "the integrity and quality of the credit rating process, as well as the role and impact of credit rating agencies in the economy, in order to enable investor confidence and a [need for] proper functioning of the capital markets".[132] Flight, as a critique, expresses reservations about the NRSRO regime in that it does not prevent "the worst predatory excesses, dysfunctional behaviour, performance failures, and damaging effects arising from their current activities to be eliminated".[133]

4.2.12.2 Competition and Conflicts of Interest

A challenging issue is whether competition should take precedence over conflicts of interest, as conflicts of interest are only manageable rather than eradicated. A major drawback for the Big Two KPMG and PricewaterhouseCoopers (PwC), and other accounting firms in the US wanting to gain a foothold in the credit ratings market, is the obstacle based on conflicts of interest since the clients they audit also pay them. In spite of these firms already having the technical and industry expertise and knowledge to get the work done, it is just a matter of processing the information in a new way. What KPMG has done is to consider passively such a move rather than actively debating it, although it has the skills, knowledge and people to provide credit ratings. The value that KPMG, PwC and other auditors can add to credit ratings is in providing subjective feedback on a company's position rather than a list of statistics and figures. KPMG is aware of the conflicts of interest, and this probably makes it impractical for them to enter the market immediately, but they are potentially strong rating players should they wish to enter the market in future.[134]

According to KPMG, auditors as a matter of course should provide forward-looking assessments of a business' risks as well as backward-looking reviews of its numbers, and this would be a step towards improving the credit rating process. "It is something that we [KPMG] talk about as a plausible thing to do. It is effectively something we [KPMG] would be proficient at doing . . . but it's not on the agenda at the moment".[135] Bearing in mind that there are the Big Three CRAs and potentially the Big Four accounting firms,[136] in total there will be seven large firms providing

[131] Becker and Milbourn (2009). See also HBS Working Paper.

[132] Letter written to the SEC on 25 July 2003 dealing with Rating Agencies and the Use of Credit Ratings Under the Federal Securities Laws. See http://www.sec.gov/rules/concept/s71203/aflight072503.htm.

[133] Ibid.

[134] Financial Times (2010).

[135] J. G. Jones of KPMG in an interview with the Financial Times, see Shah (2010).

[136] Namely, Deloitte (Revenue $32.4 billion), PwC (Revenue $32.1 billion), Ernst & Young (Revenue $25.8 billion) and KPMG (Revenue $23.4 billion) See "Big Four (audit firms)" http://en.wikipedia.org/wiki/Big_Four_%28audit_firms%29.

rating services and competing with each other. This is only possible when accounting firms both in the US and the UK apply and get permission to register as NRSROs to open up competition in the ratings market.

Whereas both CRAs and accountancy firms have conflicts of interest, this author's contention is that accountancy firms, which act as auditors and audit the corporations' accounts, have added advantages over the CRAs. The advantages are that, first, large accounting firms are more aware of a corporation's operational aspects and ability as a going concern to pay their debts. Second, the accountancy firms' liability in negligence[137] is well known and documented in judicial pronouncements, and, unlike CRAs, they have enough of a deterrent in the form of negligence liability in the performance of their duty to their clients and third parties, and this ensures they perform their job responsibly. Third, CRAs have to hold Professional Indemnity Insurance (PII); this is for their protection; it does not mean that courts would hold them liable as the law provides CRAs with adequate protection. Therefore, CRAs do not have to worry about claims without merit being filed against them.

4.2.13 *Is There a Better Way of Compensating CRAs?*

Conflicts of interest have arisen because of the issuers-pay model. Listokin and Taibleson[138] propose a unique incentive-based compensation in which CRAs receive payment based on the securities they rate, incentivising them to issue accurate ratings. They suggest that "[i]nstead of receiving cash for their rating of a security, the agencies should receive some of the [security] debt that they are rating", believing that "incentive compensation creates conditions under which inaccurate ratings hurt the agencies' profitability, giving them greater incentive to rate accurately".[139] This means that if a CRA overrates a debt, then it suffers a financial penalty because the security debt the CRA receives as compensation is less valuable than the cash compensation that the debt is replacing. They believe that this reform, though imperfect, would be more likely to generate accurate ratings to the advantage of investors than other credit rating reform proposals [140] and that it would create incentives for CRAs to underrate securities. They propose a solution for this in the form of CRAs writing "put and call" options on a predetermined amount of the debt they rate.[141] Several problems emerge with their assertion. Firstly, the CRAs claim that they are issuing opinions and as the

---

[137] Salzedo and Singla (2015).

[138] Listokin and Taibleson (2010).

[139] Ibid., p. 94.

[140] Ibid.

[141] Ibid., p. 95.

future is uncertain, they cannot guarantee that the securities will retain their initial ratings when circumstances change. Secondly, CRAs will have a cash flow problem because they will be holding the intangible securities of various corporations they rate. Thirdly, it is unclear whether CRAs would accept this type of compensation, and if they did, CRAs would want a large chunk of it to compensate them for the trouble and uncertainty. Lastly, for how long should CRAs hold these securities, and if they were to sell them before a possible downgrading, would they be committing the offence of insider trading? Faced with these difficulties, one can, therefore, expect that the present *status quo* of compensating CRAs through cash payments from issuers will remain intact for the near future.

In England, insider dealing has been a criminal offence since 1980 (the law is now contained in Part V of the *Criminal Justice Act 1993*). Although the regulator has increased its enforcement work in recent years, successful prosecutions have not been straightforward. The Financial Service Authority (now Financial Conduct Authority) believes that within the City, professional insider dealing rings as well as rogue individuals exist and are regularly trading on inside information not available to the rest of the market.[142]

4.2.14 Interim Conclusion

The main thrust of the Reform Act is to minimise conflicts of interest, and it does this by requiring the CRAs to identify situations in which conflicts of interest arise and then take remedial action to eliminate them. The provisions of the Reform Act examined, in theory have succeeded in providing transparency, objective standards and a reasonable approach to the regulations of CRAs. The provisions of the Reform Act are meant to make CRAs act responsibly and competently and to issue reliable ratings so that investors may directly benefit. The CRAs need to abide by the essence of the Reform Act to prevent gatekeeper failure. However, the drawback of the Reform Act is that it has failed to provide avenues to encourage competition in the marketplace. The next section, Sect. 4.3, discusses and analyses additional new statutory regulations imposed under Dodd-Frank.

[142] Pinset Masons, "Insider dealing", http://www.out-law.com/page-11115; see also Clarke (2013) and Dubow and Monteiro (2006).

4.3 Dodd-Frank Wall Street Reform and Consumer Protection Act 2010 (Dodd-Frank)[143]

4.3.1 Introduction

Hsiao[144] submits that inefficient supervision and oversight of the financial system is not limited to the financial crisis but rather the managerial decisions and banking practices that can cause financial losses that in turn feed on the inherent instability of financial assets. The role of the regulator is in preventing further deterioration in the market and global economic system. A precondition for orderly markets requires the regulation and supervision of the financial system by public authorities based on official and law-based arrangements as a key component. Highly integrated financial markets in turn require rapid transmission of financial disturbances. "A closer international co-operation in the regulation and supervision of markets is important to the sustainable financial system and preventing erosion of prudential standards".[145]

Dragan et al. state that "[t]he financial crisis and the recession were not the result of normal economic cycles or just a run of bad luck",[146] but rather the "war to lower rating standards was at the heart of the financial crisis".[147] Structured investment mortgage-related securities were the rating agencies' golden goose.[148] CRAs earned as much as three times more for grading these complex products as for their traditional business of rating corporate bonds. In addition to revenue generated by issuing credit ratings, CRAs often earned between US $300,000 and $500,000 and an astounding figure of US $1 million to construct a structural investment vehicle.[149] By 2007, the business accounted for just under half of the total ratings revenue and all of the revenue growth at one of the largest agencies: Moody's reported revenue was US $583 million for the month ending 31 March 2007.[150] There is always a danger of missing this lucrative business, and issuers could resort to playing the Big Three CRAs off one another and shopping around to find the best ratings or otherwise threaten to move to another agency if ratings fell below their expectation.

---

[143] Pub.L. 111–203, H.R. 4173.

[144] Hsiao (2011), p. 5.

[145] Ibid.

[146] President B. Obama, http://www.nytimes.com/2011/07/19/business/dodd-frank-under-fire-a-year-later.html.

[147] Dragan et al. (2010).

[148] Birger (2008).

[149] Wayne (2009).

[150] "Moody's Corporation Reports Results for First Quarter 2007" (25 April 2007). http://ir.moodys.com/releasedetail.cfm?ReleaseID=288634.

4.3.2 *Too Big to Fail*

"Although 'too big to fail' has been a perennial policy issue, it was highlighted by the near-collapse of several large financial firms in 2008".[151] The blame for precipitating the credit crisis in 2008 goes to big losses incurred by banks for trading in the financial securities, especially mortgage-backed assets, which required a federal bailout.[152] Dodd-Frank represents Congress's response to "too big to fail" and what the House Committee on Financial Services calls "years without accountability for Wall Street [and] the worst financial crisis since the Great Depression".[153] The legislation set out to reshape the US regulatory system in a number of areas, including, but not limited to, consumer protection, trading restrictions, credit ratings, regulation of financial products, corporate governance and disclosure, and transparency. This section will examine mainly the provisions of Subtitle C of Title IX of the *Dodd-Frank Act*, which relates to "Improvements to the Regulation of Credit Rating Agencies" (Subtitle C) as it is relevant to the research conducted in that area.

4.3.3 *The NRSRO's Role*

Subtitle C of the Dodd-Frank establishes an almost wholly new framework for governing and regulating CRAs, including NRSROs. The role NRSROs play in the markets has dramatically changed. According to the Congressional findings

> [T]he systemic importance of credit ratings [is based on] ... the reliance placed on credit ratings by individual and institutional investors and financial regulators".[154] The activities and performance of NRSROs are "matters of national public interest, as [the] credit rating agencies are central to capital formation, investor confidence, and the efficient performance of the United States economy.[155]

In addition to the important role credit ratings play, the basis for Congress enactment of the Dodd-Frank is the belief that inaccurate credit ratings played a role in the mismanagement of risk by large financial institutions and investors, which in turn contributed to the crisis in the financial markets. Others blame credit ratings lapses on "an erosion of standards, a wilful suspension of scepticism, a hunger for big fees and market share, and an inability to stand up to" the investment banks issuing the securities.[156] Although the Big Three CRAs were key enablers of

[151] Labonte (2013), p. 2.

[152] *The New York Times* (4 November 2011).

[153] Nolan et al. (2010), para 1.

[154] Section 931 (1) Dodd-Frank Act.

[155] Dodd-Frank Act Sec. 931(1), Moynihan et al. (2010).

[156] McLean and Nocera (2010), p. 111.

the financial meltdown,[157] they did not play a significant role in subprime lending or the crisis, and many subprime lenders were not subject to CRA ratings.[158] Nevertheless, the Dodd-Frank, as will be seen, is to expand substantially the scope of regulation and accountability of CRAs generally and NRSROs in particular. It aims to improve the overall quality and integrity of credit ratings issued by CRAs. It requires implementing internal and external control structures, increasing the potential liability of CRAs and promoting a more transparent credit rating process. Simultaneously, it seeks to reduce the deference and reliance that investors, regulators and other users may give to such credit ratings.

The Dodd-Frank reforms address CRAs and the credit ratings they provide. It seeks to impose corporate governance guidelines, reduce conflicts of interest and improve the rating process through enhanced controls and greater transparency. In theory, at least, Dodd-Frank greatly expands SEC's oversight and enforcement powers and seeks to make it easier for investors to bring civil lawsuits against CRAs. The reforms also seek to reduce reliance on ratings as a litmus test for credit quality in favour of broader standards that encompasses multiple factors and credit criteria.[159]

4.3.3.1 Changes to NRSROs

For several years, NRSROs have been the focus of inquiry and reform efforts by Congress, the Obama Administration and the SEC, mainly because credit ratings and the practices of the agencies issuing them are widely regarded to have been factors in the 2008 credit crisis.[160] The need for the process of reform was due to a variety of conflicts of interest inherent in the existing credit rating structure and its impact on the strength of the US and global economies. Congressional concerns about credit ratings and the 2008 credit crisis led to the enactment of Subtitle C of the Dodd-Frank. The aim here is to analyse in details these provisions. In addition, the provisions also mirror those changes identified by the SEC (in its 2 February 2010 amendments) to certain disclosure and conflicts of interest requirements for NRSROs.[161] In adopting those amendments, the SEC "cited concerns about the integrity of NRSROs' credit rating procedures and methodologies in light of the role they played in the credit market turmoil".[162]

[157] "Conclusions of the Financial Crisis Inquiry Commission" (January 2010) at xxv. http://fcic-static.law.stanford.edu/cdn_media/fcic-reports/fcic_final_report_conclusions.pdf.

[158] Ibid., p. xxvii.

[159] Fernicola and Goldstein (2010).

[160] See Chap. 2.

[161] Securities and Exchange Commission. "Final Rule" http://www.sec.gov/rules/final/2009/33-9089.pdf.

[162] Moynihan et al. (2010).

4.3.4 Gatekeeper Theory Revisited

Gatekeeper theory takes a central stage in the *Dodd-Frank Act*.[163] As a ground rule similar to other gatekeepers, CRAs perform evaluative and analytical services on behalf of clients, and as their activities are fundamentally commercial in character they ought to be subjected to the same standards of liability and oversight as apply to auditors, securities analysts and investment bankers.[164] Such recognition, for the first time, highlights a critical role CRAs (including NRSROs) play as a gatekeeper in the debt market that is functionally similar to that of securities analysts, who evaluate the quality of the securities in the equity market, and auditors, who review the financial statements of firms. It was felt such a role justifies a similar level of public oversight and accountability.[165] In addition, CRAs do perform evaluative and analytical services on behalf of clients, which are similar to those offered by other financial gatekeepers. The activities of CRAs are fundamentally commercial in character, and therefore the same standards of liability and oversight should apply to CRAs as they do to auditors, securities analysts and investment bankers.[166] The importance of the recognition of gatekeepers is to correct this imbalance.[167] The role of CRAs, similar to other financial gatekeepers, is to perform evaluations and provide analytical services on behalf of their clients. However, it is not clear how effective the liability and oversight is when applied to CRAs and how it relates to the protection of investors.

4.3.5 Dodd-Frank's Regulation of CRAs

The proper functioning of the US capital markets depends on good corporate governance. Good corporate governance in turn depends on gatekeepers that serve issuers and investors with honesty and integrity.[168] The impetus for Congress's decision is to make further improvements to the regulations of CRAs and especially with regard to NRSROs, is because of several of their findings. Congress, for the first time, has recognised the fact that CRAs did play a critical gatekeeper role in the debt market as their function is similar to securities analysts, whose task is to evaluate the quality of the securities in the equity market, and

[163] See "Subtitle C – Improvements to the Regulation of Credit Rating Agencies and Section 931 Findings". http://www.gpo.gov/fdsys/pkg/BILLS-111hr4173enr/pdf/BILLS-111hr4173enr.pdf.

[164] Congress finding under the Dodd-Frank Act, http://www.gpo.gov/fdsys/pkg/BILLS-111hr4173enr/pdf/BILLS-111hr4173enr.pdf.

[165] Dodd-Frank Bill at 821 Cl (2). http://banking.senate.gov/public/_files/ChairmansMark31510AYO10306_xmlFinancialReformLegislationBill.pdf.

[166] Ibid.

[167] Walter and Daigler (2010).

[168] Walter and Daigler (2010).

auditors, whose task is to review the financial statements of firms.[169] Congress also acknowledged the importance of credit rating to investors (private individuals and institutional investors), including NRSROs, which were matters of public interest and in turn based on CRAs being "central to capital formation, investor confidence, and the efficient performance of the United States economy".[170]

Dodd-Frank requires the Commission to adopt a number of new rules concerning various issues. They range from annual reports on internal control to conflicts of interest with respect to sales and marketing practices, as well as "look-backs" when credit analysts leave the NRSRO. New rules were also needed for the imposition of fines and penalties, disclosure of performance statistics, application and disclosure of CRAs' methodologies, disclosure of data and assumptions underlying credit ratings, disclosure about third-party due diligence, analyst training and testing, consistent application of rating symbols and definitions and specific and additional disclosure for ratings related to ABS products.[171]

4.3.5.1 Reduced Reliance on Credit Ratings

The financial crisis demonstrated that reliance on credit rating "can be a cause of herding behaviour and of abrupt sell-offs of securities when they are downgraded ('cliff effects') which can in turn amplify pro-cyclicality and cause systemic disruption".[172] Dodd-Frank also opted for the removal of various statutory references to CRAs and credit ratings from numerous federal statutes, including portions of the *Federal Deposit Insurance Act*[173] and the *Investment Company Act of 1940*,[174] effective from 2 years after the date of enactment of Dodd-Frank. In its place, the responsible governmental agencies were required to establish alternative standards based on creditworthiness.

As credit ratings play a significant role in investment decisions, it suggests that CRAs receive a "seal of approval" on the quality of any particular credit rating or rating agency, including any NRSRO. In adopting Section 939A, Congress intended to "reduce reliance on credit ratings" and with it remove such a misconception. It led to the substitution of any reference to or requirement of reliance on credit rating in a regulation with the standard of creditworthiness. It also led to the removal of references to credit ratings in rules and forms promulgated under the *Securities Act 1933* and the *Exchange Act 1934*.[175] The Financial

[169] Section 931 (1*) Dodd-Frank Act*, sub-secs (1) to (4) H.R. 4173 at 497.

[170] Section 931 (1) at 497.

[171] SEC, "Credit Rating Agencies", http://www.sec.gov/spotlight/dodd-frank/creditratingagencies.shtml.

[172] Financial Stability Board (2013).

[173] See Chapter 16, 12 USC § 1811.

[174] As Amended through P. L. 112-90, approved on January 3, 2012.

[175] SEC, "Security Rating – Final Rules", http://www.sec.gov/rules/final/2011/33-9245.pdf.

Stability Board's[176] principal effort is in ending "mechanistic reliance on CRA ratings by banks, institutional investors and other market participants by reducing the 'hard wiring' of CRA ratings in standards, laws and regulations and by providing incentives for firms to develop their own capacity for credit risk assessment and due diligence".[177]

It is difficult to predict whether the alternative suggestions of substituting creditworthiness standards, investors developing their own credit risk assessment or due-diligence will lead to a better investment decisions. Also, the alternative standards may have unintended consequences like providing less cover to market participants and a greater uncertainty as to whether securities rated by CRAs will satisfy various regulatory provisions. As there is lack of an alternative to the market norms of not using ratings from the Big Three CRAs, the chances are that it will not disappear even with the removal of the statutory and regulatory references.[178]

4.3.5.2 Accountability

When CRAs compromise their independence and integrity, naturally market confidence suffers. Excessive risk taking by management led to investors suffering losses; CRAs advertised subprime mortgages as a way to diversify and thus reduce risk, while their true risks were often poorly understood and far greater than their credit ratings suggested.[179]

Congress noted that in certain other activities, like "advising arrangers of structured financial products on potential ratings", CRAs faced a conflict of interest and, as such, there was a need for careful monitoring and the need for explicitly addressing this issue in the legislation requiring the SEC to have a clear express authority. Congress also noted that the ratings on structured financial products were inaccurate, and this "contributed significantly to the mismanagement of risks by financial institutions and investors".[180] The solution was to increase CRAs' accountability because it "justifies a similar level of public oversight and accountability" like other gatekeepers.[181] It cannot be ruled out that business pressures to generate revenue may have led NRSROs to loosen their credit rating procedures or to apply them inconsistently. To mitigate conflicts of interest, the Dodd-Frank requires NRSROs to comply with a number of internal and external controls.

[176] The FSB has been established to coordinate at the international level the work of national financial authorities and international standard-setting bodies and to develop and promote the implementation of effective regulatory, supervisory and other financial sector policies. http://www.financialstabilityboard.org/.

[177] Financial Stability Board (2013), fn. 171.

[178] Hill (2010), p. 133 at 145.

[179] Walter and Daigler (2010).

[180] Section 931 (1) Dodd-Frank Act, Subsections (1) to (4) H.R. 4173 at 497.

[181] Section 932 (2) at 497.

Each NRSRO has to (a) establish and document internal policies and procedures for determining credit ratings, (b) segregate its sales and marketing personnel and efforts from its credit rating operations pursuant to rules to be issued by the SEC and (c) have a compliance officer (whose compensation may not be tied to the financial performance of the company) to monitor compliance with these policies, procedures and rules. NRSROs have a duty to report a transition to the SEC under certain circumstances.[182]

4.3.5.3 NRSRO Governance and Liability

The *Dodd-Frank Act* establishes a number of requirements regarding the governance and operations of NRSROs, including liability. The provisions of Subtitle C *prima facie* increase the risk of liability of those NRSROs that make false or misleading statements. Section 18(a) of the *Securities Exchange Act 1934*[183] mentions the liability for misleading statements. The amendments of rule, discussed below, reflect the determination of Congress that NRSROs "perform evaluative and analytical services on behalf of clients".[184] Subtitle C specifically exposes NRSROs to liability resulting from both public and private litigation because it removes the restriction on private actions against NRSROs,[185] lowers certain pleading requirements and essentially grants investors the right to seek damages stemming from an NRSRO credit rating. Subtitle C also makes several other changes. Most importantly, it rescinds the safe harbour provided under Section 21E of the *Securities Exchange Act* that protects NRSROs from potential SEC enforcement action for statements made regarding credit ratings and repeals Rule 436 (g) under the Securities Act, which excluded NRSRO ratings from being considered part of a company's registration statement under the Securities Act. Previously, NRSROs were shielded from SEC enforcement action for false statements and/or omissions made by an "expert" under Sections 7 and 11 of the Securities Act.

The fear of being liable to pay damages may lead NRSROs to refuse to allow its ratings to be included in an SEC filing,[186] thus defeating the provision of the Act. The Act requires, in a defence against a Section 11 claim, that a CRA show that it had reasonable grounds to believe, and did in fact believe, that the included credit rating was accurate.[187] Although Subtitle C creates a new requirement for NRSROs to act as a whistleblower and creates a duty to report to the appropriate law enforcement agencies or regulatory authorities any credible information received from a third party alleging that an issuer of rated securities has violated or is

---

[182] Section 931 (4) Subtitle C.

[183] "*Securities Exchange Act of 1934*". http://www.sec.gov/about/laws/sea34.pdf.

[184] Section 931 (2) and (3) of the Dodd-Frank Act. See also Moynihan et al. (2010).

[185] See accountability under Section 15E (m) of the *Securities Exchange Act 1934*.

[186] Moynihan et al. (2010).

[187] Fernicola and Goldstein (2010), p. 74–75.

violating the law, no such reported cases have emerged. The risk of potential liability that NRSROs face is through the addition of penalties that the SEC may impose and the elimination of a potential defence to an SEC antifraud action based on the SEC's prohibition against regulating the substance of credit ratings. For public deals that include an NRSRO's credit ratings in the public offering registration statements with the consent of an NRSRO, the Dodd-Frank also creates potential securities law liability when an NRSRO acts as an expert. Most importantly, the Act also provides for a private right of action against an NRSRO for securities law violations. The basis is on the NRSRO's failure either to conduct a reasonable investigation of the rated security with respect to the factual elements it relied upon in its methodology for evaluating credit risk or to obtain reasonable verification of such factual elements from other sources it considered competent and that were independent of the issuer and underwriter.

The goal of these provisions is to act as a deterrent, thus promoting more accurate credit ratings based on the accountability on the part of CRAs. The objection relates to causing some potentially undesirable effect. Stafford et al's[188] view is that the expanded liability and associated increased litigation risks that NRSROs will be facing will probably increase their business costs. It might also lead to the issuance of more transactions through private placements. In the absence of competition, some or all of the increased costs incurred by the CRAs in connection with the Dodd-Frank may have to be borne by issuers, thus increasing their costs of issuing rated securities as the ultimate borrowers.

4.3.5.4 Securities Exchange Act 1934

Dodd-Frank confirms the availability of civil remedies against CRAs by specifically making the enforcement and penalty provisions of the Exchange Act applicable to CRAs in the same manner as the provisions are currently applied to registered public accountants and securities analysts. Most importantly, Dodd-Frank excludes credit ratings from the protection of the safe harbour provisions for forward-looking statements of the *Private Securities Litigation Reform Act of 1995*. Dodd-Frank alters the pleading standards implemented by the *Reform Act of 1995* as applied to actions for money damages against the CRAs. In the context of credit ratings, the courts require plaintiffs to plead that the rating agency did not genuinely believe its opinions regarding credit quality or that the opinions lacked a basis in fact.

Plaintiffs are often unable to satisfy this pleading burden in actions against the rating agencies. Under the Act, a pleading against a rating agency would satisfy the state-of-mind requirement if it alleges facts with particularity, giving rise to a strong inference that the rating agency knowingly or recklessly failed to conduct a reasonable investigation of the factual elements relied upon in evaluating the credit

---

[188] Stafford et al. (2010).

risk of the rated security. If the increased risk of liability does prevent CRAs from issuing ratings for new products for which they have no expertise, then this is a step in the right direction. However, in reality, as the new entrant may not be able to satisfy stringent conditions to get NRSRO status, therefore, the congressional goal of fostering greater market competition based on rating accuracy is unachievable.

4.3.5.5 Sole Reliance on Credit Ratings[189]

Prior to the introduction of Dodd-Frank, institutional investors (including banks, insurers and money market funds) had permission to rely solely on credit ratings when making certain investment decisions. Dodd-Frank seeks to compel such investors to conduct their own due diligence by carrying out an independent investigation into the multiple factors that influence the risk profile of a security in order to diminish their reliance on credit ratings. This is done by replacing references to credit ratings in certain federal laws with a requirement that such investors consider the creditworthiness of a security, thus encouraging investors to consider factors beyond the security's credit rating. In addition, every federal agency is required to study regulation it has issued that requires the assessment of creditworthiness or the use of credit ratings and to replace such references to credit ratings with references to the broader standards of creditworthiness where the agency determines such changes are appropriate. The net effect is that it thrusts extra responsibility on the shoulders of investors who are required to carry out their own diligence and releases the CRAs from conducting investigation into the multiple factors that influences the risk profile of a security. Flight is not in favour of CRAs satisfying a due diligence exercise because he sees the regulation shifting "the focus of the rating agency from producing accurate investment analysis information to satisfying bureaucratic requirements in order to maintain their market dominance".[190]

4.3.5.6 Transparency Based on Disclosure

Subtitle C of Dodd-Frank includes a number of new disclosure requirements designed to make the process used by CRAs more transparent.[191] The disclosure requirements in force are as follows:

(a) NRSROs are required to disclose and publish their "ratings track record" so that "users of credit ratings [may] evaluate the accuracy of ratings and compare the performance of ratings by different [NRSROs]". This record

[189] Fernicola and Goldstein (2010).

[190] Fight (2003).

[191] For a brief summary of this, see DechertOnPoint, "Dodd-Frank Measures Affecting Credit Rating Agencies", Issue 35 (August 2010).

will present "performance information over a range of years and for a variety of types of credit ratings" that is "clear and informative for investors having a wide range of sophistication who use or might use credit ratings".[192]

(b) Any credit rating issued by an NRSRO has to be accompanied by an attestation "affirming that no part of the rating was influenced by any other business activities, that the rating was based solely on the merits of the instruments being rated, and that such rating was independent of the risks and merits of the instrument".[193]

(c) In keeping with rules to be prescribed by the SEC regarding "the procedures and methodologies, including qualitative and quantitative data and models, NRSROs will be required to disclose to the users of credit ratings: (i) the version of a procedure or methodology used with respect to a particular rating; (ii) when a material change is made to a procedure or methodology, and the likelihood that such change will result in a change to current credit ratings; and (iii) any significant error identified in a procedure or methodology that may result in credit rating actions".[194]

(d) NRSROs must publish with the issuance of each credit rating detailed information, including (i) the main assumptions and principles underlying the procedures and methodologies used to determine the credit rating; (ii) the data upon which the credit rating is based and the reliability of that data; (iii) the existence of conflicts of interest, potential limitations and risks related to the credit rating; and (iv) the use, if any, of third-party research and due diligence. This disclosure is intended to help investors and other users of credit ratings to "better understand credit ratings in each class of credit rating issued" by the NRSRO and must be presented in a format that is "easy to use and helpful for users of credit ratings".[195]

(e) With respect to their unique credit rating symbols, NRSROs must establish, maintain and enforce written policies and procedures (i) clearly defining and disclosing the meaning of all symbols and (ii) mandating the consistent application of a symbol across all types of securities and money market instruments for which the symbol is used.[196]

In addition, there is greater disclosure of credit ratings and credit rating methodology and procedures, disclosure of certain third-party information used in the credit rating process and the use of universal symbols for credit ratings. Dodd-Frank further requires each NRSRO to ensure that (1) its credit rating procedures comply with standards approved by its senior credit officer or board of directors, (2) material changes to credit rating procedures and methodologies are applied consistently to

[192] *Dodd-Frank Act* S932 (q)(1)(2)(A)(B) at 1898.

[193] S932 (q) (1)(2) and (F) at 1898.

[194] S932 (q) (3)(A)(B)and (C) at 1879.

[195] S932 (s) (1)(A)(i)(ii) and (iii) pp. 1879–1880.

[196] S938 (a) (2) and (3) at 1885.

all credit rating and (3) credit rating users are notified of any such changes. NRSROs will be required to disclose publicly their initial ratings and any changes to such ratings.[197]

The intention of transparency is to benefit investors. It will enable the investors to evaluate easily the accuracy of credit ratings, as CRAs have to stipulate the processes used by them in arriving at credit ratings. Investors will be able to compare accuracy with the ratings performance by other NRSROs that are also required to consider information received from credible outside sources when determining credit ratings. Investors had to cope with credit ratings issued by CRAs based on inconsistency and difficulty in understanding the symbols used. To redress this problem, Dodd-Frank requires each NRSRO to define clearly and disclose the meaning of any symbols used in connection with its credit ratings. Each symbol used by NRSROs to denote a credit rating has to be consistent with respect to all securities for which that symbol is used. However, NRSROs may use different symbols, designations or highlighters to identify ratings for different types of securities.

The SEC, on its part, is required to conduct a study regarding the feasibility and desirability of creating standardised credit rating terminology across CRAs and across asset classes. Based on its study, the SEC decided against standardisation as it felt that standardisation *per se* would not lead to higher levels of accountability, transparency and competition in the CRA industry, and rather it would be better to focus on the rulemaking initiatives mandated under Dodd-Frank.[198] The disclosure requirement is to help busy investors make an informed choice and enable them to decide for themselves whether they should invest in a particular security or not. Dodd-Frank was intended to promote increased transparency by incentivising the CRAs to maintain a vigorous credit rating process. To promote transparency, the CRAs have to implement several requirements, mentioned above, which is a step in the right direction.

4.3.5.7 Credit Rating Process Modification[199]

Section C of Dodd-Frank imposes new rules relating to credit rating procedures and methodologies. To increase transparency in the ratings process, CRAs will be required to use a standardised form and publicly disclose their rating methodology, a description of issuer data considered in the rating process and any additional information that the SEC may require.[200] To facilitate comparisons among rating agencies, each agency will be required periodically to disclose information demonstrating, in hindsight, the degree of accuracy of its prior credit ratings. To

[197] S938 (r)(A) and (C) at 1879.

[198] SEC (2012), pp. 2–5.

[199] Fernicola and Goldstein (2010).

[200] *Dodd Frank Act* (s) (2) (A) and (B) at 1880.

broaden the scope of information considered in determining credit ratings, the CRAs have to consider credible and significant information from sources other than the issuer.[201]

At one time, the securitisation market provided trillions of dollars of liquidity to virtually every sector of the economy. However, during the financial crisis, ABS investors suffered significant losses, causing the market for securitisation to rapidly decline.[202]

Dodd-Frank also requires the SEC to study issues relating to the credit rating process for structured finance products.[203] SEC adopted new rules related to representations and warranties in asset-backed securities offerings. The final rules enacted require (a) securitisers of asset-backed securities to disclose fulfilled and unfulfilled repurchase requests and (b) for NRSROs to include information regarding the representations, warranties and enforcement mechanisms available to investors in an asset-backed securities.[204] The rational measures for these new rules are designed to help revitalise the important asset-backed securities market by encouraging better disclosure for investors.[205]

In order to address the so-called rating shopping by issuers and underwriters of such products, the SEC has been authorised to establish a mechanism to change the initial selection of rating agency but decided against it and instead preferred to adopt measures intended to strengthen the integrity and to improve the transparency of credit ratings.[206] Changing the initial selection of rating agency would have denied the corporate issuers the opportunity to select the CRA of their choice, which for large corporate issues is normally centred on the Big Three.

4.3.5.8 Elimination of Automatic Regulation Fair Disclosure (FD) Exemption[207]

The Dodd-Frank removes an existing blanket exemption from Regulation FD for information provided to rating agencies[208] as, in particular, selective disclosure to equity analysts was widely perceived as market abuse.[209] The goal was to eliminate selective disclosure to a few privileged interested parties, and there was a need to

---

[201] Dodd Frank Act (s) (A) (iv) (I) (II) and (v) at 1880.

[202] M. L. Schapiro quoted in "SEC Approves New Rules Regulating Asset-Backed Securities" (20 January 2011) http://www.sec.gov/news/press/2011/2011-18.htm.

[203] Section 943 at 1897.

[204] SEC, "Disclosure for Asset-Backed Securities Required by Section 943 of The Dodd-Frank Wall Street Reform and Consumer Protection Act" (28 March 2011). http://www.sec.gov/rules/final/2011/33-9175.pdf.

[205] H. L. Schapiro (2011), note 204.

[206] "SEC Proposes Rules to Increase Transparency and Improve Integrity of Credit Ratings" (18 May 2011). http://www.sec.gov/news/press/2011/2011-113.htm.

[207] Fernicola and Goldstein (2010).

[208] Section 939B of Dodd-Frank. See Fernicola and Kanter (2010), para 2.

[209] Jorion et al. (2005), p. 309.

create a more even playing field for all investors. The introduction of Regulation FD is seen as controversial because "it would lead to fewer disclosures and lower the quality of analyst forecasts, and thus dramatically impoverish the information environment".[210] Companies can decide to compensate the effect of Regulation FD by increasing their public disclosures, and equity analysts can offset the loss of selective disclosure by privately searching for additional information. [211]

Regulation FD requires that material non-public information made available by or on behalf of an issuer to certain defined parties, including brokers, dealers, investment advisers, institutional investment managers, investment companies, certain persons associated with the foregoing and the holders of the issuer's securities (each a "Covered Recipient"), must also be made available to the public.[212] Since CRAs are not within these enumerated classes, and particularly since Fitch does not engage in the trading of securities as its business, Fitch does not believe that Regulation FD would prohibit selective disclosure of information by an issuer to Fitch.[213] For those CRAs deemed as Covered Recipient, Regulation FD applies to information that CRAs receive from issuers. When a CRA is as good as acting as an agent of the issuer and further thought to have disclosed non-public issuer information to a Covered Recipient on the issuer's behalf, obligation under Regulation FD is triggered.[214] However, Fitch believes that the removal of the rating agency exemption in Regulation FD does not diminish Fitch's right to receive material non-public information of the issuer and does not believe that CRAs "are within the scope of Regulation FD's prohibition".[215]

The question is whether such contractual protections can be effective in view of the Act's increased disclosure requirements related to credit ratings and the credit rating process or, in the case of certain structured finance products, where disclosure of non-public information is required to other rating agencies.[216] In light of the removal of the blanket Regulation FD exemption, issuers and underwriters seeking to avoid a Regulation FD disclosure requirement will need to evaluate carefully whether an exemption from Regulation FD applies prior to furnishing sensitive information to a CRA.

---

[210] Ibid.

[211] Ibid.

[212] Quinlivan (2010).

[213] Fitch Releases Market Letter with Perspectives on Implementing Dodd-Frank Act (23 July 2010).

[214] "Repeal of Credit Ratings Agency Exemption from Regulation FD" (11 October 2010). http://www.gibsondunn.com/publications/pages/RepealOfCreditRatingsAgencyExemptionFromRegFD.aspx.

[215] See Fitch Releases Market Letter with Perspectives on Implementing Dodd-Frank Act (23 July 2010).

[216] Rule 17g-5 (a) (3) of the *Securities Exchange Act 1934*.

The SEC requires each NRSRO to include and disclose on a prescribed form important information, which should accompany each publication of a credit rating, be easy to use, comparable across security type and readily available to credit rating users, including investors.[217] The form requires CRAs to include and disclose important information.[218] Possibly what these requirements do is to make a CRA seriously think through the rating process, and the intended result is conferring correct ratings.[219]

4.3.5.9 The SEC's Rules

Information disclosure is the bedrock for securities investors to make an informed investment decision.[220] As of mid-2013, the Commission has put in place "an entirely new regulatory regime designed to bring greater transparency and access to the securities-based swaps market, [and] adopted rules that will result in increased oversight and transparency around hedge funds and other private fund advisers".[221] It also "established a whistle-blower program which offers incentives for individuals with information regarding securities law violations to come forward".[222] The SEC has to prescribe rules requiring NRSROs to ensure that credit ratings are determined using procedures and methodologies that are approved by the board of the NRSRO, in accordance with the NRSRO's policies and procedures. NRSROs are to ensure consistent application of the material changes to credit rating procedures and methodologies, as applicable, within a reasonable period and to disclose the reasons for the change to the public. NRSROs have to notify credit rating users of the version of a procedure or methodology used to determine a particular rating when certain events occur. The events are material change to a procedure, identification of an error and the likelihood that a material change in procedure will result in a rating change. The SEC is required to issue rules designed to ensure that persons employed by an NRSRO to perform credit ratings meet standards of training, experience and competence necessary to produce accurate ratings and are tested for knowledge of the credit rating process. The SEC has proposed a series of rules designed to improve the practices of CRAs, most importantly limiting "the conflicts that may arise when NRSROs rely on client payments to drive profits and rules to monitor rating agency employees who move to new positions with rated entities".[223] The SEC has established fines and other penalties applicable to NRSROs violating the provisions of Section 15E.

---

[217] "Dodd-Frank Wall Street Reform and Consumer Protection Act: Credit Rating Agency Provisions", *Financial Markets Alert.*

[218] Section 939 (g) (3)(A) of the *Dodd-Frank Act 2010.*

[219] Section 939 (g) (3) (B) in Ibid.

[220] SEC.

[221] SEC (2013).

[222] Ibid.

[223] Ibid.

4.3.5.10 Establishment of Office of Credit Ratings (OCR)

Subtitle C of the Dodd-Frank requires the SEC to establish a new Office of Credit Ratings (OCR)[224] with the stated purposes of protecting the users of credit ratings, promoting accuracy in credit ratings and ensuring that ratings issued are free from conflicts of interest. The task of the OCR relates to the administration of SEC rules covering the credit ratings determination practices of NRSROs, promoting the accuracy of NRSRO credit ratings and ensuring that credit ratings issued by NRSROs are devoid of any conflicts of interest. The OCR is required to audit each NRSRO annually, make its inspection reports publicly available and publish its report on its essential findings of each annual NRSRO review.[225]

4.3.5.11 Examinations

The OCR will be required to conduct examinations of NRSROs at least annually to review management of conflicts of interest, internal controls, governance and implementation of its policies, procedures and rating methodologies. Most importantly, Subtitle C gives the SEC broad rulemaking, examination and enforcement authority, significantly augmenting the SEC's existing regulatory authority with respect to NRSROs. The SEC board has to issue rules to prevent "the sales and marketing considerations"[226] of an NRSRO from influencing its production of credit ratings. The SEC board has power temporarily or permanently to revoke an NRSRO's registration with respect to a class or subclass of securities if it is incapable of consistently producing credit ratings with integrity. The intention of the above measures is to improve the accuracy of credit ratings and in addition requires examination of CRAs' rectification of conflicts of interest affecting credit rating decisions. It is submitted that assuming the primarily flawed analytical models or errors in judgment caused the inaccuracy of credit ratings, simply rectifying them may not play much of a role in improving credit ratings accuracy.

4.3.5.12 Impact on Existing Federal Securities Laws

Notably, Subtitle C removes a wide variety of statutory references to credit ratings, CRAs and NRSROs and, in many cases, requires the development of new standards to evaluate creditworthiness. These amendments affect the *Federal Deposit Insurance Act*, the *National Bank Act*, the *Federal Housing Enterprises Financial Safety and Soundness Act*, certain World Bank statutory provisions, the *Securities Exchange Act* and the *Investment Company Act*.[227] The amendments to the

[224] Sec 932 (p) (1) of *Dodd-Frank Act*.

[225] Section (p) (1) (3) (A) of *Dodd-Frank Act*. See also Moynihan et al. (2010).

[226] Ibid.

[227] As per Sec. 939 of the *Dodd-Frank Act*.

Securities Exchange Act strike at the rating requirement included in the definitions of "mortgage related security" and "small business related security" and require that these securities meet creditworthiness standards established by the SEC. Similarly, the provision affecting Section 6(a) (5) of the *Investment Company Act 1940*, which provided certain exemptions for state-regulated companies that do not issue redeemable securities, has to replace NRSROs' references to standards of creditworthiness to be adopted by the SEC. These provisions of the Dodd-Frank are similar to regulatory developments, such as the SEC's 7 April 2010 proposal to remove references to credit ratings from Rule 144A under the *Securities Act*.

Under Dodd-Frank, every federal agency is to review the existing reliance and assessment of the creditworthiness of a security or money market instrument and to develop their own standards of creditworthiness[228] by using their own discretion. There is no guidance on what amounts to a reasonable creditworthiness standard, and there is a need to avoid vague standards of reasonableness. In relation to a particular security, it ought to be what a reasonable person would deem creditworthy under the circumstances regulated by the given law.[229]

Unlike the goals of Congress with Subtitle C, the SEC's July 2008 proposal and November 2009 amendments were "designed to address concerns that references to NRSRO ratings in [SEC] rules may have contributed to an undue reliance on those ratings by market participants".[230] Subtitle C does not explicitly affect the amendments to the rules governing money market funds under the *Investment Company Act 1940*[231] that the SEC adopted on 23 February 2011 in response to the extreme turbulence experienced by the money fund sector in 2007 and 2008.

4.3.6 SEC's Studies

4.3.6.1 Section 939F

The responsibility rests on the SEC to carry out a 2-year study and subsequent rulemaking on assigned credit ratings. Areas include (1) the credit rating process for structured finance products (i.e., asset-backed securities) "and the conflicts of interest associated with the issuer-pay and the subscriber-pay models" and (2) "the feasibility of establishing a system in which a public or private utility or a self-regulatory organization assigns [NRSROs] to determine the credit ratings of structured finance products".[232] The SEC study represents a compromise struck

[228] SEC, "Credit Rating Agencies", http://www.sec.gov/spotlight/dodd-frank/creditratingagencies.shtml.

[229] Moynihan et al. (2010).

[230] "Nationally Recognized Statistical Rating Organizations (NRSROs)", https://www.sec.gov/divisions/marketreg/ratingagency.htm.

[231] Pub.L. 76–768.

[232] Section 939F of Subtitle C of Dodd-Frank.

between the sponsors of the Dodd-Frank and the proposed Franken Amendment. "The Franken Amendment to the Dodd-Frank ... proposes creating a board, overseen by the SEC, which will assign rating agencies to provide initial ratings for structured debt securities".[233] Dodd-Frank would have amended the *Securities Exchange Act* to require that initial structured finance product credit ratings are determined by a centralised Credit Rating Agency Board, thus preventing seekers of credit ratings from choosing the ratings issuer and assigning pre-qualified NRSROs on a rotating basis. Dodd-Frank mandates that upon completion of the study, the SEC must adopt rules to establish the system of assigning initial credit ratings to structured finance products and to implement the Franken Amendment "unless the Commission determines that an alternative system would better serve the public interest and the protection of investors".[234]

4.3.6.2 Asset-Backed Securities (Structured Finance Products)

The focus of special attention was on asset-backed structured finance products as having caused the crisis in the first place. The SEC is required to create new disclosure rules, as well as "a new mechanism to prevent issuers of asset-backed securities from picking the agency they think will give the highest credit rating, after conducting a study and after submission of the report to Congress".[235]

Further rules were required in that within 180 days of the enactment of Dodd-Frank, the SEC is to release, among many others, rules requiring CRAs to undertake certain tasks. It includes each Asset-Backed Securities rating to issue a report describing (1) the representations, warranties and enforcement mechanisms related to the rating and (2) how the representations, warranties and enforcement mechanisms may differ from those related to the credit ratings of similar securities.[236] In respect to (2), the SEC adopted new rules relating to representations and warranties in asset-backed securities offerings, including the new Rule 17g-7, which requires NRSROs to include information regarding the representations, warranties and enforcement mechanisms available to investors in any report accompanying a credit rating for an offering of asset-backed securities.[237]

Dodd-Frank requires the SEC to conduct a study on the credit ratings process, especially for structured finance products, and the conflicts of interest associated with issuer-pay and subscriber-pay models, ways to measure the accuracy of credit ratings and alternative ways of NRSROs charging their fees that would create

[233] Bansal (2013).

[234] Section 939F.

[235] Subtitle D of Title IX of Dodd-Frank Act—"Improvements to the Asset-Backed Securitization Process".

[236] Section 943 of the Dodd-Frank Act.

[237] SEC, "Annual Reports of NRSROs" (March 2012) at 5. https://www.sec.gov/divisions/marketreg/ratingagency/nrsroannrep0312.pdf.

greater incentives for accurate credit ratings. Increased liability would act as a deterrent to CRAs, and it would compensate the investors for losses sustained from negligent credit ratings. However, CRAs may refuse to rate those debt instruments that they perceive might make them liable, thus defeating the purpose of creating increased liability.

The explicit instruction to the SEC is to evaluate the feasibility of establishing a public or private utility or self-regulating organisation that would select the NRSROs to rate structured finance transactions, including assessing appropriate methods for determining and paying fees to NRSROs. Likewise, several questions arise like whether such a system would create a moral hazard, whether there are constitutional issues associated with such a system and the means to determine the accuracy of credit ratings. After completion of this study, the SEC has to decide whether to establish such a system for assigning NRSROs to determine the initial credit ratings of structured finance products. One possible option was to introduce a different rule with regard to rating structured finance products through which the SEC should determine and appoint the NRSRO of their choice to carry out this task, thus denying issuers the freedom to appoint the NRSRO of their own choice and to negotiate an appropriate fee.

Stafford et al. sees that the drawback of the Dodd-Frank is in not providing much guidance as to how such a governmental or quasi-governmental entity would assign NRSROs to transactions and how it would assess various factors that may enter into the decision to select a credit rating agency for any individual transaction. [238] These factors are investor preference, the workload of each NRSRO and its capacity to handle the deal flow, an NRSRO's expertise with respect to a complicated or specialised security class and the fees charged by an NRSRO to rate a transaction.[239]

4.3.6.3 Studies Based on NRSROs

In addition to the rule and regulation changes, Subtitle C requires the SEC to undertake the following studies, each of which may result in further rulemaking and other developments affecting the function and role of credit ratings. Such important studies relate to strengthening credit rating independence,[240] alternative means for compensating NRSROs to create incentives to provide ratings that are more accurate[241] and the creation of an independent professional analyst organisation.[242]

[238] Stafford et al. (2010).

[239] Ibid.

[240] *Dodd-Frank Act 2010*. Sec. 939C.

[241] *Dodd-Frank Act 2010* Sec. 939D.

[242] *Dodd-Frank Act 2010*.Sec. 939C.

4.3.6.4 Costs, Regulatory Burden and Uncertainty

Dodd-Frank had created 13 new regulatory agencies but eliminated only one: the Office of Thrift Supervision.[243] The Congressional Budget Office estimated that it would cost US $2.9 billion over the next 5 years to implement Dodd-Frank,[244] whereas others claim that there could be up to US $1 trillion in broader economic costs resulting from the Act.[245] Dodd-Frank further creates more than 2,600 new positions at regulatory agencies. Some agencies, like the Office of Financial Research, have no limitations on their budgets or staffs.[246]

The SEC shares the US Commodity Future Trading Committee's responsibility for promulgating new derivative rules.[247] The Government Accountability Office (GAO) had released a study in early July 2011 stating that the US regulators do not yet know enough about Wall Street's proprietary trading to police it effectively,[248] thus adding a saga to Dodd-Frank. The concern raised by the House of Republicans relates to the new requirements under Dodd-Frank, which will put American companies at a competitive disadvantage compared to foreign firms because "neither European nor Asian regulators or legislators will establish similar proprietary trading restrictions that the Dodd-Frank Act [has] imposed on U.S. financial institutions".[249] "There is still little understanding of when most of Dodd-Frank's extensive provisions will actually be in place and how they might affect the nation's financial systems and [the] economy".[250] While Congress continues to debate Dodd-Frank's costs and regulatory deadlines, a concern is that not providing funding will expose the US economy to a cycle of collapse and crises, which will have devastating repercussions.[251]

---

[243] Boggs et al. (2011), p. 53. http://www.hblr.org/wp-content/uploads/2011/07/Boggs-Foxman-Nahill-Growing-Pains.pdf.

[244] Press Release, Representative Barney Frank (2011).

[245] Indiviglio (2010).

[246] House Financial Services Committee.

[247] Press Release, Securities and Exchange Commission (2011).

[248] U.S. Government Accountability Office (2011).

[249] S. Bachus (House Financial Services Committee Chairman) referred to GAO, quoted by Schroeder (2011).

[250] Boggs et al. (2011).

[251] M. Miller (the U.S. Treasury Department's Assistant Secretary for Financial Markets) quoted by Hopkins and Katz (2011).

4.3.7 Expert Liability and Legal Defences

4.3.7.1 Expert Liability

The unprecedented events of the last few years have changed the expectations for CRAs, and they will have to make a number of changes to their rating process to address these expectations and to act in compliance with Dodd-Frank. Historically, the *Securities Act 1933* considered CRAs as experts since ratings are inherently forward looking and embody assumptions and predictions about future events that by their nature cannot be verified as facts. The new law rescinds Rule 436 (g), thus exposing CRAs to expert liability if they consent to be named in registration statements and related prospectuses. Under Dodd-Frank, there is a lower pleading requirement for claimants' lawsuits, both in the government and private, against CRAs. Dodd-Frank also modifies the ability of CRAs to receive certain information of a material, non-public nature from issuers. The question is whether the CRAs will consent to the use of its ratings in registration statements in relation to prospectuses. While Fitch will continue to publish credit ratings and research, it would not give consent to those parties who want to include their credit ratings in a prospectus and registration statement, at least for the time being, given the potential consequences of liability.[252] While AM Best believes that many of the provisions directed toward CRA reform will benefit the capital markets as a whole, its concern is that "the new law presents a host of new requirements and legal uncertainties" that AM Best as a CRA has to address.[253]

4.3.7.2 Litigation Defences

In summary, several sections of Dodd-Frank address the potential litigation defences of NRSROs,[254] which have the potential to exonerate CRAs from liability, by taking the following steps:

(a) *Removed Antifraud Defence*: The Exchange Act provisions, which prohibit the regulation of the substance of a rating, are not a defence to antifraud liability.
(b) *Expert Liability*: NRSROs may now be liable under Section 11 of the Securities Act. Dodd-Frank overrides Rule 436, which has exempted the organisations as part of a registration statement. Accordingly, for a report to be included in a registration statement, NRSROs should consent to it.
(c) *Regulation FD*: The SEC is required to remove the exemption for CRAs under Regulation FD. The Act also requires all federal agencies to review and

[252] A. M. Best (2010).
[253] Ibid.
[254] Gorman (2010).

modify regulations to remove references or reliance on credit ratings and substitute an alternative standard of creditworthiness.

(d) *Liability*: Dodd-Frank specifies that the statements made by NRSROs are subject to liability similar to that of accounting firms and securities analysts under the federal securities laws. Investors can bring private rights of actions against agencies. Statements made by the rating agencies are not forward-looking statements.

(e) *State of Mind*: To establish liability, it is sufficient to state facts with particularity, which gives rise to a strong inference that rating agencies that acted knowingly or recklessly failed to conduct a reasonable investigation.

4.3.7.3 Reforms Introduced by Dodd-Frank

Dealing with the subject of regulation, in summary Dodd-Frank has also established important rules. They relate to the following:

(a) Disclosure: NRSROs must disclose their rating methodologies, third-party due diligence efforts and ratings record of accomplishment.

(b) Independent Information: NRSROs must consider information that comes to their attention from sources other than the organisations they rate.

(c) Conflicts of Interest: NRSROs must have compliance officers who cannot participate in the ratings, methodologies or sales and whose compensation is not dependent upon financial performance. It also establishes guidelines for disclosure and investigation when key NRSRO employees leave to work for other clients and requires separating ratings from sales and marketing functions within NRSROs.

(d) Right to Deregister: The SEC has the authority to deregister an NRSRO for bad ratings over time or for not having adequate financial and managerial resources consistently to produce credit ratings with integrity.[255]

(e) Education: Rating analysts are required to pass qualifying exams and partake in continuing education.

(f) Rating Requirements: There must be a reduction in the instances in which an NRSRO rating is required.

(g) Independent Boards: At least half of the members of an NRSRO board are required to be independent.[256] The net effect of the rules promulgated appears to ensure that CRAs do issue reliable ratings.

[255] *Dodd Frank Act* s 932 (2) at 1874.

[256] Dragan et al. (2010).

4.4 Assessment

4.4.1 Public Oversight and Accountability

A view favouring Dodd-Frank regulation postulates that it increases transparency (particularly in derivatives markets), creates a new Consumer Financial Protection Bureau,[257] improves corporate governance, increases capital requirements for banks, deters large financial institutions from providing incentives for employees to take undue risks and gives the government the ability to take failed investment institutions into receivership. It is similar to the Federal Deposit Insurance Corporation's authority regarding commercial banks[258]:

> [Dodd-Frank] creates a bureau to protect consumers from financial fraud, cuts fees banks charge for debit-card use, and sets up a means for the government to better supervise the nation's largest financial institutions to avoid expensive and catastrophic failures. And it calls public exchanges on which derivatives and other complex financial instruments are traded.[259]

> [Dodd-Frank not only] created a council of federal regulators, led by the Treasury secretary, to coordinate the detection of risks to the financial system ... [but also] created a powerful new regulator, appointed by the president, to protect consumers of financial products, which will be housed in the Federal Reserve.[260]

Congress, by recognising that CRAs play a gatekeeper role in the debt market similar to securities analysts,[261] justified the introduction of public oversight and accountability. However, a fundamental question that remains is accountability to whom. The present issuers-pay model means CRAs are in a contractual relationship with the issuers and, therefore, they, and not investors, have recourse to any breach of oversight. Although investors have no direct protection, it seems the regulations introduced would protect investors indirectly by ensuring that CRAs (including NRSROs) act responsibly in the problematic areas identified by Congress.

---

[257] The CFPB consolidates most Federal consumer financial protection authority in one place. The consumer bureau is focused on one goal: watching out for American consumers in the market for consumer financial products and services. http://www.consumerfinance.gov/the-bureau/creatingthebureau/.

[258] Report: Wall Street's Opposition to Dodd-Frank Reforms Echoes Its Resistance to New Deal Financial Safeguards (2011).

[259] *The New York Times* (4 November 2011). http://topics.nytimes.com/topics/reference/timestopics/subjects/c/credit_crisis/financial_regulatory_reform/index.html?inline=nyt-classifier.

[260] Ibid.

[261] Section 931 (3) of the *Dodd-Frank Act*.

4.4.1.1 Conflicts of Interest

With the change from the investors-pay to issuers-pay model in 1970, the issue of conflict of interest has become problematic, and the only way regulations can cure this is by imposing liability on CRAs. In its absence, it "remains to be seen whether or not the SEC's expanded role in policing NRSROs will do much, if anything to curb the conflicts of interest that fuelled the financial crisis".[262] The concern of Congress was to improve the regulation of CRAs as, *inter alia*, inaccurate ratings related to structured finance products (e.g., mortgages). It then played a significant role in the financial meltdown, and this required special attention. It cannot be said that ratings were inaccurate when issued. The CRAs, along with everyone else, failed to predict the freezing of the bond markets. The recourse chosen by Congress was to enact legislation that reduces reliance on credit ratings and at the same time adopt measures designed to increase the quality and integrity of credit ratings. In spite of the SEC's expanded role in policing NRSROs, it is doubtful if it will do much to curb the conflicts of interest that were instrumental in the financial crisis.[263]

4.4.1.2 Enforcement by the SEC

The broad, three-part mission of the SEC has been to protect investors; maintain fair, orderly and efficient markets; and facilitate capital formation. The breadth of the SEC's jurisdiction is vast.[264] A highly complex and dispersed marketplace requires intelligent and satisfactory regulation. The SEC needs to provide expert oversight cost efficiently and without undermining market volatility. Undoubtedly, there is a need to assist CRAs in keeping a better pace with the markets. In monitoring and regulating CRAs, the SEC needs to foresee and anticipate unexpected issues that may arise.[265]

The Commission needs to further strengthen the enforcement and examination functions of the SEC. Investor confidence and the integrity of the US financial markets require a strong enforcement of the securities laws in the form of sanctions that deter and punish wrongdoing and protect investors, both now and in the future. There is a need to improve compliance by regulating entities, preventing and detecting fraud, and monitoring market risks.[266] In the event of violation of federal securities laws, the SEC's enforcement division needs to investigate and bring in civil charges in federal district courts or in administrative proceedings as the case may be. Successful enforcement actions would result in sanctions, thus deterring

[262] Dragan et al. (2010).

[263] Dragan et al. (2010).

[264] See Testimony on Oversight of SEC by Chair White (Chair) (2013).

[265] Ibid.

[266] Ibid.

wrongdoing, protecting investors and resulting in penalties that when paid to the affected investors can compensate for their losses.

In Fiscal Year [FY] 2012, enforcement continued to perform at a high level, utilising its enhanced expertise and specialisation capabilities to file tough enforcement actions that sent a strong deterrent message in an increasingly complex and global securities market. In the aftermath of the financial crisis, the SEC obtained orders requiring the payment of US $3.1 billion in penalties and disgorgement in its filed enforcement actions in FY 2012, with a total of US $5.9 billion in penalties and disgorgement. [267]

4.4.2 Comments by Others

For Schwarcz,[268] Dodd-Frank fails meaningfully to address the danger of mixing politics and finance, as occurred before the financial crisis with the governmental pressure to securitise subprime mortgage loans to expand home ownership. Dodd-Frank also does not directly address the problem of overreliance on mathematical modelling by the CRAs. Dibadj submits that Dodd-Frank might contain some positive provisions; however, it ultimately fails to address the root causes of financial crises. Most importantly, Dodd-Frank does not adequately address any of the four facilitators in order to mitigate and avoid future disasters. The policymakers should, therefore, focus on remedying four pernicious facilitators to scandal: (1) the dissemination of information that is false or misleading, (2) the ability to abuse regulatory gaps, (3) the willingness to exploit credulous consumers and (4) the use of corporate size to privatise profits and socialise losses.[269] According to Bradford, the Act may reach a narrow goal of preventing a future crisis, but Congress's loftier ambition of reforming the financial industry will fail if left to the rules in the Act. [270] He suggests that the "[t]rue reformation of an industry that is so vital and central to everyday life will not come from a piece of legislation such as this. The concerns it seeks to address have been learned the hard way and the system will adapt without the legislation, for better or worse".[271]

On globalisation, Chaffee states "the Dodd-Frank Act is largely a twentieth century approach to regulating twenty-first century financial markets".[272] It has failed to address adequately the globalisation of financial markets that has occurred within the past few decades, and therefore it represents an incomplete vision for financial regulation. He sees a "need for harmonization and centralization of

---

[267] Testimony of White (2013).

[268] Schwarcz (2011–2012), p. 591 at 599.

[269] Dibadj (2011–2012), p. 79.

[270] Bradford (2011–2012), p. 290.

[271] Bradford (2011–2012), p. 290.

[272] Chaffee (2010–2011), pp. 1431–1433.

international securities regulation ... the need for a centralized global securities regulator ... [and] the need for an evolutionary approach to reforming international securities law".[273] The *Dodd-Frank Act* also fails adequately to address the new realities of the emerging global financial markets.[274] On a positive note, McNamara's view is that the "Dodd-Frank Act contains important reforms meant to reduce the likelihood of future ratings failure".[275] The Dodd-Frank does not regulate "the ratings process directly but instead relies on the traditional securities law strategies of disclosure and liability to incentivize the production of accurate ratings".[276]

4.4.3 Conclusions

The Reform Act partially tried to tackle the problem of conflicts of interest and provide transparency, objective standards and a reasonable approach to the regulations of CRAs and, most importantly, to ensure that CRAs acted responsibly and competently. Dodd-Frank, on the other hand, seeks to impose corporate governance guidelines, reduce conflicts of interest and improve the rating process through enhanced controls and greater transparency. Dodd-Frank also greatly expands the SEC's oversight and enforcement powers and seeks in theory to make it easier for investors to bring civil lawsuits against the rating agencies. In addition, the Dodd-Frank seeks to reduce reliance on ratings as a litmus test for credit quality in favour of broader standards that encompass multiple factors and credit criteria.[277] Although an indirect regulatory approach may not meet the approval of the critics of the CRAs, "It does however reflect the prevailing rule that the SEC may not regulate the substance of credit ratings and the practical limitations of legislators and regulators in this hyper-complex area".[278] The *Dodd Frank Act* contains more than 90 provisions that require SEC rulemaking and dozens of other provisions that give the SEC discretionary rulemaking authority. Of the mandatory rulemaking provisions, the SEC has proposed or adopted rules for about three-quarters.[279]

Implementation of existing government regulations more effectively is necessary. The statutory regulations introduced have vastly increased the government's power in ways that were unrelated to the recent crisis, and one view is that it may even encourage future crises rather than preventing them.[280] In truth, it is premature

[273] Ibid.
[274] Ibid.
[275] McNamara (2012), p. 665.
[276] Ibid.
[277] Fernicola and Goldstein (2010), p. 73.
[278] McNamara (2012), p. 665.
[279] SEC (2013).
[280] Taylor (2010).

to gauge the full impact of Dodd-Frank on CRAs and the market for structured finance products. The reason is that the SEC has yet to complete the remaining mandated studies in order to formulate rules and implement them, which would enable the public to make judgements on the successful workings of the rules and regulations contemplated by Dodd-Frank.[281] Some of the studies resulted in soliciting opinions and were based on the opinions received; the SEC has decided not to take any further action. The examples are regulation in relation to rating symbols and the compensation of CRAs. In addition, having critically examined the regulatory provisions of the two important US statutory provisions, their effective implementation is needed to ensure CRAs take on the responsibility of acting as a responsible gatekeeper, which will ensure ratings issued meet the reliability test. It is in the CRAs' own interest to act more responsibly in order to prevent the introduction of more regulations in the future. The same applies to the situation in the EU examined in the next chapter.

References

Aguilar, L. A. (2013, May 25). Addressing conflicts of interest in the credit ratings industry. http://www.sec.gov/News/Speech/Detail/Speech/1365171515642#.UhibRNLVAXI.

Akins, E. M., & Calabria, M. A. (2012). Regulation, market structure, and role of the credit rating agencies. *Policy Analysis, 704*, 1–35.

Bai, L. (2010). On regulating conflicts of interest in the credit rating industry. *NYU Journal of Legislation and Public Policy, 13*, 253.

Baker (Committee Chairman). (2005, June 29). Legislative solution for the rating agencies duopoly. http://www.access.gpo.gov/congress/house/pdf/109hrg/26274.pdf.

Baker, B., & Milbourn, T. (2010, November 3). *How did increased competition affect credit ratings?* (Working Paper). Harvard Business School. http://hbswk.hbs.edu/item/6517.html.

Bansal, M. (2013, May 26). Rating agency reform – An alternative for the Franken Amendment. http://seekingalpha.com/article/1461911-rating-agency-reform-an-alternative-for-the-franken-amendment.

Becker, B., & Milbourn, T. (2009, August 30). Why competition may not improve credit rating agencies. Harvard Business School. http://hbswk.hbs.edu/item/6260.html.

A. M. Best. (2010, July 23). Fitch express deep concerns over the impact of Dodd-Frank on the ratings game. http://www.reactionsnet.com/Article/2636997/AM-Best-Fitch-express-deep-concerns-over-the-impact-of-Dodd-Frank-on-the-ratings-game.html.

A. M. Best Company, Inc. (2011). Confidentiality, firewall, conflicts of interest, and securities trading and reporting policy. Policy C-5 (Revised 1 January 2011). http://www.ambest.com/nrsro/confidentialityfirewallconflictsofinterestandsecuritiestradingandreportpolicy_c-5.pdf.

Birger, J. (2008, August 6). The woman who called Wall Street's meltdown. *Fortune Magazine*. http://money.cnn.com/2008/08/04/magazines/fortune/whitney_feature.fortune/index.htm.

Boggs, J. C., Foxman, M., & Nahill, K. (2011). Dodd-Frank at one year: Growing pains. *Harvard Business Law Review Online, 2*, 52. http://www.hblr.org/?p=1614.

Bradford, A. (2011–2012). Is statutorily required that the buck stops here: Risk retention requirements in the Dodd-Frank Wall Street Reform and Consumer Protection Act. *DePaul Business & Commercial Law Journal, 10*, 267.

[281] Timothy et al.

Carnahan, I. (2005, January 26). AAA-rated oligopoly. *Forbes*. http://www.forbes.com/2005/01/26/cz_ic_0126beltway.html.

Carroll, B. (2005, September 26). Enron scandals spur proposed credit rating legislation. *The Legal Intelligencer*. http://securities.stanford.edu/news-archive/2005/20050926_Headline100915_Carroll.html.

Chaffee, E. C. (2010–2011). The Dodd-Frank Wall Street Reform and Consumer Protection Act: A failed vision for increasing consumer protection and heightening corporate responsibility in international financial transactions. *American University Law Review, 60*, 1431.

Clarke, S. (2013). *Insider dealing – Law and practice*. Oxford: OUP.

Cox, C. (2008, April 22). 'Testimony concerning oversight of nationally recognized statistical rating organizations' before the U.S. Senate Committee on Banking, Housing and Urban Affairs. http://www.sec.gov/news/testimony/2008/ts042208cc.htm.

Deb, P., & Murphy, G. (2009, November). Credit rating agencies: An alternative model (p. 5). http://personal.lse.ac.uk/debp/Papers/Ratings_Regulation.pdf.

Dibadj, R. (2011–2012). Dodd-Frank: Toward first principles? *Chapman Law Review, 15*, 79.

Dragan, G., Grossman, S., Rangnekar, A., & Yadav, N. (2010, November 29). Dodd-Frank and ratings agencies. http://picker.typepad.com/legal_infrastructure_of_b/2010/11/dodd-frank-and-ratings-agencies.html.

Dubow, B., & Monteiro, N. (2006). *FSA publishes measure of scale of market abuse* (FSA Occasional Paper 23).

Elkhoury, M. (2008, January). Credit rating agencies and their potential impact on developing countries. No. 186 (p. 4). http://unctad.org/en/Docs/osgdp20081_en.pdf.

ESMA. (2010, March 18). Credit Rating Agencies Annual Report 2012. Application of the Regulation (EC) No 1060/2009 as amended according to Article 21(5). http://www.esma.europa.eu/system/files/2013-308.pdf.

Fernicola, G. A., & Goldstein, J. B. (2010, July 9). "Credit Rating Agencies" *Skadden Commentary on the Dodd-Frank Act*. http://www.skadden.com/Index.cfm?contentID=51&itemID=2135.

Fernicola, G. A., & Kanter, S. J. (2010, October 1). SEC issues final rule release: Removal from regulation FD of the exemption for credit rating agencies. http://www.skadden.com/insights/sec-issues-final-rule-release-removal-regulation-fd-exemption-credit-rating-agencies.

Fight, A. (2003, July 25). Rating agencies and the use of credit ratings under the federal securities laws. Letter to SEC. http://www.sec.gov/rules/concept/s71203/aflight072503.htm.

Financial Times (2010, May 17). KPMG and PwC eye rating move. http://www.ft.com/cms/s/0/5ffc65b4-614c-11df-9bf0-00144feab49a.html#axzz2e11Uc6Z6.

Financial Stability Board. (2013, August 29). Credit rating agencies reducing reliance and strengthening oversight. Progress report to the St Petersburg G20 Summit. http://www.financialstabilityboard.org/publications/r_130829d.pdf.

Fitch Releases Market Letter with Perspectives on Implementing Dodd-Frank Act (23 July 2010). http://www.businesswire.com/news/home/20100723005925/en/Fitch-Releases-Market-Letter-Perspectives-Implementing-Dodd-Frank.

Gannon, J. T. Jr. (2011–2012). Let's help the credit rating agencies get it right: A simple way to alleviate a flawed industry model. *Annual Review of Banking & Financial Law, 31*(1), 1015–1051.

Gorman, T. O. (2010, August 25). Dodd – Frank: Credit rating agencies, Part II. http://www.lexisnexis.com/COMMUNITY/CORPSEC/blogs/corporateandsecuritieslawblog/archive/2010/08/25/dodd-frank-credit-rating-agencies-part-ii.aspx.

Griffin, J. M., Nickerson, J., & Tang, D.Y. (2012, May 25). Rating shopping or catering? An examination of the response to competitive pressure for CDO credit ratings. Abstract. http://www.sec.gov/divisions/riskfin/seminar/tang061412.pdf.

Grimes, R. D., & Smith, L. R. (2013, September 4). United States: Shareholder lawsuit filed against news corp. over antitrust claims and liabilities. http://www.bassberry.com/shareholder-lawsuit-filed-against-news-corp-over-antitrust-claims-and-liabilities-06-19-2013/.

Hamel, G. (n.d.). Strengths & weaknesses of pure competition in economics. http://smallbusiness.chron.com/strengths-weaknesses-pure-competition-economics-37245.html.

HBS Working Paper. Reputation and competition: evidence from the credit rating industry. http://www.hbs.edu/faculty/Publication%20Files/09-051_13e0275c-a3a4-48bd-a86a-2324d5d70b57.pdf.

Hill, C. A. (2010). Limits of Dodd-Frank's rating agency reform. *Chapman Law Review, 15*, 133.

Hopkins, C., & Katz, I. (2011, July 13). Treasury's miller warns against "Scaling Back" major parts of Dodd-Frank. *Bloomberg*. http://www.bloomberg.com/news/2011-07-13/treasury-s-miller-warns-against-efforts-to-change-dodd-frank-act.html.

House Financial Services Committee. One Year Later: The Consequences of the Dodd-Frank Act. http://financialservices.house.gov/UploadedFiles/FinancialServices-DoddFrank-REPORT.pdf.

Hsiao, M. (2011). *International banking and finance laws: Principles and regulations* (p. 5). Hong Kong: Sweet & Maxwell Asia Ltd.

Hunt, J. P. (2009). Credit rating agencies and the worldwide "Credit Crisis": The limits of reputation, the insufficiency of reform, and a proposal for improvement. *Columbia Business Law Review*, 109–209. http://www2.wiwi.hu-berlin.de/finanz/skript_semfin/t12.pdf; http://works.bepress.com/john_hunt/1.

Indiviglio, D. (2010, June 30). Dodd-Frank's derivatives rules could cost main street $1 trillion. *The Atlantic*. http://www.theatlantic.com/business/archive/2010/06/dodd-franks-derivatives-rules-could-cost-main-street-1-trillion/58989/.

Jeon, D.-S., & Lovo, S. (2011, May 10). Natural barrier to entry in the credit rating industry. http://ssrn.com/abstract=1695519.

Jones, A. (2009, April 21). A first amendment defense for the rating agencies. *The Wall Street Journal*. http://blogs.wsj.com/law/2009/04/21/a-first-amendment-defense-for-the-rating-agencies/.

Jorion, P., Liu, Z., & Shi, C. (2005). Informational effects of regulation FD: Evidence from rating agencies. *Journal of Financial Economics, 76*(2), 309–330.

Kotz, H. D. (2010). *SEC's role regarding and oversight of nationally recognized statistical rating organizations (NRSROs)*. Collingdale, US: DIANE Publishing.

Labonte, M. (2013, July 30). Systemically important or "Too Big to Fail" financial institutions. http://www.fas.org/sgp/crs/misc/R42150.pdf.

Langohr, H., & Langohr, P. (2008). The Raison d'Etr of credit ratings and their markets (Chapter 3). In H. Langohr & P. Langohr (Eds.), *The rating agencies and their credit ratings: What they are, how they work and why they are relevant* (pp. 89–125). Chichester: Wiley.

Lemke, T. P. (1986–1987). The SEC no-action letter process. *Business Lawyer, 42*, 1019.

Listokin, Y., & Taibleson, B. (2010). *If you misrate, then you lose: Improving credit rating accuracy through incentive compensation*. Faculty Scholarship Series (Paper 3877, p. 94). http://digitalcommons.law.yale.edu/fss_papers/3877.

Long, C. (2013, May 13). Should asset backed securities be outlawed? *Reuters*. http://blogs.reuters.com/muniland/tag/credit-ratings/.

Lucchetti, A., & Ng, S. (2010, February 19). "Rating Shopping" lives on as congress debates on fix. *The Wall Street Journal*. http://online.wsj.com/news/articles/SB10001424052748703315404575250270972715804.

McLean, B., & Nocera, J. (2010). *All the devils are here: The hidden history of the financial crisis*. New York/London.

McNamara, S. R. (2012). Informational failures in structured finance and Dodd-Frank's "Improvements to the Regulation of Credit Rating Agencies". *Fordham Journal of Corporate & Financial Law, 17*(3), 665.

Moynihan, M. C., Nolan, A. R. G., Pagnano, C. E., & Williamson, G. A. (2010, July 22). Financial reform bill strengthens regulation, expands potential liability of credit rating agencies. *Investment Management Alert*.

Nazareth, A. L. (2003, April 2). 'Testimony concerning rating the rating agencies: The state of transparency and competition' before the house subcommittee on capital markets, insurance, and government sponsored enterprises. Committee on Financial Services. http://www.sec.gov/news/testimony/ts040203aln.htm.

Nazareth, A. L. (2005a, April 12). Director, Division of Market Regulation, U.S. Securities & Exchange Commission, Statement before the Subcommittee on Capital Markets, Insurance and Government Sponsored Enterprises, Committee on Financial Services. http://www.sec.gov/news/testimony/ts041205aln.htm

Nazareth, A. L. (2005b, April 12). Testimony concerning credit rating agencies. https://www.sec.gov/news/testimony/ts041205aln.htm.

Nolan, A. R. G., Pagnano, C. E., Moynihan, M., & Williamson, G. A. (2010, July 22). Financial reform bill strengthens regulation, expands potential liability of credit rating agencies. http://m.klgates.com/financial-reform-bill-strengthens-regulation-expands-potential-liability-of-credit-rating-agencies-07-22-2010/.

Powell, T. C., & Arregle, J.-L. (2014, August 8). Firm performance and the axis of errors. *Journal of Management Research, 7*(2), 59–77. http://thomaspowell.co.uk/article_pdfs/Axis.pdf.

Press Release, Representative Barney Frank. (2011, March 30). Frank statement on the cost of Dodd-Frank implementation. http://democrats.financialservices.house.gov/press/PRArticle.aspx?NewsID=1410.

Press Release, Securities and Exchange Commission. (2011, July 1). SEC provides additional guidance, interim relief and exemptions for security-based swaps under Dodd-Frank Act. http://www.sec.gov/news/press/2011/2011-141.htm.

Quinlivan, S. (2010, October 10). Dealing with rating agencies after regulation FD change (Para 3). http://dodd-frank.com/dealing-with-rating-agencies-after-regulation-fd-change/.

Report: Wall Street's Opposition to Dodd-Frank Reforms Echoes Its Resistance to New Deal Financial Safeguards' (12 July 2011). http://www.commondreams.org/newswire/2011/07/12-0.

Roberts, R. Y. Commissioner, U.S. Securities and Exchange Commission Washington, D.-C. 'Formal Regulatory Handle Needed for NRSRO Designation: Part I', SIA Compliance & Legal Seminar Scottsdale (Vol. 1). Arizona (6 April 1992). http://www.sec.gov/news/speech/1992/040692roberts.pdf.

Salzedo, S., & Singla, T. (2015, April 30). Accountants' Negligence and Liability. *Bloomsbury Professional*.

Schroeder, P. (2011, July 13). GAO: "Regulators need more info before curbing proprietary trading." *Financial Times*. http://thehill.com/blogs/on-the-money/banking-financial-institutions/171309-gao-regulators-need-more-info-before-curbing-proprietary-trading.

Schwarcz, S. L. (2011–2012). Protecting investors in securitization transactions: Does Dodd-Frank help, or hurt? The 2011 Diane Sanger Memorial Lecture. *Louisiana Law Review, 72*, 591.

SEC Concept Release No. 33-8236 (2003, June 4). Rating agencies and the use of credit ratings under the federal securities laws (p. 1). http://www.sec.gov/rules/concept/33-8236.htm.

SEC Staff Report. (2012, November). 2012 Summary Report of Commission Staff's Examinations of Each Nationally Recognized Statistical Rating Organization As Required by Section 15E(p)(3)(C) of the Securities Exchange Act of 1934. http://www.sec.gov/news/studies/2012/nrsro-summary-report-2012.pdf.

SEC. (2012, September). Report to congress credit rating standardization study as required by Section 939(h) of the Dodd-Frank Wall Street Reform and Consumer Protection Act'. http://www.sec.gov/news/studies/2012/939h_credit_rating_standardization.pdf.

SEC. (2013, August 29). Implementing Dodd-Frank Wall Street Reform and Consumer Protection Act – Accomplishments. http://www.sec.gov/spotlight/dodd-frank/accomplishments.shtml; http://www.sec.gov/spotlight/dodd-frank.shtml.

SEC. The Investor's advocate: How the SEC protects investors, maintains market integrity, and facilitates capital formation. http://www.sec.gov/about/whatwedo.shtml.

Shah, O. (2010, May 17). KPMG and PwC consider move into credit rating. http://www.cityam.com/article/kpmg-and-pwc-consider-move-credit-rating.

Sinclair, T. J. (2010, November). Credit rating agencies and the global financial crisis. *Economic Sociology the European electronic newsletter, 12*(1), 4–9. http://econsoc.mpifg.de/archive/econ_soc_12-1.pdf.

Soucy, C. (2010, June 6). Credit rating agency reform act. http://www.livestrong.com/article/140584-credit-rating-agency-reform-act/#ixzz1k03NGYX8.

Stafford, T. A., Root, M. D., & Ness, B. I. (2010, August 26). Dodd-Frank measures affecting credit rating agencies. Association of Corporate Counsel. http://www.lexology.com/library/detail.aspx?g=562ad21e-d7e6-439d-8850-f630432be31a.

Stevens, P. S. (2005, November 29). Before the Committee on Financial Services United States House of Representatives (p. 1). http://www.idc.org/policy/ici_testimony/ci.05_house_nrsro_tmny.idc.

Taylor, J. B. (2010, July 1). The Dodd-Frank Financial Fiasco. *Wall Street Journal*. http://online.wsj.com/article/SB10001424052748703426004575338732174405398.html

Timothy, A. S., Root, M. D., & Ness, B. I. (2010, August 26). Dodd-Frank measures affecting credit rating agencies. Association of Corporate Counsel. http://www.lexology.com/library/detail.aspx?g=562ad21e-d7e6-439d-8850-f630432be31a.

U.S. Government Accountability Office. (2011). GAO-11-529, Proprietary Trading: Regulators Will Need More Comprehensive Information to Fully Monitor Compliance with New Restrictions When Implemented.

U.S. Securities and Exchange Commission. (2003, January). Report on the role and function of credit rating agencies in the operation of the securities markets. As Required by Section 702 (b) of the Sarbanes-Oxley Act of 2002. https://www.sec.gov/news/studies/credratingreport0103.pdf.

U.S. Securities and Exchange Commission. (2009, August 27). The SEC's role regarding and oversight of national recognised statistical rating organisation (NRSROs), Report No. 458. http://www.sec-oig.gov/Reports/AuditsInspections/2009/Report458.pdf.

Walter, E. B., & Daigler, M. A. (2010, June 21). Gatekeepers are the key to good governance. *Fobes.com*. http://www.forbes.com/2010/06/21/shareholders-risk-gatekeepers-elisse-walter-leadership-governance-ethisphere_print.html.

Wayne, L. (2009, July 15). Clapers Sues over ratings of securities. *The New York Times*. http://www.nytimes.com/2009/07/15/business/15calpers.html?_r=3&partner=rss&emc=rss&.

White, M. J. (2013, September 26). Deploying the full enforcement arsenal. Speech, Council of Institutional Investors fall conference in Chicago, IL. http://www.sec.gov/News/Speech/Detail/Speech/1370539841202#.

White, M. J. (Chair). (2013, May 16). Testimony on oversight of SEC. U.S. Securities and Exchange Commission, Before the U.S. House of Representatives Committee on Financial Services.

Wrobel, G. A. M. (2013, April 26). *A financial crisis is a terrible thing to waste: Challenges in the regulation of credit rating agencies and the use of ratings to regulate capital of financial services firms* (BA Thesis for Political Science and Public Policy Studies). The University of Chicago. http://www.sec.gov/comments/4-661/4661-22.pdf.

Chapter 5
EU Statutory Regulation

5.1 Introduction

"The financial crisis, which started as the US sub-prime crisis in 2007, escalated into a full-blown economic crisis and raised significant political challenges in Europe".[1] The European Union (EU) 2009 regulation was in response to the economic and financial crisis. There was a need to restore confidence and prevent a similar situation occurring in the future. Similar to the US, the principal aim of the regulation is to protect the stability of financial markets and give investors the information and impartiality they need from CRAs to enable them to make prudent investment decisions. Its accomplishment is expected to create growth and jobs. To ensure that credit ratings issued by CRAs are reliable requires their activities to conform to the principles of integrity, transparency, responsibility and good governance. This will in turn ensure that credit ratings are independent, objective and of adequate quality.[2]

The financial crisis led to a number of reform initiatives in the US and Europe to address the concerns raised by CRAs' activities in the context of structured finance products.[3] The Regulation in the EU is to apply to all EU countries. This chapter examines the need for statutory regulation and analyses the salient features of regulation issued in the EU (with critical comments where appropriate). It will, *inter alia*, analyse both (a) the relevant proposals and explanations contained in the

[1] Liikanen et al. (2012), p. 1.

[2] Regulation (EC) No 1060/2009 of the European Parliament and of the Council of 16 September 2009 on credit rating agencies, Official Journal of the European Union (17.11.2009), pp. 1–31. http://www.esma.europa.eu/system/files/L_302_1.pdf.

[3] See Rousseau (2009).

M. Hemraj, *Credit Rating Agencies*, DOI 10.1007/978-3-319-17927-8_5

Proposal for Regulation[4] to get valuable insight and (b) the enacted Regulation[5] that came into force on 7 December 2009. The remaining part examines different facets of regulations, ranging from managing conflicts of interest to ethos and quality of Regulation, as well as briefly the legal accountability of CRAs.

5.2 Need for Statutory Regulation

The importance of statutory regulation is to help give investors the information and impartiality needed from CRAs for them to make prudent investment decisions and prevent bubbles of excessive risk.[6] The voluntary compliance is now subject to a yearly assessment by the Committee of European Securities Regulators (CESR), an independent advisory group to the European Commission composed of the national supervisors of EU securities markets.[7] The role of the CESR is to improve coordination among securities regulators, advise the European Commission and ensure more consistent and timely day-to-day implementation of Union legislation in the member states.

5.2.1 Inadequacy of the Pre-existing Regulations in the EU

Hitherto EU law addressed only two specific aspects of credit rating. One, credit ratings are forward-looking opinions as opposed to auditors who provide backward-looking opinions on the truth and fairness[8] of the accounts prepared and do not make recommendations relating to investors purchasing corporate debt instruments within the meaning of Directive 2003/125/EC[9] implementing the Market Abuse Directive.[10] Second, CRAs were therefore required to consider adopting internal policies and procedures designed to ensure fair representation of their credit ratings.

[4] "Proposal for a Regulation of the European Parliament and of the Council on Credit Rating Agencies, Brussels (12 November 2008)", herein after called "Proposal for Regulation (2008)". http://ec.europa.eu/internal_market/securities/docs/agencies/proposal_en.pdf.

[5] "Regulation (EC) No 1060/2009 of The European Parliament and of The Council of 16 September 2009 on credit rating agencies", herein after called "Regulation (2009)". http://eur-lex.europa.eu/LexUriServ/LexUriServ.do?uri=OJ:L:2009:302:0001:0001:EN:PDF.

[6] Barroso (2009).

[7] See Commission Decision of 6 June 2001, establishing the Committee of European Securities Regulators, 2001/527/EC (OJ L191, 13 July 2001), p. 43.

[8] For the definition of "true and fair view", see Glossary.

[9] Commission Directive 2003/125/EC of 22 December 2003 implementing Directive 2003/6/EC of the European Parliament and the Council as regards the fair presentation of investment recommendations and the disclosure of conflicts of interest (OJ L 339 24 December 2003), p. 73.

[10] Directive 2003/6/EC of the European Parliament and of the Council of 28 January 2003 on Insider Dealing and Market Manipulation (OJ L 96, 12 April 2003), p. 16.

This required (a) the appropriate disclose of any significant interests or conflicts of interest concerning the financial instruments or the issuers to which their credit ratings relate[11] and (b) the Capital Requirements Directive,[12] following Basel II, providing the use of external credit assessments to determine risk weights and the resulting capital requirements applied to a bank or investment firm's exposure. Basel II, which requires risk weightings based on CRA assessments and then requires banks to set aside a proportion of capital to cover potential losses, is seen as creating an artificial market for CRAs.[13]

An external credit assessment may only be used for this purpose if the competent authorities have recognised the External Credit Assessment Institution (ECAI) providing the risk assessment.[14] The competent national authorities may only recognise an ECAI if the latter complies with requirements such as objectivity, independence, ongoing review, credibility and transparency. In order to promote convergence, the Committee of European Banking Supervisors has issued guidelines on the recognition of ECAIs.[15]

The European Council felt that restoring public confidence, as a priority, requires a proper functioning of the financial sector by a legislative proposal to strengthen the rules on CRAs and their supervision at EU level.[16] The 2009 rules introduced in the EU were hitherto largely based on the standards set by the International Organization of Securities Commissions (IOSCO) Code[17] and were meant to raise the standards for the issuance of credit ratings used in the Union.

The EU Council on 20 June 2008 and 16 October 2008 called for a legislative proposal to strengthen the rules on CRAs and their supervision at EU level. The EU legislation attempts to protect investors and European financial markets against the risk of malpractice by CRAs.[18] A uniform approach was thought necessary in order to create a framework where member states' competent authorities were required to ensure that CRAs did apply the new set of requirements consistently across the Union.[19] Arguably, failures or the lack of a regulatory framework for CRAs in one specific member state would materially adversely affect market participants and financial markets EU-wide. Therefore, sound regulatory rules applicable throughout the EU were necessary to protect investors and for markets to redress any possible shortcomings.[20]

---

[11] Recital 10 of Directive 2003/125/EC.

[12] Directive 2006/48/EC of the European Parliament and of the Council of 14 June 2006 relating to the taking up and pursuit of the business of credit institutions (recast) (OJ L 177, 30.6.2006), p. 1.

[13] Coffee and Lannoo (2010), p. 13.

[14] Recognition mechanism is outlined in Annex VI Part 2 of the Capital Requirements Directive.

[15] Guidelines on the recognition of External Credit Assessment Institutions of 20 January 2006 (GL07). http://www.c-ebs.org/formupload/41/413b2513-5084-4293-a386-16385b80411d.pdf.

[16] 20 June and 16 October 2008, Brussels (23 April 2009). http://europa.eu/rapid/pressReleasesAction.do?reference=IP/09/629.

[17] See Chap. 3.

[18] Andenaes and Deipenbrock (2012), pp. 1–17.

[19] See Article 6 (5), Proposal for a Regulation (2008).

[20] Proposal for a Regulation (2008), p. 5.

Currently, most CRAs in the EU have their headquarters outside the Union. Most member states have regulated neither the activities of CRAs nor the conditions for the issuing of credit ratings. Despite their significance in the functioning of the financial markets, in the past CRAs were subjected to Union law only in limited areas relating to insider dealing and market manipulation,[21] the taking up and pursuit of the business of credit institutions[22] and the capital adequacy of investment firms and credit institutions.[23] Rules were, therefore, necessary in ensuring that all credit ratings issued by CRAs registered in the European Community were of adequate quality and were subjected to stringent requirements. In response to the crisis, the EU adopted Regulation 1060/2009, which will be discussed later. For the first time, this set out a legally binding pan-European authorisation regime for CRAs that issue ratings that have been used by EU-based financial institutions.[24] The applicants are required to submit an application for registration to the CESR and supply information set out in Annex 11.[25] The European Parliament and the Council of the European Union in 2009 regulation wanted to ensure that credit rating activities accorded with the principles of integrity, transparency, responsibility and good governance, which would ensure independence, objectivity and adequate quality of the credit ratings used in the community.[26]

5.3 Salient Features of the Regulation

This section will critically examine the Regulation introduced, and it will be both descriptive and, where appropriate, critical.

5.3.1 Distinction Between Solicited/Unsolicited Ratings

CRAs are required, under the new rules, to identify clearly and distinguish unsolicited credit ratings from solicited credit ratings by appropriate means[27] and to indicate whether the rating issued is solicited or unsolicited. An unsolicited credit rating is a credit rating not initiated at the request of the issuer or rated entity.

[21] Directive 2003/6/EC of the European Parliament and of the Council of 28 January 2003. OJ L 96 (12.4.2003), p. 16.

[22] Directive 2006/48/EC of the European Parliament and of the Council of 14 June 2006. OJ L 177 (30.6.2006), p. 1.

[23] Ibid., p. 201 refer to the Credit Rating Agencies.

[24] Staikouras (2012), p. 71.

[25] Article 15 (1), Application for Registration, Regulation (2009), p. 14.

[26] Regulation (2009), p. 1.

[27] Ibid., p. 3.

Unlike solicited ratings, CRAs receive no payments when they issue unsolicited ratings, and the disadvantage is that the issuers do not supply information needed by the CRAs.

5.3.2 Methodologies

CRAs are required to use rating methodologies that are rigorous, systematic, continuous and subject to validation, including appropriate historical experience and back testing.[28] However, competent authorities, including the European Securities and Markets Authority (ESMA) and the member states, are prohibited from interfering with the content of credit ratings and methodologies, which were the preserve of the CRAs. ESMA is an independent EU Authority that contributes to safeguarding the stability of the European Union's financial system by ensuring the integrity, transparency, efficiency and orderly functioning of securities markets, as well as enhancing investor protection. ESMA fosters supervisory convergence both among securities regulators and across financial sectors by working closely with the other European Supervisory Authorities competent in the field of banking (European Banking Authority), as well as insurance and occupational pensions. ESMA's work on securities legislation contributes to the development of a single rulebook in Europe. This serves two purposes: firstly, it ensures the consistent treatment of investors across the Union, enabling an adequate level of protection for investors through effective regulation and supervision; secondly, it promotes equal conditions of competition for financial service providers. Part of its role is in standard setting and reducing the scope of regulatory arbitrage.[29] Similarly, the requirement that CRAs review credit ratings at least annually did not relieve CRAs from their obligation to monitor credit ratings on a continuous basis and to review credit ratings as necessary.[30]

5.3.3 Competition

The aim of the application of the stringent requirements is not to prevent new CRAs from entering the market but rather to encourage competition.[31] However, as a critique, it is difficult to see how a stringent requirement for registration for those who wish to offer rating services would ensure competence in discharging their duties; in reality, this could discourage competition. The question is whether less

[28] Regulation (2009), Clause 23, p. 3.

[29] See ESMA (2011), p. 3.

[30] Regulation (2009), Clause 23, p. 3.

[31] Ibid.

stringent requirements for registration would facilitate new entrants to provide a more competitive environment and simultaneously encouraging quality rating practices. The answer to this is that it will have two disadvantages. First, less stringent requirement, unless accompanied by liability or the need to hold a professional indemnity policy, would in effect have an adverse effect on the ratings given, thus exacerbating the situation and making ratings unreliable. For example, newcomer CRAs may not meet the requirements regarding competent staffs to deal with credit ratings, as it is expensive to recruit them. Second, more entrants to the market would mean many rating agencies will be chasing after the same number of credit rating jobs, and this might inevitably mean offering a cheaper service to get the business, leading CRAs to cut corners, which in turn will make ratings issued unreliable. To avoid rating compromises, the Regulation requires that credit ratings issued by CRAs be well founded and be firmly substantiated.

5.3.4 *Assessment*

CRAs base their assessment on a range of financial and business attributes that might influence repayment, some of which may depend on the issuer of the bond (i.e., the borrower). Other indicators a CRA might use include "economic, regulatory and geopolitical influences, management and corporate governance attributes, and competitive position".[32] From time to time, CRAs have to carry out ratings adjustments. The "reasons for ratings adjustments vary, and may be broadly related to overall shifts in the economy or business environment – or more narrowly focused on circumstances affecting a specific industry, entity, or individual debt issue".[33]

5.3.5 *Disclosure of Information and Due Diligence*

It is perceived that disclosure of information by the CRAs will bring transparency, which in turn would educate the investors as to what CRAs actually do, and the result would be that investors would act with caution when making investment decisions. The CRAs are required to disclose information to the public on the methodologies, models and key rating assumptions that they have used in their credit rating activities.[34] The level of disclosure of information concerning models requires giving adequate information to the users of credit ratings. This would enable the investors to perform their own due diligence when assessing whether or not to rely on those credit ratings.

[32] Marston (2013).

[33] Ibid.

[34] Regulation (2009), p. 3.

Before the onset of the global crisis, the users, and in particular institutional investors with expertise and resources, were reluctant to undertake their own due diligence. One plausible reason for why CRAs are required to carry out their own due diligence is that they are required to look beyond the rating. The sort of due diligence required from investors is to read the rating rationale and disclosure documents that CRAs publish for each rating. Investors should not treat credit ratings as an absolute truth. Part of the reason is that CRAs have limited access to corporate information in calculating the company's credit rating, much like an auditor would.

In rating a mortgaged-backed security (MBS), a CRA sees neither individual loan files nor information identifying borrowers or specific properties. A CRA only receives a list of credit characteristics provided by the banks issuing the original mortgages or the investment bank issuing the MBS. If a CRA receives incomplete or inaccurate information about the entity it is rating, then the rating will also be incomplete and inaccurate, and, *ipso facto*, a rating is only as accurate as the information that goes into its calculation.[35] Under the Regulation, disclosure of information concerning models used by the CRAs prevents them from revealing sensitive business information but does not seriously impede possible innovation.[36]

5.4 Regulation Dealing with Conflicts of Interest

The collapse of so many triple-A-rated structured finance products in 2007–2008 has brought renewed attention to the causes of ratings failures and the conflicts of interest in the credit ratings industry. Three aspects of conflicts of interest are (1) CRAs' conflict of interest in understating credit risk to attract more business, (2) the ability of issuers to purchase only the most favourable ratings and (3) the trusting nature of some investor clienteles who may take ratings at face value.[37] The EU Regulation, explained below, requires CRAs to avoid conflicts of interest; for example, a rating analyst employed by a CRA should not rate an entity in which he/she has an ownership interest to ensure the quality of ratings. The ongoing monitoring of credit ratings is required, rating methodologies (which must be, *inter alia*, rigorous and systematic) should provide a high level of transparency and CRAs are required to publish a transparency report every year.

[35] Bahena (2010).

[36] Regulation (2009), p. 3.

[37] Bolton et al. (2010).

5.4.1 Rating and Consultancy

The main service provided by CRAs is a credit rating service, which has been their speciality. One way to avoid potential conflicts of interest is for the CRAs to limit their activity to the issuing of credit ratings and not to simultaneously carrying out consultancy or advisory services.[38] Although there is no legal bar for this, CRAs would hesitate in making proposals or recommendations regarding the design of a structured finance instrument as investors could then sue them for fraud.[39] Investors, as market participants, would be aware of this only when a CRA discloses it. Even if investors are required to carry out due diligence, they may not wish to take such a precaution due to lack of time or inclination and may prefer to put blind faith in the CRAs. Investors may be mistaken in relying on the CRAs' reputation and thinking that CRAs would not compromise their ratings despite conflicts of interest, which do arise as CRAs are paid by the issuers and not investors. CRAs are not legally prohibited from providing ancillary services with the issuance of credit ratings if this does not create potential conflicts of interest.[40] However, the risk of providing both credit ratings and consultancy services is that it might lead to giving an unjustifiably optimistic credit rating and be a possible cause of compliancy on the part of CRAs, as investors have not succeeded in suing them for fraud. The best option for CRAs, like auditors (who provide auditing and consultancy), is to refrain from providing this dual service (that is, rating and consultancy at the same time) in order to guard themselves against the allegation of fraud by investors. Conflicts of interest emerge based on the relationship of the parties (CRAs receiving payment from issuers, whose securities they rate), and therefore it is easy to prove the existence of a conflict of interest; the difficulty, however, lies in proving that it had an impact on a decision.

5.4.2 Managing Conflicts of Interest

In reality, conflicts of interest is a thorny issue as it may arise in different guises and situations and, therefore, it is only possible to manage through regulation rather than eradicating it completely. There are various ways of managing conflicts of interest. An example is by requiring the CRAs to establish appropriate internal policies and procedures in relation to employees and other persons involved in the credit rating process. The aim is to prevent, identify, eliminate or manage and disclose any conflicts of interest to ensure at all times the quality, integrity and

[38] Proposal for a Regulation of the European Parliament and of the Council on Credit Rating Agencies, Brussels (12 November 2008), p. 12, http://ec.europa.eu/internal_market/securities/docs/agencies/proposal_en.pdf.

[39] See Chap. 6.

[40] Proposal for a Regulation (2008), p. 12.

thoroughness of the credit rating and review process. Such policies and procedures include, in particular, the internal control mechanisms and compliance function.[41] The larger global CRAs (Moody's, Standards & Poor's and Fitch) did not consider this before the onset of the global crisis and did little in response after the global crisis. To ensure their independence, CRAs are required to disclose to investors conflicts of interest in a timely manner. This requires keeping records of all significant threats to the independence of the CRA and that of its employees and other persons involved in the credit rating process, as well as applying various safeguards to mitigate these threats.[42] To eliminate conflicts of interest, a further requirement has been introduced requiring rotation of issuers every 3 years between the agencies that rate them. In addition, two ratings from two different rating agencies are required to rate complex structured finance instruments to prevent big shareholders of a CRA from simultaneously becoming a big shareholder in another CRA.[43]

5.4.3 Independence

The compensation paid to the independent members of the administrative or supervisory board within a CRA should not depend on their business performance in order to avoid conflicts of interest[44] as, otherwise, CRAs may compromise their objectivity when issuing credit ratings in order to satisfy a high-paying client. A CRA (or group of CRAs) is required to maintain arrangements for appropriate corporate governance. In determining its corporate governance arrangements, it has to ensure that credit ratings issued are independent, objective and of adequate quality.[45] To ensure the independence of the credit rating process from the business interests of a CRA as a company, CRAs have to ensure that at least one-third, but no less than two, of the members of the administrative or supervisory board are independent.[46]

Moreover, the majority of the senior management, including all independent members of the administrative or supervisory board, is required to have sufficient expertise in appropriate areas of financial services. The compliance officer within the CRA organisation, who is in charge of ensuring regulatory compliance in the carrying out of his/her duties, has to report regularly to the senior management and

---

[41] Regulation (2009), p. 4. See also Amtenbrink and De Hassan (2009), pp. 1915–1949.

[42] Regulation (2009), p. 4.

[43] European Commission, Press Release, Commission wants better quality credit ratings (15 November 2011). http://eropa.eu/rapid/pressreleaseaction.do?/reference=ip/11/1355.

[44] Regulation (2009), p. 4.

[45] Ibid.

[46] Ibid.

the independent members of the administrative or a supervisory board.[47] CRAs are required to allocate a sufficient number of employees with appropriate knowledge and experience to its credit rating activities. In particular, CRAs have to ensure an adequate allocation of human and financial resources to the issuing, monitoring and updating of credit ratings.[48] Long-lasting relationships with the same rated entities or their related third parties would naturally compromise the independence of rating analysts and persons approving credit ratings. Such analysts and persons are subjected to an appropriate rotation mechanism aimed at providing a gradual change in analytical teams and credit rating committees.[49]

5.4.4 Methodologies, Models and Key Assumptions

In the past, CRAs have failed accurately to assess the risk of loss of various structured products,[50] thus giving the impression that perhaps they were working beyond their expertise and yet have not been penalised with sanctions in the form of liability based on the various legal defences available.[51] Perhaps, due to lack of reliable data and the complexity of the structures of new types of financial instrument, in particular structured finance instruments, it did raise serious questions as to whether CRAs were able to produce a credible credit rating. According to regulation introduced, CRAs have to ensure that methodologies, models and key rating assumptions such as mathematical or correlation assumptions used for determining credit ratings are properly maintained, up-to-date and subject to a comprehensive review on a periodic basis and that their descriptions of the methodology adopted are published in a manner permitting comprehensive review. The CRAs are required to disclose changes in the quality of information available for monitoring an existing credit rating with the review of reliability, and, if appropriate, the credit rating given should be revised.[52] In a worst case scenario where CRAs are unable to produce reliable ratings, the Regulation prohibits them from issuing a new credit rating and they may be required to withdraw from an existing credit rating.[53]

In order to ensure the quality of credit ratings, a CRA should take measures to ensure that the information it uses in assigning a credit rating is reliable. For that purpose, a CRA is able to rely, *inter alia*, on independently audited financial statements and public disclosures, verification by reputable third-party services, random sampling and examining the information received. CRAs can also rely on

---

[47] Ibid.

[48] Ibid.

[49] Ibid.

[50] Milken Institute (2002), p. 1.

[51] See Chap. 6.

[52] Regulation (2009), p. 4.

[53] Ibid.

contractual provisions clearly stipulating liability for the rated entity or its related third parties. This is possible if the information provided under the contract is knowingly materially false or misleading or if the rated entity or its related third party fails to conduct reasonable due diligence regarding the accuracy of the information as specified under the terms of the contract.[54]

The 2008–2009 crises revealed the weaknesses in the methods and models used by the agencies when rating structured financial instruments by the use of financial engineering in order to give high confidence to investors. Likewise, a CRA has to communicate with the markets and investors with regard to the characteristics and limitations of the rating of structured finance instruments and the application of critical model assumptions.[55] The changes oblige CRAs to disclose ratings on a non-selective basis and in a timely manner to the public; the exception is where the distribution of ratings is by subscription. It seeks to enable investors to distinguish between ratings for structured products and for traditional products (corporate and sovereign) by requiring the use of a different rating category for structured finance instruments or the provision of additional information on their risk characteristics. Specific disclosure requirements apply to unsolicited credit ratings[56] with regard to policies and procedures adopted. It is necessary for CRAs to establish proper procedures for the regular review of methodologies, models and key rating assumptions used by the CRA in order to be able to reflect properly the changing conditions in the underlying asset markets. CRAs have to ensure transparency and disclose any material modification in the methodologies and practices, procedures and processes prior to their coming into effect under the Regulation, unless extreme market conditions require an immediate change in the credit rating.[57] A CRA is required to keep records of the methodology used for credit ratings and regularly update the changes thereto and keep a record of the dialogue between the rating analyst and the rated entity or its related third parties, etc.[58]

One of the criticisms of CRAs has been that they were slow in downgrading their rating when the circumstances had changed. An obligation imposed under the Regulation is that the CRAs must keep methods up to date and subject to (constant) review.[59] In case there is a change in the rating methodology, CRAs must immediately disclose which ratings are likely to be affected by this change and to re-rate them promptly. Significantly, the CRAs' obligation is continually to review their ratings.[60] This is understandable as it keeps the ratings up to date and responsive to changes in financial conditions. Such a provision is meant *prima facie* to prevent CRAs from concentrating their efforts and resources only on initial ratings, and

[54] Ibid.

[55] Proposal for a Regulation (2008), pp. 8–9.

[56] Ibid., p. 9.

[57] Regulation (2009), p. 5.

[58] Proposal for Regulation (2008), p. 5.

[59] Regulation (2009) para 10, p. 2, See also, Sève (2010).

[60] Regulation (2009), p. 8.

then neglecting subsequent monitoring, which can be detrimental to the ongoing quality of the ratings.

5.4.5 Risk Warning Indication

CRAs have to indicate any appropriate risk warning, including a sensitivity analysis of the relevant assumptions.[61] It requires them to explain how various market developments that move the parameters built into the model may influence the credit rating changes (for example, volatility). A CRA is to ensure that the information on historical default rates of its rating categories is verifiable and quantifiable. It should also provide sufficient basis for interested parties to understand, where applicable, the historical performance of each rating category and how rating categories have changed. The nature of the credit rating or other circumstances may make a historical default rate inappropriate, statistically invalid or likely to mislead the users of the credit rating. In such a case, a CRA is required to provide appropriate clarification, and the information supplied should be comparative to any existing industry patterns. The aim is to assist investors in drawing performance comparisons between different CRAs.[62]

5.4.6 Transparency

CRAs are to ensure that internal processes and procedures are sufficiently transparent by publicly disclosing important information like conflicts of interest, methodologies and key rating assumptions, and the general nature of their compensation policy. They must also periodically disclose data on the historical default rates of rating categories and give competent supervisory authorities certain information such as the list of the largest 20 clients by revenue.[63] To ensure that relevant, standardised data on CRAs' performance is available to allow market participants to make industry-wide comparisons, the CESR has created a publicly available central repository for such data.[64]

To restore public confidence in the rating business, CRAs must publish an annual transparency report[65] and keep records of their activities.[66] To reinforce transparency of credit ratings and contribute to the protection of investors, the

[61] Regulation (2009), p. 5.

[62] Ibid.

[63] Proposal for Regulation (2008) Article 9 and Annex I, Section E, p. 9.

[64] Ibid. Article 9 (2), p. 9.

[65] Ibid. Article 10 and Annex I, Section E, Part III, p. 9.

[66] Ibid. Articles 5–7 and Annex I, Section B, Points 7–9.

CESR is required to maintain a central repository of information on the past performances of CRAs and keep record of credit ratings issued in the past. CRAs are required to provide information to that repository in a standardised form. The CESR is required to make that information available to the public and annually to publish summary information on the main developments observed.[67]

5.4.7 Raising Awareness for Users

Structured financial instruments, under certain circumstances, may have effects that are different from traditional corporate debt instruments. It would, therefore, be misleading for investors to apply the same rating categories to both types of instruments without further explanation. The CRAs are required to play an important role in raising awareness to the users of credit ratings about the specificities of the structured finance products in relation to traditional ratings. CRAs have clearly to differentiate between rating categories used for rating structured finance instruments, on the one hand, and rating categories used for other financial instruments or financial obligations, on the other, by adding an appropriate symbol to the rating category.[68]

5.4.8 Prohibition of Forum Shopping

CRAs are to take measures to avoid situations where issuers request a preliminary rating assessment of a structured finance instrument from a number of CRAs in order to identify the one offering the best credit rating.[69] Issuers are also required to avoid applying such practices; however, as this is an inspiration standard, it is hard to detect and police. My submissions are as follows: (a) there is a possibility that rating shopping is being practised, but it is difficult to prove unless a CRA resorts to whistleblowing issuers who resort to such a practice; (b) the fact that there are a few main providers of credit rating, opinion shopping is not expected to be rampant because the issuers have limited choice in selecting one of the Big Three CRAs; (c) the only way CRAs can avoid approaches by the issuers is to make it very clear, at the outset, to the issuers that they strongly reject any such approach based on rating shopping and will report such matters to the regulatory body; and (d) to deter issuers from adopting such malpractice, a regulator needs to be able to apply some sort of sanction, which is presently absent.

[67] Regulation (2009), p. 5.
[68] Ibid.
[69] Ibid.

5.4.9 Registration

In order to ensure a high level of investor and consumer confidence in the internal market, registration was brought about as a prerequisite for CRAs to issue credit ratings meant for regulatory purposes in the EC. This required laying down harmonised conditions and the procedure necessary for the granting, suspension and withdrawal of such registration.[70] The Regulation did not replace the established process of the External Credit Assessment Institutions (ECAIs),[71] which had received recognition in the EC, but CRAs have to apply for registration in accordance with this Regulation.[72] As CRAs registered by the competent authority of the relevant member state are allowed to issue credit ratings throughout the Union, a single registration procedure for each CRA, which is effective throughout the Union, has been established. The registration of a CRA becomes effective once the registration decision issued by the competent authority of the home member state has taken effect under the relevant national law.[73]

It became necessary to establish a single point of entry for the submission of applications for registration. The CESR receives applications for registration and provides advice in respect of the completeness of the application. The examination of applications for registration is carried out at a national level by the relevant competent authority. In order to deal efficiently with CRAs, competent authorities must set up operational networks (colleges) with an efficient information technology infrastructure. The CESR has to establish a subcommittee specialised in the field of credit ratings for each of the asset classes rated by CRAs.[74] The Regulation did not exclude a CRA from its duty to protect the right to privacy of natural persons with respect to the processing of personal data[75] and on the free movement of such data.[76]

5.4.10 Penalties for Infringing the Provisions of Regulation

To ensure the implementation of provisions of Regulation, member states have to lay down rules on penalties applicable to their infringements. These penalties are required to be effective, proportionate and dissuasive,[77] which seems to be a

[70] Ibid.

[71] In accordance with Directive 2006/48/EC.

[72] Regulation (2009), p. 5.

[73] Ibid.

[74] Ibid.

[75] In accordance with Directive 95/46/EC of the European Parliament and of the Council (of 24 October 1995) Regulation (2009), p. 5.

[76] OJ L 281 (23.11.1995), p. 31.

[77] Regulation (2009), p. 7.

formidable task as it is difficult to establish a fool proof system. The CESR is required to establish guidelines on the convergence of practices within the EU relating to penalties.[78] These penalties, at the minimum, were to cover cases of gross professional misconduct and lack of due diligence.

5.4.10.1 Criminal Penalties

It is possible for member states to provide for administrative or criminal penalties.[79] Most importantly, any claim against CRAs in relation to any infringement of the provisions of the Regulation is to be made in accordance with the applicable national law on civil liability, without prejudice to the application of Community law.[80] No mention has been made of the criminal liability of CRAs that arises based on fraud, perhaps because this is obvious. The status of the provisions of the Regulation is unknown. The CRAs, when questioned concerning assuming liability for faulty sovereign ratings, threatened to withdraw ratings for those perceived to be from high-risk economies in the EU. In reality, perhaps investors would prefer to sue CRAs directly in order to recover losses sustained and would not be interested in regulators imposing mere penalties on CRAs as they derive no benefit.

5.4.10.2 Civil Actions

A stricter and clearer legal framework within which CRAs operate was deemed necessary, as it will facilitate recourse to civil actions against the CRAs in appropriate circumstances and in accordance with the applicable regimes of liability of the member states.[81] Recital 69[82] states that infringement of the Regulation is to be dealt with in accordance with the applicable national laws on civil liability. This would "possibly result in forum shopping, when CRAs or issuers choose jurisdictions under which civil liability for infringements of CRA Regulation [is not harsh] or found to be less likely".[83] What is needed in future is CRAs to incur liability when they negligently or intentionally infringe the provisions of the Regulation, which results in incorrect ratings and investors incurring losses due to basing their investment decision on incorrect ratings.[84] Also, a liability should apply when a CRA has given unjustifiably high ratings or when they fail to make a timely downgrade of ratings. It should be limited further to solicited ratings

---

[78] Ibid.

[79] Ibid.

[80] Ibid.

[81] Proposal for Regulation (2006), Article 16.

[82] Regulation (2009), p. 7.

[83] EC, Public Consultation of CRAs (5/11/2010), p. 24.

[84] Ibid.

(of corporate debts) as opposed to unsolicited ratings (of sovereign debts). The reason is that CRAs receive payment for solicited ratings, and this might result in conflicts of interest, but as no payments take place in cases of unsolicited ratings, the issue of conflicts of interest does not arise.

5.4.11 Rotation of CRAs

Similar to audit, CRAs' independence, objectivity and scepticism are necessary for the proper functioning of capital markets, and this requires rotation of CRAs. It is submitted that regulators dealing with CRA regulation in the US and EU could have benefitted by examining how auditors were being regulated and then adopting their practices in regulating CRAs. However, whether or not CRAs should be rotated has its own supporters and detractors. The argument for rotation is based on the belief that it promotes objectivity because new personnel are not tied down by judgments, compromises and personal relationships of the past. New CRAs bring in a fresh set of eyes and have the opportunity to raise issues overlooked or settled in the past. They are better able to identify issues, alter their judgments and bring issues up for discussion when they are not personally committed to prior decisions.[85] Other arguments for the rotation of CRAs were as follows[86]: (1) setting out a maximum duration of the contractual relationship between the issuer that is rated or that issued the rated debt instruments and the CRAs would remove the incentive for issuing favourable credit ratings with respect to that issuer, (2) requiring the rotation of CRAs as a normal and regular market practice would effectively mitigate the problem of the lock-in effect and (3) it would have positive effects on the credit ratings market, as it would facilitate new market entries and offer existing CRAs the opportunity to extend their business to new areas.

The argument against rotation, similar to audit, is that the quality of rating is determined not only by CRA independence but also by many other factors—such as the quality of standards, education, expertise, committees, corporate governance, discipline, liability and a host of other institutional features of the CRA environment. Attempts to promote some of these desirable attributes of rating often degrade the others, making attainability of a "perfect" rating impossible. The focus of public policy, therefore, should be to aim for the best overall quality rating and not to fixate on any subset of the determinants of rating quality. In spite of its obvious appeal, mandating rating firm rotation would be a bad policy. Indeed, such a change may impair CRAs' independence, weaken expertise and undermine corporate governance.[87] Another argument against rotation relates to associated

[85] Tan (1995), pp. 113–135.

[86] European Union, The Council of European Parliament, "Regulation of The European Parliament and of the Council amending Regulation (EC) No 1060/2009 on credit rating agencies" (22 April 2013), p. 11, http://register.consilium.europa.eu/pdf/en/12/pe00/pe00070.en12.pdf.

[87] Ball et al. (2015), p. 1.

costs. For example,[88] (1) frequent rotation could result in increased costs for issuers and CRAs because the cost associated with rating a new entity or financial instrument is typically higher than the cost of monitoring a credit rating that has already been issued; (2) it takes a considerable amount of time and resources to get established as a CRA, whether as a niche player or covering all asset classes; and (3) ongoing rotation of CRAs could have a significant impact on the quality and continuity of credit ratings. Therefore, the implementation of a rotation mechanism requires sufficient safeguards to allow the market to adapt gradually by limiting the scope of the mechanism to re-securitisations, which is a limited source of bank funding, before possibly enhancing the mechanism in the future.

There are arguments in favour of and against regulators determining rating criteria. The argument in favour contends that regulatory authorities should play an active role as it would help to ensure the integrity and transparency of the credit rating industry. Requiring CRAs to explain publicly their methodologies and allowing regulators to ensure that proper procedural hurdles have been cleared would ensure that methodologies are sound, have a rational basis and are sensible policies that help inspire greater confidence in ratings, especially to help new entrants establish a place in the industry.[89] The registration and supervision should continue to focus on the proper procedural requirements and disclosure necessary for the sound operation of CRAs.

The argument against regulation relates to the following: (a) the determination of ratings criteria by regulators would likely undermine the global utility or comparability of ratings; the credit rating industry is global, and opening up the ratings process substantively to the views of local regulators would make comparability of ratings across jurisdictions difficult if other regulators instituted similar domestic approaches; (b) the regulatory fragmentation of standards would make the job of cross-border investors more difficult, as they would have to judge the meaning of ratings according to various domestic regulations and could negatively affect the liquidity of international bond markets; (c) the rotation could impair or render obsolete the long-term historical methods used to understand rated investments; if there is a break in coverage, CRAs would have less incentive to invest the human labour and capital into continuing their analysis of relevant products, thus undermining the quality of research involved; and (d) even assuming that rotation achieves its goal of increased competition, it could dis-incentivise and would not encourage the quality research and analysis that competition is hoped to realise. By opening the gates to new entrants and less-established CRAs, these agencies could seek to increase their market share by probably offering ratings that are more generous—a perverse outcome resulting from imposed rotation.[90] There is a strong correlation between new entrants in the credit ratings industry and reduced quality

[88] European Union, The Council... (2013), p. 12.

[89] Milken Institute (2012), p. 5.

[90] Ibid., p. 6.

of ratings; measures will be required to prevent such development should the EU proposals become law.[91]

The 2007–2009 crisis highlighted, among other things, the need for better oversight of CRAs because of the financial crisis and the failure of securitised products. It was felt that rotation would reduce reliance on any one CRA and introduce more competition. To mitigate the risk of conflicts of interest, the Regulation requires CRAs to disclose publicly if a shareholder with 5 % or more of the capital or voting rights holds 5 % or more of a rated entity. To ensure the diversity and independence of credit ratings and opinions, the Regulation prohibits ownership of 5 % or more of the capital or the voting rights in more than one CRA, unless the agencies concerned belong to the same group.[92]

5.4.11.1 Rotation in Securitisation

A successful securitisation requires a high credit rating by one of the Big Three CRAs; otherwise, most securitisation would be unsold in the primary market.[93] Issuers prefer high investment grade ratings for their securities for the reasons of easy marketability, liquidity and paying lower interest rates on the securities issued.[94] As certain categories of investors are prevented from buying speculative assets, investment grade ratings, therefore, remained an important requirement in marketing structure financial product to a broader investor base.[95] First, in Europe, securitisation is the sector of the European securitisation market that has underperformed since the financial crisis, and it is, therefore, the one in which the need to address conflicts of interest is greatest. Second, while the credit risk on debt instruments issued by, for instance, corporates to a high degree depends on the debt servicing capacity of the issuer itself, the credit risk on re-securitisations is generally unique to each transaction. Therefore, when a re-securitisation is created, the risk of knowledge being lost by hiring a new CRA is not high. Although at present there are only a limited number of CRAs active in the credit ratings market for re-securitisations, the market is open to competition; a rotation mechanism could be a motive for creating a more dynamic market. Third, a few large CRAs dominate the credit ratings market for re-securitisations, but there are other players that have been building up expertise in this area.

The Council of European Union on 13 May 2013 amended Regulation 1060/2009 to introduce a mandatory rotation rule obliging issuers of structured finance

---

[91] See Becker and Milbourn (2011), p. 493; and Bolton et al. (2012), pp. 85–111.

[92] "Regulation (EU) No .../2013 of the European Parliament and of the Council of Amending Regulation (EC) No 1060/2009 on credit rating agencies". http://register.consilium.europa.eu/doc/srv?l=EN&f=PE%2070%202012%20INIT.

[93] Flood (2005), pp. 154 and 160–171.

[94] Hill (2004), pp. 43 and 53.

[95] Committee on Global Financial System (2008), p. 9.

products with underlying re-securitised assets that pay CRAs for their ratings (issuers-pay model) to switch to a different agency every 4 years. It is prohibited for an outgoing CRA to rate the re-securitised products of the same issuer for a period equal to the duration of the expired contract, though not exceeding 4 years.[96] Due to the complexity of structured finance instruments and their role in contributing to the financial crisis, the Regulation also required issuers to engage at least two different CRAs for the rating of structured finance instruments. Under the rules approved, investors or issuers will be able to claim damages from a CRA if they suffer a loss due to an infringement committed by the agency intentionally or with gross negligence.[97] The Commission is to review whether it is appropriate to maintain a limited rotation mechanism or to apply it to other asset classes as well. As EU provision relating to the rotation of CRAs is not found in US, the US would benefit from adopting such a provision.

5.4.12 Who to Blame: Investors or CRAs?

The aim of the Regulation is to improve the quality of credit ratings, but it sent a mixed message. The CRA retains full responsibility for the ratings issued. There is no wish to jeopardise the independence of the rating process, and at the same time investors were not being relieved from exercising judgment and diligence when relying on ratings in making investment decisions. The criticism levelled against the users of credit ratings is for blindly relying on them. They are required to take care and perform their own appropriate analysis and conduct appropriate due diligence at all times regarding their reliance on such credit ratings.[98]

The CRAs' aim is to maximise both profits and shareholder's value, and in that respect ratings is supposed to represent the initial reference point in the due diligence process.[99] In reality, however, when the financial markets grew increasingly complex, borrowing opportunities expanded dramatically and the ability of a lender to obtain full information about potential borrowers became ever more difficult. Through economies of scale, rating agencies are able to offer cost-effective information services and promote liquidity in markets, thus increasing financial activity and reducing costs.

In practice, what some investors in the US and EU did was to rely "too heavily on NRSRO ratings",[100] especially those investors who were required to hold only securities with specific ratings. In doing so, investors had ignored previous warning signs such as the CRAs' failure to downgrade ratings on Enron and other troubled

[96] Council of the European Union (2013), p. 2.
[97] Council of European Union (2008), p. 2.
[98] Regulation (2009), p. 2.
[99] Gavras (2012).
[100] US Investors' Working Group (2009), p. 2.

companies until they were on the brink of bankruptcy.[101] Two situations arise: first, "Eliminating these safe harbours over time or clarifying that reliance on the rating does not satisfy due diligence obligations, [and] would force investors to seek additional and alternative assessments of credit risk".[102] Second, the blame for the financial meltdown falls on the shoulder of CRAs, as they were key enablers because investors relied on their ratings, often blindly.[103]

5.4.13 Reducing Reliance on Ratings

Ratings currently have a quasi-institutional role, and there was a need to reduce reliance on them. In July 2011, the numbers of references to external ratings were reduced, requiring financial institutions to do their own due diligence. In addition, reducing reliance led to the incorporation of a general obligation for investors to do their own assessment. CRAs needed to disclose more and better information underlying the ratings, by the rated entities themselves to enable professional investors to be better informed, and this would help them to make their own judgments. "[M]ost striking about ESMA is the unprecedented scope of its power, encompassing both law-making and supervisory power".[104] CRAs have to communicate their ratings to the ESMA by making accessible all available ratings for a debt instrument on the market by publishing under a European Rating Index, which is made freely available to investors. The CRAs, on their part, have to consult issuers and investors on any intended changes to their rating methodologies. The ESMA is to be informed of such changes to enable it to check whether applicable rules of form and due process have been abided by.[105]

Arguably, CRAs have not accepted their responsibility when the ratings turn out to be blatantly unreliable. *Prima facie*, blaming both parties, i.e. CRAs and investors, or shifting the blame onto investors may be a technical move preferred by some academic writers and the regulators alike. However, this does not absolve CRAs from their failure in carrying out their role of protecting investors. Instead of a call for investors to reduce reliance on ratings, an alternative option is an imposition of a legal liability on CRAs to act as a deterrent. The best adjudicators, in this regard, arguably are the courts and the judges rather than the regulators.

---

[101] Ibid.

[102] Ibid., p. 3.

[103] *Final Report of the National Commission on the Causes of the Financial and Economic Crisis* (January 2011), p. xxv, http://www.gpo.gov/fdsys/pkg/GPO-FCIC/pdf/GPO-FCIC.pdf.

[104] Cane et al. (2012), p. 1122.

[105] European Commission, Press Release, Commission wants better quality credit ratings (15/11/2011). http://eropa.eu/rapid/pressreleaseaction.do?/reference=ip/11/1355.1.

5.5 Ethos of Regulations

5.5.1 Regulatory Convergence

There is a need to lay down a common framework of rules regarding the enhancement of the quality of credit ratings, in particular the quality of credit ratings to be used by financial institutions and persons regulated by harmonised rules in the European Community. A common framework is necessary to avoid divergence in the form of application of different rules to financial institution in different member states, locally and internationally, as divergence has a negative impact and creates obstacles to a good functioning of the internal market. In addition, divergent credit quality rating requirements would lead to diversification rather than uniformity in investor and consumer protection and the users being deprived of the ability to compare credit ratings issued in the Community with credit ratings issued internationally.[106]

5.5.2 The Applicable Law

Whether the applicable law is that of the country where the rating agency is registered or the country in which it is operating as a subsidiary is a conundrum. The applicable law (and provision of arbitration), in the case of breaches of terms of contract, is normally mentioned in a contract. In the EU, the proposal for a Regulation explicitly states that CRAs should obey the laws and regulations of the jurisdictions in which they operate and that these laws may include direct regulation of CRAs and, unlike the US, may incorporate elements of the IOSCO Code.[107] Arguably, implicitly, although not explicitly, this is an attempt to ensure that in the EU, the defence of rating agencies acting akin to a reporting journalist based on First Amendment immunity from liability, which is available in the US, will not be available in the EU as they do not form part of the law. However, on whether this means that the liability of CRAs in the EC will be rampant or not is difficult to deduce.

5.5.3 Globalisation: Need for a Level Playing Field

In the US, as mentioned in Chap. 4, where most of the CRAs with significant EU activities have their parent companies, CRAs have been subjected to regulation and

[106] Regulation (2009), p. 2.
[107] Proposal for a Regulation (2008), p. 3.

supervision since summer 2007. The US Reform Act came into force on 27 June 2007, establishing a legal framework for the registration of NRSROs.[108] The Commission felt that it is important, given the global nature of the rating business, to create a level playing field between the EU and the US by setting up a regulatory framework in the EU comparable to that applied in the US[109] and arguably based on the same principles. What was required was that the EU regulatory framework had to converge, rather than diverge, with the US regulatory principles, arguably based on a common sense of bringing in a unified approach. Shareholders, based on the common laws (contract and tort) of both these jurisdictions, have no legal recourse against CRAs, and hence the laws do converge.[110]

5.5.4 *Self-Regulation*

The legislative option adopted has clear advantages over the other policy options, especially with regard to its effectiveness and certainty, because the other options (self-regulatory approaches or a recommendation) cannot produce legally binding rules as an enforcement mechanism. Although self-regulatory approaches *per se* may have no place in the corporate world, and in particular in the capital markets, what is important is the willingness of CRAs to abide by both the letter and the spirit of the self-regulation.[111] In order to compel CRAs to abide by self-regulation (i.e., a code of conduct), there is a need for imposition of liability when self-regulation is breached; however, it may be difficult to achieve this, as it has no legally binding effect. Statutory regulation is, therefore, the best option to ensure a common framework throughout the Community.[112]

5.6 Quality Credit Rating

The EU Regulation on CRAs,[113] which has been in force since December 2010, is part of Europe's response to the commitments made by the G20 at the November 2008 Washington summit. This Regulation was amended in May 2011, to create

[108] See Chap. 4.

[109] This was mentioned in the Proposal for a Regulation (2008), p. 3.

[110] See Chap. 6.

[111] See Chap. 3.

[112] Proposal for a Regulation (2008), p. 5.

[113] Regulation (EC) No 1060/2009 of the European Parliament and of the Council of 16 September 2009 on credit rating agencies, OJ L 302 (17.11.2009). Regulation (EC) No 1060/2009 is often referred to as CRAI Regulation.

and establish a European Securities and Markets Authority (ESMA).[114] The registration and supervision of CRAs is examined below to see how the regulators were able to tackle them.

5.6.1 Registration

A CRA is obliged to fulfil a number of obligations on the conduct of its business intended to ensure the independence and integrity of the rating process and to enhance the quality of the ratings issued. The ESMA have been entrusted, since July 2011, with the responsibility of registering CRAs in the EU. Initially, 28 CRAs (some of which belong to the same group) were registered with the ESMA.

5.6.2 Supervision

Since July 2011, the ESMA has started exercising exclusive supervisory powers over CRAs registered in the EU. It is endowed with comprehensive investigative powers, including the ability to demand any document or data, to summon and hear persons, to conduct on-site inspections and to impose administrative sanctions, fines and periodic penalty payments.[115] This centralises and simplifies the supervision of CRAs at a European level[116] and ensures a single point of contact for registered CRAs; significant efficiency gains are due to a shorter and less complicated registration and supervisory process and a more consistent application of the rules for CRAs.[117] CRAs are at present the only financial institutions that are directly supervised by a European supervisory authority. The EU rules are to apply to ratings of public entities not only within the EU but also outside the EU if a CRA registered in the EU issues sovereign ratings.[118]

The European Commission[119] noted that despite the adoption of European legislation on CRAs in 2009 and 2010 as mentioned above, recent developments in the context of the Euro debt crisis has shown that the existing regulatory framework is inadequate.[120] The reasons are that CRAs are major players in today's

---

[114] Regulation (EU) No 513/2011 of the European Parliament and of the Council of 11 May 2011 amending Regulation (EC) No 1060/2009. Regulation (EU) No 513/2011 is often referred to as CRAII Regulation. http://eur-lex.europa.eu/LexUriServ/LexUriServ.do?uri=OJ:L:2011:145:0030:0056:EN:PDF.

[115] European Commission, Press Release, Commission wants better quality credit ratings (15/11/2011). http://eropa.eu/rapid/pressreleaseaction.do?/reference=ip/11/1355.

[116] Ibid.

[117] Ibid.

[118] Ibid.

[119] Ibid.

[120] Ibid.

financial markets, with rating actions having a direct impact on the actions of investors, borrowers, issuers and governments. The Commission cited an example of a corporate downgrade where there are consequences for the capital a bank must hold. A downgrade of sovereign debt can make a country's borrowing more expensive. It meant that there is a need for proposals to be put forward "to toughen that framework further and deal with outstanding weaknesses".[121] Important goals included sovereign debt ratings,[122] a need for investors and financial institutions to carry out due diligence and eliminating conflicts of interest.

5.6.3 *Sovereign Debt Rating*

Although the links between a credit rating downgrade and increased borrowing costs for the sovereign are not always clear, credit rating downgrades in Greece, Ireland, Italy, Portugal and Spain have coincided with turmoil in European financial markets and increased borrowing costs for the downgraded countries. Sovereign credit ratings have effects on sovereign borrowing costs, risk assessments in relation to the probability of default and the market for sovereign debt.[123]

With regard to the European sovereign debt market, credit rating downgrades have a spill-over effect and affect not only the financial market in the downgraded country but also the markets in other Euro area countries as well. Downgrades in some European countries can have far-reaching effects on the financial market and the economy. Global uncertainty results in sluggish business investment. The downgrade of a sovereign credit rating may also have other repercussions like decreased solvency of financial institutions that hold a large amount of a sovereign debt, an economic slowdown resulting from reduced government spending related to higher borrowing costs and decreased liquidity in the financial sector.[124]

5.7 Legal Accountability

The European Commission had proposed to establish civil liability of CRAs in the case of gross negligence or impropriety on a uniform basis throughout the EU.[125] In cases of wilful intent or gross negligence with regard to breaches of the Regulation, a reversal of the burden of proof would have applied, but this never materialised.[126]

[121] Ibid. Para 1.

[122] EC Press Release (2011), no. 2.

[123] Mahabir and Stuckey (2011).

[124] See Arezki et al. (2011).

[125] Andenaes (2012), pp. 302–304.

[126] Stuwe et al. (2012).

Establishing a uniform civil liability within the EU requires liability rules to converge. The idea of reversing the burden of proof, as explained below, was opposed. Reversing a burden of proof is not a new phenomenon. It already exists in other areas of EU law like consumer protection (where the burden of proof is on the seller—not the consumer—to prove that the product sold conformed to the contract of sale),[127] passenger rights[128] and sexual discrimination[129] cases. In a number of cases, the European Court of Justice has sought to address the problem of adducing proof by reversing the burden of proof, requiring the employer to prove that a particular practice is not discriminatory.[130]

The reversing of burden of proof would have meant that CRAs had to prove the non-infringement of the rules rather than investors proving that they did infringe the rules. There is a possibility that such a rule would have acted as a deterrent and prevented CRAs from issuing incorrect ratings. The problem investors face is that there is no way for them to know the internal procedures a CRA has used and how it decided on the rating that was issued. What a judge/competent court have to do is to take into consideration the fact that the investor or issuer may not have access to that information, which is entirely within the domain of the CRA.

The fear of reversing the burden of proof expressed by CRAs is that it will protect large investors, and not small investors, who have deep pockets to sue, and this will make large investors less responsible for the risks they take. This may not be true as investors, who rely entirely on a CRA's opinion for an investment decision and not on a multiple sources of information, would find it difficult to convince a judge or jury that they had acted reasonably.[131] In addition, a reversal of burden would not have been fatal for the CRAs, as investors are still required to prove the existence of some sort of damage in the first place.[132]

Fitch Ratings argues that placing the burden of proof on CRAs would make it cheaper and easier for plaintiffs to bring frivolous claims against a CRA, and this would be costly for the CRAs to defend. Fitch Ratings insists that ratings are opinions about events/circumstances in the future, implying a relative default

---

[127] See "Consumer protection in the European Union: Ten Basic Principles", p. 6. http://ec.europa.eu/consumers/cons_info/10principles/en.pdf.

[128] Regulation (EC) No 261/2004 of the European Parliament and of the Council of 11 February 2004 establishing common rules on compensation and assistance to passengers in the event of denied boarding and of cancellation or long delay of flights, and repealing Regulation (EEC) No 295/91.

[129] See, for example, Council Directive 2000/43 implementing the principle of equal treatment between persons irrespective of racial or ethnic origin; and Council Directive 2000/78 establishing a general framework for equal treatment in employment and occupation. See Glossary for the meaning of "Burden of Proof".

[130] See for example, *Handels-og Kontorfunktionaerernes Forbund i Danmark v. Dansk Arbejdsgiverforening (acting for Danfoss)*, Case 109/88, [1989] ECR 3199; *Enderby v. Frenchay Area Health Authority*, Case 127/92 [1993] ECR 5535. The rule was codified in Council Directive 97/80/EC on the burden of proof in cases of discrimination based on sex (Article 4(1)).

[131] Froymovich (2012).

[132] Ibid.

probability.[133] Blackrock is one of the world's pre-eminent asset management firms and a premier provider of global investment management, risk management and advisory services to institutional and retail clients around the world. Blackrock's stand against the reversing of burden of proof is because of the fear of unintended consequences on the competition (by reducing the number of issues rated, and this would increase the rating cost). In the case of Europe, as an example, it would be to the detriment of "issuers and end-investors and potentially undermines the Commission's stated goals of avoiding over-reliance on ratings".[134]

According to Hopkins,[135] there are other ways of achieving better ratings. He suggests a sensible regulation backed by sensible supervision. A Commission's proposal to impose an EU-wide standard of civil legal liability[136] would be detrimental in not encouraging a potential new entrant to come into this market and become a competitor,[137] and the EU seems to have chosen this option. Presently, investors find it difficult to make CRAs legally accountable for their losses, especially when CRAs breach the provisions of the Regulation. Reversing the burden of proof would have relieved investors, as litigants, of adducing the proof that CRAs were negligent, say for their failure to abide by the current Regulation in place, as the CRAs would have the burden of proving that they were not negligent.

Prior to 2009, there was no recourse against CRAs when they infringed any of the laid down regulations. With the introduction of the Regulation in the EC,[138] a CRA would now be liable if it infringed, intentionally or with gross negligence, the CRA Regulation, thereby causing damage to an investor who has relied on the rating that followed such an infringement. Liability does not cover ordinary negligence of CRAs. With the shift in burden of proof, the burden now rests on CRAs, and it means CRAs have to prove that they did not infringe the regulations and investors do not have to prove that the CRAs did it. The problem not addressed is that the exculpatory exclusion clauses will protect CRAs even if investors are able to bring civil liability claims before the national courts. Presently, the judges would examine the exclusion clauses only to see if they are reasonable or not, and if found reasonable, they would be upheld by the court.

A special provision is required that would make the courts either ignore the disclaimer of liability clauses put by the CRAs or make such a provision null and

[133] "Fitch Ratings" Comments on European Commission's Proposal (15 November 2011) for Further Amendments to the Credit Rating Agency Regulation, http://www.fitchratings.com/web_content/credit_policy/reg_affairs/Fitch_CRA3_Jan2012_vFINAL.pdf.

[134] Blackrock, View Point, "Reform of Credit Rating Agency Regulation in Europe: An End-investor Perspective" (April 2012), p. 3. http://www.blackrock.com/corporate/en-gb/literature/whitepaper/credit-rating-agency-end-investor-perspective-apr-2012.pdf.

[135] Stated by Wishart (2012).

[136] Ibid.

[137] Ibid.

[138] Regulation (EU) No 462/2013, amending the Regulation (EC) No 1060/2009 on credit rating agencies, the 2nd Reform Regulation. The 2nd Reform Regulation has introduced a civil liability regime for credit rating agencies at the level of European Union law.

void, as is the case in France.[139] South Africa has introduced a provision relating to liability. It means a CRA may be liable in tort to an investor for any loss, damages or costs sustained. It does not affect any additional or other liability of a CRA to an investor or member of the public arising from a contractual relationship or the application of any law or any additional or other liability of a CRA to an investor or member of the public arising from a contractual relationship or the application of any law. Furthermore, a CRA is prohibited from limiting or reducing the liability incurred through a contract or agreement or in any other way or in terms of the common law.[140] On 23 October 2010, the French, under the law regulating banking and finance, enacted a provision making any contractual exclusion of liability of the CRAs invalid, thus creating a deterrent effect on the part of CRAs. However, it might create unintended consequences such as CRAs refusing to give controversial opinion, CRAs reducing their coverage and CRAs not disclosing ratings to the public at large, which might discourage new entrants.[141]

5.8 Conclusion

There was a need to restore market confidence and increase investor protection. In the EU, CRAs are considered to have failed to reflect the worsening market conditions early enough in their credit ratings. The European Commission felt that correction of such a failure required putting in place measures related to conflicts of interest, the quality of the credit ratings, the transparency of the CRAs and the internal governance and surveillance of the activities of the CRAs. The users of credit ratings, on the other hand, were not expected to rely blindly on credit ratings; rather, they were required to take utmost care. The proposal for regulation in the EU had four overall objectives aimed at improving the process of issuance of credit ratings relating to avoiding conflicts of interest; improving the quality of the methodologies; increasing transparency; setting disclosure obligations, an efficient registration and a surveillance framework; avoiding forum shopping; and regulatory arbitrage between EU jurisdictions.[142] Undoubtedly, they are commendable.

Regulations in the EU required the CRAs to not only comply with strict standards of integrity, quality and transparency but also be subject to ongoing supervision by public authorities. The aim of the Regulation was to provide investors with the information, integrity and impartiality they needed from CRAs if they were to make prudent investment decisions. The Regulation is expected to

[139] See also Haar (2013), p. 4.

[140] Minister of Finance, Republic of South Africa, Credit Rating Service Bill (7 February 2012) Secs. 19 (1), (2) and (3).

[141] Gracia and Del Pozo (2012), p. 257.

[142] Ibid., p. 4.

significantly improve the conduct of CRAs with clear benefits to the integrity and stability of the financial markets. Most importantly, the Regulation has also put in place a common regulatory regime for the issuance of credit. Undoubtedly, the Regulation will have a major impact on the activities of CRAs.[143] However, unresolved issues regarding the well-balanced instrument require fine-tuning in certain fields, including rating shopping, financial ties with rated entities, abuse of inside information, transparency and CRAs' accountability.[144] It is also difficult for the users/investors of credit ratings in the EU to independently decide whether opinions issued by CRAs are reliable or not and to what extent those opinions should affect their investment choices without any need for them to carry out further due diligence tests.

Where the EC directive does leave us? With regard to their reliance on such credit ratings, investors are required to perform their own analysis and conduct due diligence,[145] but the legal basis for this is not clear. Regulation, because of its direct effect, is the best instrument to ensure a consistent and uniform approach throughout the EU. Undoubtedly, a statutory regulation, which introduces a comprehensive registration and surveillance regime for the issuance of credit ratings, is a step in the right direction. Nevertheless, the Directive leaves a member state a degree of flexibility in deciding how to adapt its national legal orders; it would therefore create divergence rather than uniformity and is unproductive.[146] Most importantly, as CRAs are not barred from using exclusion clauses to exculpate them from liability, the new EC approach will have a limited effect.

References

Amtenbrink, F., & De Hassan, J. (2009). Regulating credit ratings in the European Union: A critical first assessment of regulation 1060/2009 on credit rating agencies. *Common Market Law Review, 46*, 1915–1949.

Andenaes, M. (2012). Credit rating agencies: Their regulation and civil liability in the European Union. *Law and Economics Yearly Review*, 302–304.

Andenaes, M., & Deipenbrock, G. (2012). Regulating and supervising credit rating agencies in the European Union. *International and Comparative Corporate Law Journal, 9*(1), 1–17.

Arezki, R., Candelon, B., & Sy, A. N. R. (2011, March). *Sovereign rating news and financial markets spill overs: Evidence from the European debt crisis* (IMF Working Paper). http://www.imf.org/external/pubs/ft/wp/2011/wp1168.pdf.

[143] Europa Press Release (2009).

[144] Staikouras (2012), p. 71.

[145] The Capital Requirements Directive/Capital Requirements Regulation which came into force on 1 January 2014. http://ec.europa.eu/internal_market/rating-agencies/docs/140512-fsb-eu-response_en.pdf.

[146] I Proposal for a Regulation (2008), p. 7. bid.

Bahena, A. J. (2010). Part 5 III, "What role did credit rating agencies play in the credit crisis". 2B. http://blogs.law.uiowa.edu/ebook/uicifd-ebook/part-5-iii-what-role-did-credit-rating-agencies-play-credit-crisis.

Ball, T. C., Glover, J., Jamal, K., Kassam, R., Kouri, K., & Paterson, D. B., et al. (n.d.). Audit firm rotation: A joint academic and practitioner perspective (p. 1). http://faculty.som.yale.edu/shyamsunder/Research/Accounting%20and%20Control/Presentations%20and%20Working%20Papers/AuditFirmRotation/Audit_Firm_Rotation_%20Dec30_Jamal.pdf.

Barroso, J. M. (2009, April 23). Commission President. Brussels. http://europa.eu/rapid/pressReleasesAction.do?reference=IP/09/629.

Becker, B., & Milbourn, T. (2011). How did increased competition affect credit ratings? *Journal of Financial Economics, 101*, 493.

Bolton, P., Freixas, X., & Shapiro, J. (2012). The credit ratings game. *Journal of Finance, 67*(1), 85–111.

Bolton, P., Freixas, X., & Shapiro, J. (2010, May). The credit ratings game. http://www.recercat.net/bitstream/handle/2072/88007/1221.pdf?sequence=1.

Cane, M. B., Shamir, A., & Jodar, T. (2012). Below investment grade and above the law: Past, present and future look at the accountability of credit rating agencies. *Fordham Journal of Corporate & Financial Law, XVII*, 1122.

Coffee, J. C., & Lannoo, K. (2010). OECD hearing, competition and credit rating agencies (p. 13). http://www.oecd.org/daf/competition/sectors/46825342.pdf.

Committee on Global Financial System. (2008, July). *Ratings in structural finance; what went wrong and what can be done to address shortcomings* (Bank for International Settlements, CGFS Paper No. 32, p. 9).

Council of the European Union. (2013, May 13). Council adopts new rules on credit rating agencies (p. 2). http://www.consilium.europa.eu/uedocs/cms_data/docs/pressdata/en/ecofin/137078.pdf.

ESMA (2011, January 3). Frequently asked questions, a guide to understanding ESMA (p. 3). http://www.esma.europa.eu/system/files/2011_009.pdf.

Europa Press Release. (2009, April 23). Approval of new Regulation will raise standards for the issuance of credit rating used in the community. Brussels. http://europa.eu/rapid/pressReleasesAction.do?reference=IP/09/629.

Flood, J. (2005, July 1). Rating, dating, and the informal regulation and the formal ordering of the financial market. In M. B. Likosky (Ed.), *Privatising development: Transnational law, information and human rights* (pp. 154, 160–171). Martinus Nijhoff Publishers.

Froymovich, R. (2012, August 30). Ratings firms and burden of proof. *Wall Street Journal*. http://blogs.wsj.com/brussels/2012/08/30/innocent-until-proven-guilty-not-always/

Gavras, P. (2012, March). Ratings game. *Finance & Development, 49*(1). http://www.imf.org/external/pubs/ft/fandd/2012/03/gavras.htm

Gracia, R. C., & Del Pozo, J. R. (2012). *Credit rating agencies on the watch list: Analysis of European regulation* (p. 257). Oxford: OUP.

Haar, B. (2013, January 9). *Civil liability of credit rating agencies – Regulatory all-or-nothing approaches between immunity and over-deterrence* (University of Oslo Faculty of Law Research Paper No. 2013-02, p. 4). http://dx.doi.org/10.2139/ssrn.2198293.

Hill, C. A. (2004). Regulating the rating agencies. *Washington University Law Quarterly, 82*, 43, 53.

Liikanen, E., Bänziger, H., Manuel Campa, J., Gallois, L., Goyens, M., Pieter Krahnen, J., et al. (2012, October 2). *High-level Expert Group on reforming the structure of the EU banking sector* (p. 1). Final Report. Brussels. http://ec.europa.eu/internal_market/bank/docs/high-level_expert_group/report_en.pdf.

Mahabir, M., & Stuckey, B. (2011, November 16). Sovereign credit ratings: A profile. Parliament of Canada. http://www.parl.gc.ca/content/lop/researchpublications/2011-110-e.htm.

Marston, R. (2013, February 5). What is a rating agency. http://www.bbc.co.uk/news/10108284.

Milken Institute. (2002, April 10). *Credit rating agencies regulation: A roundtable discussion on the implication for issuers and investors* (p. 1). Discussion Report. http://www.milkeninstitute.org/pdf/CRA-Paris.pdf.

Milken Institute. (2012). p. 5. http://www.milkeninstitute.org/pdf/CRA-Paris.pdf.

Rousseau, S. (2009, July 23). *Regulating credit rating agencies after the financial crisis: The long and winding road toward accountability* (Capital Markets Institute Research Paper). http://dx.doi.org/10.2139/ssrn.1456708.

Sève, M. (2010). Credit rating agencies: Post-crisis regulatory measures adopted by the European Union Regulation of 16 September 2009. *The Journal of Regulation*. http://www.regulatorylawreview.com/II-6-4-Credit-Rating-Agencies-Post.html.

Staikouras, P. K. (2012). *A theoretical and empirical review of the EU regulation on credit rating agencies: In search of truth, not scapegoats* (p. 71). New York University Salomon Centre and Wiley Periodicals, Inc.

Stuwe, A., Weib, M., & Philipper, J. (2012). Rating agencies: Are they necessary, superfluous, a necessary evil or harmful? *Permanent Working Group*. Financial Policy, Taxation, Budgets and Financial Markets of FES Managerkreis.

Tan, H. (1995, Spring). Effects of expectations, prior involvement, and review awareness on memory for audit evidence and judgment. *Journal of Accounting Research*, 113–135.

US Investors' Working Group. (2009, October 21). *Letter to the US House of representative on regulation of credit rating agencies* (p. 2). http://www.cfainstitute.org/ethics/Documents/iwg_letter_us_congress_credit_rating_agencies.pdf.

Wishart, I. (2012, January 13). Ratings firms seek changes to tough regulation plans. *European Voice*. 6th Para. http://www.europeanvoice.com/article/imported/ratings-firms-seek-changes-to-tough-regulation-plans-/73186.aspx.

Chapter 6
US Case Law Regulation

6.1 Introduction

In 2007, credit rating agencies (CRAs) had provided triple-A ratings to many securitised bond issues financed by subprime mortgages, and as a result investors had suffered losses when some of the bond issues failed. They include legal action investors can take against CRAs based on tort law and the potential drawback to corrective and distributive justice, the third-party beneficiary rule, liability for false statement in public registration, legal protection afforded to CRAs (including First Amendment protection) and claims lodged by issuers against CRAs. It examines the deterrent effect that the law has on CRAs and their responsibility to investors as gatekeepers. This chapter will only examine the US position as this is where the subprime mortgage crisis has emerged and because it is based on common law. The position in the EU is that most of the countries have adopted a civil law system that is not compatible.

6.2 Tort Law and Corrective Justice: Compensating Investors

In most cases, a CRA's contract is with the issuers and not investors who are third parties. Therefore, investors cannot sue CRAs for breach of contract, and any legal remedy they may claim lies in tort and specific statutory provisions. This analysis examines the merit of imposing tort liability on CRAs based on "corrective justice". As a vehicle for compensation, tort law adjusts "losses and afford[s] compensation

M. Hemraj, *Credit Rating Agencies*, DOI 10.1007/978-3-319-17927-8_6

for injuries sustained as a result of the conduct of others".[1] The overall objective of tort law is "justly to hold one party liable to compensate the other".[2] Legal theorists and philosophers, in their analyses, have used the term "corrective justice" to mean "a system of rights and duties that are correlative between identified persons and stem particularly from a particular event".[3]

6.2.1 Corrective Justice and Distributive Justice

The distinction between corrective justice and distributive justice is that the function of liability in the former is seen as "a redress for a wrong committed to a victim" and in the latter as redress for the losses suffered by the victims because of misfortune.[4] Legal theorists have argued that corrective justice is distinct both conceptually and normatively from distributive justice. In particular, they contend that it is an error to view corrective justice as ancillary to distributive justice, necessary only to maintain or restore a preferred allocation of benefits and burdens. The dependence thesis holds that a normative account of the occasions of corrective justice is dependent on a larger theory of distributive justice. An alternative normative account of the occasions of corrective justice offered by legal theorists supports the autonomy of corrective justice from distributive justice.[5] "The principle of corrective justice imposes agent-specific reasons for acting".[6] It relates to a duty to make a victim's loss whole if the loss is wrongful and the actor is responsible for having brought about the loss. What is unclear is what brings "the conduct within the ambit of corrective justice?"[7] Other problems with the concept of corrective justice are, first, due to its infancy, there is a lack of a "systematic account of tort law based on corrective justice"; second, the legal community finds "various economic approaches more persuasive or compelling compared to distributive justice"; and, third, unlike one economic theory of tort law based on economic efficiency, there is "disagreement among moral theorists of torts about the content and demands of corrective justice".[8]

[1] See Harlow (2005), p. 27; Fleming (1998); Jones (2002); Markesinis and Deakin (2008); Steele (2007).

[2] Harlow (2005), p. 28.

[3] Ibid.

[4] Englard, Izhak (1993), Corrective Justice and Distributive Justice (1993), p. 11–20.

[5] See Lippke (1999), pp. 149–169.

[6] See Coleman (1995), p. 56.

[7] Ibid., p. 58.

[8] Ibid., p. 57.

6.2.2 *Balancing of Interests*

There has always been a justifiable concern about opening the floodgates (of liability) wide enough to hold professional people such as auditors in the UK, the US and Australia liable in order to compensate a third-party victim for economic loss.[9] This reluctance continues today in the context of representative actions against, for example, auditors. If the theoretical problems identified are justified, at the heart of the problem lies the serious issue of the balancing of interests in the form of not making the position of CRAs untenable and at the same time compensating investors for losses when unreliable ratings are issued. CRAs have escaped liability, and as such the current system of regulation (self-regulation and statutory regulation in the US and EU) has had no deterrent effect on the underperformance of CRAs.

A cynic might ask why CRAs should exercise care and issue reliable ratings when unreliable ratings will have no repercussion in the form of liability being imposed on them. CRAs are able to pocket revenues generated from the fees charged with impunity, irrespective of whether the ratings issued by them were reliable or not. The counter argument is that CRAs are not insurers and, if they were held liable to compensate investors for every loss they incur, they would be acting as such. This is perhaps an exaggerated statement as no one is suggesting that CRAs should be held liable for all the losses but only those losses caused by unreliable ratings produced in haste or beyond their expertise.

6.3 Cause of Actions: Options Open to Investors

What are the options open to investors in recovering losses as third parties who have relied on CRAs' ratings that were undeservingly optimistic or deserving ratings that had not been downgraded when the situation changed? This section analyses investors' legal actions based on (a) common law fraud, (b) negligent and fraudulent misrepresentation made by CRAs and (c) the third-party beneficiary rule.

6.3.1 *Common Law Fraud in the US*

6.3.1.1 Scienter (Knowingly)

Common law fraud[10] is the intentional misrepresentation of material facts presented to and relied upon by another party to his detriment. Intentional

[9] See *Caparo Industries plc v Dickman* [1990] 1 All ER 568; *Credit Alliance v Arthur Anderson and Co* 483 Need 110 (1985); *Billy v Arthur Young & Co* 834 P 2d 745 (1992); *Esanda Finance Corp Ltd v Peat Marwick Hungerfords (reg)* (1997) 142 ALR 750; Nguyen and Rajapakse (2008).

[10] See R. Lord, *Williston on Contracts,* 4th Edition, Lawyers Cooperative Publishing (2012) § 69:2.

"misrepresentation is fraudulent if the maker (a) knows or believes that the matter is not as he represents it to be, (b) does not have the confidence in the accuracy of his representation that he states or implies, or (c) knows that he does not have the basis for his representation that he states or implies".[11] Common law fraud is the established version of fraud through the traditional application of English common law by local courts for hundreds of years. It is difficult for a plaintiff to win on the allegation of fraud because a plaintiff has not only to satisfy several elements of fraud but also a *scienter*. *Scienter* (Latin word meaning "knowingly") is a guilty knowledge that is sufficient to charge a person with the consequences of his or her acts. *Scienter* has a broader application than *mens rea* (guilty mind) because it also describes knowledge required to assign liability in many civil cases. *Scienter* denotes a level of intent on the part of the defendant. *Scienter* is relevant to the pleadings in a case, and plaintiffs have to allege that the defendant acted with some knowledge of wrongdoing or guilt.[12] The definition of *scienter* in *Ernst*[13] was fashioned in the context of a financial dispute, where the US Supreme Court described *scienter* as "a mental state embracing intent to deceive, manipulate, or defraud". In the *Ernst* case, investors in a brokerage firm sued an accounting firm after the principal investor committed suicide and left a note revealing that the brokerage firm was a swindler. The investors in *Ernst* did not allege that the accounting firm had intended to defraud the investors. Rather, they alleged only that the accounting firm had been negligent in its accounting and that the negligence constituted a violation of the Securities Exchange Act. The Supreme Court ruled that an allegation of negligent conduct alone is insufficient to prove a violation of the Securities Exchange Act and that plaintiffs have to prove *scienter* on the part of the defendant to establish a claim under the act.

In a fraud case, in pleading a plaintiff has to state with particularity an allegation of fraud and the circumstances constituting the fraud.[14] In other words, "a plaintiff, at a minimum, must 'allege the time, place, and content of the alleged misrepresentation on which he or she relied; the fraudulent scheme; the fraudulent intent of the defendants; and the injury resulting from the fraud'".[15] *Scienter* may be stated generally by a plaintiff, or it can be inferred from circumstantial evidence.[16] In the context of a financial dispute, the US Supreme Court[17] described *scienter* as "a mental state embracing intent to deceive, manipulate, or defraud".

---

[11] *Restatement (Second) of Torts,* American Law Institute (1977–2009), § 526.

[12] See Glossary for the meaning of "scienter".

[13] *Ernst and Ernst v. Hochfelder,* 425 U.S. 185, 96 S. Ct. 1375, 47 L. Ed. 2d 668 (1976).

[14] Under Rule 9(b), Fed. R. Civ. P.

[15] In order to comply with Rule 9(b), of the *Federal Rules of Civil Procedure 2010* (as amended), See *Walburn v. Lockheed Martin Corp.,* 431 F.3d 966, 972 (6th Cir.2005) (quoting *Coffey v. Foamex L.P.,* 2 F.3d 157, 161–162 (6th Cir. 1993).

[16] *See* Fed.R.Civ.P. 9(b); *S.E.C. v. Blackwell,* 291 F.Supp.2d 673, 696 (S.D.Ohio 2003).

[17] *Ernst and Ernst v. Hochfelder,* 425 U.S. 185, 96 S. Ct. 1375, 47 L. Ed. 2d 668 (1976).

A requirement is that the allegations must give rise to a "strong inference that the defendant acted with the required state of mind".[18] The strong inference standard is satisfied if the complaint "allege[s] facts from which, if true, a reasonable person could infer that the defendant acted with the required intent".[19] It is not sufficient that a reasonable inference be the basis of a complaint's allegations about the requisite state of mind. Rather, to determine whether a complaint's *scienter* allegations can survive threshold inspection for sufficiency, a court must engage in a comparative evaluation; it must consider not only inferences urged by the plaintiff but also competing inferences rationally drawn from the facts alleged. An inference of fraudulent intent may be plausible yet less cogent than other, non-culpable explanations for the defendant's conduct.

The US Supreme Court[20] had discussed Section 10(b)'s *scienter* requirement and set the following guidelines for analysing whether a complaint sufficiently pleads *scienter*. "First, faced with a Rule 12(b) (6) motion to dismiss a § 10 (b) action, courts must, as with any motion to dismiss for failure to plead a claim on which relief can be granted, accept all factual allegations in the complaint as true.[21] Second, courts must consider the complaint in its entirety . . . [and] Third, in determining whether the pleaded facts give rise to a 'strong' inference of *scienter*, the court must take into account plausible opposing inferences".[22]

In addition to common law fraud, the more general developments regarding the standards governing private rights of action under the securities laws affect CRAs. The CRAs receive a significant measure of protection from the strict pleading standards imposed by the *Private Securities Litigation Reform Act 1995* by requiring plaintiffs to plead with particularity facts giving rise to a strong inference of fraud.[23] The problem with fraud claims under the common law and §10 (b) of the *Securities Exchange Act of 1934* is that although it requires that plaintiffs have a higher pleading standard under *Federal Rule of Civil Procedure* 9 (b), nevertheless plaintiffs have more success at the pleading stage. In some cases,[24] the judges upheld common law fraud claims against S&P and Moody's for assigning allegedly false and misleading high ratings to certain structured finance products.

[18] *In Re National Century Financial Enterprises, Inc.*, 541 F. Supp. 2d 986—Dist. 2007).

[19] The US CA, 437 F.3d 588, 602 (2006).

[20] *Tellabs, Inc. v. Makor Issues & Rights, Ltd.*, 127 S.Ct. 2499, 168 L.Ed.2d 179 (2007).

[21] 127 S.Ct. at 2509.

[22] Ibid.

[23] Coffee Jr. (2006, 2007).

[24] *Abu Dhabi Commercial Bank v. Morgan Stanley & Co. Inc.* and *Kings County, Washington v. IKB Deutsche Industrie Bank AG.*

6.3.1.2 Abu Dhabi[25] and King County[26]

Investors in the *Abu Dhabi* and *King County* cases had accused Moody's and S&P of collaborating with banks in arranging for structured investment vehicles (SIVs) to receive ratings as high as triple-A, although much of the underlying collateral was of low quality or of subprime mortgage debt. The *Abu Dhabi* case involved the collapse of an SIV[27], which had been at the heart of the recent US credit crisis. The plaintiffs claimed the defendants' CRA had given inflated ratings by working with the issuer (Morgan Stanley) to structure the investment products and their claim was based on the notes receiving the desired ratings. The investors claimed Moody's and S&P were involved in the structuring, rating and monitoring of the Cheyne SIV and the issuance of Capital Notes and were negligent in giving ratings that it should have known were inaccurate. The court rejected the CRAs' claim of First Amendment immunity distinguishing past cases based on special circumstances of the case. Here, the ratings were disseminated to a select group of investors in connection with a private placement and not to the public.

The CRAs, on their part, in *Abu Dhabi* had argued that the plaintiffs have not pleaded an actionable misrepresentation because CRAs are entitled to immunity under the First Amendment and CRAs and are not liable as their ratings are non-actionable opinions.[28] The US District Judge Scheindlin rejected the CRAs' argument that the ratings were non-actionable opinions on the basis that plaintiffs had sufficiently pleaded that the CRAs did not genuinely or reasonably believe that "the ratings they assigned to the Rated Notes were accurate and had a basis in fact".[29] In relation to a disclaimer, the Judge held that a disclaimer by the CRAs in the Information Memorandum was insufficient to protect the CRAs from liability for issuing misleading ratings.[30] The plaintiffs had argued that in 1975, the SEC created a special status to distinguish the most credible and reliable rating agencies, identifying them as nationally recognized statistical rating organizations (NRSROs) to help ensure the integrity of the ratings process. Granting of such a status meant that "the rating organization is recognized in the U.S. as an issuer of credible and reliable ratings by the predominant users of securities ratings" and that part of awarding the NRSRO label to the company hinges on "the rating organization's independence from the companies it rates".[31] The Judge found that the plaintiffs' reliance upon the CRAs was reasonable based on the market's reliance on CRAs,

---

[25] *Abu Dhabi Commercial Bank et al v. Morgan Stanley & Co et al*, U.S. District Court, Southern District of New York, No. 08-07508.

[26] *King County, Washington et al v. IKB Deutsche Industrie bank AG et al*, U.S. District Court, Southern District of New York, No. 09-08387.

[27] *Abu Dhabi* at 1.

[28] *Ibid.* at 175.

[29] Ibid.

[30] Ibid. at 176.

[31] Ibid. at 165.

given "their NRSRO status and, at least in this case, the rating agencies' access to non-public information that even sophisticated investors cannot obtain".[32] Investors in both cases accused the ratings agencies of collaborating with banks in arranging for SIVs to receive ratings as high as triple-A, even though much of the underlying collateral was low quality or subprime mortgage debt. The lawsuits accused CRAs of negligent misrepresentation over their activities regarding the Cheyne and Rhinebridge SIVs in concealing risks in two mortgage-related deals that collapsed during the financial crisis.

In *King County*, plaintiffs' claims in the Cheyne case were for common law fraud against the CRAs, aiding and abetting fraud against Morgan Stanley, and negligent misrepresentation against Morgan Stanley. The alleged misstatements at issue are the credit ratings assigned by the CRAs on the Cheyne SIV Notes. Part of the plaintiffs' theory of fraud is that the ratings masked "the actual risks associated with the securities included in the SIV's investment portfolio". The first case centred on a SIV Cheyne Finance,[33] created by Morgan Stanley and rated by S&P and Moody's. Less than a week before the scheduled start of the appeal trial, the parties agreed to settle the claims for an undisclosed amount in that they had defrauded investors in subprime mortgage vehicles created on the eve of the US housing bust. The SIV vehicle purchased billions of dollars of subprime mortgage derivatives and other debt between its launch in 2004 and its collapse in 2007, which caused investor losses. The stakes in the cases were highest for S&P, although it did not admit liability because of the likelihood that the jury's rulings would have influenced potential settlement negotiations with the US Department of Justice. The US government in its US $5 billion fraud ongoing suit against S&P is claiming that S&P, despite knowing that risks were building in underlying subprime mortgages, continued to hand out gold-plated triple-A credit ratings to SIV in order to win fees.[34]

Similarly, in the second claim the same parties (Morgan Stanley, which marketed both SIVs and helped structure the Rhinebridge SIV, and the two CRAs—S&P and Moody's) had given favourable ratings. All the parties jointly agreed to pay about US $225 million to settle lawsuits, claiming that they had concealed risks in two mortgage-related deals that collapsed during the global financial crisis.[35]

In two other different cases, the judges had reached different conclusions on similar facts. There in a private placement, Moody's and S&P had announced their ratings at the time of the private placement on their websites and through various financial media. A limited number of investors purchased investments, and although they were not disclosed in SEC filings, it constituted public dissemination

[32] Ibid. at 181.

[33] *Abu Dhabi*, District Court of N.Y. http://docs.justia.com/cases/federal/district-courts/new-york/nysdce/1:2008cv07508/331416/602/0.pdf?1363876053.

[34] Foley (2013).

[35] Wall Street (2013).

requiring protection.[36] The main distinguishing feature was that the rating announcement took place on the CRAs' website and in the financial media, which constituted information disseminated to a large group of investors, so CRAs needed protection. The reasoning is unpalatable. Although potential investors at large have the ability to make investments, such investments are normally finite and therefore the losses sustained by investors is of a known amount, which is the amount of money issuers want to raise through placement.

6.4 Negligent and Fraudulent Misrepresentation

Negligent misrepresentation arises where someone makes a statement without any grounds for knowing whether it is true or not, and an aspect of carelessness is involved.[37] In general, negligent misrepresentation refers to a situation in which someone makes a false statement for the purpose of making a deal, without any grounds for knowing whether it is true or not and an aspect of carelessness is involved, resulting in the person who relies on the statement experiencing harm.[38] With regard to a high rating issued to corporate debt instruments, investors may wish to bring an action in tort by alleging that CRAs were guilty of negligent misrepresentation when they gave issuers high ratings in light of the information then known to them. In contrast, fraudulent misrepresentation (as opposed to negligent misrepresentation) is an instance of false statement where (1) the party making the statement is aware that it is false or disregards the possibility of it being false (2) the party making the statement does so to induce another party to enter into a contract and (3) the other party enters the contract as a result of the statement and consequently suffers a loss.[39]

6.4.1 Reasonable Reliance and Disclaimer

The treatment of the reliance element is different, depending on whether the suits are for negligent misrepresentation or for fraud. In a fraud case, reliance must be reasonable, compared with a misrepresentation case, although the requirement of reliance is required in both fraud and misrepresentation cases. An issue about the justification for the plaintiffs' reliance on negligent misrepresentation[40] is "a factor

[36] *In re Nat'l Century Fin. Enters. Inc. Inv. Litig.*, 580 F.Supp.2d 630, 639–640 (S.D. Ohio 2008) and *Cal. Public Employees Ret. System*, No. CGC-09-490241, slip op. at 10 (Cal. Super. Ct. S.F. Cty. 1 June 2010).

[37] See Glossary under the term "misrepresentation".

[38] Ibid.

[39] Ibid.

[40] *Board of Education v. A, C and S, Inc.*, 131 Ill.2d 428, *137 Ill.Dec. 635*, *546 N.E.2d* 580 at 593.

to be considered in determining whether a plaintiff's reliance is foreseeable and justifiable",[41] and in such a case there is a need to show reasonable reliance.[42] With regard to ratings of subprime mortgages, the CRAs may claim that plaintiffs could not have justifiably relied on the alleged misrepresentations because of a general disclaimer with regard to ratings given. The CRA general disclaimer is that the ratings are opinions and should not be the sole basis of reliance by a potential investor to make investment decisions. On the subject of disclaimers, Lohman and Westeinde submit that absence of recommendation and disclaimer will not protect CRAs if there are materially false factual components. "The disclaimers will be less effective if they are simply included in the codes of conduct than if they are actually included in the rating itself".[43] Therefore, for a disclaimer to be effective, CRAs have to ensure that such a stipulation appears in their ratings and draw it to the attention of investors.

The validity of a disclaimer was an issue in the *Bathurst* case.[44] There, a pertinent observation of Judge Jagot in the Federal Court of Australia was that a CRA does not require the arranger/issuer to include a disclaimer when advising potential investors of the rating. In such a case, an arranger/issuer would be unaware of whether or not investors had seen this disclaimer. In addition, such a disclaimer is not simply ensuring that potential investors were aware that the CRA was not giving them financial advice as to their investments. Moreover, CRAs did not disclaim the exercise of any skill or care in forming the opinion expressed in the rating as this would make ratings futile and self-defeating.[45] It is uncertain whether other judges in the other jurisdictions like the US and England and Wales will accept such an argument. The *Bathurst* case, arising from the Australian jurisdiction, is of a persuasive nature only rather than of a binding nature,[46] and there might be a fear of expanding the liability of CRAs.

6.4.2 Third-Party Beneficiary Rule

The doctrinal standards of third-party beneficial rule have been widely used in professional liability cases in the US,[47] principally based on the tests of

---

[41] In *Perschall v. Raney*, 137 Ill. App.3d 978, 92 Ill.Dec. 431, 484 N.E.2d 1286, 336*336 1290 (1985).

[42] *Kuch & Watson, Inc. v. Woodman*, 29 Ill.App.3d 638, 331 N.E.2d 350, 354 (1975).

[43] de Savornin Lohman and van't Westeinde (2007).

[44] *Bathurst Regional Council v Local Government Services Pty Ltd (No. 5)* [2012] FCA 1200.

[45] Allen & Overy, "Rating agencies on the firing line" (11 January 2013). http://www.allenovery.com/publications/en-gb/Pages/Rating-agencies-in-the-firing-line.aspx.

[46] See B. Bintiff, "Mandatory verses Persuasive case" (2001). http://faculty.law.lsu.edu/toddbruno/mandatory_v__persuasive.htm.

[47] Powers (1993).

Restatement Section 133 and Restatement (Second) Section 302[48] "and [as] a more general test, which is stated as the intent to confer an enforceable benefit to the third party".[49] A claim by a non-contractual third party can only succeed if a plaintiff can show that he/she is a third-party beneficiary of the contract and if a state law where the case is litigated allows this. For example, Illinois has the "intent to benefit" rule, that is, third-party beneficiary status, but even then what needs to be determined by the court is whether the contracting parties intended to confer a benefit upon a non-party to their agreement.[50] It might be very difficult for an investor to prove intent to benefit as a third party based on "a strong presumption that parties to a contract intend that the contract's provisions apply to *only* them and not to third parties".[51] The basis of the best evidence a party can adduce is on the express language in the contract identifying a third-party beneficiary as an intended beneficiary. However, courts have also accepted an implied showing where "the implication that the contract applies to third parties [is] so strong as to be practically an express declaration".[52] In principle, without an express declaration or with ambiguous language, a contract will not suffice to make someone a third-party beneficiary. In the US, contract claims based on third-party beneficiary status have been successful in Medicaid[53] and Medicare, housing and prisoner cases.[54]

In the case of CRAs, in their contracts with issuers, they must identify the identity of specific investors as the beneficiaries of the rating contract because CRAs' very existence as an independent rating agency depends on investor reliance on its ratings.[55] This is how security markets operate, and it would be unrealistic to drive a wedge between the value the issuer receives from a credit rating service and the value that the purchasers receive. Without potential purchasers, the ratings would be a sham existing in a vacuum and benefitting no one. An investor may argue that as an intended beneficiary of the obligation, a CRA undertook to provide "continuous monitoring and surveillance" of the debt instruments of an issuer.[56]

Investors generally derive valuable information from CRAs, both at the time of purchase and during the time they purchased securities like bonds. The pertinent question, according to the court,[57] is whether the actual issuer and CRA contract

[48] Prince (1984).

[49] Feinman (2000), p. 44.

[50] *XL Disposal Corp. v. John Sexton Contractors Co.*, 168 Ill.2d 355, 213 Ill.Dec. 665, 659 N.E.2d 1312, 1316 (Ill.1995).

[51] *Harbor Drive Condominium Ass'n v. Harbor Point, Inc.*, 209 Ill.App.3d 631, 154 Ill.Dec. 365, 568 N.E.2d 365, 375 (1991).

[52] Ibid.

[53] See "What is Medicaid?" http://dhss.alaska.gov/dhcs/Pages/medicaid_medicare/default.aspx.

[54] See Bobroff and Tobin (2008); Hitov and Deford (2002).

[55] *Maurice L. Quinn, Plaintiff-Appellant v. The McGraw-Hill Companies, Inc., Defendant-Appellate*, No. 97-3269, United States Court Of Appeals, Seventh Circuit, 168 F.3d 331 (1999).

[56] Ibid.

[57] Ibid. at 334.

contains either express language identifying purchasers as named beneficiaries or its functional equivalent. Otherwise, as a matter of law it is insufficient for an investor to state a claim for breach as a third-party beneficiary. Investors may be indirect beneficiaries of ratings issued by a CRA in that an issuer may not capture the full benefit of the rating, but an investor may underestimate the direct value of a rating of the issuer. Contracts between two parties may generate information that is valuable to third parties like investors. However, judges are reluctant to infer in the sense that just because ultimately consumers benefit from such contracts, they do not automatically become third-party beneficiaries of such contracts and are not entitled to sue for breach.[58]

6.5 Drawback to Investors' Lawsuits

6.5.1 *Motion to Dismiss and Standard of Review*

In the majority of investors' suits filed against CRAs for having lost money by relying on unreliable ratings, the first line of defence adopted by a CRA's lawyer is that there is no case to answer. They would claim the plaintiffs' failure to state a claim and ask the court to dismiss the case. When considering a motion to dismiss,[59] a court normally construes the complaint in the light most favourable to the plaintiff and accepts all well-pleaded material allegations in the complaint as true.[60] A complaint may be dismissed for failure to state a claim only where "it appears beyond a doubt that the plaintiff can prove no set of facts in support of his claim which would entitle him to relief".[61]

At a pleading stage, Rule 8 of the *Federal Rules of Civil Procedure* does not impose a probability requirement and, as such, the court is not required to accept as true unwarranted legal conclusions or factual inferences.[62] Although the complaint need not contain detailed factual allegations, the factual allegations must be enough to raise the claimant's right to relief above mere speculation and create a reasonable expectation that discovery will reveal evidence to support the claim.[63] The court needs to be satisfied that a plaintiff will be able to produce evidence in support of the case. The court, on its part, is not "bound to accept as true a legal conclusion

[58] Ibid. at 335.

[59] Under Fed.R.Civ.P. 12(b) (6).

[60] See *Scheuer v. Rhodes,* 416 U.S. 232, 236, 94 S.Ct. 1683, 40 L.Ed.2d 90 (1974); *Roth Steel Prods. v. Sharon Steel Corp.,* 705 F.2d 134, 155 (6th Cir.1982).

[61] *Conley v. Gibson,* 355 U.S. 41, 45–46, 78 S.Ct. 99, 2 L.Ed.2d 80 (1957).

[62] *Morgan v. Church's Fried Chicken,* 829 F.2d 10, 12 (6th Cir.1987).

[63] See *Bell Atlantic,* 127 S.Ct. at 1964–1965, 167 L.Ed.2d 929; *Associated Gen, Contractors of Cal, Inc. v. Carpenters,* 459 U.S. 519, 526, 103 S.Ct. 897, 74 L.Ed.2d 723 (1983).

couched as a factual allegation".[64] What the court does, when determining cases brought before it, is to carry out a balancing act, involving the interests of both parties. In addition, in several cases where defendants have made a motion for the dismissal of cases, judges have been liberal by allowing plaintiffs to amend their pleadings.

6.5.1.1 Amending Pleadings

This section examines amending pleadings in litigation in the US district courts in the context of CRAs. It examines the circumstances under which a court has granted leave to amend pleadings and where a court has refused to accede to such a request. A pleading[65] is a formal written statement of a party's claims or defences to another party's claims in a civil action. In the US, a complaint is the first pleading[66] filed by a plaintiff, which initiates a lawsuit. A complaint sets forth the relevant allegations of fact that give rise to one or more legal cause of action, along with a prayer for relief and sometimes a statement of damages claimed (an *ad quod damnum* clause).

Where litigants have requested leave to amend pleadings to redress any deficiencies identified by a court, Rule 15(a) (2)[67] stipulates that a "court should freely give leave [to amend] when justice so requires".[68] Indeed, "[w]hen a motion to dismiss is granted, the usual practice is to grant leave to amend the complaint".[69] This is especially true when a defendant requests that a complaint be dismissed for lack of specificity (specifying a particular claim) under Rule 9(b)[70]; claims are usually not dismissed without leave to amend. Where re-pleading constitutes a second bite at the apple, a court has permitted litigants to amend the complaint in order to rectify deficiencies found by the court.[71] There are situations where a court may deny leave to amend pleadings either where it would be futile[72] or where a

[64] *Papasan v. Allain,* 478 U.S. 265, 286, 106 S.Ct. 2932, 92 L.Ed.2d 209 (1986); *accord Morgan,* 829 F.2d at 12.

[65] Civil Procedure Rules (CPR) governs pleadings in England and Wales. The CPR rules and directions incorporating 67th update that came into force on 13 November 2013. http://www.justice.gov.uk/courts/procedure-rules/civil/rules.

[66] Federal Rules of Civil Procedure (as amended to December 1, 2013) govern pleading in United States federal courts. http://www.law.cornell.edu/rules/frcp.

[67] Federal Rules of Civil Procedure, Title III, Pleading and Motions, Rule 15 Amended and Supplemented.

[68] "Rule 15. Amended and Supplemental Pleadings" http://www.law.cornell.edu/rules/frcp/rule_15.

[69] *Ronzani v. Sanofi S.A.,* 899 F.2d 195, 198 (2d Cir.1990).

[70] Federal Rules of Civil Procedure, *Luce v. Edelstein,* 802 F.2d 49, 56 (2d Cir.1986).

[71] For pleading requirements for fraud under Fed.R.Civ.P. 9(b), see *LaSalle Nat. Bank v. Duff & Phelps Credit Rating Co., 951 F. Supp. 1071 – Dist. Court, SD New York* (1996), pp. 1081–1082.

[72] *Jefferson City School District No. R-1 v. Moody's Investor's Services* 175 F. 3d 848—Court of Appeals 10th Circuit 1999.

litigant fails to specify additional facts that would result in a litigant not succeeding in a trial.[73]

In *re Moody's Corporation*[74] and *Abu Dhabi*,[75] leave to amend pleadings was granted. In *re Moody's Corp*., the court had already found that two of the plaintiff litigant's causation arguments were insufficient. It was possible for the litigant to cure the deficiencies by averring facts demonstrating that statements regarding meaning and source of structured finance securities were false or that the defendant's staff possessed the requisite *scienter* knowledge that is sufficient to charge a person with the consequences of his or her acts. Therefore, the court in tune with its general policy allowed leave to amend. Moreover, such a request is granted liberally in cases alleging securities fraud.[76]

In *Abu Dhabi*, two institutional investors, King County, Washington, and Abu Dhabi Commercial Bank together brought a class action to recover losses stemming from the liquidation of notes issued by a structured investment vehicle between October 2004 and October 2007. The plaintiffs' claims were of common law fraud, negligent misrepresentation, negligence, breach of fiduciary duty, breach of contract and related contract claims, unjust enrichment and aiding and abetting against defendants. Defendants moved to dismiss the First Amended Complaint for lack of subject matter jurisdiction and for failure to mention a claim upon which relief can be granted. The district court gave plaintiffs' permission to amend pleadings and to remedy this deficiency within 20 days.[77] It (the District Court) felt that given another opportunity, the plaintiffs could more clearly allege their aiding and abetting claims to each defendant and the remaining common law fraud and contract-based claims.

Courts will generally allow litigants who were able to remedy any deficiency found in their complaint to file an amended complaint.[78] It will also impose a time limit on the filing of an amendment, calculated from the date of the court's order. When a litigant is granted leave to amend his/her complaint, a court may impose certain requirements, which the litigant has to fulfil. In *Allen,*[79] the litigant was required to clearly separate his claims and indicate the defendants against whom each claim was asserted. In addition, in seeking to establish a violation of any statutory scheme, the litigant was required to clearly indicate alleged violation by indicating the specific statutory requirements and sub-sections. In *Compuware,*[80] the plaintiff had amended its complaint, which alleged a breach of contract claim

[73] *In re Lehman Bros. Mortgage-Backed Securities* 650 F. 3d 167 at 188—Court of Appeals (2nd Circuit 2011).

[74] *In re Moody's Corp. Securities Litigation*, 599 F. Supp. 2d 493—Dist. Court, SD New York 2009.

[75] *Abu Dhabi* (2009).

[76] *In re Moody's Corp* (2009) at 518.

[77] *Abu Dhabi* (2009) at 163–164 and 187–8.

[78] In *King County, Wash. v. IKB Deutsche Industriebank AG* 708 F. Supp. 2d 334—Dist. Court, SD New York 2010.

[79] *Allen v. United Financial Mortgage Corporation* (2009) at 1099.

[80] *Compuware Corp. v. Moody's Investors Servs., Inc*, 499 F. 3d 520—Court of Appeals, 6th Circuit 2007 at 534.

based solely on Moody's agreement to publish a ratings report and Compuware's belief that Moody's breached its implied contractual duty to perform in a workmanlike manner. The plaintiff did not succeed in its claim because of its failure to show actual malice on the part of Moody's, which was necessary to win the case.

The US courts generally dislike lengthy pleadings. In *Re Merrill Lynch*,[81] the court had earlier recognised problems with regard to the litigant's original complaint and gave the litigant an opportunity to properly frame and assert her complaint, rather than opting for an outright dismissal. However, it transpired that the amended complaint of the litigant was too lengthy as it contained 12 pages and had 424 paragraphs. The court considered that this was a violation of *Federal Rule of Civil Procedure* 8(a),[82] which mandates that pleadings shall consist of a "short and plain statement of the claim showing that the pleader is entitled to relief". The court found that a straightforward complaint expressed in so many pages was against Congress' intention to eliminate it in the *Private Securities Litigation Reform Act 1995* under the heading of "abusive litigation".[83]

The discussion has revealed the circumstances where a court will allow claimants to amend their pleading and what conditions they have to fulfil. It also examined the reasons and the circumstances where the court will disallow an amendment of the pleading. Amending pleadings is important as it allows plaintiff litigants, in deserving cases, to restate their pleadings, to accord with the legally recognised claims, rather than the court penalising them by dismissing their claim because of poor drafting. A need to amend pleading also arises in the light of a response to the pleadings.

6.5.2 Pleading and Liability Standards Under the Reform Act

Depending on the cause of action, investors may or may not be successful in suing CRAs. It may help investors if the US government lowers the pleading and liability standards. Investors, on their part, can sue CRAs on the basis that they have perpetrated securities fraud and have acted recklessly under the securities laws the Senate and the House of Representative passed in 1995 by overriding President Obama's veto. Generally, it is difficult for investors to allege and succeed on the claim of fraud on the part of CRAs. In the past, in the securities class action plaintiffs often sought to prove fraud by hindsight.[84] Companies are, therefore,

---

[81] *In Re Merrill Lynch & Co., Inc. Research Reports* 272 F. Supp. 2d 243—Dist. Court, SD New York 2003; 272 F.Supp.2d 243 (2003).

[82] See *McCormick v. Kopmann*, 23 Ill. app. 2d 189, 161 N.E.2d 720 (1959).

[83] "An Act to reform Federal securities litigation, and for other purposes". 22 December 1995—H. R. 1058, http://www.gpo.gov/fdsys/pkg/PLAW-104publ67/html/PLAW-104publ67.htm; See also *In Re Merrill Lynch & Co*, (2003) at 267.

[84] For the definition of "hindsight", see Glossary.

hesitant to issue projections for fear of a securities lawsuit if the projections are not realised.[85]

An enactment of safe harbour provision for forward-looking statements is found in the *Private Securities Litigation Reform Act of 1995*. It allows a company to make good faith projections without the fear of plaintiff's counsel resorting to second-guessing a company's projections. Similarly, CRAs can use this provision to prevent plaintiff's counsel from second-guessing them. Presumably, a CRA will not be liable for any forward-looking rating statement in a securities fraud action instituted by an investor. This requires the CRA to identify the statement and include meaningful cautionary statements identifying important factors that could cause actual results to differ materially from those in the forward-looking statement.

6.6 Liability for False Ratings Statements in Public Registration

6.6.1 *Pleadings*

Investors, on their part, have had difficulty suing CRAs because of the pleading standard. The *Dodd-Frank Wall Street Reform and Consumer Protection Act*[86] relaxes the pleading standard in private securities cases against CRAs and rescinds a Securities and Exchange Commission (SEC) rule that previously had exempted CRAs from liability for false ratings in public registration statements.[87] *Prima facie*, the new law increases CRAs' future exposure to civil liability in private lawsuits seeking money damages from a CRA. It enhances accountability by lowering the pleading standard for damage claims against CRAs based on losses attributable to faulty ratings.[88]

CRAs are careful to avoid liability, and, therefore, many CRAs have already announced that they will not consent to the use of their ratings in registration statements because of their fear of exposure to additional legal liability. CRAs have also reportedly begun seeking indemnification from issuers and underwriters of new asset-backed bonds.[89] In S&P's view, the heightened standard will have several implications, including (a) inadvertently reducing the quality and timeliness of ratings and (b) being to the detriment of global capital markets. The reason is that the fear of liability would make CRAs decline to adjust outstanding ratings and may only rate well-established issuers.[90]

---

[85] Roake and Davidson (1996).

[86] H.R. 4173, http://www.sec.gov/about/laws/wallstreetreform-cpa.pdf.

[87] Section 933.

[88] Jickling (2010), p. 6.

[89] Ibid, Column 1, Para 5 at 2.

[90] Sack and Wilderman (2010), p. 243.

6.6.2 *States of Mind in Private Actions: Section 933*[91] *of the* Dodd-Frank Act

Changes in Dodd-Frank relates to two issues: (a) the accountability of CRAs and (b) the state of mind of CRAs, and it required amending the *Securities and Exchange Act of 1934*.[92] The enforcement and penalty provisions of this title apply to the statements made by a CRA, in the same manner and to the same extent as such provisions apply to statements made by a registered public accounting firm or a securities analyst under the securities laws. Such statements are not deemed as forward-looking statements for the purposes of Section 21E.[93]

In the case of an action for money damages brought against a CRA or a controlling person under this title, it is sufficient for purposes of pleading cases any required state of mind in relation to such action.[94] The complaint should state with particularity facts giving rise to a strong inference that the CRA had knowingly or recklessly failed to (1) conduct a reasonable investigation of the rated security with respect to the factual elements relied upon by its own methodology for evaluating credit risk or (2) obtain a reasonable verification of such factual elements (verification may be based on a sampling technique that does not amount to an audit) from other sources, which the CRA considers competent and independent of the issuer and underwriter.[95]

The implications of the legislation, according to commentators,[96] are that, first, the SEC can impose fines and censure a CRA for failure to ensure that credit ratings remain current and reliable. Second, the SEC will require a form associated with the issuance of each rating. The form will disclose a wide range of information pertaining to quantitative models, qualitative inputs, data and assumptions about the correlation of defaults across obligors for structured products. Third, CRAs will be subject to the same legal liability that auditors and security analysts face. To claim economic damages, it is sufficient to show that the CRA knowingly or recklessly violated the securities law.

---

[91] *Dodd-Frank Wall Street Reform And Consumer Protection Act*, http://thomas.loc.gov/cgi-bin/cpquery/?&sid=cp111SXv12&r_n=hr517.111&dbname=cp111&&sel=TOC_1713897&.

[92] By amending Sections 15E (m) and 21D (b) (2) of the *Securities Exchange Act of 1934*. (15 U.S.C. 78o-7(m).

[93] By amending Section 15E (m), Ibid.

[94] By amending Section 21D (b) (2), Ibid.

[95] Exception in ibid.

[96] Goel and Thakor (2011).

6.7 Protection Afforded to CRAs

In a typical suit filed by an investor, as previously outlined, CRAs would normally file a motion to dismiss the case by arguing that their credit ratings were predictive opinions of creditworthiness. They would also contend that their credit rating opinions were not guarantees or statements of fact on which plaintiffs can base a claim for common law fraud or securities fraud under federal and state laws.

6.7.1 First Amendment Protection of Expressions of Opinion

The CRAs have long enjoyed near complete immunity from liability for bad ratings based upon an old line of cases that found the rating business—assigning and reporting ratings—to be a form of journalism subject to free speech protections under the First Amendment.[97] Where investors bring litigation, CRAs have long invoked First Amendment free speech protection[98] to defend lawsuits filed against their ratings. These agencies have consistently argued that the Constitution protected them from such claims. The CRA First Amendment will continue to remain CRAs' core defence in the US[99] as Congress is barred from curtailing freedom of speech, or freedom of the press.[100] It seems that CRAs prefer invoking First Amendment protection as an easy way out, rather than defending themselves based on lack of privity. This has led to, as examined below, judges developing exceptions to the First Amendment defence.

---

[97] Froeba (2009).

[98] U.S. Const. amend. I. "The First Amendment of the United States Constitution protects the right to freedom of religion and freedom of expression from government interference. Freedom of expression consists of the rights to freedom of speech, press, assembly . . . and the implied rights of association and belief. The Supreme Court interprets the extent of the protection afforded to these rights".

"The most basic component of freedom of expression is the right of freedom of speech. The right to freedom of speech allows individuals to express themselves without interference or constraint by the government. The Supreme Court requires the government to provide substantial justification for the interference with the right of free speech where it attempts to regulate the content of the speech".

". . .[T]he right to freedom of the press guaranteed by the first amendment is not very different from the right to freedom of speech. It allows an individual to express themselves through publication and dissemination. It is part of the constitutional protection of freedom of expression. It does not afford members of the media any special rights or privileges not afforded to citizens in general". Legal Information Institute, Cornell University Law School, http://www.law.cornell.edu/wex/first_amendment.

[99] *In Re National Century Financial Enterprises, Inc., Investment Litigation*, 580 F.Supp.2d 630 (2008).

[100] See the U.S. Const. amend.1. See also http://www.law.cornell.edu/wex/first_amendment.

6.7.2 Litigation by Issuers

The chances of CRAs being sued by issuers is minimal due to the fact that the issuers have had no cause for complaint and they are happy with the inflated ratings given by the CRAs to their corporate debt instruments; otherwise, they might resort to changing their provider. However, the situation is different with regard to unsolicited ratings given to, say corporate or sovereign debt, as no money is paid. The problem arises when CRAs subsequently downgrade the ratings as it then impinges on the reputation of the business of an issuer to issue future debt instruments at a reasonable cost. The issuers will have to pay higher interest rates to attract investors based on a theory that a lower rating is risky and investors will demand a higher interest rate. In such a scenario, an issuer might want to sue a CRA for defamation, rather than in contract, on the basis that First Amendment protects free speech. The First Amendment arises from a provision of constitutional law, and so state laws cannot abrogate this fundament right. The law of defamation (discussed below) and the First Amendment serve competing social values. The former protects an individual's interest in his or her good name, providing a cause of action for damage to reputation caused by false statements.[101] The latter protects freedom of expression and "was fashioned to assure unfettered interchange of ideas for bringing about political and social changes desired by the people".[102] Beginning with Justice Brennan's landmark opinion in *Sullivan*,[103] the Supreme Court has held that the First Amendment's guarantee of freedom of expression is paramount and it limits the scope of state defamation laws to amend this fundament right.[104] Thus, the First Amendment generally prohibits public officials, public figures and journalists from recovering damages for false and defamatory statements unless they can demonstrate that the statement was made with actual malice.[105] During the pre-1971 period, the CRA used to publish a magazine detailing ratings of different corporations; investors could subscribe to them, and as such they were performing a journalism role. The CRAs have retained their journalist status even though it is limited to displaying ratings on their web page.

[101] *See Milkovich v. Lorain Journal Co.*, 497 U.S. 1, 11–14, 110 S. Ct. 2695, 111 L.Ed.2d 1 (1990) (summarising the history of defamation law).

[102] *New York Times v. Sullivan*, 376 U.S., 254, 269, 84 S. Ct. 710, 11 L.Ed.2d 686 (1964).

[103] Ibid.

[104] *Milkovich*, 497 U.S. at 14, 110 S. Ct. 2695.

[105] See *Milkovich* (discussing *Sullivan* and *Curtis Publishing Co. v. Butts*, 388 U.S. 130, 87 S. Ct. 1975, 18 L.Ed.2d 1094 (1967).

6.7.3 Exceptions to First Amendment Defence

The enforcement of First Amendment protection appears in cases.[106] NRSRO-registered CRAs have successfully resisted third-party discovery. In a private litigation, the aim of a third-party discovery is to force the opposing side to reveal information. In several such cases, courts have found that the CRAs are entitled to the same privileges as journalists, notwithstanding the fact that CRAs had generally issued inflated ratings on more than US $5 billion of securities issued in 2006 and 2007 and backed by loans from lenders. Judges have, on occasions, attempted to try to create exceptions to the First Amendment protection afforded to CRAs by distinguishing previous cases from the cases at hand based on particular distinguishing feature(s).

6.7.3.1 LaSalle National Bank[107]

In *LaSalle National Bank*,[108] an Offering Memorandum[109] had contained negligent ratings given by the defendant and was distributed to a select group of qualified and "accredited" investors rather than to the public at large. A first court declined First Amendment protection to permit Duff & Phelps, a CRA, to assert journalistic privilege because the service related to rating a private transaction. Twenty-six institutional investors (plaintiffs), who had purchased approximately US $200 million of bonds offered by subsidiaries of Towers Financial Corporation in connection with its Ponzi scheme,[110] brought an action against the defendant and Shawmut Bank Connecticut N.A. The Southern District New York court (comprising Bronx, Dutchess, New York, Orange, Putnam, Rockland, Sullivan and Westchester Counties) denied the defendant's motion to dismiss the plaintiffs' claim based on counts one, three and four but succeeded with regard to count two. Count one had alleged that Duff & Phelps violated § 10(b) of the *Securities and Exchange Act of 1934*, 15 U.S.C.; count three alleged that the defendant committed common law fraud; and count four alleged negligent misrepresentation by the defendant. Count 2 had alleged that the defendant had aided and abetted a violation of RICO, 18 U.S.C. § 1964(c). Additional counts were lodged against Shawmut but not against the CRA.

---

[106] Such as *In re Pan Am Corp.*, where the court held that publisher of credit worthiness ratings of corporate and governmental debt instruments was protected by privilege, 161 B.R. 577, 581-83 (S.D.N.Y. 1993), and *In re Scott Paper Co. Sec. Litig.*, 145 F.R.D. 366, 370 (E.D. Pa. 1992).

[107] *LaSalle National Bank, et al., v. Duff & Phelps Credit Rating Co. and Shawmut Bank Connecticut, N.A.*,951 F. Supp. 1071 (1996).

[108] Ibid.

[109] For the definition of "offering memorandum", see Glossary.

[110] For definition of "Ponzi scheme", see Glossary.

In purchasing and retaining bonds,[111] the plaintiffs had relied upon the AA rating assigned to the bonds by the defendant CRA. The plaintiffs' losses would have been averted if the CRA had properly performed the initial investigation and the post-issuance monitoring that it claimed to perform had identified any of the numerous occurrences (both prior and subsequent to the issuances of the bonds) that materially adversely affected the likelihood of timely payments of the principal sum and interest with respect to the bonds. The CRA had a choice of either assigning appropriately a lower rating to the bonds or refusing to rate them at all. Subsequently, the CRA should have either lowered the initial rating or withdrawn the rating given, but it chose not to take any action. As it was a solicited rating and the CRA had received compensation, the court found that it had failed to fulfil its duties to the bondholders as investors.[112]

The CRA had rated each bond series before issuance. It had substantial influence in the design of each bond program and in drafting the program's operational documents and drafting the documents' pursuant to which the program was to operate. It also played a critical role with respect to the Funding Corporations' bond issuances. As the program was structured, each CRA's rating was necessary to sell the bonds and to assure investors of their initial and continuing investment quality. The CRA was required, as a condition, to give AA ratings to the initial issue of each series of bonds. It meant a modest risk, although it may have varied slightly from time to time because of economic conditions. Generally, it meant bonds had high credit quality and strong protection factors. The risk was modest, but prior to the issuance of each series of bonds, the CRA assigned a rating of AA to each bond issue and consented to the use of its name and the assigned rating in connection with the disclosure documents, advertisements and description of the issue.[113]

It is normal for a CRA, as a defendant, to present a motion for the dismissal for various reasons, including the case being time barred. However, in his analysis, Senior District Judge Whitman Knapp, on a motion to dismiss the plaintiffs' Section 10(b)/Rule 10b-5 and common law fraud claims, found that the Statute of Limitations did not bar plaintiffs' Rule 10b-5 claim. The judge found plaintiffs had (a) adequately alleged actionable misrepresentations in connection with the sale of a security and (b) sufficiently alleged *scienter* (knowingly, with full knowledge or awareness). However, the plaintiffs failed to allege sufficiently the CRA's aiding and abetting RICO liability.[114] With regard to the claim based on negligent misrepresentation, the plaintiffs (a) had sufficiently alleged a common law negligent misrepresentation claim and (b) sufficiently stated a claim for negligent

[111] For definition of "bond", see Glossary.

[112] *LaSalle National Bank, et al.* at pp. 1075–1076.

[113] Ibid. at 1076.

[114] *Racketeer Influenced and Corrupt Organizations Act (RICO) (1970)* Chapter 96, Title 18, United States Code, §1961–1968, Title IX of the Organized Crime Control Act of 1970, Pub. L. No. 91-452, 84 Stat. 941 (Oct. 15, 1970), *codified at* 18 U.S.C. Ch. 96, §§1961–1968. http://itlaw.wikia.com/wiki/Racketeer_Influenced_and_Corrupt_Organizations_Act.

misrepresentation and that the CRA was not immunised from liability as a publisher. The judge was able sufficiently to distinguish previous past cases from the present one and refused to grant First Amendment defence to the defendants.

6.7.3.2 Burden of Proof

The burden of proof, also known as the onus of proof, refers to the obligation or responsibility to prove, in a case before the courts, the assertions made by a complainant.[115] The general rule is that the burden of proof lies with the party who makes the allegation. The burden of proof (Latin term *onus probandi*) is a legal duty upon a litigant to introduce evidence of preponderating weight on an issue to overcome the proof offered on that issue by the opposite party. Burden of proof is merely a question of policy and fairness; a party has to prove or disprove a disputed fact, and generally, the burden of proof is satisfied by evidence. Moreover, the burden of proof always lies with the person who lays charges (Latin maxim *semper necessitas probandi incumbit ei qui agit*). The weight of burden of proof is dependent upon whether the trial is civil or criminal. In civil law cases, the burden of proof requires a claimant to convince a judge or jury of the claimant's entitlement to the relief sought. The burden of proof is on the claimant to show by a "preponderance of evidence" or "weight of evidence" that all the facts necessary to win a judgment are probably true. The claimant must prove each element of the claim, or cause of action, in order to recover. In a criminal trial, say involving a fraud, the burden of proof is on the prosecutor to prove that the defendant had committed the specified crime(s) *beyond a reasonable doubt*, a higher burden of proof than the civil "preponderance of evidence" standard.[116]

6.7.3.3 Genesee County Employees' Retirement System[117]

Traditionally, CRAs have often defended themselves against investors' suits by arguing that the Constitution protects them from claims that they issued inflated ratings. Investors brought a lawsuit against Standard & Poor's, Moody's, Fitch and others. In addition to S&P, Credit Suisse Group AG and the Royal Bank of Scotland Group Plc. were among the other defendants in the case. The investors claimed that the CRAs had issued investment-grade ratings that were false and misleading with respect to Thornburg securities and that they were paid substantial sums of money for doing so. Specifically, investors claimed that the CRAs had issued inflated ratings on more than US $5 billion of securities over the course of two years. Judge

[115] Haynes (2013), pp. 365–397.

[116] http://civilprocedure.uslegal.com/trial/burden-of-proof/.

[117] *Genesee County Employees' Retirement System et al v. Thornburg Mortgage Securities Trust 2006-3 et al*, U.S. District Court, District of New Mexico, No. 09-00300 (12 November 2011).

James Browning of the US District Court of New Mexico ruled in favour of investors in that they had sufficiently alleged that the CRAs can be liable under the New Mexico Securities Act. The plaintiffs sufficiently pleaded allegations about material misrepresentations or omissions with respect to defendant S&P but not against Fitch and Moody's as defendants. Most importantly, the judge held that the First Amendment of the US Constitution did not bar the plaintiffs' claims against the CRAs.

6.7.3.4 In re Fitch Inc.[118]

The American Savings Bank (ASB) agreed to a deal of putting investment capital into a trust, which would then issue Trust Certificates to ASB. Between 1999 and 2000, ASB invested approximately US $83 million in the Trust Certificates. Not long after the completion of the final transaction, the Office of Thrift Supervision informed ASB that the transaction was illegal because the collateralised loan obligations did not constitute investment grade as required by regulations and it ordered ASB to dispose of the investment. ASB attempted to return the Trust Certificates to PaineWebber (the issuer), who refused to accept them. ASB then sued the issuer in the US District Court for the District of Hawaii, seeking recession of the investment agreements and damages for negligence and breach of warranty.

Fitch, on its part, appealed against the US District Court for the Southern District of New York (Keenan, J.) finding that it was in contempt for refusing to comply with a subpoena issued by that Court in connection with original litigation in the District of Hawaii. The appeal presented a question about the outer boundaries of the statutory protection against non-party subpoenas[119] in a civil case that New York has created for professional journalists and the extent to which information-gathering organisations that are not traditionally considered part of the media may claim that privilege. The US Court of Appeal affirmed the judgment of the district court and rejected Fitch's claim that the district court had abused its discretion. The court noted that although both New York State Law and Federal Law recognise journalists' privileges in varying degrees, it found that those privileges did not apply under the facts of that case. The court rejected Fitch's claim that it was engaged in protected "news gathering" and found that Fitch's rating was based on client needs and not on a judgment about newsworthiness. What Fitch did was play an active role in planning the transaction and communicating with PaineWebber regarding how best to structure that transaction to reach the desired rating, a role that is inconsistent with traditional journalism. Although, *prima facie*, Fitch's activities were not improper, under the circumstances Fitch could not invoke journalists' privileges for two reasons. First, unlike a business newspaper or magazine, which would cover any transactions deemed newsworthy, Fitch only

[118] 330 F.3d 104 (2d. Cir. 2003).

[119] For the definition of "subpoena", see Glossary.

covered its own clients, and this practice weighed against treating Fitch as a journalist. Second, Fitch had taken an active role in the planning of the transactions it had analysed, again a role that is inconsistent with traditional journalism. In granting the motion to enforce the subpoena, the Court of Appeal, based on the reasons stated, held that Fitch could not assert the newsgathering privilege codified in New York's Shield Law. A shield law gives reporters protection against being forced to disclose confidential information or sources in state court.

6.7.3.5 State of Connecticut v Moody's Corporation et al[120]

The State of Connecticut (the State) in an ongoing suit has filed separate actions against Moody's, Fitch and S&P (the McGraw-Hill Companies) in Connecticut Superior Court, seeking redress. The action was based on the defendants' alleged "unfair, deceptive and illegal business practice of systematically and intentionally giving lower credit ratings to bonds issued by states, municipalities, and other public entities as compared to corporate and other forms of debt with similar or even worse rates of default".[121] The State had alleged that the defendants' actions had harmed these public bond issuers. They were compelled either to purchase bond insurance to improve their credit rating or had to pay higher interest costs on their lower rated bonds. These costs, the State alleged, were ultimately borne by all Connecticut taxpayers. The State alleged that the defendants had violated the Connecticut Unfair Trade Practices Act.[122] The Connecticut Attorney General, on behalf of the State of Connecticut,[123] sought restitution, disgorgement and civil penalties for the injuries suffered by the State of Connecticut and all issuers of public debt in Connecticut, as well as other injunctive and equitable relief to prevent these unfair, deceptive and illegal business practices from continuing.

The defendants moved to strike the plaintiff's complaint in its entirety based on a number of reasons, *inter alia*, that the statements attributed to them were protected speech under the First Amendment and, therefore, was not regulated by the State through this action. The CRAs argued that the statements upon which the State's claim was based constituted part of their rating opinions that were protected speech under the First Amendment. J. Bright of the Superior Court of Connecticut, Judicial District of Hartford, disagreed. The basis of disagreement was a distinction where the State was not challenging the substance of Moody's et al ratings, which may have First Amendment protection. The basis for the present claim was that Moody's et al did not abide by their statements about their independence and objectivity and

---

[120] *State of Connecticut v. Moody's Corporation et al.* No. X04HHDCV106008836S, 54 Conn. L. Rptr. 116, (2012 WL 2149408 (Conn.Super.) (10 May 2012). http://www.cafalawblog.com/Case%208%20Connecticut%20v%20%20Moody%27s%20Corp%20.pdf.

[121] Ibid.

[122] Conn. Gen. Stat. §§ 42-110a et seq.

[123] Pursuant to Conn. Gen. Stat § 42–110m.

the policies and procedures they claimed to follow to protect those qualities. The First Amendment protection did not permit the defendants to misrepresent to consumers (i.e., investors) the manner in which they operate their business or arrive at their opinions, and this was the basis of the State's claim.[124]

To conclude, the four cases above illustrate how the judges attempted to deny First Amendment journalist privileges to CRAs based on particular factual situations. They include, first, where ratings are issued to a select group of investors and not to the public at large; second, where a material misstatement or omission was made; third, where a subpoena issued for the purposes of a disclosure document at a discovery stage are refused to be abided by and relates to a litigation and/or when a CRA acts both as a consultant and a rating agent; fourth, when statements about CRAs' independence and objectivity and the policies and procedures it claims to follow to protect those qualities are false'.[125]

6.8 The Protection Afforded by New York Shield Law

The Shield Law defines "professional journalist" as one who is in the "processing and researching of news intended for dissemination to the public".[126] The *Re Fitch*[127] case depicts the attitude of the court. A Second Circuit Court of Appeal stated, "[T]he ability of the press freely to collect and edit news, unhampered by repeated demands for its resource materials, requires more protection than that afforded by the disclosure statute".[128] Furthermore, the court took judicial notice of the practical burdens on time and resources on CRAs and their impact on the free press. To protect the press from the burdens of non-party discovery, both federal and New York courts have recognised a special privilege that can be asserted by journalists. New York codified its journalistic privilege in Shield Law.[129] Shield Law protects journalists from contempt for refusing to comply with a non-party subpoena when the subpoena seeks to discover information conveyed to the journalist in confidence.[130] There is also a common law privilege recognised by the New York Court independent of Shield Law.[131] Regulations forbid savings banks

---

[124] *State of Connecticut v. Moody's Corporation et al* (2012) at p. 9.

[125] Stoel Rives, LLP. "How Does a Lawsuit Work? Basic Steps in the Civil Litigation Process" (24 January 2012) http://www.stoel.com/showarticle.aspx?show=963.

[126] N.Y. Civ. Rights Law § 79-h (a) (6).

[127] *In re Fitch, Inc.*, 330 F. 3d 104—Court of Appeals, 2nd Circuit 2003, 330 F.3d 104 (2003).

[128] Para 17, Ibid.

[129] N.Y. Citv. Rights Law § 79-h (McKinney 2002).

[130] Ibid. § 79-h (b).

[131] *See Gonzales v. Nat'l Broad. Co., Inc.*, 194 F.3d 29, 32 (2d Cir.1999), endorsing journalistic privilege for non-confidential information; *in re Petroleum Prods. Antitrust Litig.*, 680 F.2d 5, 7 (2d Cir.1982) (per curiam), recognising privilege for confidential information.

like American Savings Bank (ASB) from buying and holding securities that are either not liquid or are not investment grade.[132] In addition to Fitch, ASB had also subpoenaed Moody's, and Moody's initially also resisted on the grounds of Shield Law. After filing a motion to enforce a subpoena by ASB, but before Moody's reply was due, the two sides reached a settlement[133] of an undisclosed amount. If a defendant does not fall under the category of being a journalist, no protection is afforded under the New York Shield Law.[134]

6.8.1 *What Constitutes Journalism Privileges?*

When deciding on journalism protection, US judges tend to examine whether or not a CRA's ratings are for all public debts or on a selective basis. The justification seems to be that rating all securities is more risky than selective ratings should the ratings turn out to be unreliable. S&P rates nearly all public debt issuances regardless of whether it is hired and paid to do so or not.[135] Fitch's regular practice is not to rate transitions for which initially the issuers do not pay. The vast majority of Fitch's rating activities are initiated by client request. The occasional Fitch-Initiated Rating is usually a follow-up to a security that Fitch has previously rated or a transaction Fitch and a client had discussed rating but failed to agree.[136] With this difference in Fitch's rating approach, it would be very difficult for Fitch to claim journalism privilege. Courts are not suggesting that an ostensible news gathering organisation is required to cover all events in order to qualify as journalists. The reason is that part of a journalist's job is to exercise judgment about which events are newsworthy and which are not.[137]

On disclosure, in *Von Bulow*,[138] the Court of Appeal decided that in some cases, the public's interest requires a free and active press and this outweighs its interest if it is compelled to disclose information held by journalists. In such instances, the Court of Appeal held that a journalist is to be afforded a privilege against compelled disclosure.[139] Stated another way, an applicant must establish that a person was "professionally engaged in news gathering" at the time it received the information that is sought to discover.[140] Once this is satisfied, then the journalist's privilege

[132] *See* 12 C.F.R. § 560.40 (2002).

[133] *In re Fitch Inc. v USA PaineWebber*, 330 F. 3d 104 (2003), footnote 1.

[134] *Von Bulow v. Von Bulow*, 811 F.2d 136 (2d Cir. 1987).

[135] *In re Pan Am Corporation*, 161 B.R. 577 (1993) at 583.

[136] The testimony of Kevin Duignan mentioned in *In re Fitch, Inc.*, 330 F. 3d 104—CA, 2nd Circuit 2003, 330 F.3d 104 (2003) at 110.

[137] *In re Fitch, Inc.*, 330 F. 3d 104—CA, 2nd Circuit 2003, 330 F.3d 104 (2003), p. 110.

[138] *Auersperg v. von Bulow,* 811 F.2d 136 (2d Cir.), *cert. denied,* 481 U.S. 1015, 107 S.Ct. 1891, 95 L.Ed.2d 498 (1987).

[139] *Von Bulow*, 811 F.2d at 144.

[140] *Don King Prods., Inc. v. Douglas*, 131 F.R.D. 421, 424 (S.D.N.Y.1990).

encompasses not only that information that a journalist actually intends to publish, but it extends to protect unpublished resource material as well.[141]

Federal courts applying federal law have held, on occasion, that CRAs are journalists protected by the reporter's privilege. In *re Pan Am Corporation*,[142] the court held that there was no limitation to S&P Ratings Group's use of the information for its own publication activities.[143] This means that S&P functions as a journalist when gathering information in connection with its ratings process and that, specifically, a CRA functions as a journalist when it intends to use the material to disseminate information to the public.[144] The Court concluded that "[a]s a publisher of publicly distributed financial ratings, analysis and commentary; S&P, as a matter of law, deserv[ed] ... the full breadth of First Amendment safeguards".[145] There are, however, as already mentioned, exceptions to the general rule. A CRA would also lose its journalist privilege when it makes suggestions to the companies it rates as to how to structure their offerings and then plays an active role in structuring the transaction in question.[146] In other words, a CRA loses its journalist protection when it acts as a consultant and then rates the securities in question.

Most large credit rating agencies perform consulting and advisory services in addition to issuing credit ratings.[147] An SEC report[148] raised conflict of interest concerns about the agencies' performance of these services for the entities they rate. However, the report emphasised that such advisory services represented a very small portion of total agency revenues. On a regulatory front, the SEC adopted in 2007—and updated in 2009—rules that prohibit NRSROs from issuing or maintaining credit ratings for securities issuers for whom they had performed a narrow category of consulting services, but it did not prohibit other types of consulting or advisory work.[149] The SEC report found that services other than credit ratings were a *significant* revenue source for NRSROs and suggested that further restriction on such services may be in the public interest. It recommended further investigation of the matter by the SEC's Office of Compliance Inspection and Examinations.

[141] *Von Bulow*, 811 F.2d at 142.

[142] 161 B.R. 577, 580–582 (S.D.N.Y. 1993).

[143] 161 B.R. 577 (1993) ag 582.

[144] *In re Pan Am Corp* (1993) at 582.

[145] Ibid.

[146] *In re Fitch, Inc.*, 330 F. 3d 104—CA, 2nd Circuit 2003, 330 F.3d 104 (2003), p. 110.

[147] Kotz (2009).

[148] U.S. Securities and Exchange Commission (2003). http://www.sec.gov/news/studies/credratingreport0103.pdf.

[149] Securities and Exchange Commission 17 CFR Parts 240 and 249b (2 February 2009), by adding new paragraph to Rule 17g-5 at pp. 38–39. http://www.sec.gov/rules/final/2009/34-59342.pdf.

6.8.2 *The Private Securities Litigation Reform Act 1995*

The Act does several things: it alters control of investor cases brought as class actions, encourages voluntary disclosures, provides sanctions in certain circumstances if claims are unsupported, limits liability proportionate to responsibility and contains audit requirements designed to provide added protections against fraud. The reform proposed by Congress was in response to frivolous strike suits alleging securities law violations that were increasing the cost of raising capital and had a chilling effect on corporate disclosures to investors.[150] Congress wanted to reassert legislative control over securities fraud litigation. It felt there was a need to restore the securities litigation system's ability to promote "public and global confidence in the nation's capital markets, deter wrongdoing, and guarantee that corporate directors, officers, auditors, lawyers and others properly perform their jobs".[151]

The Act, in order to achieve these objectives, does several things. It changes the discovery to minimise costs incurred pending a motion to dismiss or a motion for summary judgment. It requires attorneys, as parties in class actions, to give an undertaking for attorney fees and costs. It codifies the standard for pleading securities fraud. In an action for money damages, it allows written submission of interrogatory (request for further information) to the jury on the issue of state of mind at the time of the violation. It limits damages to losses caused by fraud but not by other market conditions. It removes securities fraud as a predicate offence in a civil action under RICO. It compels the purchasers of securities suing under Securities Act civil liability provisions to prove that the alleged misstatements or omissions actually caused their loss, and lastly it requires the SEC to report on protections for senior citizens and qualified retirement plans.

6.9 Claims by the Issuers

6.9.1 *Defamation*

An issuer is a legal entity (such as a corporation, investment trust, government or government agency) that is authorised to issue (offer for sale) its own securities.[152] In reality, when CRAs downgrade an issuer's bonds, an issuer will have to offer higher interest on its future debt instruments to attract investors to buy securities or may even need to offer security to sell the bonds or take out bond insurance, which in this situation would prove expensive. Aggrieved issuers may, therefore, wish to sue CRAs for having defamed their reputation. Historically, investors used to subscribe to the magazine issued by CRAs in which the ratings of various

[150] Schoengold & Sporn, "Summary of the Private Securities Litigation Reform Act (PSLRA) of 1995", http://www.spornlaw.com/faqs/pslra.php.

[151] Ibid.

[152] For definition of "issuer", see Glossary.

corporations were given, but this practice has since been abolished. However, the CRAs still fall under the category of a member of the press as such ratings are available on their website. In defamation actions against media defendants, the First Amendment requires that a plaintiff (investor) bear the burden of proving that the statement in question (i.e., a rating) was false and that the defendant had a requisite state of mind.[153]

In *Milkovich v. Lorain Journal Co*,[154] the US Supreme Court addressed another important limitation on the scope of defamation laws where a media defendant is involved. The Court concluded that "a statement on matters of public concern must be provable as false before there can be liability under state defamation law".[155] Thus, "a statement of opinion relating to matters of public concern which does not contain a provably false factual connotation will receive full constitutional protection".[156] What the issuers can do is to challenge the opinion expressed by a CRA. The chances of issuers suing CRAs when higher ratings are given are very slim indeed because, *prima facie*, higher ratings are to their advantage. Even where, in a few cases, the CRAs have been held negligent, it has resulted in the partial refund of the rating fees paid by the issuers.[157] It may seem puzzling that CRAs, based on past experiences, are in the habit of giving high ratings when they do not have to be afraid of liability, based on defamation, when there are occasions when low ratings are justified. However, the answer lies in (a) the inherent conflicts of interest as CRAs are being paid by the issuers and (b) the failure of investors to successfully sue CRAs based on the present legal regime. This has resulted in the gatekeeper failure of CRAs and in them not acting in the interest of the investors.

6.10 Breach of Contract and Professional Negligence Claims

According to common law, in many US jurisdictions and in England and Wales, in order to establish a claim for professional negligence, a plaintiff must demonstrate, firstly, the duty of the professional to use such skill, prudence and diligence as other members of his profession commonly possess and exercise; secondly, a breach of that duty; thirdly, a proximate causal connection between the negligent conduct and the resulting injury; and, finally, actual loss or damage resulting from the professional's negligence. [158]

---

[153] *Philadelphia Newspapers, Inc. v. Hepps,* 475 U.S. 767, 777, 106 S.Ct. 1558, 89 L.Ed.2d 783 (1986).

[154] 497 U.S. 1, 110 S.Ct. 2695.

[155] *Milkovich* at 19–20.

[156] Ibid. at 20.

[157] See below Sect. 6.10.2 for "out-of-court settlement".

[158] *In re Daisy Sys. Corp.*, 97 F.3d 1171, 1175 (9th Cir.1996) (citing *Jackson v. Johnson,* 5 Cal. App.4th 1350, 1355, 7 Cal.Rptr.2d 482 (1992).

6.10.1 *County of Orange v. McGraw Hill Companies, Inc.*[159]

The *County case* is unusual; a plaintiff's issuer challenged S&P's decision to award higher ratings for their short-term debt instruments. The plaintiff contended that it had contracted S&P solely for a rating and S&P had breached that contract by inadequately performing the analytical services underlying the ratings. The plaintiff argued that this duty to perform contract services "in a competent and reasonable manner", that is the professional standard, is inherent in all contracts[160] and constituted a special circumstance taking the contract claim out of the range of actual malice protection.[161]

The Court found that the plaintiff had raised genuine questions of material fact on S&P's assignment of ratings to the *County's* 1994 debt but not of its 1993 debt. The Court reasoned, "while a reasonably prudent rating agency might have been more cautious in assigning top ratings to the *County's* 1993 debt, the evidence shows the *County's* track record for repaying its debt had been good to that point but not with regard to *County's* 1994 debt as it has raised triable issues".[162] S&P, in its defence, contended that it could not have known its ratings were false because Moody's also gave the *County* a high rating. The Court viewed that it did not support a conclusion that, as a matter of law, S&P's ratings were false. In the Courts' view, there was sufficient evidence that S&P knew of factors, of which the *County* was not the source, that could have alerted S&P to the dangers of the *County's* investment practices. S&P further attempted to persuade the Court that its ratings are opinions that are not provably false. The Court stated that it rejected this argument in the past and did it again.

6.10.2 *Out-of-Court Settlement*

Parties to the litigation may prefer an out-of-court settlement as it has several advantages. The advantages to the CRAs is that the matter is amicably resolved "without costly and protracted litigation",[163] avoiding any bad publicity. It allows further healthy relationships between the parties to continue and would allow them to rate state and local government bonds on the same scale as corporate securities

[159] 245 BR 151—Dist. Court, CD California, 1999. It is a political subdivision of the State of California.

[160] *See, e.g., Michaelis v. Benavides,* 61 Cal.App.4th 681, 687, 71 Cal.Rptr.2d 776 (1998).

[161] The actual malice standard supplies the breathing space the First Amendment requires. See *New York Times Co. v. Sullivan*, 376 U.S. 254 (1964) and *Hustler Magazine v. Falwell*, 485 U.S. 46, 56, 108 S.Ct. 876 (1988).

[162] *County of Orange* at 161.

[163] McLaughlin and Faux (2011).

on the condition that they rectify the rating grades given to the municipal bonds. In one such instance, an out-of-court settlement was reached resolving claims by Connecticut based on the claim that CRAs had unfairly given lower ratings to public bonds. The CRAs agreed to credit Connecticut with about US $900,000; the intention was to offset the expense of obtaining future ratings on the future sales of state bonds.[164] In another case, the SEC agreed to settle without Citigroup admitting any wrongdoing on its part. The settlement amount was US $380 million, when investors had actually lost US $700 million. The settlement reflects the terms that the SEC reasonably believed they could obtain if the case had gone for trial and succeeded. In addition, if an actual trial had proceeded, it would have meant unnecessary delay and no guarantee of a successful outcome as far as litigation was concerned. Equally important was that a settlement would preserve resources that the SEC could use to tackle other frauds and protect other victims.[165]

When cases are filed against CRAs or they lose a case, their share prices tend to lower initially but then finally pick up. The news that 16 states and the District of Columbia were suing S&P for fraud led to its shares falling by as much as 8.9 % on 5 February 2013 after dropping to 13.8 % on 4 February 2013.[166] When CRAs win cases or cases against them are dismissed, their shares will go up. A case in point is when the Second US Circuit Court of Appeal confirmed a settlement between the SEC and Citigroup, Citigroup shares went up from US $1.13, or 3.2 %, to US $36.34 on the New York Stock Exchange.[167] *Prima facie*, settlement does not reflect that ratings issued were fair and transparent, but it reflects that CRAs are prepared to reassess their ratings and take remedial action, if need be, to ensure there is no future impact on income derived from providing rating services.

6.10.3 More Suits Follow

The US Department of Justice is committed to using every available legal device to respond to fraud; it takes many different forms to bring those responsible for the financial crisis to justice.[168] It epitomises the US government's intention to hold CRAs accountable for the financial crisis and to get justice for the investors.[169] The Attorney General has filed a civil lawsuit in the Central District of California, home to the now defunct Western Federal Corporate Credit Union (WesCorp), on

---

[164] Ibid.

[165] Stempel and Viswanatha (2012).

[166] Viswanatha and LaCapra (2013).

[167] See Stempel and Viswanatha (2012).

[168] *In USA v Standard and Poor's*, in US District Court, California, Case No. CV13-00779 (4 Feb 2013), the US Department of Justice has filed a case against S&P as compensation for civil money penalties. http://www.justice.gov/iso/opa/resources/849201325104924250796.PDF.

[169] Barrett (2014).

5 February 2013 against McGraw-Hill Companies, Inc., and its subsidiary, Standard & Poor's (S&P). The government is seeking US $5 billion in its civil lawsuit against S&P, accusing the ratings service of defrauding investors in one of the most ambitious cases yet from the Justice Department over conduct tied to the financial crisis.[170] The Mississippi Attorney General Jim Hood has stated, "I am pleased that the U.S. Department of Justice and attorneys general from across the nation are joining us in our efforts to hold the credit rating agencies accountable by initiating lawsuits".[171]

The allegation is that S&P had engaged in a scheme to defraud investors in structured financial products known as residential mortgage-backed securities (RMBSs) and collateralized debt obligations (CDOs). WesCorp was the largest corporate credit union in the country. Following the 2008 financial crisis, it collapsed after suffering massive losses on RMBSs and CDOs rated by S&P. Many of the investors were federally insured financial institutions and lost billions of dollars on CDOs for which S&P issued inflated ratings that misrepresented the securities' true credit risks. S&P falsely represented that its ratings were objective, independent and uninfluenced by S&P's relationships with investment banks. However, in reality it seems S&P's desire, from 2004 to 2007, was to increase revenue and market share, and this led to favouring the interests of these banks over investors by issuing inflated ratings on hundreds of billions of dollars' worth of CDOs.[172]

The complaint seeks civil penalties under the *Financial Institutions Reform, Recovery, and Enforcement Act of 1989* (FIRREA) and alleges that S&P had committed three forms of fraud: first, mail fraud affecting federally insured financial institutions[173]; second, wire fraud affecting federally insured financial institutions[174]; and, third, financial institution fraud.[175] According to the Attorney Generals (Eric Holder and Tony West):

> Today's actions against CRAs are considered as an important step forward in our on-going efforts to investigate – and – punish the conduct that is believed to have contributed to the worst economic crisis in recent history. It is just the latest example of the critical work that the President's Financial Fraud Enforcement Task Force is making possible[176]

[170] Viswanatha and LaCapra (2013).

[171] Quoted by J. M. Karmasek, "New S&P suits welcomed by Miss. AG Hood", Legal Newsline (13 February 2013).

[172] *United States of America v McGraw Hill Company, Inc., and S&P*, Case No. CV13-00779-Doc. https://s3.amazonaws.com/s3.documentcloud.org/documents/566542/united-states-of-america-v-mcgraw-hill-companies.pdf.

[173] In violation of U.S. Code—Title 18- Crime and Criminal Punishment, Chapter 63—Mail Fraud and other Fraud Offences, § 1341. http://www.law.cornell.edu/uscode/text/18/part-I/chapter-63.

[174] Ibid. § 1343.

[175] Ibid. § 1344.

[176] The US Department of Justice, "Department of Justice Sues Standard & Poor's for Fraud in Rating Mortgage-Backed Securities in the Years Leading Up to the Financial Crisis" (5 February 2013). http://www.justice.gov/opa/pr/2013/February/13-ag-156.html.

"S&P's concerns about market share, revenues and profits drove them to issue inflated ratings, thereby misleading the public and defrauding investors".[177] FIRREA authorises the Attorney General to seek civil penalties up to the amount of the losses suffered because of the alleged violations. The government has so far identified more than US $5 billion in losses suffered by federally insured financial institutions in connection with the failure of CDOs rated by S&P from March to October 2007.[178] While these cases are still pending, the questions that arise are as follows: why did investors not perform due diligence when such large amounts of money were involved? Do the motives in fraud cases solely depend on increasing market share and concurrently profits as in the case of S&P? Can S&P protect itself from liability based on the exclusion clause? The judge will have to decide these issues if raised by S&P.

The attitude of CRAs can be gauged when one examines an online April 2007 email conversation between S&P employees, discussing ratings and the actual risk involved, when an employee stated an investment "could be structured by cows and we would rate it".[179] The problem with suing CRAs is that they have often claimed that the lawsuit instituted is without merit and have argued that their ratings are opinions protected by the First Amendment. A Manhattan Federal judge, Jed Rakoff, has dismissed a class-action lawsuit accusing Moody's and S&P of defrauding investors relating to the safety of US $63.4 billion of mortgage debt.[180] The reasoning was that investors have generally not succeeded in their claims against CRAs.

The plaintiffs, in *Ohio Police & Fire Pension Fund et al. v. Standard & Poor's Financial Services LLC et al.*,[181] in the US District Court for the Southern District of Ohio, were five pension funds operated by the State of Ohio for public employees (the Funds). The Funds invested hundreds of millions of dollars in 308 MBSs between 2005 and 2008, all of which had received a triple-A rating or equivalent credit rating from one of the three major CRAs (i.e., S&P, Moody's and Fitch). The value of the MBSs collapsed during this period, leaving the Funds with estimated losses of US $457 million. In an effort to recoup some of these losses, the Funds brought a suit against the CRAs under Ohio's "blue sky" laws and negligent misrepresentation under a common law, alleging that the CRAs' ratings were false and misleading and that placing reasonable reliance on those ratings caused the Funds' losses. The complaint contained three counts: (1) common law negligent misrepresentation, (2) violation of Ohio Rev. Code § 1707.41 and (3) violation of Ohio Rev. Code § 1707.43.

---

[177] Ibid.

[178] Leonard (2013).

[179] McLaughlin (2013).

[180] "Court Throws Out Suit Against Moody's and S&P", *New York Times* (1 April 2010). http://www.nytimes.com/2010/04/02/business/02credit.html?_r=0.

[181] Case number 2:09-cv-1054 (2009).

Judge James Graham granted the CRAs' motion to dismiss the entire complaint against the three CRAs and ruled that the ratings provided by the defendant agencies were not "actionable misstatements". The ratings were predictions, according to Judge Graham, not statements of fact. The Judge also dismissed the plaintiffs' state law claim under the Ohio Securities Act because the Act applies only to sellers of securities. On Appeal to the US Court of Appeal for the Sixth Circuit in *Ohio Police & Fire, et al. v. Standard & Poor's Fin., et al*,[182] the judge concurred with the District Judge's finding and ruled that the "predictive opinions" of CRAs could not result in liability based on their reliance on the opinions when purchasing mortgage-backed securities. The District Court was found to have correctly held that the appellants lacked a viable claim under either Ohio or New York law because the plaintiffs did not properly allege a duty owed by the CRAs to the Funds, and the ratings were not actionable misrepresentations.

6.10.3.1 Settlement with the Banks[183]

CRAs were not the only guilty parties. State Attorney Generals agreed to a US $25 billion settlement with five large US banks accused of abusive foreclosure practices. The Attorney Generals in 49 states and the federal government agreed a pact with the banks in February 2012. The design of the settlement was to help about one million borrowers through measures such as loan modifications and principal reduction.[184] What this suggests is that the claims against bank lenders have been successful when a State Attorney General on behalf of the borrowers lodges them. It is doubtful whether a similar result would be achieved if claims were lodged by an Attorney General on behalf of investors because of the First Amendment defence available to CRAs.

6.10.4 Damages Awarded Against CRAs

CRAs have successfully defended themselves in the majority of cases where they have been sued. In a few cases, where CRAs were found to be blameworthy, the damages awarded against them have not been excessive. For example, in Parmalat,[185] an Italian court ruled that the CRA S&P had to pay back 784,000 Euros (US $1.14 million) to a dairy group from the original claim of 4 billion Euros. S&P had given an investment grade rating on Parmalat a week before the group collapsed in December 2003 under a 14 billion Euro deficit in its accounts. As

---

[182] Case: 11-4203, File 12a0398p.06 (17 September 2011).

[183] Ibid.

[184] Kravitz (2012), p. 1, 17th para.

[185] Aloisi (2010).

already stated, in another case, CRAs had agreed to credit the State of Connecticut with about US $900,000 for underrating state bonds, and it would be used to offset the expense of obtaining ratings on the future sales of state bonds.[186] When one examines claims lodged by the issuers, it has resulted in CRAs refunding part or the whole fees they had received from issuers in rating the debt instruments.[187] In yet another case, although not against CRAs, the SEC had brought civil charges against Citigroup, which had sold US $1 billion of risky mortgage-linked securities in 2007 without telling investors that it was betting against the debt, causing investors more than US $700 million of losses. The SEC agreed to a settlement of a US $285 million payout, including restitution and a US $95 million fine. In reality, the settlement was mere "pocket change" for the third-largest US bank, Citigroup.[188]

6.11 Contractual and Tortious Liability in England

6.11.1 Privity of Contract

The theory of privity of contract is based on the usual independence of the will and the adherence to reasonable expectations of the contracting parties. It is unacceptable that a third party should benefit and the assessment of damages for breach of contract is compensatory. A plaintiff, who contracts with a defendant for making payment, or to confer some other benefit on a non-privity party, could therefore not recover damages from a defendant for breach of that obligation. The plaintiff could only recover his/her own loss.

The contract of conducting and reporting credit rating is between issuers (corporations who want to raise money by issuing debt instruments) and CRAs. A privity of contract "is the mechanisms by which the contractual rights and liabilities are limited to the parties to the contract".[189] In theory, "contract is based upon the agreement and therefore only the parties to that agreement have consented to the contractual responsibility".[190] Only a promiser, who provides value in the form of consideration[191] under a contract, can enforce that contract.[192] An investor, as a third party, cannot sue or be sued under a contract. The common law doctrine of privity means that a "contract cannot, generally, confer rights or impose obligations arising under it on any person except the parties to it".[193] The doctrine of privity of

[186] Gosselin (2011).

[187] See McLaughlin and Faux (2011).

[188] Lattman (2013).

[189] Brown and Chandler (2005), p. 244.

[190] Ibid.

[191] See Glossary.

[192] Turner (2007), p. 382.

[193] Chitty (2004), p. 1075, paras 18-003.

contract is premised on it being unfair to subject parties to a contractual obligation without their consent. This rule has been the subject of much criticism[194] by academics and the judiciary alike because the privity doctrine imposes certain restrictions mentioned above. Courts have expressed a desire for major reforms to the rule denying third parties the right to enforce contractual provisions made for their benefit, and this requires legislative reform.[195] In the case of credit ratings, although issuers commission ratings, it is generally for the benefit of investors as a third party who rely on such ratings.

CRAs perform two functions, first, for the benefit of issuers who are a contractual party and, second, ensuring that responsibility in the market place is not endangered. Owing to the restrictions of the doctrine of privity of contract, the real practical problem facing investors, who have lost money after relying on the opinions of CRAs, relate to the reparations they can seek against the CRAs. A rational legal system requires that one who has caused a loss should compensate the other party. To prevent an inequitable result, one way in which courts can circumvent privity is the use of common law[196] and the statutory third-party beneficiary rule.[197]

6.11.2 Third-Party Beneficiary Rule

The third-party beneficiary rule is an exception and is aimed at mitigating the harshness of the privity rule. Rights in favour of third parties to enforce terms in a contract is where a contract expressly provides that the third party should have such a right or a contractual term purports to confer a benefit. For the potentially diverse investors wishing to purchase corporate debt instruments, a contract would not expressly identify them as they do not exist before issuers market the securities, and therefore investors have no legal recourse against CRAs.

Where a contract *prima facie* confers a benefit on a third party, a rational legal system requires one who has caused a loss to compensate that other party. Courts have recognised an exception where a plaintiff contracts as an agent or as a trustee for the third party or when a person is enforcing the rights of a beneficiary based on a fiduciary relationship.[198] A further exception is found in *Dunlop v Lambert*,[199] where the House of Lords applied an exception found in *St Martin's Property Corp Ltd v Sir Robert McAlpine Ltd*[200] to provide a remedy where no other remedy was

[194] Ibid., p. 1229, paras 18-001.

[195] Lavelle (2007), para 30, page 9.

[196] See *Dunlop v Lambert* (1839) 6 Cl & F 600; *St Martin's Property Corp Ltd v Sir Robert McAlpine Ltd* (1994) AC 85; *Darlington BC v Wiltshire Northern Ltd* [1995] 1 WLR 78.

[197] For English statutory provision, see *Contracts (Rights of Third Parties) Act 1999.*

[198] L. J. Dillion, in *Darlington BC v Wiltshire Northern Ltd* [1995] 1 WLR 78.

[199] (1839) 6 Cl & F 600.

[200] (1994) AC 85.

available. *St Martin's* case concerns the effect of prohibition on assignment without consent and whether such prohibition is contrary to the public policy. It also examined the conditions in which the original parties to a contract could enforce contractual terms on behalf of third parties, where the original party had suffered no loss. Courts have frequently resorted to devices such as an agency or a trust in order to allow a third party to enforce a benefit conferred upon such contracts. However, such a measure has been criticised as being artificial and contrary to the parties' intention to benefit a third party.[201]

In *Marc Rich*,[202] a surveyor acting on behalf of the classification society had recommended that after the carrying out of repairs specified by him, a vessel would be seaworthy, but it sank. The trial judge held that on that basis, the classification society owed the cargo owners a duty of care capable of giving rise to a liability in damages. On appeal, the House of Lords held that the cargo owners could not recover damages from the classification society, as there was no contract between them. There was no claim that the cargo owners knew of the survey; they simply relied on the owners to keep the vessel seaworthy and to look after the cargo. The decision turned essentially on considerations of policy in relation to the role of a classification society in the context of the insurance of risks. Classification societies are independent entities operating for the sole purpose of promoting the safety of lives and ships at sea. It was felt that a duty of care in this case would have severe consequences for both marine insurance and freight costs. Furthermore, it might lead to the classification society refusing to survey high-risk vessels with potentially harmful consequences for public safety at sea. If the *Marc Rich* case is extrapolated to CRAs (should a court hold that CRAs owe a duty to investors), will it have a negative effect and lead to higher rating costs and CRAs refusing to rate high-risk securities, resulting in severe consequences to the rating industry? It may be so, but on the other hand it may lead to a positive effect in CRAs being compelled to exercise extra care when intending to issue a triple-A rating to a debt instrument.

6.12 Tort Liability

Lord Atkin, in *Donoghue*, had unified the elaborate classification of duties in a single general theory.[203] A contract that includes a negligent statement may give rise to an action for damages in the tort of negligent misstatement.[204] However, a

[201] Lavelle (2007), para 76, page 19.

[202] (Lord Lloyd dissenting) *Rich (Marc) & Co AG v Bishop Rock Marine Co Ltd*, The Nicholas H [1996] AC 211, [1995] 3 All ER 307 HL.

[203] *Donoghue v Stevenson* [1932] AC 562 at 579–580. Negligence is a common word and refers to a type of fault and is synonymous to carelessness.

[204] *Hedley Byrne & Co. v Heller Partners* [1964] AC 465.

successful suit is dependent upon an investor's proof of the existence of a special relationship with the CRAs.[205] The basis for negligent tort liability requires investors satisfying certain elements. They are as follows: (a) the special circumstances must give rise to a duty of care; (b) there is a breach of that duty (based on carelessness or negligence), which results in loss; (c) the risk was foreseeable; and (d) no defence is available to the defendant to exculpate himself/herself for the said breach. Unlike common law, a statutory law does not require a representee to establish a duty of care.[206]

6.12.1 Caparo and CRAs

Judges have tried to use common law to extend a duty of care to a non-contracting third party. *Donoghue*[207] had established a "neighbour principle" as a test of discovering whether one party owed a duty of care to the other with reference to a faulty product and not based on economic loss. *Hedley Byrne*[208] is an English tort law case on pure economic loss, resulting from a negligent misstatement based on "assumption of responsibility" rather than from a contractual relationship. On whether the tort rulings apply to the CRAs, in *Caparo* judges reverted to a more cautious and realistic approach that necessitated the departure from *Anns*.[209]

Investors do suffer economic losses when their investment results in losses when they rely on faulty ratings issued by CRAs; however, based on the *Caparo* ruling, investors are required to satisfy a third "close proximity" requirement. The decision of the *Caparo* case, by coincidence, came at the time of worldwide recession and a wave of corporate failures. There was a general worry (which similarly applies to CRAs) in that auditors could get away with liability, even if negligent, where the parties affected were other than the audited company, its shareholders and (where appropriate) a third party for whom specifically the audit was carried out.

After years of mounting litigation against the audit profession, what *Caparo* did was to reduce auditors' exposure to potential liabilities by requiring third parties to satisfy the threefold test[210] in order for a duty of care to arise in negligence. In a suit brought by investors against CRAs, the better option is for the judges to apply a *Caparo* test rather than totally exempting or absolving CRAs from liability, which is presently the case. The reason is that it is the fear of liability that will act as deterrence and make CRAs use extra care, caution and diligence when issuing

[205] *Esso Petroleum Co. Ltd. v. Mardon* [1976] QB 802.

[206] Section 2 (1) of the Misrepresentation Act 1967.

[207] [1931] UKHL 3, 1932 SC (HL) 31, [1932] UKHL 100, [1932] AC 562. http://www.bailii.org/uk/cases/UKHL/1932/100.html.

[208] *Hedley Byrne & Co Ltd v Heller & Partners Ltd* [1964] AC 465.

[209] *Rowling v Takaro Properties Ltd* [1988] AC 473 at 501.

[210] Earle (1990), pp. 80–81.

ratings. As and when legal liability is imposed on the CRAs, they can defend their cases using *Caparo* principles as precedents. What *Caparo* did was to present an attractive option by narrowing the scope of liability when the House of Lords formulated the three-stage approach for determining duty. Namely, a plaintiff could establish a duty of care by proving that (1) the causing of the damage was reasonably foreseeable, (2) a relationship of proximity existed and (3) in all circumstances of the case it was fair, just and reasonable to impose a duty of care on the defendant. As the investors will have to satisfy the three requirements, there is no cause for the CRAs to worry about a litigation explosion, as any impending thought of liability may never materialise. Even though *Caparo's* tripartite test is applied as the test of duty in every case where duty has been an issue, *Caparo* has not denied the operation of established categories and at the same time provided the litigants with needed certainty. The judges, on their part, have interpreted the *Caparo* tests in conjunction with other established categories.[211]

Although the "neighbour principle" led to a general recognition of tortious liability for physical harm caused by negligence,[212] Lord Atkins was cautious about open-ended liability. *Anns v Merton LBC*,[213] *Caparo Industries v Dickman*[214] and *Marc Rich*[215] both have the common element of a policy doctrine that tries to limit the scope of duty or remove it altogether based on policy grounds.[216] The House of Lords in *Marc Rich*[217] went one step further and made no distinction between cases of direct physical damage and indirect physical or economic loss. Moreover, in spite of sufficient proximity between the cargo owners and the classification society, it was considered not fair, just and reasonable to impose such a duty in view of the effects it would have on international trade. As a policy matter, imposing liability on CRAs might *prima facie* result in adverse consequences for issuers. Issuers will face liquidity problems when they are unable to raise money should CRAs refuse to assign ratings for fear of liability. The CRAs, on their part, have a simple choice of either sacrificing excessive revenue that issuing commercial ratings generate, which is unlikely to be a preferred option, or issuing reliable ratings, which is the only likely option, to escape from liability.

---

211 *Attorney-General v Carter* [2003] 2 N.Z.L.R. 160. See also Hemraj (2004), p. 119.

212 *Donoghue v Stevenson* [1932] AC 562, See also Turner and Hodge (2010), p. 23.

213 [1978] A.C. 728; [1977] 2 All E.R. 492; [1977] 2 W.L.R. 1024, See also, Richard Kinder, "Resiling from the Anns Principle: The Variable Nature of Proximity in Negligence" (1987) 7 *Legal Studies* 319.

214 *Caparo Industries v Dickman* [1990] 1 All ER 568, HL. See also Hemraj (2006), pp. 82–89.

215 (Lord Lloyd dissenting) *Rich (Marc) & Co AG v Bishop Rock Marine Co Ltd*, The Nicholas H [1996] AC 211, [1995] 3 All ER 307HL.

216 *Junior Books Co Ltd v Veitchi Co Ltd* [1883] 1 AC 520.

217 *Rich (Marc) & Co AG v Bishop Rock Marine Co Ltd* [1996] HL.

6.13 Duty of Care in Australia: *Bathurst* Case

Bathurst[218] is the first case in the world where an Australian court found a CRA accountable for the rating opinions when paid to assign to financial products. Investors had incurred losses due to S&P erroneously awarding triple-A status and for which S&P were found liable for their breach of duty. The Federal Court found that the Rembrandt notes were sold to local councils in Australia with triple-A rating, implying that S&P had exercised reasonable grounds and reasonable care and skill but which was untrue and S&P were aware of it. The local councils lost huge sums of money on the collateralised debt instruments when the financial crisis ensued.[219] *Bathurst* at first instance laid down a precedent that even in the absence of contract, a CRA owes a duty of care to investors in rated instruments.[220] The basis of the verdict reached by J. Jagot was as follows:

(a) No reasonably competent CRA would have given "3-A" rating. S&P therefore owed a duty of care to potential investors for negligently rating the notes (security) and such a loss was reasonably foreseeable.
(b) Whilst S&P's had expressed rating as an "opinion", the rating conveyed an "extremely strong" representation that S&P actually believed that the notes were capable of meeting all financial obligations, such belief is required to be reached through the exercise of reasonable care. The S&P had failed to exercise reasonable care as in its knowledge this was not true, and
(c) The council investors were not sophisticated investors. They were not sufficiently sophisticated to understand the CPDO (security) investments, which was "grotesquely complicated".

Having identified a number of flaws in the rating process and the assumptions that were adopted by S&P in issuing the triple-A rating, S&P (together with ABN Amro) were found to have breached this duty and to be liable to each of the investors for their losses.

On appeal, the Full Federal Appeal Court of Australia in *ABN AMRO Bank NV v Bathurst Regional Council*,[221] based on the common law, found S&P liable as it owed a duty of care to investors in a rated financial product.[222] The Full Federal Court's finding based on the application of established legal principles to the facts was similar to those imposing duty of care under the English law.[223] However, according to conservative approach adopted by the English courts, when a party is in a position to provide protection from suffering harm and selects not to do so, the

[218] *Bathurst Regional Council v Local Government Financial Services Pty Ltd (No 5)* [2012] FCA 1200.

[219] Smyth and Fleming (2014).

[220] Platford.

[221] [2014] FCAFC 65.

[222] Freehills (2014).

[223] Freehills (2014).

court will not impose a duty of care to a non-contractual party.[224] Rather than raising significant issues of law and policy, the *Bathurst* concerns the application of established and undisputed legal principles found in Australia.[225] For there to be a duty to exercise reasonable care in making a statement or giving advice, (1) S&P must realise, or the circumstances must be such that S&P ought to have realised, that the recipient of the information or advice intends to act on that information or advice in connection with some matter of business or serious consequence and (2) the circumstances must be such that it is reasonable in all the circumstances for the recipient to seek, or to accept, and to rely upon the utterance of S&P.[226]

The reasonableness of the acceptance of and of the reliance by the recipient upon the words of S&P and the assumption of responsibility or known reliance (or conversely, vulnerability)[227] are sufficient grounds for the imposition of duty.[228] They are as follows: (1) S&P knew that if its opinion as to the credit-worthiness of the notes was carelessly given, investors were likely to lose the money they had invested in the notes[229]; (2) a duty is owed to an identifiable class,[230] although it is not necessary that the person making the statement knows the identity of the persons who may rely on it and suffer loss[231] and the person making the statement or giving the advice has some special expertise[232]; (3) a duty is owed even where there has been no direct relationship between the person who owed the duty and the person to whom the duty was owed[233]; and (4) S&P knew that ABN Amro obtained and paid for the rating for the sole purpose of communicating the

[224] Edwards (2013), p. 90.; a sophisticated litigant is required to prove dishonesty according to Hamblen J. in *Cassa di Risparmio della Repubblica di San Marino v Barclays Bank* [2011] EWHC 484 (Comm): www.bailii.org/ew/cases/EWHC/Comm/2011/484.html.

[225] *ABN AMRO Bank NV v Bathurst Regional Council* [2014] Para [572].

[226] Para [573].

[227] *Woolcock Street Investments Pty Limited v CDG Pty Limited* (2004) 216 CLR 515 at 530–531 [23]–[24] (Gleeson CJ, Gummow, Hayne and Heydon JJ).

[228] *ABN AMRO Bank NV v Bathurst Regional Council* [2014] Para [575].

[229] Ibid. Para [593].

[230] *Esanda Finance* at 252 (Brennan CJ) and 302 (Gummow J) approving *Al Saudi Banque v Clark Pixley* [1990] Ch 313 at 330. Para [577].

[231] *Kestrel Holdings Pty Limited v APF Properties Pty Limited* (2009) 260 ALR 418 at 435–436 [94]; *BT Australia Limited v Raine & Horne Pty Limited* [1983] 3 NSWLR 221 at 232 approving *Derring Lane Pty Limited v Fitzgibbon* (2007) 16 VR 563 at 571–572 [41]-[48]; *Caparo Industries Plc v Dickman* [1990] 2 AC 605 at 638 and *Hedley Byrne & Co Limited v Heller & Partners Limited* [1964] AC 465, where Lord Oliver noted that the identity of the person to whom the information was to be conveyed was not known by the defendant bank.

[232] *Esanda Finance* at 265; *San Sebastian Pty Ltd v The Minister* (1986) 162 CLR 340 at 357 and *Henderson* at 180.

[233] Authorities quoted by the appeal court were *Caltex Oil (Australia) Pty Ltd v The Dredge "Willemstad"* (1976) 136 CLR 529 at 573–574; Hedley Byrne [1964]; *Henderson v Merrett Syndicates Ltd* [1994] UKHL 5; *Aiken v Stewart Wrightson Members Agency Limited* [1995] 1 WLR 1281; *Kestrel Holdings; Dartberg Pty Ltd v Wealthcare Financial Planning Pty Ltd* (2007) 164 FCR 450 and BT Australia, at Para [616(2)].

rating to "interested parties" so that those parties could consider the rating in deciding whether to invest in the notes.[234] The duty of care does not extend to anyone who might come across ratings on any security, as this would turn S&P's predictions about the future into guarantees.

With regard to disclaimers, the Full Federal Court held that it might negate a duty that would have otherwise been owed.[235] S&P's disclaimers fail[236] because a disclaimer whose effect is absolving S&P from responsibility for the function or task it was engaged to perform would render the rating absence of content or meaningless and thus rendering the rating "content-less, futile and self-defeating".[237] Therefore, there are limits on the protection disclaimers can give as, to be effective, the disclaimer has to be in a clear explicit language and displayed noticeably.[238]

The court ordered S&P, ABN Amro and another entity to pay Aus $30 million in damages for losses incurred by investors. S&P had breached a duty of care owed to the investors under common law principles of negligence. Unless enacted as a statutory provision, the decision in other common or civil law jurisdictions is of a persuasive nature only. Owing to the complexity of the products, it could not be independently analysed and the court found the claimants had reasonably relied on the CRA's Notes' ratings.[239]

6.14 Threat of Civil Liability

In reality, what CRAs really fear is litigation, not legislation, as they do not want to see the removal of the tissue-thin veneer in the US that they are just expressing opinions protected by the First Amendment.[240] A credible civil liability threat, which is presently lacking, is required to act as deterrent and will have a positive effect in forcing CRAs to be more vigilant and thus guard against negligence, recklessness and fraudulent practices.

Whereas in present times most financial markets and professional gatekeepers like auditors, solicitors and company directors have faced litigation, the threat to CRAs, as the evidence suggests, has been minimal. They have been sued relatively infrequently, and even in these few cases, they have escaped from liability.[241] The

[234] Para [616(3)] at 156.

[235] Evatt at 570 (Barwick CJ); Hedley Byrne at 492–493 (Lord Reid) and 504 (Lord Morris) and Derring Lane at 570 [36]-[38] (Ashley JA, Buchanan JA and Kellam AJA agreeing).

[236] Para [603].

[237] Para [613].

[238] Freehills (2014).

[239] Werlen and Gaila (2014).

[240] Hallman (2013).

[241] Partnoy (2006).

inability of investors to litigate against CRAs has been because of statutory provisions and judicial precedents that limit the liability of NRSROs. This limitation is in the judicial decisions accepting "the rating agency's assertion that ratings are merely 'opinions' which, under the First Amendment, should be afforded the same free speech privileges as the opinions of publishers".[242]

Investors consider CRAs responsible for unjustifiably awarding high credit ratings (i.e., issuing faulty ratings) to the issuers' debt instruments and then failing to downgrade them promptly with changing circumstances,[243] and yet investors cannot make CRAs legally accountable.[244] The judges are quite capable of adjudicating cases lodged against CRAs by investors and holding them liable in deserving cases. The present trend seems to be favouring CRAs by allowing them what can be termed as "blanket immunity from liability".

Bathurst[245] is a case originating from Australia and makes a CRA liable to investors. The basis of the verdict reached by J. Jagot, relevant to this book's discussion, was the statements relating to the following: no reasonably competent CRA would have given a triple-A rating, an "opinion" about the rating had conveyed an "extremely strong" representation and investors were not sophisticated. Most importantly, the *Bathurst* case has laid down a precedent that even in the absence of contract, a CRA owes a duty of care to investors in rated instruments. The Court of Appeal upheld the case on appeal,[246] it is binding on Australian judges but not US judges as for them this case is only of a persuasive nature. Persuasive authority means the sources of law that the court consults in deciding a case. It means that the reasoning advanced in support of the holding is analytically compelling.[247] It is not a binding precedent on the court under common law legal systems such as English law. Appellate courts may look to rulings in other jurisdictions as persuasive authority.[248] It seems that CRAs have ammunition arising from the case, which they can exploit. They could exculpate themselves from liability by pleading that those investors were sophisticated investors, which is the state of affairs in the majority of the cases.

[242] Darbellay and Partnoy (2012), p. 16.

[243] Partnoy (1999).

[244] See Ellis et al. (2012), pp. 175–222.

[245] *Bathurst Regional Council v Local Government Financial Services Pty Ltd (No 5)* [2012] FCA 1200.

[246] *ABN AMRO Bank NV v Bathurst Regional Council* [2014] FCAFC 65.

[247] See *State v. Southers*, 1988 Ohio App. LEXIS 4648 (Ohio Ct. App., Pickaway County (23 November 1988).

[248] For definition of "persuasive authority", see Glossary.

6.15 Professional Indemnity Insurance (PII)[249]

What influences some judges to impose liability is the fact that the defendant carries indemnity insurance. For example, Lord Griffiths, the UK judge, recognised that the "availability of insurance is an important relevant consideration"[250] for judges. His Lordship further stated, "[E]veryone knows that all prudent professional men carry insurance, and the availability and cost of insurance must be a relevant factor when considering which of the two parties should be required to bear the risk of a loss".[251] The probability is that the judges will be reluctant to impose liability on CRAs because they do not carry insurance. Big institutions (banks and pension funds) lodge such claims where large amounts are involved. Should it transpire that the imposition of liability on the CRAs would make their position untenable based on the excessive cost of getting an indemnity policy, then the judges, based on policy grounds maintained by the defendant, would not impose liability.

The CRAs have insisted that investors should carry out their own due diligence because in assigning ratings they are merely expressing an opinion. The CRAs are arguably trying to distinguish between the actual existence of a duty of care and causation for the loss. In the English Law of negligence, causation proves a direct link between the defendant's negligence and the claimant's loss and damage. For these purposes, establishment of liability in negligence is when breach of the duty of care owed by the defendant to the claimant causes loss and damage and it is reasonable that the defendant should compensate the claimant for that loss and damage.[252]

A genuine fear is that the extent of the insurance cover required by CRAs would probably be un-financeable and, therefore, they would declare themselves insolvent for several reasons. However, judges have held professional people liable in negligence, *albeit* only those to whom they owe a duty of care, which is a limited responsibility. In reality, changes in the law would not make CRAs face huge liability when compared to other professions[253]: first, as already discussed, CRAs can resort to several legal defences available to them; second, reduction of damages is awarded to the investors based on contributory negligence (i.e., the failure of shareholders to carry out their own due diligence); third, similar to auditors, the court should exclude CRAs' damages for claims relating to past and future investors; and, fourth, based on the present state of laws that absolve CRAs from liability, it would be cheaper for CRAs to get PII[254], as the premium costs will be lower and which they can easily recover from the issuers. Having examined the positive, the negative aspect relates to the rise of the premium cost based on the

249 See also Hemraj (2002), pp. 397–410.

250 *Smith v Eric Bush* [1990] 1 AC 831 at 858.

251 Ibid.

252 For definition of "negligence", see Glossary.

253 American Medical Association (2002).

254 For definition of PII, see Glossary.

increase in CRA claims even where cases are dismissed. The cost of insurance underwriting to cover the risk of class action litigation for negligence in the US would be enormous.

Unlike other professions like solicitors and accountants, who are compelled to purchase PII, there is no requirement for CRAs to hold a compulsory PII. Investors, on their part, have not received compensation for losses suffered. Professional peoples' insurers have compensated parties who have lost money. In reality, it is the investors who are indirectly paying for the services of CRAs (when this is factored into the issuer's cost), and they need to be compensated for loss of money through reliance on the credit ratings for their investment decisions. Although it is the insurers, under the PII, who pay for the damages rather than it coming from the professional people's own pockets, nevertheless it led to a better result. The professionals like auditors and solicitors were compelled to re-examine their practices and have tried to rectify their shortcomings by making necessary changes to ensure protection against any possible future liability.

It is the deterrence that will force CRAs to act responsibly. This is only possible if CRAs fear a potential threat of the institution of civil liability against them. This is not the case at present, and it may be the reason why CRAs are complacent. A possible option is for regulators to compel all those CRAs registered as NRSROs to carry a compulsory PII. CRAs can then add the PII premiums to the cost of rating debt instruments and require the issuers to pay for it. However, as PII will protect CRAs from paying damages directly for the consequences of their actions, this might create a problem with the deterrence rationale.[255]

PII helps protect professional advice- and service-providing individuals and companies from bearing the full cost of defending against a negligence claim made by a client and damages awarded in such civil lawsuits. PII sometimes also provides for the defence costs, including when legal action turns out to be groundless, but excludes criminal prosecution. Presently, as CRAs are not liable to the third-party investors, they do not carry any PII, although the money paid for insurance premiums could have been easily accounted as a business expense. Similarly, the CRAs also do not have to worry about the possibility of any future increase in the premiums, which arises because of potential increases in the liability.

6.16 Due Diligence

The banks, especially some of the larger ones, have in-house rating experts, and also the pension funds and large investors can all afford to carry out their own independent ratings (and also carry out due diligence) rather than exclusively rely on the ratings issued by CRAs. However, the court should compensate small

[255] Griffith (2011), p. 337.

investors or non-expert investors who solely rely on ratings given by the CRAs, as it is fair, reasonable and just to impose liability on CRAs on the basis that there is no fear of imposing excessive liability on them. In an Australian case,[256] J Jagot rejected S&P's various disclaimers as the council members were unsophisticated investors. However, in reality, some fund managers do pool securities of different categories of ratings in their portfolio (investment grade and some containing junk status) and do rely on the ratings issued by CRAs. In such instances, investors have no say in this matter. What they do is to make a decision on which fund manager to invest in. Two scenarios emerge here: either a manager in charge of collective investment is granted a *locus standi* on behalf of small investors to bring legal proceedings against CRAs or such managers should carry out their own due diligence. There is no evidence that the investors have directly sued the fund managers.

Another suggestion is that regulators should revert to the previous investors-pay model and let investors request and pay CRAs for conducting credit ratings[257] as this will create a contract between investors and CRAs. Investors would then be able to sue CRAs for their breach of contract if they negligently issue unreliable ratings. The difficulty lies in how the investors would share the costs of ratings and whether they would succeed in their suits, as the claim of CRAs is that they do not give investment advice. Derby and Murphy have suggested reverting to the previous investors-pay model (in which investors pay CRAs for the rating service) as a solution to the problem of conflicts of interest; however, in my opinion, the issuers-pay model is expected to remain the preferred option.[258]

6.17 Liability Conundrum

There are reasons in favour of and against introducing liability. The positive attribute of liability is that if "CRAs are [made] liable for negligent ratings, they will be less likely to be negligent, and will improve the quality of their credit ratings. Placing liability on CRAs undoubtedly increases their incentives to avoid negligent ratings".[259] The negative attribute of liability is that "[s]uch liability, however, may work too well. Liability is an extremely blunt instrument for improving ratings quality. A single negligent rating may cause billions of dollars in losses, causing instant bankruptcy for an agency".[260] Should CRAs refuse to rate those debt instruments where there is a potential fear that a liability may be imposed on

[256] *Bathurst Regional Council v. Local Government Financial Services Pty Ltd (No. 5)* [2012] FCA 1200 (5 November 2012).

[257] See Deb and Murphy (2009).

[258] See Pagano and Volpin (2009); Wessendorf (2008–2009), p. 155.

[259] Listokin and Taibleson (2010), p. 101.

[260] Ibid.

them, the corporate issuers will suffer in not being able to raise funds, and this will in turn affect the business and the economy.

In case of the audit profession, *Caparo Industries plc v Dickman*[261] has greatly restricted their liability. In the US, auditors cannot limit liability for their own negligence. The company law in England also does not allow auditors to limit their liability on the basis that "as in other walks of life, auditors should be held liable for the consequences of their own actions"[262] for several reasons:

> First, a tendency to sue based on perceived ability to pay rather than degree of fault has spread across the Atlantic. Second, auditors are required to have professional indemnity insurance when others involved in the financial reporting process are not. Third, the principle of joint and several liability entrenched in UK law allows someone who is only partly responsible for a loss to be pursued for the whole loss if other parties cannot pay.[263]

The CRAs, with the introduction of a cap in liability, would get the same treatment. The adverse effect of not imposing liability is that there will be no improvement in the quality of ratings. A better option would be for the SEC to ensure that the CRAs either have in place a professional indemnity policy or should introduce a statutory liability cap or both.

6.18 Conclusion

This chapter examined the civil liability of CRAs in the US, and briefly in England, and the position of investors wishing to sue CRAs. It also briefly looked at the position of issuers in the US. It explains why the present laws (dealing with contract and tort) act as a safe harbour for CRAs (though not in Australia where the situation is slightly different). The preferred option is to correct this anomaly by judges adopting the rulings of the *Bathurst* case and, better still, if it is enshrined in a statutory provision in the US and in England.

CRAs have been criticised for some time for their role in contributing to the global financial crisis, especially for assigning high ratings to subprime structured finance instruments, which did not reflect their true risk, and globally CRAs face a number of claims whose outcomes are still pending. The CRAs have used the defences available under the existing law to exculpate themselves from liability from suits filed by the issuers and investors alike. The current liability position is that no court has ever found a CRA liable for bad ratings, and CRAs are terrified of losing that protection.[264] This chapter has examined the civil liability of CRAs in

[261] [1990] 2 AC 605, House of Lords decision. For a summary of the judgement, see C. Mills, *The Caparo Decision: A Summary of Judgement*, London, Coopers & Lybrand Deloitte (April 1990).

[262] "Auditors liability conundrum – The need for auditor liability limitation in the UK", *Accountancy* (August 2008). http://www.icaew.com/en/technical/audit-and-assurance/working-in-the-regulated-area-of-audit/audit-liability/auditors-liability-conundrum.

[263] Ibid.

[264] Submission of Professor D. Reiss at Brooklyn Law School mentioned by Hallman (2011).

the US and England and the position of investors, should they wish to sue CRAs. It also briefly looked at the position of issuers. It explains why the present laws dealing with contract and tort act as a safe harbour for CRAs. In examining the contract and tort laws, the evidence suggests that the CRAs, in the US, as the law presently stands, have nothing to fear as the present legal regime (contract and tort) favours CRAs. The CRAs have also included an exclusion clause(s) in their attempt to exclude their potential liability with the investors, should they breach their duties. What this means is that presently there is a lack of sufficient deterrence on the part of CRAs, which would oblige them to act responsibly towards the investors. CRAs in the US have an advantage over the investors as they have successfully pleaded the First Amendment defence. Investors have failed to sue successfully CRAs and thus have had to bear personally the monetarily losses. Despite the current regulations in place, a thorny issue regulators face is how to eradicate conflicts of interest and lack of competition. The next chapter evaluates the success and failure of the regulations introduced in previous chapters and what regulators should do to tackle the gatekeeper failure of CRAs responsible, which may be due to lack of a deterrence.

References

Aloisi, S. (2010, July 5). Court orders S&P to reimburse Parmalat rating fees. http://www.reuters.com/article/2011/07/05/parmalat-sp-idUSLDE7641IJ20110705?feedType=RSS&feedName=marketsNews&rpc=43.

American Medical Association. (2002, April 24). Professional liability insurance: Clamoring for relief. http://ama-assn.org/ama/pub/article/3216-6145.html.

Barrett, P. M. (2014, January 16). A $5 billion U.S. fraud case against standard & poor's enters critical phase. *Bloomberg Business Week*.

Bobroff, R., & Tobin, H. J. (2008). Third-party beneficiary claims: Recent cases against private parties and local agencies. *Clearinghouse Review, 42*, 99.

Brown, I., & Chandler, A. (2005). *Law of contract – Questions & answers* (5th ed.). Oxford: OUP.

Chitty, C. (2004). *Chitty on contracts* (29th ed.). London: Sweet & Maxwell.

Coffee, J. C., Jr. (2006). *Gatekeepers: The professions and corporate governance* (pp. 295–296). Oxford, UK: OUP.

Coffee, J. C., Jr. (2007, September 20). The mortgage meltdown and gatekeeper failure. New York Law Journal, 2 and 5.

Coleman, J. L. (1995). The principles of corrective justice. In D. G. Owen (Ed.), *Philosophical foundations of tort law*. Oxford: Clarendon Press.

Darbellay, A., & Partnoy, F. (2012, April). *Credit rating agencies and regulatory reform* (University of San Diego Legal Studies Research Paper Series, Research Paper No. 12-083). http://ssrn.com/abstract=2042111.

de Savornin Lohman, H. A., & van't Westeinde, M.G. (2007, May). Control and liability of credit rating agencies under Netherlands law, EJCL. *Netherlands Comparative Law Association*, 1–22. http://www.ejcl.org/111/art111-18.pdf.

Deb, P., & Murphy, G. (2009, November). Credit rating agencies: An alternative model (p. 5). http://personal.lse.ac.uk/debp/Papers/Ratings_Regulation.pdf.

Earle, V. (1990). Accountant liability: Cardozo remembered in the House of Lords. *CPA Journal, 60*, 80–81.

Edwards, H. (2013, March). Liability for the rating and sale of structured credit products: Australian cases and their (much) wider implications. *Law and Financial Markets Review, 7*, 88–96. http://sites.herbertsmithfreehills.vuturevx.com/34/4732/landing-pages/harry-edwards-article.pdf.

Ellis, N. S., Fairchild, L. M., & D'Souza, F. (2012). Is imposing liability on credit rating agencies a good idea? Credit rating agency reform in the aftermath of the global financial crisis. *Stanford Journal of Law, Business and Finance, 17*(2), 175–222.

Englard, I. (1993, January 7). Corrective justice and distributive justice (Chapter 2). In I. Englard (Ed.), *The philosophy of tort law (applied legal philosophy)*. Aldershot: Dartmouth Publishing Co. Ltd.

Feinman, J. M. (2000). *Professional liability to third parties* (p. 44). Chicago: Aba Professional Education.

Fleming, J. G. (1998). *The law of torts* (9th ed.). Andover: Sweet & Maxwell.

Foley, S. (2013, April 27). Standard & Poor's and Moody's settle US subprime lawsuits. *Financial Times*. http://www.ft.com/cms/s/0/27a59708-af46-11e2-ac6f-00144feabdc0.html#axzz2fjE4i6oZ.

Freehills, H. S. (2014, June 10). Liability of Credit Rating Agencies confirmed by Australian Appeal court.

Froeba, M. (2009, September 29). Rating agency legal liability standards. http://expectedloss.blogspot.com/2009/09/rating-agency-legal-liability-standards.html.

Goel, A. M., & Thakor, A. V. (2011, March 15). Credit ratings and litigation risk. http://ssrn.com/abstract=1787206 or http://dx.doi.org/10.2139/ssrn.1787206.

Gosselin, K. R. (2011, October 14). Jepsen settles with credit agencies. *The Hartford Courant*

Griffith, S. J. (2011). Shareholders litigation and deterrence. In C. A. Hill & B. H. McDonnell (Eds.), *Research handbook on the economics of corporate law* (p. 337). Cheltenham: Edward Elgar.

Hallman, B. (2013, April 2). S&P lawsuit first amendment defense may fare poorly, experts say. *Huffington Post*. http://www.huffingtonpost.com/2013/02/04/sp-lawsuit-first-amendment_n_2618737.html.

Harlow, C. (2005). *Understanding tort law* (3rd ed., p. 27). London: Sweet Maxwell.

Haynes, A. (2013). The burden of proof in the market abuse cases. *Journal of Financial Crime, 20*(4), 365–397.

Hemraj, M. B. (2002). Professional indemnity insurance: International demand, affordability and the insurance market. *International and Comparative Corporate Law Journal, 4*(4), 397–410.

Hemraj, M. B. (2004). Economic loss: Tests for liability in negligent misstatements. *Comparative Law, 25*, 119–120.

Hemraj, M. B. (2006). Taking stock of Caparo. *Company Lawyer, 27*(3), 82–89.

Hitov, S., & Deford, G. (2002). The impact of privatization on litigation. *Clearinghouse Review, 35*, 590.

Jickling, M. (2010, November 24). *The Dodd-Frank Wall Street Reform and Consumer Protection Act: Title IX, investor protection* (Congressional Research Paper). http://www.llsdc.org/attachments/files/260/CRS-R41503.pdf.

Jones, M. A. (2002). *Textbook on torts* (8th ed.). Oxford, New York: OUP.

Kotz, H. D. (2009, August 27). The SEC's role regarding and oversight of nationally recognized statistical rating organizations (NRSROs). *U.S. Securities and Exchange Commission*. http://www.sec-oig.gov/Reports/AuditsInspections/2009/Report458.pdf.

Kravitz, D. (2012, February 9). States, banks reach $25 billion foreclosure-abuse settlement, 17 para at 1. http://www.katu.com/news/business/States-banks-reach-25-billion-foreclosure-abuse-settlement-139036839.html.

Lattman, P. (2013, February 8). Court hears arguments on Judge's rejection of S.E.C.-Citigroup Deal. http://dealbook.nytimes.com/2013/02/08/appeals-court-hears-arguments-over-judge-rakoffs-rejection-of-citigroup-settlement/.

Lavelle, M. (2007). *Privity of contracts and third party beneficiaries*. Alberta Law Reform Institute, Charlottetown, Prince Edward Island. http://www.ulcc.ca/en/2007-charlottetown-pe/216-civil-section-documents/574-privity-of-contract-and-third-party-beneficiaries-2007?showall=1&limitstart=.

Leonard, B. (2013, February 5). Standard & poor's sued by U.S. for fake ratings, Courthouse News Service. http://www.courthousenews.com/2013/02/05/54588.htm.

Lippke, R. L. (1999). Torts, corrective justice and distributive justice. *Legal Theory, 5*(2), 149–169.

Listokin, Y., & Taibleson, B. (2010). *If you misrate, then you lose: Improving credit rating accuracy through incentive compensation.* Faculty Scholarship Series (Paper 3877, p. 94). http://digitalcommons.law.yale.edu/fss_papers/3877.

Markesinis, B., & Deakin, S. (2008). *Markesinis and Deakin's tort law* (6th ed.). Oxford, New York: OUP.

McLaughlin, D., & Faux, Z. (2011, October 14). *Moody's, S&P, fitch settle ratings dispute with Connecticut.* http://www.bloomberg.com/authors/AP8pAjHCRc8/david-mclaughlin.

McLaughlin, D. (2013, February 6). *S&P analyst joked of bringing down the house before crash.* http://www.bloomberg.com/news/articles/2013-02-05/s-p-analyst-joked-of-bringing-down-the-house-ahead-of-collapse.

Nguyen, V., & Rajapakse, P. (2008). An analysis of the auditors' liability to third parties in Australia. http://www98.griffith.edu.au/dspace/bitstream/handle/10072/23782/51198_1.pdf?sequence=1.

Pagano, M., & Volpin, P. (2009, September). Credit ratings failures and policy options. http://www.eief.it/files/2009/12/credit-ratings-failures-and-policy-options.pdf.

Partnoy, F. (1999). The Siskel and Ebert of financial markets: Two thumbs down for the credit rating agencies. *Washington University Law Quarterly, 77*, 619–712. http://dx.doi.org/10.2139/ssrn.167412.

Partnoy, F. (2006). *How and why credit rating agencies are not like other gatekeepers* (University of San Diego Legal Studies Research Paper Series No. 07-46, pp. 59–102). http://ssrn.com/abstract=900257.

Platford, C. Federal court ruling a landmark decision against credit ratings agency. http://www.clmr.unsw.edu.au/article/risk/federal-court-ruling-landmark-decision-against-credit-ratings-agency.

Powers, J. F. (1993). Expanded liability and the intent requirement in the in third party beneficiary contracts. *Utah Law Review*, 67.

Prince, H. G. (1984). Perfecting the third party beneficiary standing rule under section 302 of the restatement (second) of contracts. *Boston College Law Review, 25*(5), 5.

Roake, T. K., & Davidson, G. K. (1996, January). The Private Securities Litigation Reform Act of 1995. http://www.fenwick.com/docstore/publications/corporate/sec/corp_sec_01-00-96.pdf.

Sack, J. S., & Wilderman, K. (2010, 15 September). Civil liability of rating agencies: Past success, future danger? *New York Law Journal, 234*(53), 1–2.

Smyth, J. & Fleming, S. (2014, June 6). S&P loses Australia appeal over misleading investors. http://www.ft.com/cms/s/0/681d754a-ed1f-11e3-8963-00144feabdc0.html#axzz3JLBh3vmx.

Stempel, J., & Viswanatha, A. (2012). SEC, Citigroup may win appeal in fraud case. Reuters. http://uk.reuters.com/article/2012/03/15/us-citigroup-sec-idUSBRE82E0VB20120315.

Turner, C. (2007). *Unlocking contract law* (2nd ed., p. 382). Abingdon: Hodder Arnold.

Turner, C., & Hodge, S. (2010). *Unlocking Torts* (3rd ed., p. 23). Abington: Hodder Education.

U.S. Securities and Exchange Commission. (2003, January). Report on the Role and Function of Credit Rating Agencies in the Operation of the Securities Markets.

Viswanatha, A., & LaCapra, L. T. (2013, February 5). U.S. government slams S&P with $5 billion fraud lawsuit. *Reuters.* http://uk.reuters.com/article/2013/02/05/us-mcgrawhill-sandp-civilcharges-idUSBRE9130U120130205.

Wall Street Journal. (2013, April 29). Cost of rating suits: $255 million. http://online.wsj.com/article/SB10001424127887323528404578453292918428224.html.

Werlen, T., & Gaila, Y. (2014). ABN AMRO Bank NV v Bathurst Regional Council Rating Agencies. Duty of Care to Investors'.

Wessendorf, E. M. (2008–2009). Regulating the credit rating agencies. *Entrepreneurial Business Law Journal, 3*(1), 155. http://moritzlaw.osu.edu/students/groups/oseblj/files/2013/04/3-9.pdf.

Chapter 7
Regulation: Success or Failure?

7.1 Introduction

This book has taken a holistic view by examining various regulations ranging from self-regulation, statutory regulation and common law regulation in the US and EU. The intention of regulation is to solve the problems of conflicts of interest, lack of competition and lack of accountability on the part of credit rating agencies (CRAs). The regulation consists of soft laws, statutory regulations and common law. The book's premise is that for any regulation to play an effective role, it needs to have a deterrent effect in the form of imposing gatekeeper accountability on CRAs, thus compelling them to issue reliable ratings. Although this was critically examined in the preceding chapters, this last chapter aims to highlight the key issues, which hinge on whether or not regulation introduced in the US and EU is a success or a failure, and to consider the conclusions reached and make recommendations.

7.2 Regulation: Revisiting the Research Agenda

The first key issue to consider is the choices that were open to the regulators on the types of regulation they were able to introduce and whether or not regulation is robust enough to enable the CRAs to perform a gatekeeper role of protecting investors' interests. This book has taken a broad research focus by critically examining different types of regulation relating to CRAs (rather than having a narrow focus, limiting it to a particular country or sub-topic) in the US and EU. Previous researchers, guided by the nature of their research questions, have adopted a narrow focus. The broader focus of this book is an attempt to examine and to redress the deficiencies found in "soft-laws" in the form of self-regulation, "hard laws" in the form of statutory regulation and common law. Common law defences

M. Hemraj, *Credit Rating Agencies*, DOI 10.1007/978-3-319-17927-8_7

are intact, and in practice the regulators neither have lobbied for nor have suggested any changes to the US common law position examined, which currently absolves CRAs from any liability towards the investors, thus retaining the *status quo*. The research contributes to the proper understanding of these various regulations, the impact on CRAs' gatekeeper role and whether or not investors have benefitted from them, given that the prime purpose of introducing or utilising these regulations is to prevent abuses (which were identified by the regulators) from recurring in the future.

7.3 Reaping Profits Without Risking Capital

A report commissioned by the US Senate[1] in 2002 had reached the following conclusions. First, under the then current system, in many respects CRAs were acting like government agencies, although their ratings were generally accurate when produced perhaps on technical grounds. Nevertheless, as the subprime mortgage and its worldwide impact have indicated, the consequences can be serious. Second, CRAs with their special access and strong market power were in a perfect position to act as a referee and raise a "red flag" but failed to do so. Third, reputational concerns were a sufficient incentive for CRAs to be diligent in their work. The plausible explanation as to why they failed to achieve these things may be found in considering conflicts of interest, lack of competition and lack of accountability.

What the 2007–2008 subprime mortgage crisis has shown is that the CRAs did have conflicts of interest. The issuers-pay model meant that it was issuers and not investors paying CRAs, which probably meant CRAs were not very much concerned about their reputation and, therefore, had little incentive in doing a diligent job. There was no incentive for CRAs to catch a few issuers who were possible wrongdoers, even though it might have a huge consequence to the market. The majority of companies are deemed to be honest and do not resort to fraudulent accounting. In reality, when the external auditors have failed to discover fraud, the CRAs may feel that they are not in a better position to do so. It may also be due to the fact there is no accountability on their part for their failure to detect fraud. Arguably, the CRAs are only able to rely on the financial statements if companies are honest. Perhaps legal defences available to CRAs and their entrenched position of power may mean that they did not go to additional lengths to try to act as a responsible gatekeeper. This meant that a few corporations lack accountability when they give wrong or unreliable information to CRAs. The crux of the matter seems to be that "the raters answer to no authority. In addition, unlike a government agency, they profit from every transaction they rate, thereby reaping the benefits of the capital markets without risking any capital".[2] Added to this, under the

[1] Financial Oversight of Enron (2002), p. 98.

[2] Ibid.

issuers-pay model, CRAs' reputation seems to be geared towards pleasing issuers rather than protecting investors' interest. While the SEC in the US now supervises CRAs as mentioned in Chap. 4 and the European Securities and Markets Authority (ESMA) in the EU, mentioned in Chap. 5, the *status quo* of CRAs reaping profits without risking any capital remains.

7.4 Subprime Mortgage Crisis and Structured Financial Products (SFP)

An important question is whether these regulators have succeeded in making CRAs the investors' gatekeeper. Chapter 2 showed that the Big Three CRAs had given risky structured financial products (SFPs) favourable ratings. The SFP consisted of mortgage-backed securities, off-balance-sheet vehicles, derivatives and the like. "Structured products" refers to combinations of individual financial instruments, such as bonds, stocks and derivatives. At first glance, most of these composite products are very similar to plain vanilla coupon bonds. SFPs tend to involve periodical interest payments and redemption at maturity. What sets them apart from bonds is that both interest payments and redemption amounts depend in a rather complicated fashion on the movement of stock prices, indices, exchange rates or future interest rates. SFPs are made up of simpler components, are usually broken down into their integral parts when there is a need to value them or assess their risk profile and any hedging strategies. This facilitates the analysis and pricing of the individual components.[3] The SFPs needed high triple-A ratings, and CRAs easily gave them. According to Buckley, by mixing 80 % of the risky subprime mortgage debts together with a pool of 20 % of collateralized debt obligation (CDO) debts,[4] which were considered less risky because of some associated securities in order to minimise the overall risk,[5] issuers attracted investors to buy these securities.

Banks purchased SFPs to reduce their capital requirements, and so did money market funds and pension funds, and they all, as a result, suffered huge losses. As was observed in Chap. 2, in some instances, CRAs were rating products for which they lacked expertise, and yet they were willing to give favourable ratings. They then failed to downgrade these products when the circumstances changed, or at least to downgrade them quickly enough, which resulted in creating huge investors' demand for these products and some banks retaining them in their portfolio. Ryan[6]

---

[3] Lamb (2013). See also Glossary for definition of "structural products".

[4] CDO consisted of private equity debt, auto debt, credit card debt, etc. See Glossary for definition of CDO.

[5] See Buckley (2011), p. 69. See also Chapter 8 "Why Everyone Loved Moody's" in McLean and Nocera (2010).

[6] Ryan (2012a).

questions the credibility of CRAs, and in his view there is a need to strengthen the accuracy of credit ratings and reduce systemic risk.

Several factors relate to why CRAs gave triple-A ratings to these risky products. Conflicts of interest arose because of issuers paying CRAs to rate their debt instruments, and CRAs may have cared less about maintaining their reputation, as they wanted to appease issuers to get future rating business. In addition to conflicts of interest, there was also a lack of rivalry in the form of competition in the marketplace, including an absence of any liability threat from investors. Following the aftermath of the crisis and the introduction of various regulations examined in the preceding chapters, it is submitted that these regulations generally lack a deterrent effect on CRAs due to an absence of liability when they are breached. Investors, in spite of inducement to invest based on the highly rated debt, had to bear the losses. CRAs have repeatedly insisted, despite the regulations, that they are only providing opinions and do not give investment advice on the debt instruments they rate, which partly may be because of future uncertainty on the creditworthiness of the corporations concerned. Assuming that the CRAs' submissions are true, one would have expected that they would have erred towards caution by exercising extra care before readily awarding triple-A ratings. In addition, the CRAs have opted not to verify the information provided by the issuers and chosen to accept its accuracy without question.

CRAs want investors to carry out their own due diligence and collect other necessary relevant information in order to make an informed choice rather than blindly rely on the (high) ratings given. The implication for this is that it allows CRAs to behave as if nothing has changed. CRAs have refrained from taking any responsibility for investors. What regulatory authorities have done is to ensure that CRAs have put into place procedures addressing internal controls, credit rating methodologies and employee conflicts of interest as precautionary safeguards aimed at maintaining rating accuracy, which is a step in the right direction. Ryan[7] proposes that the regulatory authority should rank CRAs in terms of performance, in particular on the accuracy of their ratings, which is worthy of adoption by the regulators.

7.5 Have Credit Rating Agencies Lost Trust?

A problem that arises is whether CRAs can be trusted. The behavioural pattern of the investors was to rely on the triple-A ratings as indicating a safe investment with the minimum risk of default. It is the ease with which the CRAs were issuing triple-A ratings to corporate debt instruments that should naturally be a cause for concern to potential investors. CRAs are interested in investors buying debt instruments issued by the issuers, but they can only do so if investors are able to trust and rely on

[7] Ryan (2012b), p. 19.

their ratings. If investors cannot do this, then high ratings would become meaningless and the investors, in spite of high ratings given by the CRAs, would demand issuers pay them a higher rate of interest for the risk associated with these instruments. However, perhaps as banks are required to comply with the capital adequacy requirement under Basel II and Basel III, which is dependent on holding securities with triple-A ratings, there is a possibility that the rating is relied upon as a formality only.[8] It is a fallacy to assume that in regulations that require CRAs to act as the investors' gatekeeper, regulators were unnecessarily trying to punish or to financially overburden the CRAs with the need to abide by various regulations. Ryan[9] suggests that the regulators should use their inspection, examination and regulatory authority. This would ensure CRAs do not assign higher ratings to the risky financial debt instruments whose performance is difficult to predict reliably. This can happen due to a variety of reasons ranging from the novelty and complexity of the product to reliance on assets from parties and corporate borrowers with a poor record for issuing quality assets.

7.6 Soft Law

7.6.1 Self-Regulation

Self-regulation relies on ethical principles when discharging duties. The advantage for the regulators following this avenue is that some of these provisions were already in existence, were enshrined and implemented by the Three Big agencies in their respective codes of conduct. The regulators, rather than calling for CRAs to improve their ethical doctrines, as already examined in Chap. 3, came up with their own suggestions and insisted that CRAs adopt and incorporate additional provisions contained in the IOSCO Code into their own codes of conduct. These consisted of the quality and integrity of the rating process, their independence, avoidance of conflicts of interest and their responsibilities to the investing public and issuers. None of the Big Three had objected, arguably for the simple reason that there were no adverse legal implications if they did breach, or failed to abide by, the provisions of the IOSCO Code.

Investors, on their part, could not successfully sue CRAs because of exclusion clause(s) that CRAs had introduced. Some additional provisions in their codes, as examined in Chap. 3, were to clarify the expectation gap. Most importantly, it relates to the role they actually perform of expressing an opinion rather than giving investment advice. This meant that investors ought not to rely blindly on ratings issued, even if they were given triple-A ratings, but should exercise caution and perform due diligence. The basis of the problem is the issuers-pay model where

---

[8] Haynes (2013).

[9] Ryan (2012b), p. 19.

issuers pay CRAs; CRAs enter into a contractual relationship with issuers but not with investors. In that sense, even when a conflict can be managed and the CRAs fail to do so, the investors are not a party to the contract entered into by the CRAs and the issuers and, therefore, do not have any legal recourse against CRAs. The effect is that investors' interests have been unprotected when CRAs have failed to discharge their duties of issuing credit ratings accurately. Investors had to suffer losses without any recompense from CRAs, in terms of damages suffered.

7.6.2 *Criticisms of Self-Regulation*

Several criticisms of regulators relate to the manner of the adoption of self-regulation and the way the regulators went about introducing it. The criticisms are, first, regulators failed to insist that CRAs ratify the mess they helped to create. The achievement of this required the Big-Three CRAs to meet together and devise strategies and recommendations to redress the harm caused to investors for the regulators' approval, similar to the brilliant piece of UK Cadbury Code with reference to company directors.[10] Second, regulators preferred micro-regulations detailing what these regulations were, rather than macro-regulations. To illustrate with an example, what the regulations ought to have done is to adopt a macro-regulation stating that "Credit Rating Agencies shall avoid conflicts of interest" and then let CRAs, rather than the regulators, develop detailed micro-regulations on how to achieve it.

In cases where CRAs did breach these regulations, the investors need a right to litigate. Judges, on their part, should decide on their culpability based on the neighbour proximity negligence principle[11] for breaching their own code of conduct. That is whether, in the given circumstances, CRAs were competent enough to issue reliable ratings, on the justification of higher ratings issued and on their failure to downgrade them when the circumstances had changed. The judges should then compensate those investors who have suffered losses based on their reliance on inaccurate credit ratings, through no fault of their own. The failure by investors to carry out their own due diligence, if a court might find such due diligence were necessary, could be the basis of comparative/contributory negligence leading to a reduction in damages awarded to investors.[12]

[10] Cadbury (2000).

[11] *Donoghue (or McAlister) v Stevenson*, [1932] All ER Rep 1; [1932] AC 562 (House of Lords).

[12] See Chap. 6.

7.6.3 Disclaimer by CRAs

Presently, investors cannot litigate by suing CRAs for breaches of ethical principles. Litigation based on breaches of ethical principles is possible, as it does not bar litigation. What bars litigation is the disclaimer by CRAs contained in their code of conduct, thus preventing investors from successfully suing CRAs. The theoretical ruling by the courts in favour of investors requires a statutory rule, which bars an application of the exclusion clause(s). The UK prohibits auditors from including and relying on such exclusion clauses in their audit report, and the *Caparo Industries v Dickman*[13] decision ensures that liability of auditors is only to the company they are auditing and its present shareholders (past and future shareholders are excluded). Similarly, if applied to CRAs, it means only present investors, with the exclusion of past and future investors, should be able to bring a successful claim.

Company directors in the UK cannot have a disclaimer clause in the company's Articles of Association absolving them from fiduciary duties and the duty of care and skill (but with the shareholders' approval, the US allows exclusion of duty of care but not for breaches of good faith and loyalty). Shareholders have a statutory right to sue directors in a derivative action on behalf of the company for negligence, default (including breaches of statutory obligations), breach of duty or breach of trust, subject to the court allowing the action to proceed.[14] Shareholders can bring a derivative action against directors for negligence even if the directors concerned have not benefited from their negligence.[15] The *UK Companies Act 2006* generally prohibits a UK company from indemnifying a director against his liability for negligence, default, breach of duty or breach of trust in relation to the company or an associated company.[16] Any provision in the company's articles of association or in any other agreement with the company that purports to exempt its directors or the directors of its associated companies from such liability will not be valid.[17] Conflicts can be consented to by a mere declaration of interest.[18] It also permits a company at its own cost to purchase and maintain insurance for its directors or the directors of its associated companies.[19] Professional Indemnity Insurance will ensure CRAs are not out of pocket should judges decide possible liability of CRAs based upon breaching their own codes of conduct.

Judges have to adjudicate whether a disclaimer is justified when applied to inaccurate ratings. The exclusion clause(s) may be preventing CRAs either to act responsibly by issuing accurate ratings or to pay damages to investors. By declaring exclusion clause(s) invalid (say by a statutory provision or by judges), then it will

[13] [1978] AC 728, [1977] 2 All ER 492, [1977] 2 WLR 1024.

[14] Part 11 of the *UK Companies Act 2006*.

[15] Cf *Pavlides v Jensen* [1956] 1 Ch 565.

[16] Section 232 (1) of the *UK Companies Act 2006*; See also Morse et al. (2007), p. 214.

[17] Section 232 (2) of the *UK Companies Act 2006*.

[18] Section 177 of the *UK Companies Act 2006*.

[19] Section 234 Ibid. See also Morse (2007), p. 215.

be for judges to decide and fix the amount of compensation CRAs have to pay to the investors who have relied on incorrect ratings.

7.7 Statutory Regulations

In Chaps. 4 and 5, this book examined statutory regulations in the US and EU. This section will recap the important issues of competition, reliance, globalisation and conflicts of interest.

7.7.1 NRSRO Registration and Competition Concern

With regard to the statutory provisions in the US and EU requiring CRAs to register as NRSROs, its advantage, it seems, is for the regulators to have a control over CRAs. However, in the pre-Enron failure period, "[t]he registration did not involve intrusive intervention by the SEC and there was no close oversight of the rating process".[20] All governments historically have chosen to regulate less rather than more.[21] While Enron's decline is considered to be a market failure, it is likely that the events surrounding the firm in 2001 was a case in which the market worked to ferret out deception and poor judgment on the part of Enron's management.[22] Following the Enron saga, the SEC implemented an oversight programme based on a degree of regulatory changes. In adopting the CRA provisions of the *Dodd-Frank Act*, Congress noted the systemic importance of credit ratings to debt markets, concluding that rating agencies' status as gatekeepers justified a degree of oversight and accountability similar to more heavily regulated securities analysts and auditors.

Even if the regulators did succeed in fostering accountability and transparency on the part of CRAs and thereby indirectly protect investors,[23] the fact that only a few CRAs were able to meet the criteria laid down by the regulators for registration in turn created a non-competitive environment. It has, therefore, defeated one of the purposes for enacting the US Reform Act, which relates to fostering competition. Moreover, anti-competitive behaviour occurs when large CRAs buy small rival CRAs. The EU prohibits this for 10 years after the enactment of the relevant regulation, and this prohibition is limited to only those CRAs with over 20 % of the market in the EU.[24]

[20] Davies (2010), p. 123.

[21] Tombs and Whyte (2015).

[22] See Clayton et al. (2002). See also, Dembinski et al. (2006).

[23] Dodd-Frank Act § 931. Martin and Franker (2011), p. 6. See also Coskun (2008), p. 264.

[24] "EU plans to shake up rating agencies", *Reuters* (15 November). http://us.mobile.reuters.com/article/topNews/idUSTRE7AE1KA20111115?irpc=945.

7.7.2 Competency and Competition

It is impossible for the regulators to regulate in such a way that would achieve the dual purpose of ensuring competency and simultaneously encouraging competition on the part of CRAs. The reason is that there is a trade-off between ensuring CRAs do act competently (when discharging their duties) and competition (i.e., allowing market participants to compete). It seems the regulators chose competency at the expense of and sacrificing competition. However, if competition as an alternative is to be preferred, then obviously there is a need to have less stringent and demanding criteria for registration that would either make it easier for new CRAs to apply and be accepted as an NRSRO or alternatively, as an extreme case, entirely abolish the need for registration. There might be a fear that competition based on limited corporate debt issuers and many CRAs in the marketplace will lead to the unintended consequence of CRAs undercutting each other and some of them, when trying to save time and costs, inevitably issuing inaccurate ratings. To prevent it, regulators should adjudicate on whether or not CRAs have issued accurate ratings. This will then allow investors to litigate and win.

Investors can successfully litigate if, as already suggested, there is a provision to invalidate any exclusion clause(s), and this requires a specific statutory provision. Judges would then carry out a monitoring role instead of the regulators, and the US government could save a huge amount of taxpayers' money on monitoring costs conducted by the SEC. The same principle should apply with regard to the EU.

As mentioned in Chap. 4, the objective of the *Dodd-Frank Act* (Dodd-Frank) was to achieve several purposes, including improving the overall quality and integrity of the credit ratings issued by CRAs. The *Dodd-Frank Act*'s rescission of Rule 436(g), the *Securities Act of 1933*, would have meant that CRAs would be subject to the same standards of liability and oversight as apply to auditors, securities analysts and investment bankers. However, the largest NRSROs had the upper hand by announcing that they would decline issuer requests to provide consent to references to their ratings in Securities Act registration statements or prospectuses[25]; any attempt by the regulator to impose a potential liability of CRAs was defeated.

Other objectives were to promote a more transparent credit rating process and to reduce reliance on credit ratings. Under the Dodd-Frank, CRAs are required to prepare a report and include the rating, methodology and assumptions used in determining the rating and the limitations and uncertainties regarding the rating.[26] The Dodd-Frank also sought to impose corporate governance guidelines, reduce conflicts of interest and improve the rating process through enhanced controls and

[25] "Fitch Comments on U.S. Financial Reform Act's Implication for Credit Rating Agencies", *Reuters* (19 July 2010). http://www.reuters.com/article/2010/07/19/idUS132937+19-Jul-2010+BW20100719.

[26] Dodd-Frank Act, § 459–463.

greater transparency. In addition, Dodd-Frank greatly expanded the SEC's oversight and enforcement powers and sought to make it easier for investors to bring civil lawsuits against CRAs, although in theory not in practice. These are commendable acts, but the success depends on their practical implementations by the regulators.

7.8 Reduce Reliance on Ratings

The general effect of the various regulations that were introduced is that the CRAs have had the upper hand. In the midst of the 2007–2008 financial crisis, policymakers began to consider structural changes in oversight and regulation of financial markets, including the potential removal of credit ratings from regulation, but the SEC took limited action to remove some references to credit ratings from its regulations. SEC's effort was relatively discreet, based on the tension between concern over investor overreliance on credit ratings and the utility of credit ratings to prudential financial regulation.[27]

Ryan's[28] suggestion is that regulators should reduce a government's reliance on privately issued credit ratings. However, it is counterproductive as there are many reasons why investors and others rely on them, not least the requirements of Basel II that necessitated resorting to credit ratings to determine a bank's capital requirements. CRAs, on their part, have to ensure that the US and EU do not take further action in reducing reliance on ratings. Should this happen, then it would spell their death knell as they would forego lucrative income generated through ratings. It means CRAs have no choice but to organise their affairs properly.

The future survival of the CRAs depends on them taking appropriate responsibilities by verifying the information that they have asked for and been supplied by the issuers and also in carrying out every aspect of due diligence themselves, rather than expecting the investors to do so. This will mean the CRAs will have to carry out extra work, and they can certainly demand higher fees for carrying out additional tasks associated with ratings from the issuers (including the cost of indemnity insurance premiums) for the work done. The issuers, on their part, will be able to add this extra cost by reducing interest rates paid to the investors when issuing these debt instruments to the public. The investors are likely to accept lower interest rates based on the robust and reliable ratings that, as depicted by the subprime mortgages crisis, were lacking. It is a fallacy to assume that issuers are in favour of higher ratings at any cost. Indeed, an unsustainable future higher rating would mean that issuers will have to pay high interest rates when present debt instruments mature and when attempting to raise money by issuing another trench of corporate debts.

[27] Martin and Franker (2011), pp. 3 and 4.

[28] Ryan (2012a, b).

7.9 Globalisation and the Convergence of the Regulation

Chapter 3 revealed that the "soft laws" promulgated by the IOSCO are applicable to both the US and EU and as the same provisions apply, the regulations in reality do converge. In addition, as was discussed in Chap. 5, the general objective of the European Commission's proposal, which was then enshrined in the EC Regulation, is to contribute to reducing the risks to financial stability, restoring the confidence of investors and other market participants in financial markets and ensuring ratings quality. These proposals are similar to the US *Dodd-Frank Act* and are commendable as, based on globalisation, the regulations in the US and EU need to be identical in nature as both are facing identical problems. An important regulation brought into force in the EU, and which is akin to the US regulation, is improving the quality of ratings by reinforcing the independence of the CRAs and promoting sound credit rating processes and methodologies. They are commendable; however, with regard to reducing reliance on ratings, as already mentioned, it will be counterproductive.

7.10 Conflicts of Interest and Independence

7.10.1 Conflicts of Interest

The root cause of why CRAs were motivated to issue high credit ratings of corporate debts, which this study is about, and why they had lagged behind in downgrading them is that of conflict of interest.[29] Conflicts arise in the case of corporate debts where ratings given are for solicited ratings when corporations approach CRAs to rate their debt instruments for sale to the market, and for which the issuers pay the CRAs. The position with reference to solicited rating is that CRAs can get information from the issuers with regard "to corporate strategies and specific business risk, financial risk and corporate governance aspects".[30]

Suggestions on reforms needed to address the problems of conflicts of interest include lowering barriers to entry, holding CRAs liable for their ratings, having a taxpayer-funded CRA, having a ban on shopping for favourable ratings and consulting services, and making ratings more informative.[31] However, the most effective method of preventing conflicts of interest, in this author's view, is in holding CRAs legally liable for their unreliable ratings, which the regulators seem to be shying away from. This would presumably require legislative intervention. Deterrence should take central stage, as it will force CRAs to act responsibly.

[29] See Chapter 23 "Conflict of Interest: Credit Rating Agencies", in Davies (2010), pp. 123–130.

[30] For definition of "solicited ratings", see Glossary.

[31] Deb and Murphy (2009), p. 5.

7.10.2 *Independence*

With regard to the issue of independence, notwithstanding the actions taken by the regulators in the US and EU to address this issue, the compromise of independence is due to the ownership structure and the long tenure of the business relations of issuers with the same CRA. Resolving the issue of independence requires the fixing of conflicts of interest. One way around this is for the regulators to concentrate their efforts in ensuring reliable ratings for corporate debts and not to be unduly concerned with unsolicited ratings of sovereign debts (and European banks) where conflicts do not arise because no payment changes hands.

7.11 Imposition of Liability

Presently, based on the US common law examined in Chap. 6, investors are unable to sue CRAs when they suffer losses for relying on the optimistic ratings issued. This section will examine the liability issue and the ensuing debate.

7.11.1 *Breaches of Statutory Duties*

An important issue relates to what happens if the CRAs breach their statutory duties. When examining breaches of self-regulations, the finding was that investors have had no legal recompense. Regulations *per se* are meaningless if the regulators are not vigorously enforcing them. Regulators have tried to impose meagre fines on the CRAs, and the money so raised is utilised as regulatory expenses leaving investors uncompensated for their losses. The regulators are in a strong position because of their power to sue CRAs. In addition to or instead of imposing fines, they can suspend or de-list CRAs from NRSRO membership for breaching statutory regulations. This has not happened in practice; rather, the regulators have opted to impose fines, arguably because the Big Three CRAs, which are the subject of this book, are too big to be de-listed. Ryan[32] suggests that the regulatory authority needs to facilitate and enable investors to hold CRAs accountable, in civil lawsuits, when they issue inflated credit ratings and where a CRA knowingly or recklessly fails to conduct a reasonable investigation of the rated security but does not specify how to achieve it.

[32] Ryan (2012a, b).

7.12 Reputational Risk

When credit opinions do not stand the test of time, the CRAs have nothing to risk except their reputations. A study reveals how a financial guru can build a reputation and ultimately cash in on it by manipulating market prices in one direction and trading in the opposite direction.[33] Other market participants involved in the transactions that failed in the subprime crisis (investment banks, investors and collateral managers) have had some financial stake in these transactions. Having a significant financial risk is enough to warrant separate pleading and liability standards for these market participants.[34]

In the past, reputation risk alone did provide the CRAs with the same kind of incentives as financial risk. The bankruptcy of Enron within 4 days of losing its investment grade ratings did some damage to the reputation of the CRAs, but it did little to affect and hurt their business. In reality in the aftermath of Enron, the CRAs have enjoyed some of their most profitable years ever. Thus, fear of reputational damage after Enron did nothing to discipline CRAs, and it has not prevented them from issuing investment grade ratings that caused the subprime mortgage crisis. The plausible explanation is that globally more corporations (old and newly established) have resorted to raising more money by issuing debt instruments, and this has led to unprecedented demand for ratings by the Big Three CRAs to conduct ratings.

The subprime crisis had an impact on the global economy and investors alike but did not cause any reputational damage to CRAs in terms of a decrease in its ratings. CRAs have to reform themselves and to ensure greater quality and accuracy of their ratings to prevent further regulation. Reputation risk *per se* may not work unless CRAs have to face personal liability. Personal liability, if imposed, will compensate those investors who have suffered losses in reliance to unreliable ratings and would incentivise CRAs to act more responsibly. Arguably, it is the fear of legal liability, rather than concern with tarnishing their reputation, that may provide a proper check and balance.

7.13 Investors-Pay Model to Issuers-Pay Model

More than 40 years ago, the First Amendment defence had some merit. CRAs assigned ratings to bonds and then reported all of their ratings in periodicals sold to subscribers who were investors. Bond issuers were not obliged to pay the CRAs. It was in the 1970s that CRAs largely abandoned this model. The new issuers-pay model shifted the cost of the rating from subscribers/investors (who were eager for the most accurate rating) to bond issuers (who were eager for the highest rating).

[33] Benabou and Laroque (1992), pp. 921–958.

[34] Froeba (2009).

The issuers-pay model did change CRAs' incentives when real journalism could not make a similar business model switch.[35] It is necessary to restore confidence in the financial markets, and this can only be possible with the restoration of confidence in the quality and integrity of credit ratings.

The reason for overreliance on ratings is natural and is due to banks, investment funds and others being required to invest in products based on a certain minimum rating criteria, even though CRAs claim that they are only expressing an opinion.[36] More accountability might help in the development of rating in a professional manner,[37] especially where CRAs have failed to scrutinise properly ratings issued to ensure their reliability. If investors are able to prove such failure on the part of CRAs, then liability should fall to them. Competition in the EU could be encouraged by introducing a European agency or even another rating agency elsewhere, such as an Asian agency.[38] Dagong is a global CRA based in China and is functioning well, and it is one of the few notable non-US-based CRAs.

7.14 Recommendations

"The ultimate goal of reform should be to ensure credit rating accuracy".[39] An ideal solution would have been abolishing the protection afforded by the First Amendment, but which is not possible. In this section, the recommendations will consist of abolishing disclaimer and requiring compulsory professional insurance policy for CRAs and CRAs acting as responsible gatekeepers, which would in theory and practice prevent regulatory failure:

(a) First Amendment—the regulators have not directly interfered with the provisions of common laws (contract and tort laws). They have not suggested the introduction of appropriate changes to remedy the situation where laws continue to favour CRAs. CRAs, through the various defences available to them, effectively have "litigation immunity", and as such investors are unable to institute litigation and make claims against them. It is impossible to abolish the first Amendment in the US, as it is a constitutional provision: however, the issue is whether CRAs are acting in a journalist capacity. This is doubtful because of a change from a previous investor-pay model where CRAs did act in a journalistic capacity by issuing a magazine depicting various corporate ratings, and investors used to subscribe for such a publication. Under the present issuer-pay model, ratings are displayed on CRAs' website and are

[35] Froeba (2009).

[36] Klintz (2011).

[37] Ibid.

[38] See Hume (2013).

[39] Gannon (2011–2012), pp. 1015–1017.

available on subscription to subscribers, rather than for public consumption, which seems to negate this notion. First amendment defences are inapplicable in the EU, and yet it has not brought about a flood of litigation. CRAs claim that they have been inundated with legal suits and, based on the US legal system, they cannot recover the cost of their defence even if they win a case. In reality, "the credit rating agencies have been sued by their own shareholders, individual and institutional investors in structured finance securities, state attorney generals and potentially the US Securities and Exchange Commission".[40] In reality, while the current debate has focused excessively on generous ratings, which is alleged has been given in the past, opening up the CRAs' liability to investors could have the opposite effect in that CRAs may be tempted to give lower ratings. Should this happen, then CRAs may expect a threat of proceedings from the issuer companies, who might think that their ratings were too low and then use legal proceedings, or at least a threat of them, to try to get them raised.[41] In the US, each party is responsible for its own legal costs, but in practice most cases are settled in favour of CRAs at the preliminary hearing and without a full trial. A solution is for the US government to enact a statutory provision that forces a losing party to pay the costs of a winning party, similar to the position in the UK to align the US position with the UK. The advantage of this is that it will prevent unmerited cases going to court.

(b) On disclaimers—an enactment of a statutory provision in the US and EU is needed to make disclaimers of liability by CRAs invalid for breaching the regulations (soft self-regulation laws and hard statutory laws) when it relates to investors lodging third-party suits. CRAs might claim that a disclaimer of responsibility or liability is necessary to protect their interests; otherwise, they will be inundated with a flood of legal suits. This is untrue based on the several defences that are available to the CRAs, which were examined in Chap. 6.

7.14.1 *Prevention of Regulatory Failure*

Some are sceptical as to whether CRAs can be regulated.[42] The critical examination of various regulations introduced in this book in the context of a gatekeeper theory has had some impact in ensuring that CRAs discharge their responsibility efficiently. However, regulations have not been as effective as anticipated because the regulators have failed to eliminate conflicts of interest and address the issues of lack of competition and legal accountability. CRAs have escaped playing the role of an effective investors' gatekeeper, thereby protecting investors' interests. Regulators

[40] Zhou and Kumar (2012), p. 1.

[41] Haynes (2014).

[42] Richardson and White (2009), pp. 101–116.

should implement the various suggestions (and some changes in common laws) proposed in the various chapters of this book, including this chapter. CRAs are required to have a professional attitude towards investors. This requires them to take some personal initiative that goes beyond their moral and ethical duties in working towards protecting the interests of those investors who are directly affected by their actions by becoming their gatekeepers and to stop introducing and relying on their disclaimers. The advantage of such a move will be that investors will continue to rely on ratings. This will also prevent the US and EU regulators from taking drastic action in the future, introducing more regulations and more legal accountability and reducing reliance on rating, which will benefit the Big Three CRAs, bearing in mind that rating is their main source of income. The book concludes that there is no deterrent for the CRAs as the common law and regulations (self-regulation and statutory regulations) act as a safe harbour by shielding them from liability and thus preventing them from acting as the responsible gatekeepers of investors.

7.15 Other Related Issues

It was inevitable that the book takes an ambitious and holistic approach and focuses on examining the three types of regulation: the self-regulation and statutory regulation that were introduced and the present common law defences found in the US. This was necessary in order to avoid research bias and to arrive at a reliable conclusion. This has meant that there were other issues relating to CRAs; these are worth mentioning in closing and are discussed below in a summary form rather than in detail.

7.15.1 Sovereign Ratings

This book mainly concentrates on corporate ratings rather than sovereign ratings as corporate ratings have been problematic due to conflicts of interest. It arises because of the nature of soliciting ratings where the issuers approach the CRAs and pay fees for conducting those ratings. No such problem arises in the case of sovereign ratings, as their issuance is rooted on a non-solicited basis.[43] The governments neither approach CRAs, nor do they pay them for their service. CRAs are cautious when issuing sovereign ratings and resort to instant downgrading, and this has increased the cost of government borrowing. Governments tend to think that borrowed money is safe and would be repaid because of their ability to raise future taxes and print currency notes if the circumstances

[43] See Glossary for definition of "unsolicited ratings".

demand. Printing currency notes will increase inflation, and raising taxes will reduce consumer purchasing power. In both these cases, it would affect the economy.

7.15.2 Globalisation

Based on the globalisation of the world's securities markets, there is a need for regulations introduced in the US and EU to converge to ensure uniformity in practice.[44] "The current [globalisation] lingo includes the terms 'national recognition,' 'equivalence', 'convergence' and, finally, 'harmonization.' Significantly, it isn't the global form of the markets that is novel; it is the regulation of that global marketplace that produces the difficulties".[45] Both the SEC and EC regulators have the same concerns relating to investor protection, financial stability and free and fair competition.

7.15.3 Legal Enforcement

Regulation *per se* will be of no benefit if legal enforcement to prevent the wrongdoing that the regulators had identified and were trying to tackle is not effective. At present, the SEC in the US and the ESMA in the EU carry out the enforcement of the regulation, but perhaps judges can also perform this role.

It is doubtful if a "threat that both regulators and market actors will switch to alternatives to ratings could force rating agencies to behave more like information intermediaries than providers of 'regulatory licenses'".[46] At present, there is no alternative system in place and, unless the auditor firms join in, the Three Big CRAs (Fitch, S&P and Moody's) have a monopoly over ratings. The dilemma relates to the failure of reputational constraint working for novel debt instruments, as CRAs are being paid by the issuers and in situations where CRAs lack special expertise, they have issued high ratings[47] to the detriment of investors. What is required is either a special regulatory control mechanism to prevent CRAs from performing a task where they lack proper expertise, for example, in rating novel financial products. In such a situation, perhaps CRAs should act with caution by issuing low ratings, or failing that, the investors ought to have redress in a court of law.

As a contribution, this book has analysed both extensively and critically various regulations introduced in the US and EU, including the drawbacks of common laws

---

[44] For general discussion see Held and McGrew (2000).

[45] Campos (2004).

[46] Darbellay and Partnoy (2012), p. 16.

[47] Hunt (2009), pp. 109–209.

and difficulties in solving the problems of conflicts of interest and lack of competition that have resulted in the gatekeeper failure. The recent civil liability[48] introduced in the EU for gross negligence, based on the reckless behaviour of senior management within the rating firms and the test for reasonable reliance on the part of investors, perhaps is to introduce deterrence on the part of CRAs. However, it would not act as a sufficient deterrent to prevent CRAs from issuing unreliable ratings. As stated:

> Legal measures, such as breach of contract and negligence, may offer CRAs incentives to make every reasonable effort to prepare adequate credit ratings and to update ratings in a timely manner. It is nonetheless difficult (in the context of liability) to make an objective assessment because CRAs, too, must work under uncertain relationships.[49]

Sufficient deterrence through liability may be required as found in the Netherlands[50] and in other professions like auditors and solicitors. In addition, CRAs should be compelled to hold PII to meet their potential legal liability as a condition for granting NRSRO status. However, CRAs may object to such moves if taken by the regulators.

7.16 Formulation of a New Statutory Liability

The book proposes for regulators to formulate the following new statutory liability rules for CRAs to resolve the issue of conflicts of interest and to act as deterrence.

Preamble: "Civil liability of rating agencies has to strike a balance between over-deterrence and overly lax behaviour control".[51]

1. A credit rating agency (CRA) has a duty of care to investors to ensure that there is a reasonable basis for issuing a rating, notwithstanding that there is no contract between them.[52]
2. Where a CRA issues a rating without a reasonable basis, or where there are significant flaws in the methodology and model used, this shall constitute a breach of duty; the CRA is liable for the total loss of investor's investment.
3. A CRA shall incur liability to investors on the court's finding that ratings issued were either misleading or deceptive or constitute a misrepresentation.
4. An investor who suffers loss because of investing in rated products where a CRA has committed, intentionally or with gross negligence, a breach of the standards

---

48 Statutory Instruments, 2013 No. 1637 Financial Services and Markets, "The Credit Rating Agencies (Civil Liability) Regulations 2013", which came into force on 25th July 2013.

49 Duffhues and Weterings (2011).

50 See Duffhues and Weterings (2011). de Savornin Lohman and van't Westeinde (2006).

51 Haar (2013).

52 Points 1 to 3 and 5 are based on *Bathurst*; see Harding-Farrenberg and Donovan (2013), p. 190.

prescribed by the Regulation, a cause of action shall arise when an investor acts reasonably in reliance of the rating and has suffered a detriment.

5. For a disclaimer to be effective, a CRA shall not defeat the purpose for which a task given is to be performed, and a disclaimer shall be set out in a clear explicit language and shall be noticeably displayed.
6. In every 3 years, a CRA shall rotate and not continue to perform the task of ratings on behalf of the same issuer.[53] Moreover, when an issuer requests rating a complex instrument (like structured finance), two CRAs shall perform the task.
7. A CRA shall incur a civil liability when either intentionally or with gross negligence, it commits any of the infringements specified in the European Regulation. An infringement is committed with gross negligence if the senior management of the rating agency are reckless in asserting whether the infringement has occurred.[54]
8. The measure of damages for a claim by an investor where there is no contract with a CRA shall be the damages that would be recoverable if the investor succeeded in a claim for negligence (i.e. a claim in tort) against the CRA.[55]
9. A limitation on liability is allowed, where it is reasonable and proportionate in relation to all the relevant circumstances. In addition, damages awarded against CRA shall be reduced when a claimant fails to mitigate its own losses.[56]

7.17 Summary of the Key Issues

The book ends with a summary of key issues. CRAs fulfil an important function in evaluating and assessing the creditworthiness of issuers and the probability of them making timely payments (of interest and capital) on the securities issued and therefore *prima facie* and impliedly is fulfilling the role of a gatekeeper. One of the limitations of credit ratings is that it carries inference for credit risk and does not include the assessments of the liquidity or the market price. CRAs have been criticised for their role in contributing to the global financial crisis, especially for assigning ratings to subprime structured finance instruments, which did not reflect their true risk, and a number of claims have been filled globally against CRAs.[57] CRAs' failure to correctly rate subprime mortgages led to the lawmakers and regulators to introduce reform, intending to enhance the accountability and effectiveness of CRAs by adopting market- and regulatory-based strategies.

In the US and EU, the IOSCO standards and statutory regulations have dealt with the issues of competition, reputation, independence, conflicts of interest, quality of

[53] Such a provision already exists in the EU aiming at eliminating conflicts of interest.

[54] The Credit Rating Agencies (Civil Liability) Regulations 2013.

[55] Ibid.

[56] Ibid.

[57] Cooper et al. (2013), p. 1.

ratings, disclosure and transparency.[58] Certain shortcomings of regulatory approaches, however, remain and relate to lack of competition, lack of deterrence and conflicts of interest. An anti-competitive environment is due to the Big-Three CRAs dominating the rating market. In terms of reputation, unreliable ratings have had no adverse consequences on the revenue generated by CRAs. On the contrary, after the short-lived crisis, the numbers of securities CRAs rate have increased steadily, and so have the revenues it generates. Conflicts of interest have arisen due to issuers, rather than investors, requesting and making payment for ratings issued by CRAs, and the *status quo* remains. CRAs are not legally accountable to investors as it is difficult to attribute a duty of care on them, and this has created a lack of deterrence and arguably lack of motivation for ensuring the issuance of reliable ratings.[59] CRAs are only private bodies undertaking private functions. When CRAs issue unreliable ratings, the absence of duty of care and the accessibility of various defences available to CRAs have resulted in investors bearing the losses. There is a need for accountability in the form of liability.[60] in order to strike a balance between over-deterrence and to control overly lax behaviour. It will ensure that CRAs act responsibly, and it will remedy at the same time the problems of absence of competition and conflicts of interest.

References

Benabou, R., & Laroque, G. (1992). Using privileged information to manipulate markets: Insiders, gurus, and credibility. *Quarterly Journal of Economics, 107*(3), 921–958.

Buckley, A. (2011). *Financial crisis: Causes, context and consequences* (p. 69). Sussex: Pearson Education Limited.

Bussani, M. (2010, January). Credit rating agencies' accountability: Short notes on a global issue. *Global Jurist, 10*(1).

Cadbury, A. (Sir). (2000, May). *The combined code principles of good governance and code of best practice*. http://www.ecgi.org/codes/documents/combined_code.pdf.

Campos, R. C. (2004, September 17). *Speech by SEC commissioner: The global marketplace and a regulatory overview*, Para 4. http://www.sec.gov/news/speech/spch091704rcc.htm.

Clayton, R. J., Scroggins, W., & Westley, C. (2002, Spring). Enron: Market exploitation and correction. *Financial Decisions*. Article 1. http://www.financialdecisionsonline.org/current/clayton.pdf.

Cooper, J., Millington Jones, Z., Imhoff, J., Kirk, N., Eagles, R., Edmond, J., et al. (2013, March). *Tide is turning against credit rating agencies* (p. 1). Clyde & Co, FI & D&O. http://www.clydeco.com/uploads/Files/Publications/2013/CC002768_FI_and_DO_Review_20_03_13.pdf.

[58] Rousseau (2009), pp. 36–37.

[59] Bussani notes, "CRAs still are almost immune from any form of civil liability, and the regulatory approaches [in the US and EU] still use... the same administrative tools that have so far proved to be largely ineffective", Jones (2010), pp. 201–231. See Bussani (2010).

[60] Refer to the Model of a Formulation of a New Statutory Liability. Kerwer (2004), pp. 1–27.

Coskun, D. (2008). Credit rating agencies in a post-Enron world: Congress re-visits NRSRO concept. *Journal of Banking Regulation, 9*(4), 264. http://www.kvdl.nl/wp-content/uploads/2013/01/Deniz-Coskun-credit-rating-agencies-in-a-post-Enron-world.pdf.

Darbellay, A., & Partnoy, F. (2012, April). *Credit rating agencies and regulatory reform* (University of San Diego Legal Studies Research Paper Series, Research Paper No. 12-083, p. 16). http://ssrn.com/abstract=2042111.

Davies, H. (2010). *The financial crisis: Who is to blame?* (pp. 123–130). Cambridge: Polity Press.

de Savornin Lohman, H. A., & van't Westeinde, M. G. (2006). Control and liability of credit rating agencies under Netherlands law. EJCL, *Netherlands Comparative Law Association*, 1–22. http://www.ejcl.org/111/art111-18.pdf.

Deb, P., & Murphy, G. (2009, November). *Credit rating agencies: An alternative model* (p. 5). http://personal.lse.ac.uk/debp/Papers/Ratings_Regulation.pdf.

Dembinski, P. H., Lager, C., Cornford, A., & Bonvin, J. M. (Eds.). (2006). *Enron and world finance: A case study in ethics*. Basingstoke: Palgrave Macmillan. http://www.strongwindpress.com/pdfs/TuiJian/Enron%20and%20World%20Finance%20-%20A%20Case%20Study%20in%20Ethics.pdf.

Duffhues, P. J. W., & Weterings, W. C. T. (2011, May 26). The quality of credit ratings and liability: The Dutch view. *International Journal of Disclosure and Governance* (advance online publication).

Financial Oversight of Enron: The SEC and Private Sector Watchdogs. (2002, October 7). *Report prepared by the staff of the committee on governmental affairs* (p. 98). United States Senate. http://www.gpo.gov/fdsys/pkg/CPRT-107SPRT82147/pdf/CPRT-107SPRT82147.pdf.

Froeba, M. (2009, September 29). *Rating agency legal liability standards*. http://expectedloss.blogspot.com/2009/09/rating-agency-legal-liability-standards.html.

Gannon, J. T. (2011–2012). Help the credit rating agencies get it right: A simple way to alleviate a flawed industry model. *Annual Review of Banking & Financial Law, 31*, 1015–1017.

Haar, B. (2013, January 9). *Civil liability of credit rating agencies after CRA 3 – Regulatory all-or-nothing approaches between immunity and over-deterrence* (Research Paper No. 2013-02). University of Oslo Faculty of Law. Available at SSRN: http://ssrn.com/abstract=2198293 or http://dx.doi.org/10.2139/ssrn.2198293.

Harding-Farrenberg, R., & Donovan, K. (2013). Figure 1, p. 190.

Haynes, A. (2013). The burden of proof in the market abuse cases. *Journal of Financial Crime, 20*(4), 365–397.

Haynes, A. (2014, March 26). Discussion.

Held, D., & McGrew, A. (Eds.). (2000). *The global transformations reader* (2nd ed.). Cambridge: Polity Press.

Hume, T. (2013, June 25). Hong Kong-based credit rating agency launched to challenge 'Big Three'. *CNN*. http://edition.cnn.com/2013/06/25/business/universal-credit-rating-group.

Hunt, J. P. (2009). Credit rating agencies and the "Worldwide Credit Crisis": The limits of reputation, the insufficiency of reform, and a proposal for improvement. *Columbia Business Law Review*, 109–209.

Jones, R. (2010). The need for a negligence standard of care for Credit Rating Agencies. *William & Mary Business Law Review, 1*(1), 201–231. http://scholarship.law.wm.edu/wmblr/vol1/iss1/8.

Kerwer, D. (2004, December). Holding global regulators accountable: The case of Credit Rating Agencies. In *School of Public Policy Working Paper Series Working Paper 11*, University College, London, pp. 1–27. https://www.ucl.ac.uk/spp/research/publications/downloads/spp-wp-11.pdf.

Klintz, W. (2011). *European Parliament Special Committee on the Financial, Economic and Social Crisis*. http://www.europarl.europa.eu/document/activities/cont/201109/20110901ATT25750/20110901ATT25750EN.pdf.

Lamb, K. (2013, October 4). *An introduction to structured products*. http://www.investopedia.com/articles/optioninvestor/07/structured_products.asp

Martin, D. B. H., & Franker, M. C. (2011, December). Rating agency regulation after the Dodd-Frank Act: A mid-course review. *Insights, 25*(12), 6.
McLean, B., & Nocera, J. (2010). *All the devils are here: The hidden history of financial crisis.* London: Penguin Ltd.
Morse, G. (2007). *Palmer's Company law: Annotated guide to the Companies Act 2006* (p. 215). London: Thomson/Sweet & Maxwell.
Morse, G., Davies, P., Worthington, S., Morris, R., Bennett, D. A., Hudson, A., et al. (2007). *Palmer's company law annotated guide to the Companies Act 2006* (p. 214). London: Thomson/Sweet & Maxwell.
Richardson, M., & White, L. J. (2009, April 2). The rating agencies: Is regulation the answer? (Chapter 3). In V. Acharya & M. Richardson (Eds.), *Restoring financial stability: How to repair a failed system* (pp. 101–116). John Wiley & Sons.
Rousseau, S. (2009, July 23). *Regulating credit rating agencies after the financial crisis: The long and winding road toward accountability* (pp. 36–37). Capital Markets Institute Research Paper. Available at SSRN: http://ssrn.com/abstract=1456708 or http://dx.doi.org/10.2139/ssrn.1456708.
Ryan, J. (2012a, January 12). *How credible are the credit rating agencies?* http://www.publicserviceeurope.com/article/1341/how-credible-are-the-credit-rating-agencies.
Ryan, J. (2012b, January 1). *The negative impact of the credit rating agencies and the proposals for better regulations* (p. 19). Working paper. http://www.swp-berlin.org/fileadmin/contents/products/arbeitspapiere/The_Negative_Impact_of_Credit_Rating_Agencies_KS.pdf.
Tombs, S., & Whyte, D. (n.d.). Corporate crime stalks the globe. *Nerve*. http://www.catalystmedia.org.uk/issues/nerve2/corcrime.htm.
Zhou, B., & Kumar, P. (2012, April). *Economic considerations in litigation against the credit rating agencies* (p. 1). The Brattle Group, Inc. Discussion Paper.

Glossary

Accounting Standards They enable investors to make comparisons on a like-for-like basis and provide assurance of the assessment and report of the key elements of a company's financial controls and systems. http://www.frc.org.uk/Our-Work/Who-What-We-Regulate/Accountants.aspx.

Actual Malice It is defined as "knowledge that the information was false" or that it was published "with reckless disregard of whether it was false or not". See *New York Times Co. v. Sullivan*, 376 U.S. 254 (1964). Under this standard, a publisher will not incur liability for a false statement of fact unless the statement is made with actual malice. See *Hustler Magazine v. Falwell*, 485 U.S. 46, 56, 108 S.Ct. 876 (1988).

Arbitration A dispute, by agreement of the parties, is submitted "to one or more arbitrators who make a binding decision on the dispute in a procedure. In choosing arbitration, the parties opt for a private dispute resolution procedure instead of going to court". WIPO, "What is Arbitration?" Compared with court cases, arbitration is less costly and with an added advantage of matter being adjudicated quickly. http://www.wipo.int/amc/en/arbitration/what-is-arb.html.

Basel II It is a "set of banking regulations put forth by the Basel Committee on Bank Supervision, which regulates finance and banking internationally. Basel II attempts to integrate Basel capital standards with national regulations, by setting the minimum capital requirements of financial institutions with the goal of ensuring institution liquidity". http://www.investopedia.com/terms/b/baselii.asp.

Binding Precedent It is also known as mandatory precedent or binding authority. It is a precedent of a higher court, which all lower courts must follow.

Bond It is a debt investment in which an investor loans money to an entity (corporate or government) that borrows the funds for a defined period at a fixed interest rate. Companies, municipalities, states, and the U.S. and foreign governments to finance a variety of projects and activities issue bonds. Bonds or fixed-income securities (as generally referred to) are one of the three main asset

M. Hemraj, *Credit Rating Agencies*, DOI 10.1007/978-3-319-17927-8 classes, along with stocks (shares) and cash equivalents. http://www.investopedia.com/terms/b/bond.asp.

Burden of Proof It "refers to the obligation or responsibility to prove, in a case before the courts, the assertions made by a complainant. The general rule is that the burden of proof lies with the party who makes the allegation". http://www.eurofound.europa.eu/areas/industrialrelations/dictionary/definitions/burdenofproof.htm.

Capital Requirements Directive (CRD) It is an EU directive that regulates the capital adequacy of banks and other financial institutions and is based on Basel II, which is a set of international guidelines for banks' capital adequacy. The CRD replaced the previous rules in 2007 (Basel I). In July 2011, there came a proposal for a revision of the CRD (CRD IV) based on the new Basel III standards, among other things.

Cash Flow It is the "incomings and outgoings of cash, representing the operating activities of an organisation". http://www.businessdictionary.com/definition/cash-flow.html. CRAs need cash to pay for salaries, rents and rates, office expenses and other expenses of running a business.

Collateralized Debt Obligation (CDO) This is an insurance-like contract and is sold as protection against default on loans. A CDO is not an ordinary insurance; rather, it is a private bet. It is "an investment-grade security backed by a pool of bonds, loans and other assets. CDOs do not specialize in one type of debt but are often non-mortgage loans or bonds. Similar in structure to a collateralized mortgage obligation (CMO) or collateralized bond obligation (CBO), CDOs are unique in that they represent different types of debt and credit risk. In the case of CDOs, these different types of debt are often referred to as 'tranches' or 'slices'. Each slice has a different maturity and risk associated with it. The higher the risk, the more the CDO pays". http://www.investopedia.com/terms/c/cdo.asp. "In CDOs, not all investors share risk equally and every participatory group has different risk profiles". CDOs usually buy securities that are backed by loans. "Later on, CDOs became toxic assets for these banks and investors". *Times of India* (1 February 2009) http://articles.timesofindia.indiatimes.com/2009-02-01/open-space/28008882_1_cdos-mutual-funds-toxic-assets.

Consideration It is an essential element for the formation of a contract, and it is something of value given by both parties to a contract that induces them to enter into the agreement to exchange mutual performances. http://legal-dictionary.thefreedictionary.com/consideration.

Cost Benefit Analysis It is a "process by which business decisions are analyzed. The benefits of a given situation or business-related action are summed and then the costs associated with taking that action are subtracted". http://www.investopedia.com/terms/c/cost-benefitanalysis.asp.

Credit Default Swap (CDS) It "is a financial swap agreement that the seller of the CDS will compensate the buyer in the event of a loan default or other credit event... Credit default swaps have existed since the early 1990s, and increased in use after 2003. By the end of 2007, the outstanding CDS amount was

$62.2 trillion, falling to $26.3 trillion by mid-year 2010 but reportedly $25.5 trillion in early 2012… During the 2007–2010 financial crisis the lack of transparency in this large market became a concern to regulators as it could pose a systemic risk". https://en.wikipedia.org/wiki/Credit_default_swap.

Credit Spread It is "the difference between yields on treasuries and those on single A-rated industrial bonds. A company must offer a higher return on their bonds because their credit is worse than the government's". http://www.investopedia.com/terms/c/creditspread.asp.

Critical Thinking It requires questioning, evaluating, making judgements, finding connections and categorising rather than passively accepting everything. "In the arts, social sciences and commerce it can include asking questions, identifying problems and solutions, relating theory to practice, stating an argument and supporting it with evidence, making comparisons and evaluating". "In science and technology it can include asking questions, identifying problems, describing, predicting, analysing, categorising and establishing cause and effect". http://www.deakin.edu.au/current-students/study-support/study-skills/handouts/critical-analysis.php.

Deep Pocket It is an American slang term. It means "extensive financial wealth or resources". The term is utilised in reference to big companies or organisations, although it can also refer to individuals. In the context of a lawsuit, the deep pocket is often the target defendant, even when the true (moral) culpability is with another party, because the deep pocket has money to pay damages. http://en.wikipedia.org/wiki/Deep_pocket.

Derivative It is a "security whose price is dependent upon or derived from one or more underlying assets. The derivative itself is merely a contract between two or more parties. Its value is determined by fluctuations in the underlying asset. The most common underlying assets include stocks, bonds, commodities, currencies, interest rates and market indexes. Most derivatives are characterized by high leverage. Futures contracts, forward contracts, options and swaps are the most common types of derivatives. … Derivatives are generally used as an instrument to hedge risk, but can also be used for speculative purposes". http://www.investopedia.com/terms/d/derivative.asp.

Deterrence The notion of deterrence underlines the criminal justice systems in most democratic societies, although punishment and incarceration traditionally have a variety of goals—including incapacitation, punishment, deterrence and rehabilitation. In the United States in particular (and also in other Western democracies), sentencing policy initiatives have often been enacted with the goal of enhancing the deterrent effect. https://en.wikipedia.org/wiki/Deterrence_%28legal%29.

Disclaimer A disclaimer is a statement intended to limit someone's liability in the event of loss or damage. The terms "disclaimer", "warning", "exclusion clause" and "exemption clause" are often used interchangeably, and a disclaimer is generally any statement intended to specify or delimit the scope of rights and obligations that may be exercised and enforced by parties in a legally recognised relationship.

Discovery It is a process in litigation requiring compulsory disclosure of information relating to the litigation. Each party in a trial may demand discovery of the other party. Discovery is the method by which parties gather relevant information from each other or from third parties. During discovery, the parties ask each other and third parties for information about the facts and issues of the case. http://www.stoel.com/showarticle.aspx?show=963.

Estoppel It is a legal principle that bars a party from denying or alleging a certain fact owing to that party's previous conduct, allegation or denial. http://legal-dictionary.thefreedictionary.com/estoppel.

Ethical Codes They "are often adopted by management because they are seen as pragmatic necessities for running an organization in a complex society in which moral concepts plays an important part. Often, acts that violate ethical codes may also violate a law or regulation and can be punishable at law or by government agency remedies". http://en.wikipedia.org/wiki/Ethical_code.

Ethical Standards They are principles that when followed promote values such as trust, good behaviour, fairness and/or kindness. Ethical standards are not always easily enforceable by regulators, as they are frequently vaguely defined and somewhat open to interpretation. http://www.businessdictionary.com/definition/ethical-standards.html#ixzz2UDznzcQq.

Fixed Income Security It is "[a]n investment that provides a return in the form of fixed periodic payments and the eventual return of principal at maturity... are known in advance". http://www.investopedia.com/terms/f/fixed-incomesecurity.asp.

Fraud It is "a deception deliberately practiced in order unfairly to secure gain or advantage, the hallmarks of which are misrepresentation and deceit, though affirmative misrepresentation is not required, as concealment or even silence can under certain circumstances constitute fraud". *Williston on Contracts,* 4th Edition (2012) § 69:2.

Gatekeepers They are professionals who are positioned to be able to prevent wrongdoing by withholding necessary cooperation or consent. Generally, "Gatekeepers can also be seen as institutions or organizations. In a political system there are gatekeepers, individuals or institutions which control access to positions of power and regulate the flow of information and political influence... Media gatekeeping showed that decision-making is based on principles of news values, organizational routines, input structure, and common sense. Gatekeeping is vital in communication planning and almost all communication-planning roles include some aspect of gatekeeping. The gatekeeper's choices are a complex web of influences, preferences, motives and common values. Gatekeeping is inevitable and in some circumstances it can be useful". http://www.utwente.nl/cw/theorieenoverzicht/Theory%20clusters/Media,%20Culture%20and%20Society/gatekeeping.doc/.

Hindsight It refers to a "perception of the significance and nature of events after they have occurred"; "the ability to understand, after something has happened, what should have been done or what caused the event"; the "recognition of the nature or requirements of a situation, event, etc., after its occurrence"; the "wisdom or knowledge got only after something (*usually* bad) has happened". http://www.thefreedictionary.com/hindsight. http://definitions.uslegal.com/l/locus-standi/

Insider Trading It is the buying or selling of a security by someone who has access to sensitive material and non-public information about the security. "[I]t is illegal when the material information is still non-public [and] trading while having special knowledge is unfair to other investors who do not have access to such knowledge". http://www.investopedia.com/terms/i/insidertrading.asp.

Issuer It is "A legal entity that develops, registers and sells securities for the purpose of financing its operations. Issuers may be domestic or foreign governments, corporations or investment trusts. Issuers are legally responsible for the obligations of the issue and for reporting financial conditions, material developments and any other operational activities as required by the regulations of their jurisdictions. The most common types of securities issued are common and preferred stocks, bonds, notes, debentures, bills and derivatives". http://www.investopedia.com/terms/i/issuer.asp.

Lender of Last Resort It is a "Central bank of a country that has the authority and financial resources to act as the ultimate source of credit. In emergencies (such as a run on banks), it extends loans to solvent but illiquid depository institutions whose failure to obtain credit would have a destabilizing effect on the national or regional economy. Central banks have their government's backing to make such loans for retaining the public's confidence in the country's financial system. When central banks themselves get into difficulties, the IMF may act as a lender of last resort". http://www.businessdictionary.com/definition/lender-of-last-resort.html."The lender of last resort functions both to protect individuals who have deposited funds, and to prevent panic withdrawing from banks that have temporary limited liquidity... Commercial banks usually try not to borrow from the lender of last resort because such action indicates that the bank is experiencing financial crisis". J Redwood (2009) at 27. In "the UK it is the Bank of England and in the US it is the Fed (Federal Reserve)... [that] lend the money in cases when financial institutions have no other means of raising the cash they need to stay afloat and their failure to get credit would dramatically (and adversely) affect the economy". See http://peo.cambridge.org/index.php?option=com_content&view=article&id=383:new-lender-of-last-resort&catid=10:jargon-buster&Itemid=4.

Locus Standi In law, it "means the right to bring an action, to be heard in court, or to address the Court on a matter before it. Locus standi is the ability of a party to demonstrate to the court sufficient connection to and harm from the law or action challenged to support that party's participation in the case".

Malice Either expressed or implied, it is a legal term referring to a party's intention to do injury to another party.

Market It means both the primary market and the secondary market. The **primary market** refers to the market where securities are initially created, while the secondary market is one in which they are traded among investors. http://www.investopedia.com/articles/02/101102.asp. The **secondary market**, also called aftermarket, is the financial market in which previously issued financial instruments such as stock, bonds, options, and futures are bought and sold. http://en.wikipedia.org/wiki/Secondary_market. Without them, the stock market would be much harder to transact and much less profitable.

Materiality It is one of the basic and major concepts of auditing. The concept of materiality recognises that some matters, either individually or taken together, are relatively important for true and fair presentation of the financial information in conformity with recognised accounting policies and practices. An auditor's responsibility is to apply the concept of materiality in planning and performing an audit of financial statements. http://my.studyindenmark.dk/profiles/blogs/easy-understanding-about-the-audit-risk-materiality.

Misrepresentation "In general, misrepresentation refers to a situation in which someone makes a false statement for the purpose of making a deal, resulting in the person who relies on the statement experiencing harm. In the case of **negligent misrepresentation**, someone makes a statement without any grounds for knowing whether it is true or not, and an aspect of carelessness is involved... In **innocent misrepresentation**, someone making a statement believes that a statement is true when it is not. This person may be relying on outdated information or incorrect information from someone else, which that person has reason to believe is true. In **fraudulent misrepresentation**, the statement is a lie and someone knows that it is a lie or disregards evidence that it is a lie". http://www.wisegeek.org/what-is-negligent-misrepresentation.htm.

Mortgage-Backed Securities These are a "type of asset-backed security that is secured by a mortgage or collection of mortgages. These securities must also be grouped in one of the top two ratings as determined by an accredited credit rating agency, and usually pay periodic payments that are similar to coupon payments. Furthermore, the mortgage must have originated from a regulated and authorized financial institution". http://www.investopedia.com/terms/m/mbs.asp.

Negligence It is a common word, refers to a type of fault and is synonymous to carelessness. It is a "conduct [of a corporation or a person that] falls below the standards of behavior established by law for the protection of others against unreasonable risk of harm. A person has acted negligently if he or she has departed from the conduct expected of a reasonably prudent person acting under similar circumstances". http://legal-dictionary.thefreedictionary.com/Negligence+%28law%29.

Off-Balance-Sheet Financing It "does not appear on a company's balance sheet because it is not strictly a debt (so liabilities and associated assets are excluded from the balance sheet). In certain circumstances, this can have a flattering effect on important accounting ratios such as leverage and return on assets. Accordingly, published financial statements may fail to provide a full and transparent representation of the underlying activity of the reporting entity; in particular, reported results may suggest less exposure to liabilities than really exists. Common off balance sheet financing mechanisms include[s] consignment stock, sale and repurchase (or leaseback) arrangements, debt factoring, securitisation, creation of special purpose entities, and leasing". http://lexicon.ft.com/Term?term=off-balance-sheet-financing.

Offering Memorandum Also known as "private placement memorandum", it is a "legal document stating the objectives, risks and terms of investment involved with a private placement. This includes items such as the financial statements, management biographies, detailed description of the business, etc. An offering memorandum serves to provide buyers with information on the offering and to protect the sellers from the liability associated with selling unregistered securities". http://www.investopedia.com/terms/o/offeringmemorandum.asp.

Oligopolistic It is an economic condition in which there are few suppliers of a rating service, and that one supplier's actions can have a significant impact on prices and on its competitors.

Oligopoly "Similar to a monopoly, it is one in which only one company exerts control over most of a market. In an oligopoly, there are at least two firms controlling the market". http://www.investopedia.com/terms/o/oligopoly.asp.

Persuasive Authority It "means sources of law that the court consults in deciding a case. It may guide the judge in making the decision in the instant case. But it is not a binding precedent on the court under common law legal systems such as English law. Persuasive precedent may come from a number of sources such as lower courts, horizontal courts, foreign courts, statements made in dicta, treatises or law reviews". http://definitions.uslegal.com/p/persuasive-authority/. Appellate courts may look to rulings in other jurisdictions as persuasive authority, but persuasive authority means that the reasoning advanced in support of the holding is analytically compelling. See *State v. Southers*, 1988 Ohio App. LEXIS 4648 (Ohio Ct. App., Pickaway County Nov. 23, 1988).

Pleading The Federal Rules of Civil Procedure were completely rewritten, effective from 1 December 2007, and effective 1 December 2009 substantial amendments were made to some of the rules. Thirty-five states have adopted procedural codes based on the Federal Rules, but sometimes there are slight variations. Rule 8(d) maintains that each allegation should be "simple, concise, and direct" but allows "2 or more statements of a claim or defense alternatively or hypothetically". If a party makes alternative statements, the pleading is sufficient if any one of them is sufficient. A party may state inconsistent (even mutually exclusive) claims or defences. *McCormick v. Kopmann*, 23 Ill. app. 2d 189, 161 N. E.2d 720 (1959).

Ponzi Scheme It is "an investment scam that appears to be actually paying high returns by paying the supposed returns out of victims' own capital... A typical Ponzi scheme promises investors a high rate of return in a short time. The money that is collected from investors is used to pay the return. This means the scam can run for some time, because investors appear to be making the promised return. Early participants can profit, as they can with a pyramid scheme". http://moneyterms.co.uk/ponzi-scheme/.

Professional Indemnity Insurance It is also called professional liability insurance or errors & omissions in the US, which "helps protect professional advice- and service-providing individuals and companies from bearing the full cost of defending against a negligence claim made by a client, and damages awarded in such a civil lawsuit. The coverage focuses on alleged failure to perform on the part of, financial loss caused by, and error or omission in the service or product sold by the policyholder... Professional liability coverage sometimes also provides for the defense costs, including when legal action turns out to be groundless. Coverage does not include criminal prosecution, or a wide range of potential liabilities under civil law that are not enumerated in the policy, but which may be subject to other forms of insurance". http://en.wikipedia.org/wiki/Professional_indemnity_insurance.

Racketeer Influenced and Corrupt Organizations Act RICO makes it a federal crime for any person to conduct or participate, directly or indirectly, in the conduct of the affairs of an enterprise engaged in, or the activities of which affect, interstate or foreign commerce through the collection of an unlawful debt or through a pattern of racketeering activity. http://itlaw.wikia.com/wiki/Racketeer_Influenced_and_Corrupt_Organizations_Act.

Rating Trigger It is a "provision in a loan agreement or bond indenture allowing one party or the other to take a certain action if the borrower's credit rating changes for any reason. For example, if a bond issuer's credit rating falls, a rating trigger may release bondholders from certain obligations specified in the indenture". http://financial-dictionary.thefreedictionary.com/Rating+Trigger. A rating trigger is a "Clause present in a loan agreement that outlines what actions may be taken if a borrower's credit score declines to an unsatisfactory level over the course of the loan. If the borrower's credit score declines to this level, this terms of this clause may require an elevated interest rate or procedural requirements that the creditor may force the borrower to complete, so that the creditor can protect itself". http://www.investorwords.com/8315/rating_trigger.html.

Ratio Decidendi It is the principle of law on which a decision is based. A judge, in delivering a judgement, outlines the facts proved on the evidence and applies the law to the facts and arrives at a decision, for which he gives the reason.

Scienter [Latin term knowingly] It is guilty knowledge that is sufficient to charge a person with the consequences of his or her acts. "The term *scienter* refers to a state of mind often required to hold a person legally accountable for her acts.... *Scienter* has a broader application because it also describes knowledge required to assign liability in many civil cases. *Scienter* denotes a level of intent on the part of the defendant.... *Scienter* is relevant to the pleadings in a case. Plaintiffs and prosecutors alike must include in their pleadings allegations that the defendant acted with some knowledge of wrongdoing or guilt. If a legislative body passes a law that has punitive sanctions or harsh civil sanctions, it normally includes a provision stating that a person must act willfully, knowingly, intentionally, or recklessly, or it provides similar *scienter* requirement... .Most courts hold that reckless conduct may also constitute *scienter*. The definition of *reckless* includes conduct that reasonable persons know is unsafe or illegal. Thus, even if a defendant did not have actual knowledge that his behavior was criminal, *scienter* may be implied by his reckless actions". http://legal-dictionary.thefreedictionary.com/scienter.

Solicited Ratings They "are requested by the rated entity or related third parties and are made publicly available" through CRAs' site". Solicited rating "is characterized by a strong interaction between rating analysts and the management of the rated entity. The rating is assigned after a due diligence process, which involves the acquisition and verification of a series of information provided by the company, with particular reference to corporate strategies and specific business risk, financial risk and corporate governance aspects". http://www.creditrating.crif.com/site/en/Credit-Rating/Ratings-issued-by-CRIF-Credit-Rating-Agency/Pages/Solicited-Ratings.aspx.

Special Purpose Vehicle (SPV) It is also "referred to as a 'bankruptcy-remote entity' whose operations are limited to the acquisition and financing of specific assets. The SPV is usually a subsidiary company with an asset/liability structure and legal status that makes its obligations secure even if the parent company goes bankrupt. ... A corporation can use such a vehicle to finance a large project without putting the entire firm at risk. Problem is, due to accounting loopholes, these vehicles became a way for CFOs to hide debt. Essentially, it looks like the company doesn't have a liability when they really do". Enron bankruptcy indicates that if things do go wrong, the results can be devastating. http://www.investopedia.com/terms/s/spv.asp.

Structured Products They "are synthetic investment instruments specially created to meet specific needs that cannot be met from the standardized financial instruments available in the markets. Structured products can be used: as an alternative to a direct investment; as part of the asset allocation process to reduce risk exposure of a portfolio; or to utilize the current market trend. Structured investments arose from the needs of companies which want to issue debt more cheaply". http://www.hedgefund-index.com/d_structured.asp. Structured products can provide enhanced return and increased diversification and are purchased by high-net-worth individuals and retail investors around the world.

Subpoena It is a word derived from the Latin phrase *sub poena*, meaning *under penalty*. A subpoena is a court-issued command for an individual or corporate representative to appear before the court or to provide specific evidence. Failure to comply with a subpoena without good reason can result in contempt-of-court charges. http://searchfinancialsecurity.techtarget.com/definition/subpoena.

The Federal Rules of Civil Procedure It governs civil procedure (i.e., for civil lawsuits) in United States district/federal courts. Rule 8 provides general rules for pleading. Rule 8(a) sets out the plaintiff's requirements for a claim: a "short and plain statement" of jurisdiction, a "short and plain statement" of the claim and a demand for judgment. It also allows relief in the alternative, so the plaintiff does not have to pre-guess the remedy most likely to be accepted by the court. Rule 8(b) states that the defendant's answer must admit or deny every element of the plaintiff's claim. Rule 8(c) requires that the defendant's answer must state any affirmative defences. Rule 8(d) maintains that each allegation should be "simple, concise, and direct" but allows "2 or more statements of a claim or defense alternatively or hypothetically". http://en.wikipedia.org/wiki/Federal_Rules_of_Civil_Procedure.

True and Fair View Although there is no statutory definition of "true and fair", it "means that the financial statements under review (audit) are materially accurate and can be used by the user to make informed decisions; that is not the same as saying the statements are accurate. It means that there are no misstatements or errors of such magnitude that they render the statements useless to a user or would cause a user to make an incorrect decision". http://www.frc.org.uk/Our-Work/Codes-Standards/Accounting-and-Reporting-Policy/True-and-Fair.aspx. The "accounting principle states that a firm should provide a true and fair view in regard to financial conditions and also its operating results. The concept of true and fair view does not necessarily mean the absolute and total truth about the firm. Financial statements are after all the product of different management's judgments and various estimates. The principle of true and fair view requires that the comparative truth is given about the firms' position". http://www.tuition.com.hk/dictionary/t.htm.

Unsolicited Ratings It is a credit rating not initiated at the request of the issuer or rated entity or other third parties and is assigned without participation by the issuer or any related third party.

Watchdog It is a term used in the audit profession. 'A watchdog is a person or committee whose job is to make sure that companies do not act illegally or irresponsibly.' Collins English Dictionary.

Whistleblowing It "is when a worker reports suspected wrongdoing at work. Officially, this is ...'making a disclosure in the public interest'. A worker can report things that are not right, are illegal or if anyone at work is neglecting their duties". https://www.gov.uk/whistleblowing.

Index

M. Hemraj, *Credit Rating Agencies*, DOI 10.1007/978-3-319-17927-8

MIX
Papier aus verantwortungsvollen Quellen
Paper from responsible sources
FSC® C105338

If you have any concerns about our products,
you can contact us on
ProductSafety@springernature.com

In case Publisher is established outside the EU,
the EU authorized representative is:
Springer Nature Customer Service Center GmbH
Europaplatz 3, 69115 Heidelberg, Germany

Printed by Libri Plureos GmbH
in Hamburg, Germany